BILLY FOST

The Victoria Flash

... plus a walk through the history of motor racing in British Columbia

Bob Kehoe

Copyright © 2019 by Bob Kehoe

All rights reserved. No part of this publication may be reproduced, distributed or transmitted in any form or by any means, without prior written permission.

Author: Bob Kehoe
          Hillsboro, Oregon; Eloy, Arizona
          (bkehoe51@gmail.com)

Book Layout © 2017 BookDesignTemplates.com

Jacket Design by Joe Santana, MKTX, Inc.

Billy Foster/Bob Kehoe – First Edition (rev. 0)

ISBN 978-1-7970524-4-1

Printed in the United States of America

To the entire Foster family for putting their faith in me to present this tribute to Billy.

In addition, I would like to thank all of Billy's friends, associates and fans for your amazing contributions to this effort. Without your input, I could not have undertaken this project.

"Rejoice, O young man, in thy youth"

- Ecclesiastes

ACKNOWLEDGEMENTS

Billy Foster's family, close friends, fellow competitors and fans assisted me with this effort, and it would be nearly impossible to acknowledge all of them individually. To those that I may have overlooked, I extend my gratitude.

However, there are a few that I would like to mention, beginning with Gordon Alberg. 'Gordy' was a godsend in putting me in touch with the right sources around the Victoria area, and I'm indebted to his willingness to help in so many ways. In the same thought, my thanks to his lovely wife Sarah for her great hospitality!

I would also like to extend my gratitude to Bev, Debra, Billy Jr. and Kelly Foster for their support and assistance during this long effort. Additionally, a big shout-out to Billy's cousin Daryl Foster for his memories and family photo archives.

I conducted a number of interviews with Billy's close friends and competitors, including Mario Andretti, Dave Cooper, Ray Pottinger, Jimmy Steen, Phil Hendry, Dick Hansen, Harvey Chipper, Eldon Rasmussen, Norm Ellefson, Irv and Scott Hoerr, John Feuz, Don Robison, Fred Sewall and Jay Koch. These fellows' personal input and story-sharing played a big part in this undertaking. Though the years may shade their exact memories of events, believe me – I enjoyed every minute of it! I'm sure Billy would have been appreciative of your thoughts.

Many of the photos were sourced from the Daryl Foster archives and the Victoria Auto Racing Hall of Fame and Museum, but I would also like to thank many others for their photo contributions.

My thanks also to my Facebook friends who were happy to share their knowledge. You have all been a valuable resource. Additional credit to Judy (Pollard) Dippel for her expert suggestions and proof-reading.

In closing, I have been diligent in verifying the facts and circumstances surrounding the events recorded in this book. At the same time though, I realize some may find slight errors here and there. If so, please contact me at bkehoe51@gmail.com and I will be happy to make those corrections.

Bob Kehoe
March 2019

p.s. I certainly can't close without extending my love to my wife Karen for her support, patience and understanding of all the hours I spent on the keyboard.

I would like to acknowledge the following media outlets that provided valuable content for this book through their archives:

Competition Press	The Los Angeles Times	The Vancouver Sun-Telegram
Racing Wheels	The Nanaimo Free Press	The Victoria Daily Colonist
Sports Illustrated Magazine	The News-Herald	The Victoria Daily Times
The Associated Press	The Oregonian	The Victoria Times-Colonist
The Charger	The Players' Tribune	Vintage Motorsports Magazine
The Deseret News	The Spokane Daily Chronicle	Yesterday's Wheels
The Edmonton Journal	The Spokane Spokesman-Review	
The Indianapolis Star		
The Lafayette Journal & Courier		

Websites:

Grant King Racers (www.grantkingraceshops.com)
Greater Vancouver Motorsports Pioneers Society (www.gvmps.org)
Racing Reference (www.racing-reference.info)
Racin' Thru the Raindrops (befastpast.blogspot.com)
The Jalopy Journal (www.jalopyjournal.com)
Victoria Auto Racing Hall of Fame (victoriaautoracinghalloffameandmuseum.com)

Photo Credits

My thanks to all those who graciously provided photos for this book:

Barrie Goodwin	Goldstream Media	Ralph Hunt
Bill Throckmorton	Grant King Racers	Ray Pottinger
Bob Glenny	Harvey Chipper	Stock Car Racing Magazine
Brian Pratt	Idaho Historical Racing Society	Ted MacKenzie
C.V. Haschel	Jay Koch	The Foster Family
Canada Track and Traffic	John Feuz	The Hoerr Family
Canadian Racer	Legends of the San Jose Speedway	The Pollard Family
Daryl Foster	Len Sutton	The Tipke Family
Don Robison	Midwest Racing Archives	Tom Osborne
Doug Dempsey	Norm Ellefson	USAC Archives
Eldon Rasmussen		Victoria Auto Racing Hall of Fame
Ford Total Performance		

CONTENTS

Preface by Bob Kehoe 1
The Foster Family 3
Billy's Friends Remember – Dave Cooper 17
Billy's Friends Remember – Dick Hansen 25
Victoria's Auto Racing Heritage – The Willows 28
Billy's Friends Remember – Ray Pottinger 39
Victoria's Auto Racing Heritage – Langford Speedway 46
Swede Lindskog 64
Victoria's Auto Racing Heritage – Shearing Speedway 71
Kajia Kalevala 80
Billy's Friends Remember – Phil Hendry 85
Billy's Friends Remember – Harvey Chipper 87
Victoria's Auto Racing Heritage – Western Speedway 91
Ed Kostenuk 102
Victoria's Auto Racing Heritage – Grandview Bowl 107
Billy and the Mt. Douglas Hillclimb 131
Billy's Friends Remember – Dick Varley 134
Billy's Friends Remember – Gordon Alberg 137
The Canadian-American Modified Racing Association 141
Billy's Friends Remember – Eldon Rasmussen 151
Billy's Friends Remember – Norm Ellefson 161
1964 – Billy's Debut in the Champ Car Series 176
The 1965 Champ Car Season – First Half 179
Key Members of the Vollstedt Champ Car Team 182
The 1965 Indianapolis 500 219
The 1965 Champ Car Season – Second Half 230
Billy's Friends Remember – Mario Andretti 237
1965 – Billy's Start in the USAC Stock Car Series 243
The Rudy Hoerr Family 246
The 1965 USAC Stock Car Season 250
The 1966 Champ Car Season – First Two Races 254
The 1966 Indianapolis 500 – Prerace 256
The First Lap Incident 260

1966 Indy 500 – Conclusion	269
1966 USAC Champ Car Season – Second Half	271
Billy's Friends Remember – Jay Koch	279
The Story of 'Old Bess'	281
The 1966 USAC Stock Car Season	287
January 20th, 1967 – The Last Lap	296
A Fitting Tribute	305
Billy Foster's Championship Car Results	309
Billy Foster's USAC Stock Car Results	313
The Victoria Auto Racing Hall of Fame and Museum	317
About the Author	397
Index	398

PREFACE

I never had the opportunity to meet Billy Foster, nor to watch him race, but I wish I had. When he was killed in Riverside, California in January 1967, I was a high school sophomore in my home town of Portland, Oregon.

Being a car guy and racing enthusiast living in the Pacific Northwest, I was familiar with more localized open-wheel racers such as Rolla Vollstedt, Len Sutton, Bob Gregg, Palmer Crowell and Bill Hyde. Billy's name would pop up now and then when he appeared at the Portland Speedway, but since he hailed from Victoria, I didn't follow him as much.

There was always the Memorial Day tradition of gluing myself to the radio for the broadcast of "The Greatest Spectacle in Racing" – the Indianapolis 500. In the years 1965 and 1966, Billy Foster's name became more familiar when he was associated with Sutton and Vollstedt – joining the fraternity of the premier drivers of the United States Auto Club's Champ Car Series. At the same time though, we weren't much aware of his additional involvement with USAC's Stock Car Series.

Following his tragic accident, Foster's story would slowly fade over the following decades throughout the many racing circles. Except, of course, in British Columbia, where his legend has remained strong with his family, friends, fellow competitors, crewmembers and dedicated fans.

It was shortly after I published a book on the life of Art Pollard in 2016 (*The Life and Legacy of a Gentleman Racer),* who perished in a horrific practice accident on the morning of Pole Day qualifying at Indianapolis in 1973. Each July, the local old-timers of racing, their families and friends all gather for a picnic at Blue Lake Park in Portland. It's a time to reminisce, enjoy some bench-racing and marvel over vintage race cars their owners put on display. A good time is had by all.

By chance that day, I met a gentleman named Gordon Alberg from Saanich, British Columbia. 'Gordy' was visiting friends in Portland and attended the picnic. In conversation, Gordy described his past racing exploits up in his neck of the woods, while thumbing through a copy of the Art Pollard book.

Gordy brought up Foster's name, mentioning that the two of them had run around together back in the day, and that he always thought a book about Billy's life would be in order. Coincidentally, I was ready to embark on another writing project, and a Foster biography might be an interesting endeavor. We agreed that teaming up, given Alberg's strong connections up in British Columbia, would be a big help for me.

And thus, the project began. The first step was to begin research, and Gordon's task was to put me in touch with those who could provide valuable interviews and information.

As I experienced with the Pollard book, the more people I spoke with, and the more news articles I discovered (thanks to Internet archives), the more I got to know Billy. I discovered that he was quite a guy, even as a youngster, and fully dedicated to the sport he loved. Beyond that, he was a loving husband and father to his wife Bev and children Debra, Billy Jr. and Kelly. And he loved playing jokes on everyone!

While cruising the 'information superhighway', I also learned of the rich history of motorsports – dating back to the early 1900s – in British Columbia.

I got to thinking, "Wow, this is very interesting and important history! Perhaps I should include some of this material which could help explain how and why Billy worked his way into racing."

Thus, intertwined throughout this accounting, readers will find short histories of the notable racing facilities that were found in the near-Victoria area, with descriptive reprints from period newspapers. Most of the old-timers I interviewed competed on these tracks during their heyday, not to mention that several competed against the young Billy Foster.

I hope the reader will find this track history interesting, not to mention the personal observations that were shared with me before those memories are lost to time.

I can't profess to be dead-on factual throughout this book, and based on experience, there will be discrepancies found. But as we all age, we understand that the further back in time we go, our memory becomes foggier. Years ago, a gathering of people may have been all eyewitness to an event, but today may have differing accounts.

My thanks to all – Bob Kehoe

(Ted MacKenzie photo)

ONE

The Foster Family

Victoria is the capital city of the Canadian province of British Columbia. Named after Queen Victoria of the United Kingdom, Victoria began as a British settlement in 1843 and was incorporated as a city in 1862 – establishing it as one of the oldest cities in the Pacific Northwest.

It was in Victoria on Saturday, September 18th of 1937, that a second son was born to Eric and Gladys Foster. They named this new arrival William, who would join two-year-old Stephen as a brother.

Little could anyone imagine that young Billy, as he was nicknamed, would grow up to be a race car driver - but it was perhaps inevitable given his family's shared love affair with the automobile and speed.

The extended Foster clan was large and closely-knit, with many involved one way or another in the automotive trade.

In October 1953 an article in the *Victoria Daily Colonist* spoke of Billy's uncle Phil's penchant for early automobiles and their impact on daily life:

History of Ancient Cars Deeper
Victoria Garageman Provides Interesting Facts

The automobile plays a big part in the life of Victoria's Phil Foster. It has not only provided the well-known garageman with the means of livelihood but also has furnished him with two interesting hobbies.

Mr. Foster is noted in Victoria for his fine collection of antique cars, but he has another pastime which is not so well known - recording the histories of old buggies. "I believe the most interesting part of the antique car hobby to most would be the growing pains these old cars went through," he says.

The rather lengthy article continues with obscure – but interesting – historic automotive facts Phil provided to the reporter.

Top left: Morry, Ruth and Jeannie Foster in 1950 in a 1911 Auto Carrier. **Top right:** Foster family members parading in 1950 with their 1912 Ford Model T. **Bottom:** a few years earlier, Daryl Foster with his Dad Ken in a 1906 Ford Model N.

Phil Foster's Speedway Service, on the corner of Douglas and Queens, in Victoria.

Phil Foster's #1 Buick – Before and after a race.

As they grew, Stephen and Billy shared in family gatherings along with numerous cousins. Daryl Foster was the same age as Stephen and provided his memories of those early years.

Daryl Foster:

"Our grandparents had a large family. The girls were named Gertie, Marjorie and Ruth. The boys were Ken, Alan, Phil, Morry, Lionel and Eric. Billy's mother's maiden name was Gladys Steen. Her brother, Bill Steen, was the father of Jimmy Steen – who will probably still be driving a race car when he is 100 years-old!

Until Grandfather Foster and my father Ken died in 1947, we often saw each other at family gatherings. There were seventeen Foster cousins in all. Our extended family was close and remains that way today.

Ken and Alan Foster with a Star automobile, circa' 1927.

"My first memory of Billy was at the Foster grandparent's home on Hastings Street in Victoria. Billy and his brother Stephen were having a contest to see who could sing *'Roll Out the Barrel'* the loudest. Even then Billy was a competitor, but a good loser as well."

Stephen was a great older brother to Bill, and they were close. Stephen was smart, talented and one of those all-around nice guys that everyone liked.

Stephen, age 9 and Billy, age 7.

At an early age Billy had impetigo [a highly contagious skin infection that primarily affects infants and children]. At times it was quite serious, which landed him in the Children's Hospital at Mill Bay. He eventually grew out of it.

While I was a country boy, Stephen and Bill grew up in the city, so the opportunities for us to hang out together, before we each had cars, was difficult.

Billy and Stephen.

Phil Foster ran what became the Speedway Service Station at the corner of Douglas and Queens in Victoria. Maurice and Eric worked there, but Eric soon went out on his own to operate the Fernwood Garage. I believe Eric first took over the garage by lease and later purchased it outright. Morry stayed with Phil until about 1954 when he went to work for the Saanich Municipality.

The Fernwood Garage.

I graduated from high school in 1953 and began working full-time for Phil. My dad Ken died when I was 12 years-old, and it was arranged that I would work part-time for Phil at the Speedway Service, which was a huge win for me.

Other family members were often there, along with friends and members of the racing fraternity. The huge benefit for me while working there was that Phil and Morry became my surrogate dads. Many others did so much for me, and I will be forever grateful.

Many of the racers coming from the United States would arrive at Phil's garage before Saturday's race, working on their cars or simply hanging around. Some of the racers would include personalities such as Bud and Pike Green, Del Fanning, Jack Spaulding and Digger Caldwell.

Gerry Vantreight did body work for Phil and often used the shop to work on his own race car. He also became related to the family when his sister married Maurice Foster. Local drivers would often stop and gas up on their way to the track. Corky Thomas might come by scavenging for pieces of pipe, as his 'downspout' exhaust pipes had burned out.

In the early years Phil built, drove and sponsored race cars. I don't believe Morry did, though I'm sure he helped Phil in the 1920s and '30s. For a long time Morry was the pit boss at Langford Speedway.

Billy's mildly-customized 1940 Chevrolet that Daryl Foster purchased around 1954.

It was around 1954 when I bought Billy's 1940 Chevrolet street car. Before he had his driver's license, Bill would take his dad's Model T and drive it around. Actually, he would take any of his dad's cars out for a social drive.

At one time Billy had a very nice custom '49 or '50 Ford, along with a '51 Oldsmobile Rocket 88 convertible. I was with him in that car when a little old fella' driving a Hillman made an unwise left turn in front of Bill – who was passing on the inside at well over the speed limit. I remember the

Hillman doing a 720-degree spin! Fortunately, no one was injured. The Olds was the one my wife and I drove after our wedding. It was also used as a tow car in the 24th of May parade, pulling a custom car from the Quarter Milers Club.

I became associated with the Vancouver Island Track Racing Association (VITRA) by crewing for Dick Varley in 1952 or '53. They allowed no one into the race track without a VITRA membership. That led to my serving as president for a year, but that was not due to any great talent on my part. No one else wanted the job!

It was around that time that Billy and I saw each other more often – either working on cars, at the race track or at the post-race parties. Billy's parents often hosted the parties which were enjoyed by family friends and relatives. Inside the racing crowd, these get-togethers were as important as oil and gasoline during the racing season.

There were several musicians in the group so live music was sometimes a feature. Bill's brother Stephen was a fantastic piano player. He was much more serious about life than Bill and never became involved in racing. He elected to make a career with the Royal Canadian Air Force but sadly, Stephen passed away in 1965 at the age of 30 due to leukemia.

Poor Eric and Gladys – can you imagine losing two sons, two years apart, before they were 30 years-old? No one could fully recover from such a tragedy.

Gladys and Eric Foster with their sons Stephen and Billy.

After Billy and Bev were married, I traded circle track racing for co-founding the Quarter Milers Car Club. We saw less of each other after that, but Bill and I were always close.

As long as I knew him, his interests were always the same: having fun, many types of racing and living dangerously. Billy always wanted to do it all and to stay as far away from work as possible.

He was a great hockey player and that might have been a career for him, but his size was against him. In those days they underrated how valuable a smaller play could be. Someone who could stick-handle the puck and make the big guys appear to be chumps standing still.

And that is a good analogy to Bill's personality – living life faster than those around him and being good at things that held his interest. People that he associated with, aside from family, were friends or others who wished to befriend him. Even the few he may have pissed off at one time or another could not be angry with Bill for more than a short time.

I was at work when I heard about Billy's fatality on the news. His final services were held at Hatley Memorial Gardens, and it appeared that the entire town was in attendance.

It was a terrible day."

Gladys, Stephen and Eric Foster

(All photos in this section courtesy of the Daryl Foster Collection)

Bev Foster:

"We met in the eighth grade," says Beverly about the couple's early start. "We went to the same school and, through friends, began seeing each other and carried on from there. Later, when Billy began racing, we'd be at the track every Saturday night."

During their high school years, sometimes the couple had an on-again, off-again relationship. As their eldest daughter Debra related with a smile, "Every time Dad and Mom broke up and she wanted to date someone else, Dad would come over and ruin it – he made the guy high-tail it out of there."

"I was 18 and he was 19 when we married in 1956," says Bev. Three children followed, beginning with Debra in 1957, Billy Jr. in 1958 and Kelly in 1962.

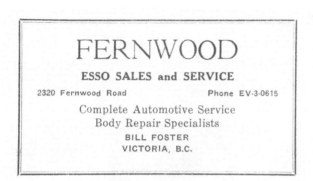

In their first years of marriage, Billy supported the family by taking over his dad Eric's garage for a time, then found a position with the Forestry Dept. That opportunity lasted only a short while due to Billy's allergies.

He then teamed up with Reg Midgley and both were car salesmen at Suburban Motors in Victoria. The pair moved on to start their own used car dealership, named Mayfair Motors. By this time though, Billy was fully committed to racing and beginning to make a name for himself throughout British Columbia and beyond.

"Financially it was working out pretty good," Bev remembers. "Actually, we were amazed. We thought we'd struggle more than we did. Billy lived for family and racing. He always made sure that the family was well taken care of."

Reg Midgley and Billy were both racing and business partners.

(Ted MacKenzie photo)

Bev continued: "We didn't do much as a family when the kids were young. He would only be home for a day or two and there was always a party going on somewhere. Sometimes I would travel with him but with the kids, it was a struggle. I would have loved to be able to go more but the kids were too little. Back in those days there wasn't a whole lot of people that could look after them, and my mother was still working."

"It was Billy's dream forever to race and becoming a full-time racer was always in his mind. He was doing so well. Rolla Vollstedt finally gave him that break, and it was great – very exciting days!"

When Billy finally reached the pinnacle of the sport at Indianapolis, the family accompanied him. The first year – 1965 – they rented a mobile home at a local trailer park and became close neighbors and friends with the young Andretti family. Both Billy and Mario were in their rookie year at the Speedway. Bev and Dee Ann Andretti quickly bonded, and their young kids played together.

Debra Foster was about 8 years-old then and recalls that: "Michael and I were friends in the trailer court, and I remember being in Andretti's trailer."

The Billy Foster family, then and today - Wife Bev with Debra, Billy Jr. and Kelly.

(Foster family collection)

At age 82, Jimmy Steen may have slowed down a bit, but still enjoys climbing into the cockpit of a race car now and then. In the fall of 2016, he drove his stock car to a third-place finish in a 75-lap race at Western Speedway. Quite the accomplishment!

Jim was a close cousin of Billy and from a very early age the two shared a love for speed.

Jimmy Steen:

"Billy's mother was my dad's sister," Jim explained. "He was born in September 1937, and I was born just one month later. He lived on one side of the school and we were on the other side. We both attended Oakland grade school, which was in Saanich. Around grade four or five my family moved to another area while Billy's folks also moved - but we stayed together in the same school. Later, we both went to the new junior high school, S.J. Willis. I think we started there in 1952."

Jimmy Steen

(Victoria Auto Racing Hall of Fame)

While Jim explained that the main sport they played was hockey, the cousins were always around race cars. In a May 2009 interview with *Thestar.com* Jim said: "Me and Billy liked to play hockey more than we liked going to class. And we liked cars even more than hockey."

"We grew up at my uncle Eric's (Billy's father) gas station – Fernwood Esso," Jim told this author. "He was a racer, building sprint cars and racing them around Victoria and Seattle. Dave Cooper was his driver."

Jimmy and Billy began racing jalopies together in 1954 at their local track, which was Western Speedway. Jim freely admits that "Billy was by far the better driver – a natural talent."

That first season, Jim suffered a major accident at the track and barely survived. "In the old days we used to run the cars pretty much as we got them," he said. "We'd strip 'em and added roll bars, but I didn't wear a safety belt. The car flipped and left me laying on the track."

He was running practice laps when the mishap occurred when the car overturned and landed on top of him. Jim was not expected to live more than an hour after the accident. His parents were rushed to the hospital with a police escort.

But Jimmy was a tough guy and, with the care he received, managed a full recovery. When he was able, Jim jumped back into racing locally. "I just stayed around Victoria," he admits. "I was a carpenter by trade, and I had a family then."

For most of his racing career, Jim was a one-man driver, crew, and car owner. And like so many others, he competed on a shoe-string budget – but was always at the track and part of the show. In the meantime, he watched as Billy moved up the racing ladder.

"It more or less started for Billy when he hooked up with Jimmy Haslam," said Jim. "They started building bigger and better cars and started traveling. They got into the modified cars, and that's what really got them going."

As Billy moved onward and upward with his racing career, he and Jimmy remained in touch with each other as much as possible. "When he was home, we used to go to his house and play poker," Jim remembers. "Billy liked having a good time. He wanted to race anything he could get his feet in."

Jim recalls the day of Billy's fatal accident. "It hit everybody really hard. We were at our grandmother's house and had to inform her. Billy was her favorite grandson and it just tore her apart."

Over the following years, Jim primarily raced stock cars locally. Driving a new car for the first race of the 1972 season, Jim was involved in a wreck that found his car flipping and rolling nine times down Western Speedway's backstretch. Fortunately, he came out unharmed, and was back at the track the following week.

Jim Steen was inducted into the Victoria Auto Racing Hall of Fame in 1991.

During the 1973 season at Western, Steen was honored with a celebration of his 20 years of continuous competition. Three years later, Jim formed a two-car team with his son, Kerry, as the driver of the second car.

Jimmy Steen holds the record of being the longest continuous competitor at Western Speedway – a record that will likely never be broken. In 1991, he was inducted into the Victoria Auto Racing Hall of Fame.

Jim still owns his cousin Billy's '65 Mustang.

A sampling of Jim's many race cars through the years.

(Victoria Auto Racing Hall of Fame)

Heather Rohn was another cousin of Billy'. We thank her for sharing some of her early memories prior to her passing in 2018.

Heather Rohn:

"Most of my memories of Billy and his family are from 1945 through 1952. Stephen and Billy visited us every summer that I can remember in Vancouver, B.C. Their parents – Eric and Gladys – usually brought them over with their bikes. Eric told my Mum that he wanted the boys to continue with piano practice while they were with us.

Stephen was exemplary, to my Mum's delight, and dutifully practiced daily. Mum taught him some duets. On the other hand, Billy – whom my Mum jokingly called "a scamp" – was not so obliging with his practicing.

One summer, while Stephen and my brother Alan discussed the merits of becoming plumbers along with other get-rich schemes, decided to make some money. We would all ride our bikes to Lulu Island to pick strawberries. Once we got started, very soon Billy found a rotten berry and mashed it in my face. Of course, I had to retaliate by picking an unripe berry and threw it at him. He winged one back, and the strawberry fight was on! We soon were caught and immediately got fired from the field. Stephen was not happy, although I'm sure my brother wasn't too upset, so we dragged on home.

There was another time when I asked my Mum if I could show Billy the Vancouver Public Library on Hastings Street, to which she gave permission. So, after riding our bikes down there we spent about five minutes at the library, and then Billy wanted to check out Chinatown and tour the alleyways.

At some point we were going through one alley where a lot of the Chinese people were smoking. Suddenly Billy said, "Let's get out of here," when two men started chasing us. These alleys were narrow and crowded with ramshackle kiosks, and we needed to get out of there to a main street.

I don't recall if Billy had tried to steal something or had bumped into someone or one of the kiosks, but the chase was on! Fortunately, as soon as we got to a main street, the pursuit was over. We were both pretty scared for a while. But in Billy's retelling of the ordeal (with much bravado), he had saved the day by getting *ME* out of there!

Other times, the four of us would often bike down to Kitsalino or English Bay to go swimming but that was not my cup of tea. I far preferred going to the Crystal Gardens in Victoria with Stephen and Billy.

Sometime before 1950 the boys were at Grandma Foster's house, along with a number of other relatives. While everyone was busy with things, Billy suggested we throw rocks at Farmer Jackson's cows out in the pasture next door, just to make them run! We thought it was hilarious – but unfortunately, we did get caught by the adults and Billy really got into trouble. I did too, but with a much milder reprimand.

It was in 1950 or '51 when I was at Eric and Gladys' house. Billy had a good sense of when he could sneak out, which he and I did one night even though Stephen tried to talk Billy out of it.

We went to Eric's garage on Fernwood. Billy, who was about 13 years-old then, knew exactly where to get a key and "borrow" a car. I'm not sure whether it was one of Eric's cars or one of his customer's.

We tooled all around Victoria for several hours. We even passed by a cop car. I think we were heading to the Tillicum Drive-In, but we didn't have the money and were a little concerned we'd get caught. Thankfully, we didn't.

These are just several examples of incidents to illustrate what an irrepressible kid Billy was – fun-loving, adventuresome, impish and lovable!

There's one other thing I should mention that took place sometime in the early 1970s. There was a pizza place in San Bernardino, California called 'The Mug'. We usually had our kids with us so didn't sit in the bar area. However, when I was in the bar and noted many sports photos on the wall, mostly of auto racing [Riverside Raceway was only a few miles from San Bernardino].

I saw one that looked like Billy and the bartender verified that. The bartender had taken the picture when he was at a race in Japan. I had never heard that Billy had raced over there. I always planned on going back to talk to the photographer, but somehow that never happened."

Sylvia Rose, whose husband Doug was a racer back in the 50s, was kind enough to share her own memories of Billy:

Sylvia Rose:

"I knew Billy right from the beginning. His family lived just up the street from ours when I was a young girl. Stephen Foster was my age and Billy was two years younger, so he was in a different age group. I attended school with Stephen.

Billy was always in and out of the solarium because of his illness. Stephen was a brainiac. He takes after his cousin David Foster. Stephen was a pilot in the air force and was a good musician, could play the piano well and was an honor student at Victoria High. Billy was more like his dad. You didn't dare him to do something, because he would go on to do it. A real dare-devil.

My husband Doug, who raced stock cars, once had an offer before one race to drive for a well-known stock car owner. Doug said he would, but that left the car he had been driving without a driver. So I called Billy and asked him if he would like to start driving again and he said yes. He took on Doug's old car, which was owned by Jimmy Haslam, and began racing again. This was around 1954.

Every Friday or Saturday we went to Western Speedway as long as Doug was racing. My dad took over Eric Foster's garage for a year.

Billy was a prankster. When Doug and I were first married, the hang-out for the VITRA racing gang was at the corner of Yates and Douglas streets in Victoria. We'd all go up-town and parked. One night I guess Billy got bored and said for everyone to follow him – there must've been 40 cars. He led us over hell's half-acre and then he went through Beacon Hills Park. We had just had a rain. My husband worked for the parks department and said you should have seen the lawn after 40 cars drove through it. That was Billy leading everybody along."

TWO

Billy's Friends Remember – Dave Cooper

As a Saanich teenager in the 1930s, Dave Cooper bought a worn-out Model T and, after hours of tinkering, got it running. He inherited his mechanical gifts from his father, and his interest in cars only increased.

Once the Langford Speedway opened in 1937, the young Cooper was often in the crowd of spectators. He was further introduced to auto racing by Eric Foster – Billy's dad – who owned the Fernwood Avenue Garage.

"I was actually a customer of Eric's back in the 1930s," Dave now recalls. "He and I hit it off pretty good. He was the president of the old Langford track and talked me into helping him out there."

Dave was a plumber by trade and had a Ford Model A work truck. "At Langford, just before the main event, they'd have a special race for anyone who wanted to run their street car – and the winner got a box of chocolate or whatever." explained Dave. "Eric talked me into running my truck, and that's what got me going."

Soon thereafter, Cooper got a chance to try his hand at driving a real race car, as he remembers: "Eric and a buddy of his had a car, but their driver wasn't doing very well. Eric talked his partner into putting me in the car. I ran second in my very first race, and that sold Eric."

"Eric knew of a race car that was for sale down in Washington and talked me into going in half with him to buy it. It was an old Ford open-wheeler that had a four-cylinder with twin carbs and all that stuff. We started at Langford Speedway and I had a good plumbing crew – they'd root me on."

When the Langford Speedway reopened in 1946 following the war years, Dave raced Eric Foster's #8 Friction-Proof car. He was now a serious big-time driver, finishing fourth-best in the 1947 Island Sprint Car Championships.

Until Langford Speedway's closure in 1950, Dave won his share of races against competitors such as Digger Caldwell, Bung Eng, Del Fanning and Gerry Vantreight. Dave raced at tracks as far away as California, scored one of his most satisfying victories at the Portland Speedway, and suffered one of his worst wrecks – a multiple end-over – in Roseburg, Oregon.

Dave Cooper in his early racing days, racing Eric Foster's Friction-Proof car.

(Victoria Auto Racing Hall of Fame)

Even today, at the age of 98, Dave still has fond memories of that era. "At some time, Eric Foster decided he wanted nothing more to do with race cars, so I was on my own. I had a racer built that was powered by a hot Ford V8 that burned alcohol. I took it down to the states and ran lots of fall races on the fairground tracks. I won a race in Oakland – 'on the wall' – as they called it."

"In Portland, I ran at both the Meadows horse track and the old Union Avenue Speedway. I drove a few races for [car owners] Vi and Art Scovell. They had a car that had run at Indy, but they put a different engine in it. I think it was a Studebaker. It blew a tire at Portland Meadows and I hit the wall.

They felt I first hit the wall which then blew the tire. I took offense to that and didn't want to drive for them anymore. I was also good friends with local Portland drivers Bob Gregg and Bill Hyde.

Because of his association with Eric Foster, Cooper has warm memories of Billy when he was just a youngster. "Billy was just a kid. He'd come to his dad's garage and sit in the car while Eric was telling me what to do. Anytime the car had to be moved out of the garage – boy, he was right there."

A young Billy Foster sharing victory lane with the hard-charging Dave Cooper.

(Victoria Auto Racing Hall of Fame)

"Billy was a natural," Dave remembers. "I'll bet you he wasn't but twelve-years-old when he first drove my plumbing truck around the race track.

Cooper's work truck did double-duty as his race car hauler.

(Victoria Auto Racing Hall of Fame)

They were still holding those special 'street car' events on Saturday nights and Dave recalled, "Billy drove my truck in one of those races and won it. I thought, 'Bill's going to be a great race car driver'. I thought the world of him!"

Because of his trade, Cooper was best known by the title "The Flying Plumber." He advertised his company with a sign on the fence in the south turn of the speedway. It turned out to be an expensive location, as the signage had to be repainted when a driver failed to make the turn and wiped out a portion of the fence and sign.

Starting with the 1953 racing season, Dave became increasingly more proficient in the sport he loved. Much of that early success came at Shearing Speedway. Articles about his winning ways appeared in the local area newspapers regularly, such as this one in the *Victoria Daily Times* on June 23rd, 1953:

Cooper Top Driver

Dave Cooper, voted most popular race car driver at Shearing Speedway last season, is piling up points in both the big car and stock car divisions this year and could easily take the track aggregate point championship title in both sections. For any driver, racing fans will quickly admit, this would be quite an accomplishment.

Dave, although known around the local track as a veteran, never really got his start driving in big meets until after the war in 1946. He first started race car driving in 1939. The first big race he ever drove in, Dave laughingly recalls, was at Yakima in 1946 when he placed second, finishing the event on a flat tire.

Since then it has been an upward surge for the "flying plumber." Racing on both sides of the border he placed third in aggregate point totals for the Northwest big cars in 1950. He was second to track champion Bob Simpson at the Cobble Hill cutoff oval last season.

Dave's driving can be likened to that of a horse racing jockey, in the respect that if he can see an opening, large or small, which he calculates his car will go through, then he goes through. Very few times he has been wrong in his judgement during the past two seasons.

In Saturday's meet both his big car and stocker were put out of action. The stock car was forced to the pits with a broken front axle and his No. 2 big car was incapacitated with a broken transmission when he locked wheels on the No. 2 turn with Bob Simpson. However, it is expected both cars will be running mainly through the efforts of mechanic, Bill Walters, for the next show.

Cooper's new car, which will be the lightest and should prove the fastest big car to hit the local scene in many years, is still in the making. With work being done on his other two cars this week, appearance of the new car at the track will be delayed that much longer. With his highly competitive spirit, fans have come to look on the colorful Cooper for a top performance and the "flying plumber" rarely disappoints.

Like most other drivers, Dave Cooper had his share of racing mishaps - such as this one at Western Speedway. Note Billy Foster standing on the right, with hands in his pockets.

(Ted MacKenzie photo)

The *Victoria Daily Times* offered the following reports on Cooper's progress during the latter part of the 1953 racing season:

Cooper Sets New Mark at Shearing Speedway

Dave Cooper experienced one of his better nights at Shearing Speedway Saturday as he cracked the track record and then went on to win all the races in which he competed in the weekly car racing meet. It marked the fifth or sixth time this season that Cooper has broken the existing mark for the oval. He completed the circuit last night in 17.42 seconds. The old mark was 17.50.

Cooper also won the A-Main event, the helmet dash and the second heat race. Displaying some masterful driving, Cooper came all the way from the back in the A-Main to take the lead, beat off some strong opposition by Ken Nelson and Bruce Passmore, and pulled away for a five car-length victory.

(Victoria Auto Racing Hall of Fame)

Cooper Increases Lead with Four Track Wins

Colorful Jack Spaulding set a new big car track record at Shearing Speedway, Cobble Hill, Saturday night but he had to take a back seat to the driving ability of Dave Cooper. Leading in the point standings of the big car division, Cooper went way out in front after Saturday night's card. He won the main event, helmet dash and first heat in the big car division and also the main event of the stock car division.

Spaulding circled the quarter-mile track in 15.28 seconds to chop more than two-tenths of a second off the record set last year by Bob Simpson. Driving Gene Fanning's Seattle car, Simpson also had a good night although he couldn't win an event. He was in the money in every race, picking up three seconds and two thirds. A field of 16 cars started in the main race of the stock car event but only six could finish, none of them pressing Cooper too strongly.

Cooper's Cars Take Point Titles in Both Big Car, Stock Divisions

Final point standings for both big car and stocks at Shearing Speedway this year were released by the British Columbia Automotive Sports Association Wednesday. The standings refer not to drivers but to individual cars as in some cases more than one driver handled the same car during the season. Point standings for drivers have not yet been released.

In big car races, Dave Cooper's No. 2 car piled up a season's total of 265.5 points for first place and the right to carry the No. 1 tag next season. Cooper edged out Verne Moore's No. 1 car by only a single point. Moore, whose car was driven for the greater part of the season by Jack Spaulding before transfer of ownership, was

11.5 points behind going into the Thanksgiving Day race and almost pulled out the lead by scoring a sweep in the big meet.

Cooper's No. 99 stock car accumulated 260.5 points to lead the stockers with Bruce Passmore's No. 48 car second with 223 points. Popular Ken Nelson's #15, a strong finisher late in the season, was third with 149 points.

In 1954, Dave repeated as the season champion for stock cars, along with holding the track record and being voted as Most Popular Driver. As the winner of the Gold Cup Race in 1955, the "Flying Plumber" also repeated as track champion.

Dave Cooper tending to his growing collection of trophies.

(Victoria Auto Racing Hall of Fame)

Moving ahead a few years, Cooper was virtually unbeatable during 1957, primarily at Western Speedway. On his way to becoming the track champion for the third time, he won the Gold Cup, the Roy White Memorial, the Six-Mile Perpetual Trophy, the Corby Cup (most main event wins) and the championship race. 1958 was a carbon copy of the previous year, as Dave repeated as track champion. In 1959 Cooper won the Dick Willoughby Memorial Trophy and ended the year fifth-place in the standings.

Dave believes it was in 1957 that he and Billy Foster first competed against each other on the track. "Bill and I raced together and had some good times," says Dave. "He was so smooth."

In one race in Roseburg, Oregon, a back-marker spun out in front of me while I was leading the race. I went over one of his back wheels and flew up in the air. Somehow Billy avoided hitting me – he was right on my ass and we were sliding around a lot."

In 1962 at the Mt. Douglas Hill Climb in Victoria, on somewhat of a whim, Billy Foster ran Jim Haslam's track roadster up the hill in winning time. Dave Cooper competed in the same event in a TVR sports car he had at the time.

TVR was an independent British manufacturer of lightweight, tube-frame sports cars with powerful engines. At one time, the company was the third-largest specialized sports car manufacturer in the world.

Cooper bought the car brand-new and shipped it over from England – less engine – to his home in British Columbia. He acquired a small-block Ford V8 from the factory and installed it. It was a rocket ship.

Dave Cooper racing and winning in his TVR

(Victoria Auto Racing Hall of Fame)

(Victoria Auto Racing Hall of Fame)

Cooper had quite a bit of fun with that TVR, which he also used as a daily driver. When Billy moved up to running the USAC Champ Cars, Dave drove down to his races at both Phoenix and Riverside. At those venues, he became acquainted with Billy's best racing buddy, Mario Andretti.

As Dave remembers, "Mario took one look at my TVR and wanted to drive it in the worst way. He just loved that thing! He put it up against a guy from California who had a Mustang. They went to a place where they stored the race cars and had a drag race. That was an interesting time."

"I always thought Billy wanted to go big-time in racing", said Dave. "When he went to Indianapolis I went back there, and he was making good times."

Dave was at Riverside International Raceway when Billy was killed. "I was there with Bob Lowe and we were on the backstretch timing him. Billy was making damn good time but losing some in the corners. Then his brake drum exploded – he was probably going about 150 mph when he crashed. It was really hard being there."

During the course of his long motorsports career, Dave Cooper played a hand in the formation of the Vancouver Island Track Racing Association – more commonly known as 'VITRA'. This organization played a major role in racing during its era. It was one of the largest and best organized motor racing clubs in the West. Dave Cooper penned the following history of VITRA for the Western Speedway program in 1961:

In 1949 a group of automobile enthusiasts met in an old home, called "The Dingle", on Gorge Road. The property was owned by Bruce Passmore, who was then the owner of the old Langford Speedway. The instigator – Jack Smith – was one of Victoria's best-known race car builders and a former driver who is now a teacher at Victoria High School.

The original idea was to build cars that could be driven on the road and still be raced. For this reason, the club was called the Vancouver Island Track Roadster Association and Jack Smith was elected the first president. Les Webb, who is now VITRA's Paymaster, filed the original papers for the club's charter, which was received in 1949.

In 1984 Dave Cooper was one of the original inductees to the Victoria Auto Racing Hall of Fame.

(Victoria Auto Racing Hall of Fame)

The club held its first races at Langford Speedway; however, these were mostly fill-in races for the Big Cars, which were very popular then. It wasn't until the Shearing Speedway opened at Cobble Hill in 1952 that the club was able to field a full event of races. It was apparent right from the start that the roadsters or home-built sports cars were in the minority, and the American-made coupes and sedans were the most popular. This created a division in the club, with the new cars being called 'Stockers'. The Stockers soon completely took over the club and, for this reason while Frank Addison was president, the roadster portion of the club's name was changed to 'Racing', as it stands today.

Most of the cars were driven with license, lights, etc. for the first few years of racing and were similar to the jalopies of today. They were also similar for the frequency of accidents. This made driving home something of a problem, and soon all cars were towed to the races. The machines used as tow cars were generally in worse condition than the stockers and towing over the Malahat overheated the engines – so it was common practice for everyone to stop at the summit. These impromptu get-togethers are probably remembered better than the races!

With the opening of Western Speedway in 1954, VITRA continued to grow. It was in 1958 that the highest purses ever were paid out, and this figure will certainly be passed in 1961.

This year is notable for a number of firsts: the first time the club has taken over a track and promoted racing; the first time in a number of years that late-model overhead-valve V8 engines have been allowed; the reorganizing of a Jalopy division with the first all-Jalopy race night; the first time a 150-lap championship race has been run; the first time a purse as large as $3,000 has been offered; and the first time cars have come from Idaho, Washington, Alberta, etc. to race here.

THREE

Billy's Friends Remember – Dick Hansen

Among the close childhood friends of Billy was Dick Hansen, and together they grew to adulthood – while also becoming business partners.

"We lived in an area called Fernwood," Dick remembers, "and we had two hills nearby - one was much steeper than the other. The neighborhood kids would get together with our old soap box cars with simple two-by-four wooden axles, and we'd use buggy wheels taken from our mother's carriages. We had a rope on the front we kinda' used to steer with."

"We'd go down the smaller hill with those rickety old cars. The only one that would go down the much steeper hill was Billy," Dick continued. "Everybody else would say, 'no, we'll just go down the short hill'. We were eleven years old, and that was our introduction to racing."

"Billy was a natural from the beginning," observed Dick. "We were all driving cars at early ages, and he was no different. There was one instance - I think Billy was only twelve or thirteen years old - at Langford Speedway.

Dave Cooper, a plumber, was there practicing with his sprint car. Somebody mentioned that Billy wanted to drive a car around the track.

Once they reached their teenage years, Dick and Billy stayed close. They played a lot of hockey together and spent weekend time racing at Western Speedway. The pair went into business together with a full-service gas station and auto repair business – Fernwood Esso – where they also bought and sold old cars on the side.

"Billy was winning races in stock cars, as we all were," says Dick, "in '34 Fords and that sort of thing at Western Speedway. The oval started out as a dirt track, but a year or two later they paved it. He gained the nickname, 'Billy the Kid Foster'. I remember him saying, 'I want to race at Indy someday'".

In the ensuing years, Billy's involvement with racing progressed. "I was married with a young family and everything, but I stayed involved with Western Speedway," Dick described. "Billy went professional racing with the CAMRA series and I struck out on my own with the repair shop. We split up at that point, but we and our wives stayed best of friends. I ended up with BC Transit as a driver-trainer for busses. I'm 79 years-old now."

 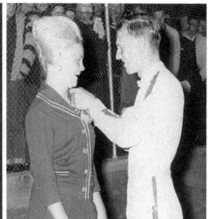 

Billy won his share of trophies around the Pacific Northwest.

(Victoria Auto Racing Hall of Fame)

Dick Hansen in his home shop.

(Author photo)

"As he got into the Indy Cars, Billy was making a living and doing quite well. But Bev (Billy's wife) had her hands full looking after their kids when he was gone racing," Dick noted. "When he was at home he would come and join the boys for a beer. Nothing ever changed about him, and he was a fun-loving guy".

"We played hockey together, and I remember one time he got clipped in the face and eye. He said, 'I have to quit this, or it could be the end of my racing career'. We didn't wear helmets or have pads on like they do these days."

Dick continued, "We did talk a lot about his experiences at Indy. Billy said, 'If you could just imagine the speed I'm going and that steering wheel – it's like holding a beer bottle in each hand with all that vibration and movement."

Reflecting on his memories of Billy Foster, Dick said, "He was well-known throughout the lower island. Running all types of cars was no big deal for him – other than the schedules. Our races up here were the hotbed of racing. Billy was eating up the coast here, along with the CAMRA circuit."

"It was terrible to hear of his fatal accident and I'm still emotional about it. He never had a chance to fully prove his capabilities. Billy's aspiration was that if he made it big, he wanted to own a Ford dealership, but that never came to be."

Dick Hansen and friends restored one of Billy's most famous race cars.

(Photos from the Victoria Auto Racing Hall of Fame and the author)

FOUR

Victoria's Auto Racing Heritage – The Willows

What is not well known is that the Victoria, British Columbia area holds a rich motorsports heritage. Automobiles first began appearing in the early 1900s and it is said the first to arrive in the area was a 1902 curved-dashboard Oldsmobile, owned by a Dr. Hurt.

A Mr. Todd owned the next car to arrive – a 1903 Stanley Steamer. Accompanied by his riding mechanic, they raced against the clock to a point on the wagon trail (15.5 miles) to a point on the Malahat Summit – in just three hours one-way!

The local automotive experience stepped up a notch in 1905 when Mr. Butchart imported a bigger and more powerful 30-horsepower Winton. About that time, Victoria's Willows horse racing track became a dirt-oval testing ground for an increasing number of motorized vehicles. It came as no doubt that sanctioned motor racing was soon to follow.

The first automotive racing event we were able to locate was previewed by this article which appeared in Victoria's *The Daily Colonist* newspaper on May 21st, 1915:

Racing Cars Had Final Practice

A big crowd watched the work-out of the fast cars on the Willows track last night. As the entry list is a long one, it took some time to get the drivers in position for practice starting, but after two or three tries, things went smoothly enough, and it is certain that some fast times may be looked for in the car races.

Every arrangement has been made to do away with delays between races, and all details are arranged to ensure the avoidance of any hitch in the carrying out of the program.

Yesterday was the last day for the cars to practice, and today the motorcycles will work out and practice starting. Word was received from Vancouver yesterday that all the riders will be over today, including the professionals. Great care has been taken of the track, and it is in such excellent shape that the crowd will certainly witness some of the fastest riding and driving ever seen on a half-mile track on the Coast.

1919 – Major racing comes to the Willows

Victoria's first structured and widely promoted automobile race took place on August 16th of 1919 at the Willows Fairgrounds. Members of the Victoria Automobile Club, along with men from the Automobile and Accessory Dealers, coordinated this life-size event.

Headlines in *The Daily Colonist* newspaper spoke of how great the event would be, and how promoters had found the greatest "Speed Kings" and "Wheel Jockeys" of the Pacific Northwest. Some described the venue as "the fastest dirt track in the world."

Local car dealers and automotive supply stores placed large ads in the local papers and sent out flyers as far up the Island as Nanaimo. The dealers' ads pushed the sale of their own vehicles, stating just how good one would look if they showed up at the races in a car of their own.

The Esquimalt & Nanaimo Railway took part in the promotion by offering a special discount to those who wanted to go down-island to attend the event. A train pass purchased on Friday was still valid on Monday, meaning more people could stay the weekend and spend their money in Victoria's stores, restaurants and hotels. A general admission ticket to the event was $1.10, a grandstand seat was $1.65, and a box seat was $2.60

On Sunday, August 10th, 1919, *The Daily Colonist* began what would be a series of enticing articles in the days leading up to the event – written in the journalistic style of the day. In this extended opener, a few of the expected drivers and cars are described:

Real Speed Kings Entering for Races

"And I miss my guess if this race meet isn't the finest thing of its kind ever held in the Northwest" is the summary of Mr. Walter Revercomb, one of the committee members in charge of the arrangements for next Saturday's auto races at the Willows.

Details as to the entries in the professional events are coming in with every mail, and each day sees additions to the list of racers who will compete in the various classes. The latest to file an affidavit is Ernest Columbus, of Seattle, who will compete in the light car class with a machine of his own build.

The first man on the ground arrived on Thursday, when George Stacy, of Yakima, brought over a red racer. This car is running in the light car class and is a Ford with few changes which are visible, but it weighs only 340 pounds, and that tells a tale. Each of the pistons has been lightened by removal of over a pound of surplus material, and this process has been applied to every portion of the machine, which has been attracting much attention as it ran around the business district over the weekend. Another entry in the small car class is expected here tomorrow, when Mr. W.R. McConnell will bring over a Ford which is equipped with a sixteen-valve engine.

Ray Kayno has had great success with his little French Peugeot of late, in the races around Los Angeles. He claims that in a few yards he can accelerate to 105 miles per hour, and this gives him a great start with his 360-pound baby. Henry North will be the driver to pilot the Comet Special when it takes to the Willows track. At Vancouver recently, this car won a pair of races in handsome time.

Bill Giddings is doing the double event stunt. He has a special Maxwell running in the light car class and will also pilot the great Lott Special in the heavy class. This latter car was running at record setting clips some three years ago under the name of the Aubrey Special. Then Aubrey was killed in one of his speed bursts, and the man who secured possession of the monster was never able to get his wife to allow him to try it out. For the next two years it rarely left the garage, until George Lott, of Seattle, heard of the car and bought it, as much as an advertisement for his battery business as anything else. Bill Giddings will carry the hopes of lots of Victorians who want to see local men come in ahead, for he worked for several years in some of the local garages before migrating to Seattle.

The combination of Charles Latta plus E.J. Romano is due to provide lots of speed around the Willows track. Latta has a great name as a driver, while those who know say that Romano is a mechanical genius, and the special car which bears his name is one of his pet projects. It is fitted with an eight-cylinder "V" type Hali-Scott aeroplane engine and has such a flow of power that it made the 12-mile climb up Pikes Peak at Denver in 20 minutes and 23 seconds, beating all the other cars in the event by a wide margin.

The Stutz Special, which will be driven by Walter Blume, is the identical machine which won the 100-mile inter-city event at Tacoma two years running. It was built for racing and advertising purposes by Jim Parsons when he was first handling the Stutz, and it is in great part due to the reputation of this car that the Stutz got its flying start in the public appreciation.

What sort of a road burner the Duesenberg entry of Jack Ross may be is puzzling the local men. The only thing they are going on is that Ross is one of the wisest race dopesters in Seattle, where he runs a big taxi business. Jack Ross has a Mercer which has brought him lots of kudos, but he heard such remarkable stories of the new bus that he sold his faithful flyer and hustled down to San Francisco to get the new machine himself. He writes that he is more than pleased and will be driving the entry himself.

If the Vulcan Kewpie comes over from Vancouver there will be two Stutz racers in the heavy car events, each of them with a great name. This Kewpie bird was run throughout the East by Earle Cooper for the Stutz Company, and Mr. J.R. Duncan, of the Vulcan Ironworks, bought it mainly for the pleasure of having the fastest thing on wheels in Vancouver. Harry Hooper regularly drives the speeder and has earned the title of Vancouver's Pride by the manner in which he has been able to make all other mainland cars take his dust.

Silver Port Awaits Locals

Much interest centers on what local speedsters are doing to make a showing. As a starter, the Victoria Auto Dealers' Association is putting up a handsome silver cup, a real big one, which will fill the eye, for amateur racers to scramble after. There are no strings on the offer other than a ban against monkeying with the works of the entries. Any old car with a swift pair of heels is welcome to get into the running but putting a special gear in the rear end will be considered poor sport, and any such cars will be requested to go home. Gentlemen who claim that large and heavy bodies are what keep their busses from passing the flight Ford on Yates

Street hill are to have a chance to prove their words or hold their peace. They may come out without a single fixing other than a bonnet if they so desire.

In somewhat a light-hearted approach, the article continues by enticing local competitors to challenge the 'big-boys' of racing who are expected to dominate the event:

The Real Hush-Hush

In the meantime, there is a remarkable situation in the local garages. Ask any one of them, from Rennie's to Plimley's, and all over with solemn eye: "Well, we may have an entry, but there's so much darned work in fixing up a car," and all the while two or three men are feverishly working at some back bench on the innards of what is hoped will be the bacon-bringer. The fact of the matter is every last one of the garages appears to be trying to steal a march on the other fellows, and by intimating that there is nothing going to get that much of a start on the work of slicking up some dark horse.

And all the while the committee in charge of this feature sits back and says "go to it boys, but no faking. Give the civilian with a real car a chance to beat your old crocks," and the private car owner who enters a stripped chassis has a really good chance, so great has been the improvement in engine design in recent years. Such is the real meaning of the flat "thou shalt not fake."

Quite a bit of attention was directed towards preparing the Willows track in order to make this a world-class event:

Alderman Sangster Looks On

At the Willows, great improvement labor is being put in on the track. Grass-grown and rutty from four years of misuse and disuse, the oval looked poor going when the organizing committee first inspected it, but an Avery Tractor from Thomas Pilmley's depot and one of the city's graders made short work of the forage, and already the track shows that its years' old reputation as the best on the North Pacific Coast was based on fact.

Mr. Robert Hillier, of Tacoma, was one of an inspection party which visited the oval yesterday and, after a tour around the course, he said that when the improvements were completed, the Willows course would be vastly superior to the tracks existing at Vancouver, Seattle, Tacoma, Walla Walla, Yakima, or any other northwestern center, which prides itself on its motor races.

The lead-up to the Big Event continued with this newspaper article, dated August 12th, 1919, highlighting several upstanding citizens that planned to attend:

Motor Races Promise Remarkable Success

Mr. J.R. Thomas, of Portland, Maine, a capitalist tourist, has postponed his trip to Alaska, and requested Thomas Pilmley to secure for him a box at the auto races to be held at the Willows next Saturday. J.A. Virtue, of the Oak Bay Hotel, has secured two boxes. J.A. Rithet, one. Dr. Tomalin purchased his box seats, and numerous prominent residents of Victoria have reserved their seats at the rate of two and four, according to the number of their parties, and the indications are that there will not be many box seats left by noon tomorrow, so great was the demand yesterday even before the sale opened.

Mr. C.H. Willis, chairman of the executive committee, stated last night that the interest already shown in the auto races was remarkable, and that a great crowd would attend. Mr. Willis also made it plain that the free list had been entirely suspended, as the expenses of conducting the auto races would be very heavy and a part of the proceeds is to be given to the Orphan's Home. The work of putting the track in first-class condition "is progressing most satisfactorily," and it is believed that by Thursday it will be ready for the first tryouts.

Jack Ross and his great Duesenberg racing car arrived in Seattle from San Francisco on Sunday night, and will be in Victoria on Thursday. Walter Blume has notified the executive committee that he would be here on Wednesday with the Stutz Special. This is a fast car, and has many victories to its credit, but a majority of the cars that will race at The Willows have never been pitted against each other before at a race meet.
George Lott now believes that his Lott Special is a world beater on a dirt track, and the Romano Special already holds several worlds' records. "From all the information gathered as to the class and number of great racing cars, the racing of next Saturday will be the most sensational event ever witnessed in the Pacific Northwest on a dirt track," said Walter Revercomb, a member of the executive committee.

On the morning of the Saturday meet, August 16th, 1919, a pre-race newspaper report in *The Daily Colonist* brought all the details together. The City of Victoria and Canada would be on the international racing map:

Victoria Gains Much Fame from Race Meet

All Victoria is talking of the great race meet which will take place this afternoon at the Willows, and in a few weeks at most all Canada will be appraised of the fact that the finest automobile competition ever held in Canada is that which the Victoria automobile dealers have prepared for this city's benefit. The official record photographer of Canada, who has been here for some days in the course of a trans-Canada tour, has been instructed from Ottawa to take pictures of the Willows contests for dissemination throughout Canada and the Old Country, as typifying one of the sports which this city offers among its many attractions.

Track conditions at the Willows will be as nearly perfect as constant work can make them. All through the night two shifts of men wetted the track, heavy rollers have been steadily packing the surface into a solid bed, and this work will be maintained right up to the moment when the first event is called.

Chairman C.H. Willis said last night that the committee was more than pleased with the way the track has come under attention. "The Willows oval was never designed to withstand speedy motor traffic. It has been allowed to get into a chocking condition, and we are all surprised by the results we have attained," he said. "Of course, there will be a little dust after the afternoon wear has loosened up the surface, but practically all of the loose material was removed yesterday, and the watering and rolling will have the track just fine."

George Lott, who runs the Lott Special for the advance of motoring at a staggering yearly maintenance cost, said last night that the half-mile Willows track absolutely outclassed Vancouver and Tacoma, in spite of the latter course being a mile long. "There is only one improvement I can see is needed, paint the fence posts white," he said, and forthwith Chairman Willis had the work put in hand.

To educate those spectators who had never attended a sporting event of this nature, the article explained:

Spectators Must Help

There are two points on which the Auto Dealers' Association is asking the cooperation of the public. In the first place, the spectators are asked to come early, as the advance ticket sales indicate that there will be thousands of people to be handled before the races commence, which will be as soon after 2:30 o'clock as possible.

The second and more important assistance which the spectators can give is in connection with any possible misadventures which may occur. It must be constantly borne in mind that if, for any reason whatever, one of the racers drops out of the running the rest of the entries continue their speeding at the top of their motor's power. Under these conditions the people in the center of the oval are asked to obey one simple rule, "Pick a view point and stay there." Don't move around unduly, and above all do not press towards any point where a car is stopped.

Inside the track fence has been marked a clear white line, thirty feet back from the rail on the straights and forty feet away on the bends. This line will be patrolled by all the police who can be spared from the city and Oak Bay forces, but unless the crowd implicitly obeys instructions and refrains from crowding toward centers of excitement, it will take a battalion of soldiers to keep people from getting too close to danger, and such action would spoil the success of a meet on which all the Northwest has its eyes today.

The article continued by describing some of the confirmed race cars and their drivers – as if reporting on an upcoming horse race:

A Dozen Cars Entered

The last of the racing cars to arrive will be the Seattle Special which Charlie Latta is bringing over this morning. All the other cars were out at the Willows yesterday afternoon to try out the track and tune up, and all spoke well of the course.

Gus Duray put his Stutz No. 4 through an easy workout; Jack Ross trod on his special for half a lap, and brought his half-mile time to 35 seconds, and George Lott ran around the track in 33 seconds. By the way, the Lott Special will be handled in all the races except the one-mile dash by Bill Giddings. In this mile event the car will be pushed to the limit by George Lott himself, as he wants to show that the car has the speed legs of the whole field.

After the Vulcan Kewpie and Harry Hooper has sauntered around a couple of times her race driver gave place to Mr. J.D. Duncan, the owner of the checker board star of Vancouver, and he took it for a spin around the get the feel of the track. "You've done wonders here, this is a real track for a dirt course. I'm glad I came over," was his pleased compliment, as he alighted after a speedy run.

What Racing Really Means

Henry North took the Romano car for a turn and the sight of this car making a dash set George Lott talking. "There goes the creation of a genius. Money means nothing to Romano. He's spent thousands on what his friends call a fool idea, and today he has a machine which is a marvel, no less. That is what motor racing does. No motor races, no experimenting, no new ideas, no modern cars, no aeroplanes, no tanks, the war still on and civilization imperiled. All that from automobile races and the visionaries who build cars for them."

When the Mercer was gully-bussing around the far bend of the course she blew a tire off, and Walter Blume had got the car slowed down to a crawl before the casing hit the ground. Spectators vowed that the tire mounted over twenty feet in the air when it came off, and it made quite a queer sight as it spinned against the blue sky.

Louie Nelson took his Victoria Special for a final tryout and the performance of the local entry was watched with close attention by the other drivers. Louie appeared to be holding a bit in reserve, but of one lap on which one of the boys was holding a watch, it was remarked: "If he can keep that up, that lad's in the money all right." He made one mile in a trifle over a minute and came in as pleased as punch with his mount.

All the smaller cars made good showings, but it was apparent that none of them was being pushed, and no real line on their speed was obtainable. William McDonnell spoke for them all when he said, "Don't want to burn the track, just try out how she rides around the bends."

The most successful competitor of the event was Henry North, who picked up wins in three events. Driving a Romano Special, he was victorious in the Mile Against Time (1:09) and the eight-mile race for Heavy Cars (10:00). In a five-mile contest for Light Cars, he was first across the line with a Comet Special (6:54). Gus Duray, racing his Stutz, took home the laurels in both the five-mile Dash (6:26) and the twenty-mile Victoria Free for All (26:00).

When all was said and done, the inaugural event at the Willows track in 1919 proved to be a major victory for the promoters, competitors, fans and the city itself. Over 4,000 energetic ticket buyers watched the most popular speed demons of the time compete against local drivers.

1920 – A Return to the Willows

News of the huge success of the 1919 event at the Willows spread and plans for a repeat performance quickly gained momentum. The date for the race was set for May 22, 1920 and promised the addition of a number of drivers crossing the border from the United States.

Teams arrived with their new, technically-advanced racing machines, which were now lighter and faster than before. People around the region were eager to see the 16-valve Stutz Special that, when driven by Jack Ross, achieved an average speed of 120 miles-per-hour around the Los Angeles Motor Speedway. It was publicized that Ross had issued a $1,000 check for anyone who could beat him.

To further entice both previous and new fans of local motorsports, race organizers arranged for a parade downtown the night before the races. The parade started in front of the Legislative Buildings and toured through the town.

As it did the year before, *The Daily Colonist* newspaper helped to spearhead promotions, beginning with this short preview article on Tuesday, May 18th, 1920, preceding the race:

Fast Auto Racer Arrived Yesterday

The first racing car has arrived in town. Jack Ross, accompanied by his mechanic, Phil Yodle, came over from Seattle on yesterday afternoon's boat with his powerful 16-valve Stutz Special, and last evening spent a few minutes on the track preparing for the big race meet next Saturday.

"The track is in perfect condition and there should be some tall speeding done Saturday," declared Mr. Ross, after covering the course a few times. Mr. Ross stated that he had come over early so that he could get used to the track, and on Saturday would do his best to lower the world's dirt track record, now 1:04 for the mile. Phil Yodle is an old-time racer, having piloted cars on all the principle race courses in Canada, the United

States, and Europe. Besides being an auto expert, he loves the sport of flying, and has served overseas with the United States Flying Corp.

On the following Thursday, May 20th, 1919, the newspaper further teased its readership with this piece:

Speed Kings Arrive to Prepare for Meet

Today will see the arrival of most of the speed cars from Vancouver and Seattle to take part in the big race meet to be held at the Willows track Saturday afternoon. Gus Duray, with his Stutz Special, arrived yesterday, but had not yet had a workout.

"The track could not be in a better condition," declared Mr. C.H. Willis, president of the Victoria Auto Sports, Limited, yesterday. "Jack Ross has made the course many times and he thinks it could not be beaten. Right up till Saturday afternoon we will continue to sprinkle the track, and with the cars traveling over it, the surface will be hard and fast."

Tickets are selling at a fast rate. The box seats are nearly all sold, and a large part of the grandstand has been disposed of, according to George Little, who is in charge of this section of work. Long-distance telephone calls from Seattle, Tacoma and Vancouver accounted for many of yesterday's bookings, and the mail from up-island points continued the remarkable demand which started Tuesday.

The Erickson Special and its driver, Carl Erickson, are due to arrive on this afternoon's boat from Vancouver. This entry has caused the Mainland metropolis to take enormous interest in the races, and sports are talking of coming across in throngs to see Carl "bring back the bacon." Jim Healey, with his fast Stutz, is also expected to be over today.

Prior to making their way to the track, Victorians read this *Daily Colonist* news update on the morning of the race. The Willows Fairgrounds seemed to be *THE* place to be that day:

Speed Kings Prepared for Race Meet Today

The whole of Victoria is talking about the big race meet to be held this afternoon, starting at 2:30, at the Willows oval, which promises to be the greatest ever held on a dirt track in the Pacific Northwest. Track conditions at the Willows will be perfect. The past week it has been sprinkled, rolled and graded. All last night two shifts of men wetted the track, and heavy rollers steadily packed the surface into a solid bed. This work will be maintained right up till this afternoon just before the races commence.

Mr. C.H. Willis, president of the Victoria Auto Sports, Limited, stated last evening that he was highly delighted with the condition of the track. "Victorians will be absolutely assured there will be no dust this afternoon. Last year our chief trouble was the dust, but today things will be entirely different. The track has been well soaked, both by sprinklers and the rain of the past few days."

Final arrangements for the meet were discussed at a luncheon at the Dominian Hotel yesterday, when the speed kings were guests of the Victoria Auto Sports, Limited.

On Sunday, May 23rd, 1920, following another successful event, *The Daily Colonist* published an extensive report with the results:

Large Crowd Sees Race Meet at Willows Track

Over 4,000 race fans witnessed the big race meet held yesterday afternoon at the Willows track, and saw Jack Ross, with his 16-valve Stutz Special, capture the Pacific Northwest dirt track championship from Gus Duray. The race meet from beginning to end was a success, and the competitions were so thrilling at times that the crowded grandstand rocked with excitement.

The track was in excellent condition, and there was very little dust. Each and every event was closely contested, and some exciting races were staged. Jack Ross and Gus Duray were in a class by themselves and gave an exhibition of real fast, clever driving.

During the last race, the feature of the meet, Jim Healey of Vancouver, driving a Lott Special with mechanic "Speed" Thompson of Seattle, went through the fence at the north end of the rack and turned turtle in the bushes. Mr. Thompson was cut about the head, while Mr. Healey received a few minor injuries which were attended to on the track by Dr. J.F. Grant.

From the appearance of the parking space about the Willows there could not have been but a few members of the city's motoring clan who were not present, and in addition there were many machines from Up-Island and Mainland points, with a strong delegation from the other side of the international boundary.
From a financial standpoint the meet was a success. All the drivers received a good share of the gate receipts, and the balance will be given to the Orphan's Home and the Island Development Association. "Everyone who attended the meet today enjoyed themselves immensely," stated C.H. Willis last evening to The Colonist. "I want to thank all the officials and those who helped make the meet such a huge success."

Following these accolades, the article continued to describe, in greater detail, the outcome of the races:

The first event called was the mile against time, and with a world's record of 1:04 minutes for a half-mile dirt track as a check of the work of the drivers, the fans shouted with applause as Jack Ross brought his Stutz Special across the line in 1:06. The runner-up was Gus Duray in a Stutz. George Lott, driving the Lott Special, took third fastest time.

The five-mile race for the heavy cars resulted in a win for Jack Ross in his 16-valve Stutz, which was running like a clock. Gus Duray made second place. Ross made a wonderful getaway and kept the lead and won the race. Jim Healey, driving a Stutz, was forced out of the running owning to having trouble with his motor. George Lott, driving the Lott Special, made third. The Erickson Special, piloted by Carl Erickson, made fourth. The light cars provided some good sport in the five-mile race, with four entries. W.R. McDonnell, in a Ford Special, did some remarkably tall speeding and won.

The Oh No Special, driven by "Wild" Bill Giddings, made second, and the Buttera Special, piloted by James Buttera, came in third. The Pepp Special buzzed around the track and helped raise dust. It took the fourth place, being about a mile behind the third car.

The fourth event for the big cars proved real exciting. The race was for eight miles and the spectators were given nine minutes of real fast, close and exciting racing. Duray got away ahead of Ross and did his best to keep the lead. Ross, with his clever driving, got ahead of Duray, and hit the winning post 200 yards in the lead. The Lott Special, driven by "Wild" Bill Giddings, made third place, while Carl Erickson came in last.

The small cars had a second race with W.R. McDonnell winning first position again. Jim Buttera in his Buttera Special took second position and G.W. Stewart third. Jim Healey in the Oh No Special had motor trouble and did not finish the race.

The main event of the day packed a lot of excitement for the thousands of spectators, and it appears they got their money's worth:

The 20-mile Victoria International free-for-all was the great event of the day, and this went with flying colors to Jack Ross by a decisive margin. Getting a start on the field in the 40 trips around he managed to gain a clear mile on all entries, and by staging most of his passing stunts opposite the grandstands he garnered a continuous succession of plaudits.

The 16-valve Stutz got into the limelight. Duray, with his Stutz, gave Ross a wild chase about the track. The longer Ross' car traveled the faster it went, and Duray was unable to hit the fast pace, so dropped out of the race, his alibi being that his "engine had overheated."

About the twelfth mile Jim Healey, of Vancouver, who was driving the Lott Special, was making the north end of the track at a fast speed and it seemed that he lost control of the machine for a second and then tried to right it – and failed. He went through the fence and turned upside down in the bushes. Mechanic "Speed" Thomas, who was with him, was cut about the head, but Healey only received slight injuries. Both were about last evening and were being congratulated on not being killed.

The Erickson Special, driven by Carl Erickson of Vancouver, did not make any real fast speed, but just plugged along and made second place. W.R. McDonnell in his Ford Special came in third.
The 20-mile event was exceedingly interesting as both Ross and Duray were out for a win, do or die. From the start to the end Ross did some excellent driving. Duray did all in his power to win this event, but Ross' car was too fast and kept the lead the entire race without any trouble. When on the straight-away it seemed to fly, leaving Duray far in the background. When Duray saw that his chances were futile he threw up his hands and called it "quits."

FIVE

Billy's Friends Remember – Ray Pottinger

Like so many of his contemporaries from the Victoria area, Ray Pottinger has probably heard and seen it all when it comes to their old racing escapades.

Ray was born in Victoria where he spent his early years, but in 1954 he moved to Nanaimo when he landed a job with the *Daily Free Press* newspaper.

Pottinger had been an enthusiastic racing spectator beforehand and finally decided it was time to see what it was like behind the wheel of his own racer. In 1954, at the age of 21, he brought his 1934 Ford V8 coupe to Shearing Speedway in Cobble Hill. And, on that first run as a novice, he probably surprised even himself.

Three decades later, in an interview with the *Nanaimo Free Press*, Pottinger described that first night in the cockpit. He turned the third fastest time in the opening heats and placed second in the main event. "I got second only because I didn't know how to pass the guy ahead of me," he quipped.

(Ray Pottinger Collection)

1954 was also a transition year for many of the racing Islanders, as Shearing Speedway was closing, and Western Speedway in Victoria was opening. At the end of the 1954 season, Ray finished in sixth place in the Western Speedway points championship. The following two years, he ended up fourth overall for the year at Western, where he also won the prestigious Gold Cup race. Beyond Victoria, he additionally competed in Nanaimo, Digney, and Skagit.

Ray had become a typographer for the *Victoria Colonist* newspaper where he had served his apprenticeship. "I had a steady job that wouldn't interfere with my racing, because I was on the day shift.

(Ray Pottinger Collection)

It was during this period when Ray first became acquainted with Billy Foster.

"He ran his own stock car in 1954," Ray remembers. "That's when I met him, but I had friends who knew him. We were all young – in our 20s. In 1955 he wasn't a regular driver, and then in 1956 he drove for his cousin Jimmy Steen. I think he also did some 'catch' driving now and then."

Pottinger continued: "Bill hooked up with Jim Haslam around 1960. 1961 was the year they allowed overhead-valve engines in stock cars, which were then called modified stocks. Foster and Haslam then showed up with one of those in 1962." "Right around the first of July, which is similar to your Fourth of July weekend, they held a double-date event with one race on Saturday and the other on Monday. On Saturday, Billy drove for Haslam, and then he bought a modified car from Ed Kostenuk to run on Monday. He broke the track record with it. That's when we realized just how talented Billy was.

Billy was a natural driver, as he proved in the following years. At some point he hooked up with John Feuz, the big tall mechanic from Portland. The car got better and better.

I'm probably one of the few guys that took Billy 'out'. That was in the stock cars at Western Speedway. He'd come to the corner and then slice down across you. I let him do that two times, but the next time around I drove around him, thinking 'I wasn't going to have any more of that.' I can't recall whether I won that race or came in second. Afterwards, the officials came to me and asked, 'did you do that deliberately to Billy?' I said, 'you bet I did' and they disqualified me. I replied that if he does that again, you'll be disqualifying me again. Billy never came to me to talk about it, but I think he got the message."

Ray Pottinger in action.

(Ray Pottinger Collection)

In 1960 Ray teamed up with car owner and mechanic Dick Midgely to drive a DeSoto-powered super-modified. In 1961 they earned the season points championship in the modified division.

The first Daffodil Cup race in Victoria also took place in 1961 as Pottinger explained. "The guy who drew up the first event was president of VITRA. He thought, 'Let's put on a big show and big prize money.' They ended up with a standing-room only crowd for the 150-lap race. Eldon Rasmussen came in first, followed by Bill Crow." Billy Foster would win the Daffodil Cup in 1962 and 1963.

In 1966, Ray also found the time to become president of the Mid-Island Auto Racing Association (MIARA) and took on the promotional activities at Western Speedway. His wife Vi stepped in to help by selling tickets while their son Vance sold programs.

Pottinger continued racing his own cars throughout the Pacific Northwest well into the 1970s, plus an occasional ride for other car owners. "We used to go down to Washington and Oregon," he says, "but much of the traveling was beyond my expense account because we didn't have a sponsor. "I needed to win prize money in order to take the ferry trip back home," he chuckled.

Pottinger suffered one bad accident during qualifications in Nanaimo, driving Bob Vantreight's new roadster. Gordon Alberg, who was racing his B-Modified that same day, observed: "That was a very scary accident. At Grandview Bowl, going into turn one, there was a quite steep embankment. Ray went straight up that bank with the throttle stuck wide open. The bank just catapulted him straight up into the air. He was probably 40-feet in the air and disappeared out of sight into the parking lot and landing on a parked car."

"The throttle stuck wide open," Ray explained. "I hit the bank, went through the fence and landed upside-down on a parked car that belonged to a pit crew member. That car was also totaled. I broke my back and busted my face all up. My wife Vi rode to the hospital with me but I have no recollection at all. I was laid up a couple of months with a compression fracture. For a long time afterwards, it was hard for me to stand for long periods, but that eventually disappeared."

Later in the 1960s, Pottinger eventually sold his own car and took part in a few Canadian-American Racing Association (CAMRA) for other car owners, such as Barry White. One of those events was at Western Speedway in 1968, where he remembered, "We were doing really good, but there was a big wreck in the main event, and I drove right on top of another car. The other guy, whose name I don't recall, was from Boise."

"It didn't hurt the car much, but it broke the exhaust pipes, so Barry didn't want to continue in the race. It worried him about the car catching on fire – but not me. The car had a damn good engine with six Weber carburetors, but I never got a chance to run it again."

There was one time at the Gold Cup event in Edmonton when racing ace Al Smith arranged a ride for Pottinger – the two had been good friends. Smith was switching cars and needed to find another driver for the first car he was scheduled to race. Ray wasn't able to get in any practice laps and would have to qualify the car fast enough to make the main event. "Al told me not to worry. He walked me out to the turns and explained each racing line I should take. They gave me one hot lap, and then I had to qualify. I was a bit slower than Al, but I wasn't worried because he wouldn't bullshit me."

Ray and the odd-looking 'Flintstone Special', owned by Dick Midgley, at the Portland Speedway. As ugly as it was, it was a fast racer powered by a Buick 401 cu.in. Nailhead engine. Ray won a few races with it.

(Ray Pottinger Collection)

"During the race we were a half a lap ahead of the second-place car – I could see it on the backstretch when I was on the front straight. It was Norm Ellefson. It wasn't too long before he was right on my ass, but by then I had no brakes. He finally trapped me. Running with no brakes is a challenge, to say the least. We ended up finishing second, but who remembers that?

Shortly after the Gold Cup, Ray drove the same car in winning a CAMRA race in Spokane. After that, the car was sold. "It was a hell of a ride," says Pottinger. "Probably the most forgiving car I ever drove."

Another CAMRA race that Ray remembers was one year at Langley Speedway in Vancouver, B.C. "I had one hell of a race with Tom Sneva, who was driving that four-wheel-drive car. I beat him. He came over afterwards and said he'd tried for all those laps to get by me, but never could."

In July 1974 this interesting article about Ray appeared in the *Nanaimo Free Press*, written by Mark Kiemele:

From Rags to Riches Suits Ray Pottinger Just Fine

You'll pardon Ray Pottinger, of course, if he acts like a kid with a new toy. It's just that after over two decades of automobile racing in the Pacific Northwest, the Nanaimo driver finally thinks he has a machine that will take him places.

Pottinger has long been regarded as one of the more competent handlers of racing cars around. In the past, however, he's never quite had the machine to match his skill. His racing career began in 1953 when he took a 1934 Ford V8 coupe on to the track at the old Shearing Speedway in Cobble Hill. Although just 21 years-old and still wet behind the ears, he had been entranced by stock car racing for several years and figured he'd like to try his hand.

In his first night out on the south-Island track, Pottinger pretty much lived up to his dreams as he turned in the third quick time in the opening heats and placed second in the main event. "I got second only because I didn't know how to pass the guy ahead of me," he relates.

A year later Pottinger moved to Nanaimo to work for the Daily Free Press. In those 12 months he learned how to pass cars ahead of him and got the racing bug for good.

Until 1960 he ran stock cars at Grandview Bowl here while running his first sprint car as well. In that year he decided to devote his spare hours to the speedy little open-cockpit cars full-time. He apparently knew what he was doing. In 1960 and 1961 Pottinger was the B.C. sprint car champion, also in '61 placed seventh in the Northwest running a little flathead Ford against big Chevy and GMC V8s.

The first Daffodil race in Victoria in 1961 started the popular trend toward modified racing and a year later, Pottinger converted his own sprint car to a modified and has been there ever since.

Until 1967 he raced his own cars, but with the advent of the super-speed machines came super expenses. Pottinger loved his racing but found it a very expensive hobby. He sold his own car and began driving for other owners. In the past half-dozen years he's

(Ray Pottinger Collection)

raced cars owned by men in Victoria, Prince George, Seattle, Portland and Puyallup. A couple years ago he teamed up once again with Bob Vantreight of Victoria, one of 'The' men in auto racing in the Northwest. That relationship worked out fine with Pottinger winning his share, but finding his champagne talents often going to waste on a beer-budget machine.

Without the thousands of dollars necessary to equip a first-class car, he often found himself hurtling down the chute on an aging frame that felt like spaghetti. The running gear suffered continual breakdowns. The handling would change during a race. Safety became a factor every time he took to the blacktop, mainly because of the lack of speed.

Then last year, from out of the grease and grime of Victoria's Western Speedway stepped the spic-and-span character of Barry Bunyan. Bunyan is one of the more successful sports entrepreneurs in the capitol city; successful in the sense that he gets a real kick from sponsoring a myriad of lacrosse, hockey, soccer and other teams through his Island Pacific Oil Company.

"Barry became our sponsor last year and enjoyed racing so much he decided to build a new car," said Pottinger. It was a dream come true for the Nanaimo driver. During the winter, Vantreight, who's head mechanic as well as part owner, and Jim Cannon, a long-time partner, got together a crew to fit the pieces together. "No car is complete without a crew," said Pottinger, as he refers to the almost magical work of Vantreight, whom he calls "the chief screw," and his gang. Machininists Vantreight, Cannon and John McKie, along with Ian Smith, Gerry Vantreight and Rick Cox labored through the cold months on the automobile in a garage provided by Bunyan.

This spring the $15,000 machine got its first public showing. The frame was impeccably designed by Vantreight, the fiberglass body built by Jim Justice of Victoria. It's powered by a 400 cubic-inch Chevy V8 with a 350 cubic-inch short-stroke crankshaft, all put together by Spokane's Dick Flynn.

Pottinger and the car took to one another immediately. In the first test run at Western in June the car turned the track just below 16 seconds and not too far off the track record. "It's been several years since the old car was able to do anything close to that," Pottinger said at the time, obviously pleased with himself and his new set of wheels.

Since that first run, the car has been in two races. It's first was in Prince George, a most dramatic debut. Pottinger was leading the field in the main event when the throttle stuck going full-bore down the straightaway. The car flew off the track, went through a wooden fence, shattering the four-by-fours like matchsticks, coming to rest on a golf course a couple hundred feet away. Trips like that Pottinger can do without.

But last weekend, with the car mended from its Prince George antics, Pottinger ran in Ephreta, Washington and placed third in the main event even though he ran without brakes for almost half the race. Still not perfect, but getting there. This Sunday the Island Pacific crew will travel to the big 5/8ths-mile track at Monroe Speedway near Seattle. A week from Saturday local racing fans will get a chance to see the new car in action at Western Speedway in Victoria. If a fellow by the name of Pottinger is riding high that night, try to understand. He's earned it.

In a side-bar article, Ray added some further thoughts about his passion for racing:

Racing's Relaxing for Pottinger

Ray Pottinger has a couple of favorite ways of finding relaxation. He likes to bowl and is a steady roller in a local tenpin league.

When he isn't on the alleys, he relaxes by driving a race car at speeds sometimes reaching 140 miles-per-hour. "When a race is over, I'm super relaxed. After a race I'm soaking wet from head to toe. You've no idea how hard you wrestle out there. If you're out of shape you couldn't last 10 laps. Coupled with the heat of the engine and the physical pressure, the exertion is just tremendous. But when it's over, I'm super relaxed. I guess I race because of the element of thrill ... of going fast in a tough, competitive sport that shouldn't be contact but is – and it's violent at times too – there's few rules out there. I like that – I like to win."

Does Pottinger get scared? You bet he does, but not under ordinary circumstances. "Anyone who says he has never been scared would have something lacking. In a pure race you don't get scared. It's the things that happen and the things that you see that gives you the scare. I've always raced with the idea that I'm taking the car for a ride, not it taking me. The moment the feeling gets reversed, then I get scared."

Ray's last race came in 1976, closing out his 24-year racing career. "I hardly drove the last couple of years. I deliberately stayed away from the race track after retiring from racing. I didn't have a nickel in the bank for retirement. I knew I'd never make a living at racing – it was just a hobby."

SIX

Victoria's Auto Racing Heritage – Langford Speedway

Racing continued at least into the mid-1930s at The Willows, and its popularity gave rise to other race tracks nearby Victoria such as Hastings Park in Vancouver and Digney Speedway in Burnaby. Racers also could travel over the Malahat to tracks in Cobble Hill, Chemainus, Nanaimo and other small towns on the island. Arguably, the most significant racing facility of its time was built by Jack Taylor – Langford Speedway.

The Jack Taylor Years – 1936 to 1940

Enlisting the help of the British Columbia Automobile Sport's Association and the local Langford community, Jack Taylor is credited for bringing international sprint car racing to Canada regularly. Thus, Victoria became widely known as "Canada's Auto Racing Capital."

Jack Taylor

Jack Taylor, as a 'Big Car' owner in the early 1930s, campaigned a Ford sprint car in British Columbia Automotive Sports Association (BCASA) sanctioned meets at the Willows and the Colwood Mile. The always-capacity crowds at these venues did not escape Taylor's attention. He was eventually approached to build a speedway on a large tract of land he owned near Langford Lake, about eight miles north of Victoria proper.

The financial risks were enormous, but Taylor was willing to gamble. Actual construction began in 1935. Jack built the 2,000-seat grandstand with the help of Andre and George Cottyn.

Johnny Wright, one of the founding members of the BCASA and a correspondent for the *National Speed Sport News,* described the track's construction:

Clay was hauled, and gallons of old crank case oil were poured into the recipe and there was the track, loose as a goose and with millions of big rocks just waiting to be tossed up by the flying wheels. To make the plant perfect, a set of bleachers was erected, and a board fence wrapped around the deal, all ready for the grand opening.

Langford's first race date was June 6th, 1936. The 3/8ths-mile dirt track was an immediate success, largely due to Jack's talents as a promoter, publicist, announcer, car owner and track manager – all rolled into one. Continuing with his report, Wright provided details about that debut event:

On opening day all the city big-wigs were invited, and with their ladies' fair all dressed in spotless white, they were given preference of ringside seats. Well, the results were self-explanatory, as the field included cars from Washington and elsewhere

Langford's first main event in 1936

In an article by Brian Pratt for the website *Canadian Racer.com*, on the history of Langford Speedway, he wrote:

Seattle's Dave 'Wildman' Dippolito won the opening day's 20-lap feature, shortened due to the corners softening up. He finished ahead of Wilburn, who had been the 1935 Northwest Champion, and who would go on to win so many races in Southern California and the Midwest that his nickname would become 'Ho-Hum', as if winning was boring to all concerned, including himself.

Johnny McDowell, who would start in the Indianapolis 500 four times, was in Glen Shaw's Seattle-based car and set the track record at 22 seconds in front of 1,500-2,000 fans. Local drivers included Fritz Miller in the Jack Smith and Ed Allen-built car, Bill Pearson in Lloyd Vaio's car and Bert Sutton in his own car.

Pratt added details about Langford's second event, held on July 1st, 1936:

The Victoria newspaper reported that 'spectators bowed their heads under a rain of mud and dust'. Dippolito again won the 10-lap feature, this time in the Glen Shaw Dreyer. Fritz Miller was second.

Early on, to augment a local field of about a dozen sprint cars, Taylor offered a generous guarantee of $25 to any driver/car combination to come north from the United States. Upon hearing this offer, racing teams arrived from Seattle, Portland, California's Bay Area and even Los Angeles.

By the end of that first season of racing, Jack Taylor announced that Langford Speedways Limited had been formed with capital estimated at $15,000, and the track would be "hard-surfaced" soon. That upgrade took place in 1937 and (thanks to a $1,500 donation from Frawny Morris) Langford became the first paved track in Canada. They also installed track lighting – using 150-watt bulbs.

L to R: Jack Taylor, Glen Shaw, Frawny Morris and Frankie Rentz.

Though the field of local cars continued to grow, Jack kept up with his bounty to the southern teams to maintain the international component of his events.

Many legendary drivers of that era were drawn to Langford, such as Jimmy Wilburn, Rajo Jack, Wally Schock, Johnny McDowell, Allen Heath, Chick Barbo, Tommy Legge, Adolph Dans, "Cactus" Jack Turner and Shorty Scovell.

Over the next two years the facility came into full bloom. Eleven race dates were held in 1938 and fifteen during 1939.

Racing action at Langford in 1938.

Victoria's *The Daily Colonist* newspaper reported regularly on the action taking place at the Langford Speedway, as in this example:

Car Racing at Langford

Headed by Swede Lindskog, famous Seattle speed demon, who had captured more races here than any other American driver, at least five United States pilots will be in the city Saturday to take part in the events which will be run off at the Langford Speedway. The time trials will open the evening's racing at 7:45 and then the distance events will get underway.

Lindskog, well known for his daring driving at the local track, will be the favorite to top the field in the main races. Along with the Seattle Swede there will be Jud Taylor, Lew McMurtry and the possibility of car number 74 coming here from Yakima.

According to reports, all Victoria drivers have their cars in first-class condition and will be gunning for some of the purse money. Last Saturday the boys held a practice event at the speedway and their times were faster than previous turnouts. The track is in fine condition and therefore there is the possibility that some new records will be established during the evening. Jack Taylor, track manager, went over to Seattle to line up the best available drivers for Saturday's program and will be back in the city today with all the data on the boys.

The following Sunday, June 11th, 1939, *The Daily Colonist* published a full race report – followed up by a rather extensive review of the event. As predicted, the "Seattle Swede" took home all the laurels:

Lindskog Again Shines at Langford Speedway

Turning the Langford oval in some of the cleanest and most thrilling exhibitions of speed seen here for a long time, local and visiting drivers divided honors in last night's meet, before a packed stand of excited fans. As usual, Swede Lindskog, Seattle ace, was the pick of the speed friends, and shot his wagon across the finishing line in first position in the main, twenty-lap event in seven minutes, forty-one and one-fifth seconds.

Bert Sutton, up and coming Victoria driver, hit his stride in the final two events and chased Lindskog around the oval to take second-place honors in the feature race, in addition to capturing a special five-lapper. Jimmy Symes was another Sound City driver who was burning up the tires in the breath-taking contests. Symes wheeled his machine around the track in twenty seconds flat, to hang up the fastest time trial. The Seattle boy also captured the second heat race and trailed Sutton in the final event on the evening's card.

"Tarzan" Carson had a narrow escape from serious injury in the fourth eight-lap heat race. Trailing George White, Nanaimo, and "Digger" Caldwell, Carson went into a spin on the north corner, and his car flipped over, landing on its side. Members of the St. John Ambulance brigade rushed to the scene, righted the car, and treated the injured man for a badly-abraised arm. His wheels kicked up such a cloud of dust that it was impossible to see from the grandstand just what was happening.

In the same race, Caldwell's "horse-collar" speed machine conked out and the "Digger" spent the rest of the evening in the pits. It was a tough break as the Victoria pilot was out in front and seemed headed for a certain victory.

Gerry Vantreight, Nanaimo, had a good evening placing third in the helmet dash and the second heat race, and taking premier honors in the third heat race. White was the sole finisher in the event that saw Carson and

Caldwell wind up in the pits. Eric Whitehead and his "lizzie" romped home first in the stock car event. Munsie, in his tiny Austin, had captured the lead from Whitehead on the sixth lap but went into a spin in the eighth that put him out of the running.

A special cup was presented to Vantreight for making the fastest time in the time trials for local cars, and Bert Sutton was awarded the "Joker" Patton Cup for being the first Canadian pilot to finish in the main event.

About one month later, Swede Lindskog returned to Langford and continued his racing prowess, despite tough competition from Symes and Vantreight. The following report appeared in *The Daily Colonist* on July 16th, 1939:

Lindskog is Tops Again

After the stiffest fight that he has faced in auto races here this year, Swede Lindskog, Seattle king of the superspeedways, once more emerged victor in the main event of the Langford Speedway bill last night. Closely trailing him at the finish was Jimmy Symes, another Seattle driver, who held the lead position until the seventeenth lap of the twenty-lap race.

Symes took the first position from Gerry Vantreight, Victoria, who had the pole spot in the fourth lap, but Vantreight stayed in the fight for two more laps before yielding second position to Lindskog. Swede, winner of almost every main event here in the season's racing, pushed to the front from twelfth position at the start in the sixth lap, but only held the lead for a lap.

In the seventh, Symes saw an opening and drove past his Seattle partner in a clever maneuver that enabled him to build up a slight lead on Swede. Lindskog followed for ten laps trying for an opportunity to pass, but Symes held him until the end of lap seventeen. Even then, it was anybody's race until the last lap. Lindskog's time for the twenty laps was 8:34. Symes was only a few seconds slower, and Gerry Vantreight was a good third, with a considerable lead over Digger Caldwell, Victoria, in fourth position. Prior to the main event, Lindskog had the edge on Lew McMurtry, Seattle, in the helmet dash and first heat race. He won the five-lap helmet dash and the eight-lap heat.

Digger Caldwell, Victoria driver, who shows most promise among local pilots, won the British Columbia Automobile Association Cup for the second consecutive week for winning the second heat race. He also won the five-lap match race and beat Gerry Vantreight to the pole in a special challenge race.

Fred Carson, Duncan boy, with a car much improved over last week, turned in the surprise of the evening by qualifying with the fastest cars by completing a 19-second time trial lap, and then following through with a victory in the third heat race over Jimmy Laird, Victoria, winning the feature race.

Victim of a smash-up at the speedway last summer, Buddy Green was back on the track again for the first-time last night. He did some steady driving during the evening and placed first in the fourth heat race. Bert Sutton, Victoria boy, who usually provides the toughest competition for the fast Seattle drivers, among the local speedsters, failed to qualify in the time trials owning to wheel trouble. His car did not run during the evening.

As the 1939 season at Langford wound down into September, the two drivers from Seattle – Swede Lindskog and Jimmy Symes – continued their winning ways despite strong challenges from the local hotshots. On September 17th, 1939, *The Daily Colonist* reported:

Symes Victor in Main Race at Langford

Jimmy Symes, veteran Seattle speed artist, who two weeks ago set a new record of eighteen seconds flat for a single circuit of the Langford Speedway, came through to a comfortable win again in the main event at the auto races last night. Starting in the second position, Symes took the lead immediately and was not seriously challenged throughout the whole of the grueling twenty-lap drive. He compiled the fast time of 6:07, cutting one and one-fifth seconds off the mark he made in winning the event a fortnight ago.

Placing second in the feature race was Joe Moore, Victoria's "butcher boy", who nosed his way through from fifth position at the start to second in the third lap and held the second berth up to the finish line. Most of the thrills of the race were provided by a duel for third place fought out through fourteen laps by Digger Caldwell, Victoria, and Lew McMurtry, Seattle. McMurtry pulled by Gerry Vantreight, Victoria, in the fifth circuit, to be followed closely by Caldwell.

It was almost neck and neck for eleven laps, with the Seattle driver having the advantage of the inside position. Caldwell challenged hard at every straightaway, and finally managed to edge past McMurtry on the seventeenth lap. McMurtry was not yet beaten, however, and he came within a yard of taking third place again in the nineteenth lap. Getting every ounce of power out of his motor, Caldwell managed to make sure of his position in the last lap. McMurtry zoomed in only half a car length behind him, closely followed by Gerry Vantreight. Jack Frumento took sixth place, last of the paying positions.

Sharing the night's honors with Symes was Wes Moore, also of Seattle. After circling the track in the near-record time of eighteen and one-fifth seconds, equaled a few minutes later by Symes, Moore went out to take clean wins in the five-lap helmet dash and the first heat race, beating Symes to the pole in each case. Symes pressed hard for the lead in both events but was unable to dislodge Moore from the pole position. Moore had a good two-length advantage at the end of the helmet dash, and nearly a car length in the heat race. Digger Caldwell did some fast driving to get right in at the finish of the heat race and finished a good third just a few feet behind Symes.

Joe Moore and Digger Caldwell together were responsible for keeping a full share of the prize money in Victoria. Digger took first money in the second heat race, as well as taking the third purse in the main feature. Joe Moore, who has shown as much progress as any of the local drivers in recent meets, won the third heat and gained another victory in the five-lap match race, which he won over Caldwell, and then finished up by placing second in the main feature.

The fourth heat race of the night's bill proved even a little faster than the third, going to Lew McMurtry, driving Seth Renning's car. McMurtry had an easy win over Claude Walling, Portland.

Gerry Vantreight was awarded the British Columbia Automotive Sports Association Cup for turning in the fastest time trial of Victoria drivers. His mark for the distance was eighteen and three-fifths seconds.
The crowds never failed to cheer their approval in loud unison at the sportsmanlike gesture as Swede's car was rolled to the rear of the lineup. More intriguing yet, he put this string together at the wheel of several different race cars.

Far from being an unpopular winner, as sometimes happens, Swede's presence on a race night always brought a capacity crowd, many of whom would arrive early for the simple pleasure of seeing him time in. It has been said that this alone was worth the price of admission.

Through the fence at Langford!

As any race track promoter will tell you, sometimes a promising night of racing action will go afoul for any number of reasons. For Jack Taylor, one night went that way – as reported the following day in *The Daily Colonist*:

Ill Fortune Stalks Racing Car Drivers at Langford Track

When Digger Caldwell crashed his car through the fence at the Langford Speedway last night he wrote the last word to a chapter of accidents and mishaps that caused the postponement of the meeting before the end of the first event. Caldwell's crash gave the big crowd a thrill in the third lap of the helmet dash. He was closely following Bert Bloomgren (Seattle) at the entrance to the back stretch when the spectators saw his car suddenly leap into the air, smash into the fence and go out of sight on the other side.

The accident was brought about through Bloomgren spinning broadside across the track. Caldwell had no chance to avoid him, and his left front wheel climbed over Bloomgren's rear axle. The Victoria driver was shaken but unhurt, and his car, which climbed onto its nose behind the fence and came to rest on its side, was only superficially damaged.

Caldwell was lucky for he missed one of the main posts supporting the fence by a matter of inches. Wes Moore (Seattle) had his car put out of action temporarily before it reached the track. On the way out to Langford the trailer on which the Seattle entry was being transported came free from the towing car and ran off the road, turning over and causing some damage to the racing machine. Jimmy Symes, crack Seattle racer booked for the big event, was another who failed to reach the track, for the fuel pump of his car broke down in Seattle.

A broken piston put Jimmy Laird's Victoria car out of the running before the meeting began, and rear-end trouble prevented Joe Moore (Victoria) from entering. So, with nothing much left to offer in the way of excitement, the officials met with full approval when they suggested calling off the meeting, and the crowd was contented with tickets to the speedway next Saturday night or the Saturday following, in lieu of having their money refunded.

In May of 1940, Dr. F. Cyril James, president of McGill University in Hamilton, Ontario, was urging complete mobilization of Canada's manpower and economic resources for the growing war effort in Europe.

Despite these looming dark clouds, competitors and fans alike continued their enthusiasm at Langford Speedway. The 1940 racing season was shortened to just ten races, and further reduced to six race dates in 1941. Because the United States had not yet entered the war, teams were still crossing the border into British Columbia and included newcomers like Les Anderson and Bill Gehler.

The Daily Colonist kept up its strong support of the Langford scene, as shown in these samplings from the 1940 season:

Auto Races Are Carded

Pacific Coast speed demons who have thrilled thousands of Victoria automobile racing fans since the inauguration of the sport at the Langford Speedway, will return to the local strip Saturday evening to usher in the 1940 season. Jack Taylor, racing promoter, yesterday announced that plans are practically completed for the season's opening program, and what a card it promises to be. Such favorite pilots as Tommy Legge, Jimmy Symes and Lew McMurtry, Seattle, and Chic Barbo and Claude Walling, Portland, have already been signed for Saturday's meeting, an assurance in itself that the fans will witness plenty of action and smart driving.

Victoria's own drivers, such as Digger Caldwell, Joe Moore, Fred Carson, Jack Frumento, Buddy Green and Sid Holdridge will be in the thick of the racing, and with the added experience should take a larger share of the gold during the coming season. Jack Spaulding, former of Seattle and now a resident of this city, will greatly strengthen the local contingent of pilots and racing machines.

There has been considerable activity among local drivers during the winter and a number of smart speed wagons are ready for their seasonal christening on the Langford Speedway. As for the racing strip, it has been reconditioned while the infield has been leveled, giving a clear vision of every part of the track.
In addition to the regular racing machines, midgets will probably make their debut at Langford this season. Jack Smith and Jimmy Laird have built the smaller racing cars, and others are under construction. Special races for midgets will probably be added to the 1940 program with a view to giving the fans added entertainment.

With new speed wagons primed and ready for action, Victoria's racing pilots should give visiting American drivers plenty of real opposition this season, according to close followers of the automobile racing game. During the fall and winter months there has been considerable activity in local shops and when the curtain goes up tomorrow evening at the Langford Speedway the fans will see some brand-new machines in action. Present indications point to all events being well filled, with the possibility of between fourteen and fifteen cars facing the starting flag for the time trials. Six ace drivers from across the border have been booked for the show and with more than an equal number of Canadian speed demons ready for action the inaugural show promises to be a thriller.

The visiting contingent will include Jimmy Symes, Chick Barbo, Claude Walling, Seth Kenning, Lew McMurtry and Wes Moore, all favorites with Victoria racing fans. Digger Caldwell, top driver last season, will lead the local contingent. Gerry Vantreight, "Butcher Boy" Joe Moore, Jack Frumento, Buddy Green and Jack Spaulding will uphold this city's colors against the invading speedsters. The program will start at 7:45 o'clock with time trials. Other events will include the helmet dash, match race, heats and the thirty-lap main events.

As with the 1939 season, the thrills and spills at Langford continued its high popularity with Victorians through the summer of 1940, as in these examples from *The Daily Colonist*:

Has Narrow Escape When Car Crashes

It looked very much like the Grim Reaper had Jack Spaulding's number chalked up on the wall at the Langford Speedway last night, but the Victoria racing pilot, victim of one of the season's worst crashes lived to tell the tale – he not only lived, he was walking around and hour later with nothing more than a limp.

All the excitement occurred during the three-lap helmet dash that raised the curtain on the evening's fireworks. Digger Caldwell started on the pole with Spaulding driving beside him. From the first it was apparent that Spaulding intended taking Digger on the inside. He had a narrow squeak on the north turn, and in the southern bend again attempted to slip through. Caldwell held his position, however, and Spaulding's mount, roaring wide open, climbed right up the back of the No. 1 car. While Digger ducked to a grinding stop, Spaulding bounced off to the right, ripped down thirty-five feet of Promoter Jack Taylor's best fence and rolled over twice.

As a cloud of black dust enveloped the scene, the crowd sat with bated breath. Provincial Police and St. John Ambulance men rushed to the scene. Spaulding managed to extricate himself, while Caldwell climbed out of his car unhurt. The injured man was placed on a stretcher and taken to the hospital, where it was discovered he suffered nothing more than bruises. His machine did not fare so well, however, the radiator and engine were stove in and the machine was a wreck generally. Caldwell's left rear tire was blown and he was able to effect repairs, only to suffer motor trouble later in a special match race.

But now to the main event which Buddy Green captured in the time of 7:47. Gerry Vantreight wheeled his mount into second place and Fred Carson concluded the twenty laps in third place. Finishing fourth, fifth and sixth, respectively, were Don Vantreight, Jack Frumento and "One-Lap" Sid Holdridge.

There was a little sabotage at the track when somebody deposited three lumps of sugar in Green's carburetor prior to the main grind. After some delay mechanics got the car started and it went faster than ever.
Joe Moore captured the first heat dash of five laps when he passed Green in the final turn. Carson was third.

Gerry Vantreight blazed home first in the second five-lapper with Carson second and Holdridge third.
Eric Whitehead, taking a vacation from bicycle riding, drove his way from third place into first and walked off with the prize money in the stock car event. R. Hibberd was second and K. Dodsworth earned show.
Jumping into an early lead after starting in fourth place, Digger Caldwell beat out Frumento and Dan Vantreight in the third heat race. Digger's throttle stuck during a match race with Joe Moore and ruined his motor, writing finis to his evening's performance.

Automobile racing was curtailed world-wide during the World War Two years, but Langford Speedway was destined to return to happier days.

The Bruce Passmore Era – 1946 to 1950

Langford Speedway reopened in 1946 and a new track owner was on the near horizon. The first car to run on the track in the post-war era took place on Saturday, January 26th, 1946. Pike Green was behind the wheel of the car that won the BCASA title in 1941.

Before the war, Green had been too young to compete – instead serving as a "pit rat" by helping anyone who may let him.

During the next several years, *The Daily Colonist* newspaper continued to report weekly what was happening at the track. This article was published on July 14th, 1946:

Local Driver Again Winner of Main Event

Digger Caldwell, ace Victoria race driver, again won the feature 20-lap event at the Langford Speedway last night. Predicted stiff opposition from Seattle's Lew McMurtry failed to materialize as the American's car broke down on the third lap and he had to withdraw. Gerry Vantreight and Pike Green, both local drivers, placed second and third, respectively, and Claude Walling, of Portland, was fourth.

Vantreight headed Caldwell and McMurtry to the finish line in the helmet dash after a fine display of driving. Caldwell came right back in the first heat race with a win over Walling, Green and Vantreight. In the second heat Green built up a long lead but took a turn a little too fast and spun out, allowing Jack Spaulding to take the lead, which he never relinquished. Lew McMurtry won the next heat with Green in second place. Green's big moment of the evening came when he won a close match race with Claude Walling. Both cars turned in approximately the same time in the trials, and Green drove a smart race to beat the Portland throttle-pusher.

Another match race saw Digger Caldwell nose out McMurtry in one of the fast races on the program. Tom Williamson, driving an ancient entry by Hill's U-Drive, won the Model T event. A "show race", a ceremony honoring the memory of drivers who received fatal injuries on the speedway was held for Swede Lindskog, popular American ace who was killed last month in a racing accident in the south.

Three drivers, each representing a different city and racing group, made three laps of the oval at slow speed following which the audience was asked to observe one minute's silence.

Ron Mayall, starter, and Edward Conway, pit boss, each received a presentation from John B. Priestly, of the Lions Club, for their part in the recent Tin Lizzy Derby at Willows Park. Digger Caldwell was also commended for the assistance during the event.

In his *Canadian Racer.com* article, Brian Pratt summarized the 1946 racing season at Langford:

That first season back had eleven races, and it was Jack 'Digger' Caldwell who dominated by winning all but three of the feature events.

The Green brothers won the others, Bud with one and Pike with two. Digger took the points title in what was now called the Bert Sutton Memorial Trophy, with Pike second. Pike's rookie driving improved to the point that on the night of the 50-lap championship race, he eked out a close win over Digger, only to end up in the fence, but quite happy.

Bruce Passmore and his family moved from Moose Jaw, Saskatchewan to Victoria in 1945. The next year he became involved with an old race car and drove it in two meets at Langford. He was smitten with the sport.

In 1947 Bruce mortgaged his assets to purchase the Langford facility and held grand plans for the future. To prepare for racing every Saturday night, he installed additional grandstands, repaved the track, installed an electric eye timing device and commissioned six new race cars for the season. Not bad for a 25-year-old!

Bruce Passmore

The action at Langford in 1947.

(Brian Pratt Collection)

Passmore scheduled 17 events for 1947 and realized an impressive increase in attendance – often witnessing overflow crowds. The price of admission was $1.00.

In just the next two years, Bruce Passmore amassed a $30,000 race track, a $40,000 apartment block and a yellow convertible.

More U.S.-based drivers were taking the ferry trip to Langford because the large crowds were helping to increase the race purses. Combined with an increasing number of local racers, it was necessary to add a "B" feature race in addition to the "A" main event.

Though Pike Green had relocated to the United States, he returned to Victoria on a regular basis. He often drove cars from the U.S., but a special machine was built for him in Victoria by mechanic John Dalby, as explained by author Pratt:

Dalby had been another one of the original members of the BCASA and had worked on various cars at the speedway before the war. The two-port Riley he debuted part way through the 1947 season was special in a few ways. It had inboard brakes instead of the hand lever-type used on most other cars, and the clutch was a lever. The car was the inspiration for a young high school lad, Grant King, to build his first race car for the 1948 season.

The story has it that King was hanging around the Dalby car taking measurements, when Pike Green asked him 'what the hell was he doing?' Dalby's response was that 'that crazy kid thinks he's going to build a race car.' Grant King did build that car and many more after that, going all the way to Indianapolis in 1964.
In 1948 King's driver, Bung Eng, won a feature race at Langford with the new King car.

Pratt also mentioned another new car that appeared in 1947, built by Jack Smith. It was a rear-engine racer with a four-wheel independent suspension, which drew a lot of attention. From Smith's perspective, his design was more of an experiment to see if the technology that Ferdinand Porsche had included in the European Auto Union racing cars would work on a short track such as Langford. With rookie driver Howard Stanley at the controls the car, dubbed the 'Flying Saucer', actually performed well.

1947: Verne Bruce in the cockpit. Bruce Passmore and Jack Smith standing alongside.

The Daily Colonist provided this preview of the next event on tap at Langford on July 4th, 1947:

U.S. Cars to Race at Langford

Another evening of thrills and spills is on tap for racing fans when Promoter Bruce Passmore stages the weekly Saturday night racing program at Langford Speedway, commencing at 7:30 p.m. Last week's race produced one of the most interesting programs ever seen on the oval when Gerry Vantreight stole the show by taking top honors in the helmet dash, first heat race and the A-Main event. He also made the fastest time in the time trials.

Stiff competition is predicted this week with several United States cars on hand. Out-of-town drivers appearing will be Jack Spaulding of Vancouver, driving the Olds and Perkins entry; Gene Fanning at the wheel of his car, "The Dryer", the car which was driven by the late Swede Lindskog; and Shorty Scovell, from Portland. Four Victoria racing machines which attended a meeting at Aurora Speedway in Seattle on Tuesday finished in the money, according to Eric Foster, president of the BCASA.

Pike Green, driving Chuck House's car, from Tacoma, walked off with the fourth heat and the A-Main event. Digger Caldwell, driving George Davies' machine, took top honors in the helmet dash and first heat race. Lew McMurtry, driving Phyllis Mathews' entry, placed second in the first heat.

Gerry Vantreight, driving his own car, had bad luck when his wheel came off in the third race and during the B-Main he crashed after a car driven by Don Kain, Seattle, went end over end and landed on Jerry's engine bonnet. The car rolled off in front of Vantreight's wheels and was pushed for 50 feet. George Haslam's car dropped a valve and was not running during the evening's events.

At the conclusion of the 1947 season Digger Caldwell again won the overall points' title. He also held onto the Jimmy Laird Trophy for the most helmet dash wins. Other winners during the season included Jack Spaulding, Gerry Vantreight, Pike Green, George Haslam and Dave Cooper. Cooper co-owned his car with BCASA president Eric Foster.

The 1948 season at Langford kicked off without losing pace to the year before, and with the same tough players. A sampling of *The Daily Colonist* reports which appeared throughout the spring and summer months highlighted the action:

Green Defeats Caldwell in Auto Race Thriller

The feature 300-lap reverse handicap event at the Langford Speedway auto races last night was a duel between Victoria's Digger Caldwell and Seattle's Pike Green with the latter triumphing after a stirring race. Starting well to the rear, both drivers pushed to the front early and from there it appeared to be an even race. Green, however, had the edge and although he was close to being passed several times, held the lead and crossed the line with plenty to spare.

More than 3,000 screaming fans once more came out to Langford to see the "big cars" and their drivers put on a show which for thrills and just plain entertainment has no equal in Canada. Unlike the previous week no spills marred the evening's fun. Dave Cooper, driving his sleek racer, lost a wheel in a practice run but no serious damage was done.

Digger Caldwell took second in the main event and Eddie Kostenuk, from south of the line, came third. In a field of 13 cars which began the grueling struggle, only seven cars finished. Caldwell also scored firsts in the helmet dash, first heat race and second match race. Vantreight, McLeod and Spaulding took the wins in the second, third and fourth heat races.

Spaulding Has Big Night at Langford Race Meet

Jack Spaulding again took a monopoly on the honors at Langford Speedway last night, winning the main event and helmet dash and making the fastest time trial.

Spaulding, Don Olds of Seattle and Digger Caldwell moved up early in the main event. Spaulding soon took the lead and held it to the finish. Olds tangled with Caldwell, eliminating the latter, and then got into trouble with Cooper. Cooper held on to finish second, followed by Gerry Vantreight, Verne Bruce, Harry Greenwood and Bung Eng.

Eddie Kostenuk scored an easy triumph over Bob Simpson and Blim Johnson in the B-Main event. Olds captured the first heat race and followed Spaulding across the line. Caldwell captured the second heat, with Bruce and Brownie Brown trailing. Bert McCleod copped the third heat from Eng and Greenwood and Cooper led White and Haslam in the fourth heat.

Stock Car Event at Speedway Draws Big Entry

Racing fans are promised plenty of action in the 50-lap stock car race at the Langford Speedway tomorrow. Entry lists closed yesterday with 14 cars entered, ranging from 1930 models owned by Bob Irwin and Earl Faulkner to 1938 models owned by J. Waldson and Don Hudson.

Six entries have been received for the supporting 25-lap tin lizzie race. Two lizzies were entered by the Colwood Service Station, a 1927 Model T by J. Savory and a 1916 Model T by Don Duncan. Other entries were received from Bob Simpson and Archie Child.

Time trials to decide positions in the stock car race will begin at 7:30 p.m. and will be followed by the tin lizzie race and the stock car feature. Promoter Bruce Passmore announced last night that a 15-lap race for racing cars and match races would be added.

As the racing progressed, Bruce supplemented the popular 'Big Car' races by promoting a Stock Car race on July 1st, 1948, along with a 'Tin Lizzie' (Model T) race on the same date. The Stock Car main event was 50-laps and the Tin Lizzie main was 25-laps. Another attraction he brought in was the sixth-place finishing car from that year's Indianapolis 500 – Leo Dobrey's 'City of Tacoma'.

Among the many young enthusiasts that would regularly attend the racing events at Langford Speedway was Eric Foster's young son Billy.

Vantreight, Bruce Share Spotlight at Speedway

Although leading American cars and drivers failed to appear at Langford Speedway last night, the large crowd in attendance was treated to an evening of exciting racing with many close finishes.

Gerry Vantreight scored a popular triumph in the main event after trailing Brownie Brown for 27 laps. Vantreight made his move going into the north turn on the 28th lap, took the lead and won going away. Verne Bruce swept the early events. He set the fastest time for Canadian cars on the Langford oval in the time trials. He followed up by taking the helmet dash in the fastest time of the year and capturing the first heat race. Del Fanning and Don Olds trailed Bruce in the helmet dash and Olds and Howie Stanley followed him across the line in the first heat race.

Closest race was the second heat event when Vantreight and Stanley fought wheel to wheel all the way. Vantreight took the lead going into the final turn and barely nosed out the "Flying Saucer." Jack Spaulding finished third.

Spaulding led Fanning and Brown to the wire in the third heat, while Brown copped the fourth with Bung Eng second. Norm Ellefson spun in the fourth heat and crashed into George Matlan's car, putting both out of contention. Vantreight also copped a novel Australian pursuit race. Eight cars started with the slowest in front. As each car was passed, it dropped out of the race. Spaulding wound up second and Brown third.

Langford Speedway continued its popularity during the 1949 and 1950 seasons, with highlights such as these *Daily Colonist* reports:

Ernie Spaulding Escapes Injury in Race Crack-Up

Ernie Spaulding narrowly escaped serious injury at Langford last night as the roaring race car he was driving broke a spindle on the right front wheel, causing it to cartwheel into the air and tear down nearly 30 feet of board fence.

The accident took place in the third lap of the main event as the tightly-bunched pack was tearing down the backstretch toward the north turn. Bob Wensley, official starter, immediately stopped the race to allow pit crews to free Spaulding from the wreck. He was not seriously injured but the car was almost a total wreck. Meanwhile, Dave Cooper supplied his share of the evening's excitement when he spun out in the second lap of the main event. His throttle stuck wide open as he was entering the south turn and the car went through the fence backwards.

The excitement was not over. The race got underway again and the drivers settled down to fight out the remaining 27 laps. It was straight-forward racing for 25 laps and then the throttle on Eddie Kostenuk's car stuck on the unlucky south turn and the car went into a wild spin. Digger Caldwell made a split-second decision. He was right behind Kostenuk and to avoid what might have been a serious accident, he deliberately spun his car and smashed sideways into the stalled car. The event finally wound up with Jack Spaulding first, Bob Simpson second, and Brownie Brown third.

Ernie Spaulding was again first man in the first heat race. Brother Jack was second and Caldwell third. The second heat race saw Dave Cooper pick up top money with McLeod second and Bung Eng third. Eng romped home a winner in the third heat race with Simpson second and Brown in third place. Brown, however, had everything his own way in the last heat race as he tramped down on the gas pedal to beat Kostenuk for first place. Corky Thomas in the "Lucky Lady" was third.

Langford Track Record Set by Ernie Spaulding

Ernie Spaulding, dapper driver, had a field day at Langford Speedway last night. He took top money in every event he raced in, and also picked up $100 when he shaved seconds off the track record set by Don Olds last year. The speedy little black-and-white racer brought him home a winner. Driving like a champion, Ernie copped the checkered flag in the helmet dash after leading Don Hale and Pike Green for five fast laps. They finished in that order.

The first heat also saw the trio finish in the same order. The real race in the heats, which had the crowd on its feet, was the hard-fought duel between Bob Simpson and Digger Caldwell. Every corner was a thrill as the careening Caldwell jockeyed his black racer for a pass position. Caldwell had the lead position in the second heat race and picked up the checkered flag well ahead of Simpson. Brownie Brown was third.

Bert McLeod came into his own in the third heat race when he secured his first win of the season. Corky Thomas was second and Ken McMurtry was third.

Jack Spaulding received a big hand from the crowd as he burned up the track to win the fourth heat race. His car threw a front wheel in the time trials but was repaired in time for the event. Bung Eng and Eddie Kostenuk really put on a show for the fans with no holds barred. It looked for a while as if the Chinese boy wouldn't made second place, but he made it in the last lap.

Eight Leading U.S. Drivers Entered for Opening of Racing at Langford

With entries received from eight top-flight American drivers, Bruce Passmore will pull the wraps off the 1950 big-car racing season at his Langford Speedway Saturday night.

Among the visiting wheel-jockeys will be Del Fanning, who earned the position as No. 1 driver in the Pacific Northwest with his many victories last year. Fanning will bring over the Hal Dobry car, with which he set a new track record in winning the main event at Portland recently. Most expensive of the machines on display will be the car owned and driven by another American driver, Ralph Taylor. This newly-built, double-overdrive racer has cost Taylor better than $10,000.

Back in the racing wars despite his announced intention of retiring last season - an annual proclamation - will be Digger Caldwell, the perennial local favorite. Caldwell will pilot Grant King's car with which he placed second in the recent Portland opener. Verne Bruce will take over the wheel of the No. 2 car, owned jointly by Passmore and Jack Smith. Brownie Brown, Dave Cooper, Jack Spaulding and Roy Newton are among the other Victoria drivers expected to compete.

Passmore will inaugurate a new system of positioning cars for the third and fourth heats in a move calculated to provide the fans with additional thrills at the three-eighths-mile speedway. The cars, divided into "A" and "B" classes according to the times recorded during the time trials, will start those two heats in reverse order to their finishing order in the first and second heats.

Driver Unhurt in Spectacular Smash at Langford Speedway; Races Again

Jack Spaulding walked away uninjured last night from a crash at Langford Speedway that saw 20 feet of guard rail in front of the grandstand reduced to matchwood. Only this week track owner Bruce Passmore had the foresight to install an additional two strands of steel cable to protect the fans from just such an accident. It proved its worth and is credited with stopping the heavy No. 1 car from tearing into the stands.

The accident was over in a flash and many of the 2,600 fans hardly realized what happened. In the seventh lap of the second heat race, Spaulding tangled wheels with Verne Bruce coming out of the north turn. Traveling about 70 mph, the car flipped into the air, turned upside down and crashed into the fence. Pit crews rushed to the scene, righted the car and released Spaulding. He was badly shaken but managed to race again later.

The north corner was the scene of another accident in the 20th lap of the main event. Dave Cooper locked wheels with Lloyd Blair and flipped into the air out of control. Blair, also out of control, swerved toward the infield and smashed head-on into Brownie Brown, who was just rounding the turn. No one was injured. Bob Simpson won the event. Del Fanning, driving George Haslam's car, was second and Corky Thomas, third.

Cooper Declared Winner in Rain-Shortened Race

With the R.C.M.P in possession of their "slick" tires and with rain threatening all evening, local big-car drivers piloted their machines remarkably well on stock tires and almost completed their program before a smaller-than-average crowd at Langford Speedway last night.

Rain finally began to fall steadily during the main evet and the slippery condition of the track caused starter Bob Wensley to halt the feature race when 18 of the 30 scheduled laps had been completed. Dave Cooper, who was breezing along with a comfortable three-quarters of a lap lead, copped the event with Brownie Brown second and Verne Bruce in third place.

Cooper emerged as the big winner of the night by throttling his car to two firsts, two seconds and a third. One of his wins was scored in the five-lap backward race in which the contestants drove their machines in the reverse direction of the track.

Manager Bruce Passmore announced that stock car racing will return to the speedway next Saturday night and the Canadian big-car racing championships will be held at the Langford layout on September 4.

The government closed the Langford Speedway in 1950. The track's land was appropriated and used for the development of a new school. The people of Victoria were without a local racing facility. Drivers and race fans were forced to pass over the Malahat to take part in up-island events. But in 1954, all that would change with the addition of a brand-new racing facility.

Following the closure of Langford Speedway, Bruce Passmore retired from the sport to devote his time and energies into his newly-acquired business – Speedway Motors – the oldest Volkswagen dealership in Canada.

(Images in this chapter courtesy of the Victoria Auto Racing Hall of Fame and Museum.)

SEVEN

Swede Lindskog

Research shows that numerous – and often highly successful – racers made a name for themselves during the late 1930s and during the '40s (excepting the war years) in British Columbia. It's sometimes difficult to pick exceptional standouts from that group, but one driver certainly deserves mention.

(Photo courtesy of Canadian Racer)

Swede Lindskog became one of the most dominant and popular drivers at Langford Speedway, not to mention numerous claims to fame in Southern California.

Perhaps the best description of Swede's exploits was written by Victoria's Pike Green in March 1973 for the publication *Yesterday's Wheels*. Pike – along with his brother Bud – were successful racers in their own right around the Pacific Northwest beginning in 1946. Both were inducted into the Victoria Auto Racing Hall of Fame in 1996.

The following paragraphs are from Pike's article, interlaced with several related news clippings and other facts relating to the legacy of Swede Lindskog:

Born in Seattle on March 17, 1917, Einar T. 'Swede' Lindskog died on June 27, 1946 in a racing accident while qualifying a midget at Gilmore Stadium in Los Angeles. The tragedy occurred before 18,500 spectators while on his second lap, after having posted the season's fastest time of 14.78 on the first circuit. His prowess as a race driver still lives with us as one of auto racing's legends.

Swede attended Ballard High School in Seattle, where he made the best possible use of his time in machine shop classes by building a sprint car, his first ride. The Ballard educators felt it necessary to call in the parents of 15-year-old Einar for a discussion of the doubtful future in store for their bright young son, when it was noted that his preoccupation with auto racing had become what they considered to be an obsession.

At the age of seventeen, Swede started driving the "High School" car and immediately displayed some of the talent for which he later became famous. His performance in the first car attracted the attention of some influential people and earned him a ride in some of the era's most potent cars. He rose quickly through the ranks, soon becoming a contender for top honors.

Swede drove one of the first midgets to be constructed in the Northwest, a car owned by 'Pinky' Pinkham, and alternated between midgets and sprinters thereafter. During the 1938 season, a roll bar was added to the midget Swede was driving, and he lost no time in testing it, by way of lighting on his head. He emerged uninjured from the spill, but the roll bar was soon to be removed from the car when it became commonly called such names as "Sissy Bar" and "Girl's Car."

Swede racked up an impressive list of victories while driving for the very competitive and colorful Portland, Oregon, car owner Dorothy Gruman, widely known as the "Duchess of Auto Racing", who had a stable of both midget and sprint cars. On a swing through California in 1937, Swede startled our southern neighbors by firmly establishing himself among the top few drivers in the midget circuit there.

While racing in Los Angeles, Lindskog befriended a gentleman by the name of Roy Richter, who worked in a suburban shop named Bell Auto Parts. Richter was a successful car builder and one of the leading Californian drivers at the time, as well as racing promoter.

By virtue of his outstanding performance in the 1937 season, Swede was selected as one of a six-member U.S. race team that Richter put together to tour New Zealand. The popular young driver became a permanent member of the "Down Under" team until the outbreak of World War Two. The New Zealand fans took an immediate liking to the personable Swede from Seattle and, according to the New Zealand programs of that time; Swede was always considered a feature attraction.

The spring of 1938 found him back in the Northwest, by now a seasoned veteran at the ripe old age of twenty. In May of that year, he began the most incredible string of victories of which this writer has ever known.

On his first appearance at Victoria's Langford Speedway, Swede won the main event, followed closely by Seattle's Tony West, Jack Spaulding and the 1938 Northwest midget king, Bert Bloomgren. During his invasions of Langford, Swede was NEVER defeated in a main event, although some may recall the one program in which he failed to finish due to a broken steering gear in Glen Shaw's Dreyer.

These were the days of straight-up starts, and Swede captured the fancy and affection of all Victoria race fans after his fourth consecutive win. From then on, he voluntarily started in the last slot of each successive main, leaving his closest competitors still in the front lines. The crowds never failed to cheer their approval in loud unison at the sportsmanlike gesture, as Swede's car was rolled to the rear of the lineup. More intriguing yet, he put this string together at the wheel of several different race cars.

Far from being an unpopular winner, as sometimes happens, Swede's presence on a race night always brought a capacity crowd, many of whom would arrive early for the simple pleasure of seeing him time-in. It has often been said that this alone was worth the price of admission. He was a natural-born rim-rider, and a past master in the art. Perhaps there have been others, but of the thousands of drivers I have personally witnessed, not one has been as complete a master of his flamboyant rim-riding technique. This being judged the most difficult of all driving forms, particularly on short, paved tracks.

The *Daily Colonist* newspaper reported regularly on the action taking place at the Langford Speedway, as in this example dated June 1st, 1939:

Five American Drivers Expected to Compete at Speedway Saturday

Headed by Swede Lindskog, famous Seattle speed demon, who had captured more races here than any other American driver, at least five United States pilots will be in the city Saturday to take part in the events which will be run off at the Langford Speedway. The time trials will open the evening's racing at 7:45 and then the distance events will get underway.

Lindskog, well known for his daring driving at the local track, will be the favorite to top the field in the main races. Along with the Seattle Swede there will be Jud Taylor, Lew McMurtry, Ramsay and the possibility of car number 74 coming here from Yakima.

According to reports, all Victoria drivers have their cars in first-class condition and will be out gunning for some of the purse money. Last Saturday the boys held a practice event at the speedway and their times were faster than previous turnouts. The track is in fine condition and therefore there is the possibility that some new records will be established during the evening.

Jack Taylor, track manager, went over to Seattle to line up the best available drivers for Saturday's program and will be back in the city today with all the data on the boys.

The following Sunday, June 11th, 1939, *The Daily Colonist* published a full race report – followed up by an extensive review of the event. As predicted, the 'Seattle Swede' captured all the laurels:

Lindskog Again Shines at Langford Speedway

Seattle Race Driver Captures Major Honors After Thrilling Large Crowd – Sutton Shows Up Well – Carson Escapes Serious Injuries in Spill

Turning the Langford oval in some of the cleanest and most thrilling exhibitions of speed seen here for a long time, local and visiting drivers divided honors in last night's meet, before a packed stand of excited fans.
As usual, Swede Lindskog, Seattle ace, was the pick of the speed friends, and shot his wagon across the finishing line in first position in the main, twenty-lap event.

Bert Sutton, up and coming Victoria driver, hit his stride in the final two events and chased Lindskog around the oval to take second-place honors in the feature race, in addition to capturing a special five-lapper.
Jimmy Symes was another Sound City driver who was burning up the tires in the breath-taking contests. Symes wheeled his machine around the track in twenty seconds flat, to hang up the fastest time trial. The Seattle boy also captured the second heat race and trailed Sutton in the final event on the evening's card.

About one month later, Swede Lindskog returned to Langford and continued his racing prowess, despite tough competition from Symes and Vantreight. As the *Daily Colonist* described on July 16th, 1939:

Lindskog is Tops Again

Seattle Driver Given Battle by Jimmy Symes in Main Event

After the stiffest fight that he has faced in auto races here this year, Swede Lindskog, Seattle king of the superspeedways, once more emerged victor in the main event of the Langford Speedway bill last night. Closely trailing him at the finish was Jimmy Symes, another Seattle driver, who held the lead position until the seventeenth lap of the twenty-lap race.

Symes took the first position from Gerry Vantreight, Victoria, who had the pole spot in the fourth lap, but Vantreight stayed in the fight for two more laps before yielding second position to Lindskog. Swede, winner of almost every main event here in the season's racing, pushed to the front from twelfth position at the start in the sixth lap, but only held the lead for a lap.

In the seventh lap, Symes saw an opening and drove past his Seattle partner in a clever maneuver that enabled him to build up a slight lead on Swede. Lindskog followed for ten laps trying for an opportunity to pass, but Symes held him until the end of lap seventeen. Even then, it was anybody's race until the last lap.

Lindskog's time for the twenty laps was 8:34. Symes was only a few seconds slower, and Gerry Vantreight was a good third, with a considerable lead over Digger Caldwell, Victoria, in fourth position. Prior to the main event, Lindskog had the edge on Lew McMurtry, Seattle, in the helmet dash and first heat race. He won the five-lap helmet dash and his eight-lap heat race.

Continuing with the earlier-referenced article by Pike Green:

Swede's introduction into major league racing came on May 20, 1940 when driving license card number 167 was issued to Einar Theodore Lindskog by the contest board of the American Automobile Association.

The Los Angeles Times newspaper of May 19, 1940 even heralded this with the comment that: "This new rising young star from somewhere in Backwoods, Washington" would be on the following Thursday's program at Gilmore Stadium.

Swede Lindskog and Glen Shaw at Langford Speedway – circa' 1939.

(Brian Pratt Collection)

Three months later, the same newspaper headlined Swede as "The Man to Beat" at both Gilmore Stadium, Mecca of the midget racers, and the old Ascot Speedway, home of the sprint cars:

Such well-known drivers as national champion Rex Mays, Indianapolis stars Johnny Parsons, Sam Hanks, Mel Hansen, Johnny McDowell, Ronnie Householder and an endless list of racing greats, were to chase the Swede across the finish line throughout his rookie year in that league. San Diego newspaper records of that year indicate that Swede had also dominated most of the midget racing at their Balboa Stadium.

In his sophomore year, 1941, Lindskog became a featured personality on the sports pages, attracting national interest when the *Saturday Evening Post* ran a story predicting that he would become an Indianapolis sensation within the next few years.

Swede was listed that year as a co-favorite to win a 100-miler at Los Angeles' old Atlantic Speedway. The 1941 Ascot win column gave Mr. Lindskog's name frequent mention, culminating with a victory in the 100-lap World War Anniversary Race, which was ironically staged on the eve of this country's entry into World War Two.

The midget point chase at Gilmore became a real cliff-hanger as the season neared its close, when Swede ran up a win on October 10, 1941 to move ahead of Roy Russing by a slim margin of 1673.4 points to Russing's 1668.2. Swede was touted as a 3-to-1 favorite by the Los Angeles Times going into the final Grand Prix Racing on Thanksgiving Day. On November 20th, the rivalry between these two men was battled down to the wire, with Roy Russing emerging the victor and Swede having to settle for second.

Swede answered his country's call-to-arms after the attack on Pearl Harbor, becoming a Staff Sergeant in the Air Corps for the duration of hostilities. He fought in several battles in the South Pacific, and while engaged in the historic battle of Iwo Jima, he and several of his wartime buddies somehow found the time (and parts) to build a midget race car. Unbelievable as it may sound, this is a fact. I have personally seen photos of the car, both still and action shots, of Swede broad-sliding it on the flat sands of Iwo Jima. Whether the car ever came to this country or not, I have been unable to determine. Swede's mother told me that he sold the car for $200 before leaving Iwo Jima, and unless some reader can help me trace the car further, the story ends there.

Upon his discharge from the service, Swede took right up where he had left off four years earlier, headlined at Gilmore Stadium. In the meantime, Roy Richter decided to sell his race car in order to purchase Bell Auto Parts outright. After driving for several other car owners, Lindskog was hired to drive a new midget design being built for Captain Walt Seyerle, a Trans World Airlines pilot. Swede won the first race in that car – the same as the one he was soon killed in at the age of 29.

It was the second time that Roy Richter would lose a close friend to a racing accident. Thereafter, Richter made a commitment to work toward creating safer racing products. His efforts marked the foundation of Bell Helmets, one of the largest helmet manufacturers in the world.

A bachelor, Swede was survived by his parents and three sisters, all of Seattle. He was inducted into the National Midget Racing Hall of Fame in 2003. He gave all he had to auto racing, letting neither concerned school officials, nor a raging wartime battleground stand in his way and, in the end, gave his life as well.

A person would be hard-pressed to find anyone who knew him who could say an unkind word about Einar Lindskog – the tall, blond, handsome and quiet young race driver from "Backwoods, Washington", who possessed a rare and magic personality that infected everyone who came in contact with him.

Recently, I had the pleasure of visiting with Einar's mother and, although she understandably doesn't share our enthusiasm for auto racing, she is justly proud of the son she lost so long ago. I sincerely hope that she will gain some small measure of comfort in knowing that her son's other world of racing has not forgotten him either.

(Photo courtesy of the Legends of San Jose Speedway)

EIGHT

Victoria's Auto Racing Heritage – Shearing Speedway

When Langford Speedway closed in 1950, there became a void in auto racing in the Victoria area. During that time some did not want another track to come onboard, but along came the Shearing brothers of Cobble Hill.

Ted, Bill and John Shearing, ages 26, 24 and 23, were sturdy young loggers with a big vision. Out of the blue one day, they came up with an idea to build a racing facility on ten acres of their father's wooded property.

As the story goes, it was during the forest closure in July of 1951 when the brothers began talking about reviving racing in the lower Island area. In one interview with the *Victoria Times* newspaper, Ted said, "I just got the crazy idea if the three of us got together, we could build a track on Dad's property."

The site would be located on the old Cowichan Bay Road, about a quarter of a mile up from Dougan's Junction. They formed a company called Shearing Speedway Ltd.

Despite the naysayers, the Shearing brothers put in endless blood, sweat and tears in constructing their dream. They cleared the land, leveled it and then plotted out the race course. They designed the track to accommodate three flavors of competition: big cars, roadsters and stock cars.

Next came the banking and rolling the surface, building grandstands to seat 1,200 spectators, erecting light posts, and carving out a parking lot for 1,000 cars. The boys did all the work themselves except the final paving.

As it so often occurs with new racing facilities, there was some backlash by local neighbors who were concerned about noise and crowds. The inside story was described in this *Victoria Daily Times* article posted on June 16th, 1952:

Race Cars' Noise Held Unnoticeable

Noises from race cars won't bother anyone, say officials of the B.C. Automotive Sports Association, and they claim to have scientific evidence to prove it. Three race cars were towed to the proposed site yesterday and run at full throttle for five minutes. A portable sound equipment was unable to pick up any but the faintest sounds at distances as close as 300 yards away, they say.

A test run-off in the Colonist newsroom yesterday showed that at a distance of 3/10 miles the microphone picked up: (1) the sound of birds singing; (2) a child speaking close by; (3) a car door slamming – but no engine noises.

Several persons living within a quarter-mile radius of the site, unaware the test was being conducted, said they could hear nothing while the engines were running at top speed. Two of these people had signed the 142-name petition protesting the establishment of a track in the area, association members said.

The Shearing Brothers (left to right): Ted, Bill and John. In the ticket booth is John's wife Louise.

(Ray Pottinger Collection)

The test was held between 11 a.m. and 2 p.m. The recording may be run off for city council today. Council had already approved the track several weeks ago when the petition forced them to reconsider. A final decision is expected today.

Four check points were used during the test, two .3 miles away, one at 300 yards (near the home of a resident who gathered names for the petition) and another a half-mile away in a more thickly populated area.

Charles Flitton, president of the automobile club, said the track would serve the city in two ways – by providing an interesting diversion for several thousand people and by getting speed-minded youths off the road. "If they can't have a track, they'll build hot rods and tear around the streets anyway," he said. He added that the association would require that the cars competing be true racing cars, not hot rods. "They couldn't be driven anywhere but on the track," he said.

Finally, the word went out that the facility was ready for action. Together with the Shearing brothers, there was a happy group of idle racers who were ready to go throttle-down once again.

The inaugural night at the races took place on Saturday, August 23rd, 1952. According to the *Victoria Daily Times* article published the following Monday, August 25th, it was a smashing success for all:

Not Enough Seats for Auto-Race Enthusiasts

Auto racing returned in a roar of exhaust and a cloud of dust Saturday night at the Shearing Brothers' Speedway on the Cowichan Bay Road. Close to 3,000 fans turned out to watch the opening of a new season and if they liked what they saw, the venture will be a successful one. There were seats for only about half the fans that filled the grandstand and were three-deep in some parts of the area behind the guardrails.

There were no spills or crackups as the drivers were a little wary of the new track which was noticeably soft at the turns. Cars were forced to slow down considerably at the east corner. Seattle's Pike Green won the featured 10-lap main event with Corky Thomas of Victoria turning in a good second. Del Fanning, another Seattle-ite, was third. Green just missed taking the helmet dash but was forced out at the last turn of the fifth lap after jockeying with Bob Simpson who beat Green by yards. Green beat Simpson in a match race that replaced heat dashes.

Verne Bruce cleaned up in the stock car races but was not a popular winner as his car appeared to be a stock in name only. Built by Jack Smith, the stock seemed capable of giving any racer a fight. Bruce beat Dave Cooper's car in the main stock event and beat Bruce Passmore who was driving Smith's low-slung car in another stock feature. Wild Bill Heller had two firsts in other stock races.

In the next Saturday evening event at Shearing Speedway, Del Fanning nearly made a clean sweep in the big car contests. He finished in a dead heat with Victoria's Bob Simpson in the helmet dash, out-drove Corky Thomas and Simpson in his heat race, and edged out Brownie Brown in the main event.

In the evening's stock car events, there were a number of spinouts, two minor collisions and one car badly damaged after climbing a guard rail, but the driver was uninjured. Fifteen cars took the green flag in the stock car main event, which featured Vern Bruce throttling all the way from the last position to win over Bruce Passmore.

The night of September 8th, 1952 appeared to be another exciting evening of racing at Shearing. A new surface had been laid, which enabled speeds to increase over those of opening night.

On September 9th, 1952 the *Victoria Daily Times* issued this recap:

Piles-Up, Fire Thrill Speedway Fans

Vancouver Island car racing fans got more than their money's worth of thrills and spills at Shearing Speedway last night. There was a three-car pile-up, one car caught fire and crashed into the railing near the grandstand. No one was injured. Verne Bruce, Bill Vye and Bruce Passmore provided the pile-up. Bob Simpson's race car caught fire from the exhaust, but the fire was quickly put out, and Bill Heller's stock car threw the wheel when the wheel bolt pulled through the hub.

A benefit meet to aid Ronald Ainey, 16-year-old Victoria boy who was injured at the track the previous week, will be held in the near future. All prize money won by the drivers as well as proceeds from the gate, will go to the injured lad.

Nearing the end of the 1952 racing season at Shearing Speedway Bob Gregg, a standout driver from the Oregon/Washington scene, visited the track in stunning fashion.

Gregg merely placed first in the helmet dash, the first heat and the 25-lap main event to take home the Speedway's big-car championship. Del Fanning placed second in each of those races, followed by Bob Simpson.

The final event of the year at Shearing took place on Thanksgiving Day, when an estimated 1,000 fans filled the grandstands. Local stock car racer John Lister came from behind 15 other entries and captured the 30-lap main event and the championship trophy.

Bob Simpson received the Bert Sutton Trophy for winning the most points throughout the season in the big-car events. For the most untiring effort, George Haslam captured the Frank Cameron Trophy. Corky Thomas was awarded the Jimmie Laird Trophy for the most improved driver.

The Shearing Brothers' first season of racing proved successful, paving the way for an even greater racing year in 1953.

Fast forward to the latter part of the 1953 season at Shearing, beginning with these articles in the *Cowichan* newspaper in early August:

Phil Hendry Dogged by Ill Luck at Speedway

Phil Hendry found himself a puzzled man at the end of the Shearing Speedway racing program on Saturday evening. In every race in which he competed something went wrong, and even when he loaned his car to another driver trouble occurred. Maybe it was just coincidence, but his car happens to be number 13.

In one race Phil had almost half a lap lead in the last lap when he spun out in the second turn. In the fifth heat he again had the lead and spun out on the far side in the fifth lap. In the B-Main, Hendry once more held the lead and again spun out during the last lap. In the A-Main, he loaned his car to Dave Francis, but he spun out too.

Eddie Kostenuk lost his left rear wheel when approaching the number one turn during the time trials, the wheel running off the track and hitting a tree, finally stopping in some bushes about 50-feet from the track. The wheel was soon replaced and Kostenuk was back in the running.
In the stock car helmet dash, Dave Cooper's car hit Bruce Passmore and spun him out, but no damage was sustained.

During the third heat Duncan driver Chris Benson spun out and found himself "sideswiped" from both sides. Enough damage was done to prevent him from racing the rest of the evening. This was Benson's second appearance at the track and he was doing well until the spin-out. Alec McEwan hit the rail on the far side of the track when he lost control coming out of the first turn during the fourth heat.

Sixteen cars started in the A-Main and after Cooper and Passmore locked wheels in the last lap, only four cars crossed the finishing line. Most of the cars had motor trouble or spun out along the track. K. Nelson was the A-Main victor, followed by J. Sylvester and B. Nelson.

New Stock Car Record Made by Dave Cooper

Once again Dave Cooper made a new track record for stock cars on Saturday night at Shearing Speedway. Three weeks ago, Bruce Passmore established a record time of 17.50 seconds. On Saturday night Cooper brought it down to 17.42 seconds, with Dick Varley right behind him with 17.64 seconds and Passmore with 18.01 seconds.

Maybe Phil Hendry has broken the spell, because he placed second in the B-Main. No extensive damage was done when Passmore hit the rail in the last lap of the second heat. He was back in the racing by the fourth heat. In the fourth heat Bill Heller and Dave Miller tangled in the second turn after Miller had spun out.

Don Geyser hit the rail in the second turn of the B-Main which finished his racing for the night. In the second-to-last lap of the A-Main, Mel McDonald and Miller got tangled and went into the rail together in front of the concession stands. McDonald's front wheel went through the rail, but Miller was able to finish the race, which was won by Cooper. The B-Main winner was Ray Pottinger.

Shearing Speedway reports also appeared in the *Victoria Daily Times*. Here are some interesting samples from September 1953:

Newton Breaks Record at Shearing Speedway

Mike Newton with a new Mercury engine in his car broke Dave Cooper's stock car track record at Shearing Speedway Saturday night. Newton circled the track in 17.19 seconds, shaving one-tenth of a second off the mark set three weeks ago.

The stock A-Main event almost turned into a crash elimination race. Several of the favorites were knocked out of action in the jams and the race had to be restarted. It was finally won by Jack Rumley. Cooper, the track's leading driver in both stock and big car events, won the helmet dash, placed third in the first heat of the big car events, and picked up a first in the third heat of the stock car events. He was driving with a cast on his left foot, broken at work last week.

Newton Again Winner at Shearing Speedway

Mike Newton, a former motorcycle racer who had done little at Shearing's Speedway until Saturday night, continued to hold the spotlight by winning three events on Monday night's all-stock car program at the quarter-mile track.

Newton, who cracked Dave Cooper's stock car record Saturday night, won the helmet dash, first heat and 15-lap main event. Cooper, who held the record and is leading in points in both stock car and big car divisions, was competing in a 100-mile big car race at Portland Monday. Newton came from back in a field of 16 drivers which included Jack Spaulding, Dick Varley and Bill Nelson to take the main event by only a few feet. On the last lap, he found a hole and slid through to edge out Spaulding.

Varley Wins 'A' Main at Shearing Speedway

Dick Varley drove a spectacular race to capture the A-Main event in the weekly stock car racing program at Shearing Speedway Saturday night, edging out favored Dave Cooper in a nip-and-tuck battle. Sixteen cars started in the 25-lap event and numerous jams and spin-outs caused the race to be restarted twice.

Corky Thomas, standing on a parked car in the infield, escaped serious injury when a car careened out of control and crashed into the car on which he was standing. Thomas was severely shaken up.

Further thrills were provided in the third heat race when Bruce Passmore and Ray Pottinger tangled in front of the grandstand and slammed into the guard rail. Passmore's car was put out of commission but Pottinger returned to take second place behind Ken Nelson when the race was restarted. Pottinger also finished first in the fourth heat race.

Thomas and Varley Win; Stop Sweep for Cooper

Main-event victories by Corky Thomas and Dick Varley stopped Dave Cooper from scoring sweeps in both big car and stock car racing events at Shearing's Speedway Saturday night. Cooper, however, emerged as the big winner at the Cowichan Bay Road track boosting his seasonal points lead in both divisions as he picked up four first places and finished second in each main event.

In racing car competition, he took the checkered flag in the helmet dash and first heat race before Thomas, who had a "hot" machine Saturday, roared to his surprise victory in the A-Main. Varley out-drove Cooper in the stocker A-Main after the point leader had driven to first-place finishes in the helmet dash and first heat race.

Hank Neilson of Nanaimo rolled his stock machine into the infield after being bumped in the second heat race. Shaken up but otherwise uninjured, he returned to action in later races.

As the 1953 season wound down to the final event on Thanksgiving Day and the awarding of the B.C. Championship awards, Shearing Speedway featured its first-ever female driver as an added promotion. Her name was Kajia Kalevala – a 22-year-old who had relocated to Vancouver, B.C. from her native Finland.

For her performance at Shearing, she was supplied with a big car and a stock car by track officials. One report stated, "She may bring her Ford coupe stocker, which she describes as having 'seven cylinders - the eighth one will not go.'"

Shearing's 1953 season wrap-up was summarized in this *Victoria Daily Times* report that appeared on October 13th, 1953:

Kostenuk Sweeps Final Race Card; Newton Sets Mark; Cooper No.1

The winning of a special race by Miss Kaija Kalevala, first girl to race on Vancouver Island, a new track record by Mike Newton, a clean sweep of the big car events by Eddie Kostenuk and the presentation of the B.C. Championship award, featured the last race of the season at Shearing's Cobble Hill track Thanksgiving Day afternoon.

Miss Kalevala won a special race for guest drivers in which she demonstrated the nerve and ability which won her 21 race trophies in Finland and was warmly applauded by the fans as she added her kisses in presenting trophies and awards.

Verne Moore and Bruce Passmore drove in an exciting big car duel which was declared a dead heat as Moore caught Passmore at the tape. The big 40-lap stock car main event had to be flagged down when Nielsen from Nanaimo swerved into the path of Dick Varley, who crashed into him with Dave Cooper also piling in.

Shearing Speedway in 1953. Dick Varley #88, Phil Hendry #13, Ray Pottinger #90, Mike Newton #98.

(Ray Pottinger Collection)

Kostenuk swept the card for big cars, winning the helmet dash, the first heat and the 30-lap main. Dave Cooper's untiring efforts throughout the season brought him the Frank Cameron Perpetual Trophy and, in addition, he was chosen the leading driver of the year and the big car driver of 1953.

Ken Nelson received the Shearing Brother's Trophy as the most popular driver, with his brother Bill getting the trophy for the best-appearing stock car.

To Dick Varley, Lamont Brooks and Bobby Vantreight went the honor of being the best pit crew. All awards were made by Miss Kalevala, who was warmly applauded as she added a kiss to each presentation. Varley was also chosen by VITRA as the most promising driver of the year.

Along the way, Shearing Speedway played a major role in the early days of the Vancouver Island Track Racing Association (VITRA). The club progressed to become one of the largest and best organized motor racing clubs in the Pacific Northwest.

In 1961, veteran driver Dave Cooper penned this interesting history of VITRA that appeared in a Western Speedway program:

In 1949, a group of automobile enthusiasts met in an old home, called "The Dingle", on Gorge Road. The property was owned by Bruce Passmore, the then-owner of the old Langford Speedway. The instigator was one of Victoria's best-known race car builders and a former driver, Jack Smith. The original idea was to build cars that could be driven on the road and still be raced – and for this reason the Club was called the Vancouver Island Track Roadster Association.

Jack Smith was the first President. Les Webb filed the original papers for the Club charter, which was received in 1949. The Club held its first races at Langford Speedway. However, these were mostly fill-in races for the big cars (sprint cars) which were very popular then.

It wasn't until the Shearing Speedway opened at Cobble Hill in 1952 that the club was able to field a full event of races. It was apparent right from the start that the roadsters, or home-build sports cars, were in the minority. American-type coupes and sedans were the most popular. This created a division in the club, with the new cars being called Stockers. The Stockers soon completely took over the club. For this reason, while Frank Addison was President, the Roadster portion of the club's name was changed to Racing – as it stands now.

Most of the cars were driven with license, lights, etc. for the first few years of racing, and were similar to the Jalopy's of today. They were also similar for the frequency of accidents. This made driving home something of a problem, and soon all cars were towed to the race track. The machines used tow-cars that were generally in worse condition than the stockers and towing over the Malahat overheated the engines. It was common practice for everyone to stop at the summit, and these impromptu get-togethers are probably remembered better than the races.

With the opening of Western Speedway in 1954, VITRA continued to grow, and it was in 1958 when the highest purses ever were paid out. This figure will certainly be passed in 1961. This year is notable for a number of firsts:

- The first time the club has taken over a track and promoted racing.
- The first time for a number of years that late-model, overhead V8 engines have been allowed.
- The reorganizing of a Jalopy Division with the first all-Jalopy race night.
- The first time a 150-lap championship race has been run.
- The first time a purse as large as $3,000 has been offered.
- The first-time cars have come from Idaho, Washington, Alberta, etc. to race here.

Shearing Speedway continued to operate for several more years, but when Andre Cottyn's new Western Speedway opened in 1954, the car counts at Shearing floundered. The facility remained intact until sometime in the mid-to-late 1970s when the property was excavated and housing was built on the site.

NINE

Kajia Kalevala

Kajia (pronounced Ki-ya) Kalevala was a 22-year-old who relocated to Vancouver, British Columbia from Finland. Following her service in the Finnish army during the war years, this auto enthusiast participated in racing in her native country.

After arriving in Vancouver in 1951 and finding employment at an automobile dealership as a mechanic, she still had a desire to return to racing.

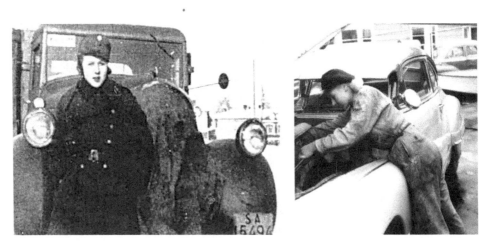

(Photos courtesy of The Greater Vancouver Motor Sports Society)

Kajia soon saved enough money to buy an old Ford coupe, which she fixed up herself, and began competing at Digney Speedway in Vancouver. She naturally garnered headlines, such as this one from *The News Herald* newspaper on July 24th, 1952:

Girl 'Stock Jock' Races Against Time – And Men

"Play for a baby" was the way Kaija looked on racing at the Digney Speedway in Burnaby until she acquired a stock car and began racing against time – and men. But the 28-year-old native of Finland, and winner of many firsts in ice and dirt track racing, soon changed her mind.

She now looks upon racing as a thrilling adventure and "fear" is a word that seldom passes through her mind. Christened Kaija Marja Kalevala of Hameelinna, the beautiful platinum blonde came to Canada eight months ago and held dreams of competing on the famous Indianapolis race track.

Five-foot-nine, 130-pound Kaija weathered two wars, serving as the only woman chauffeur in the Finnish army.

Even as a child she was interested in cars, and toy autos topped the list of playthings. She recalls driving a heavy army truck, packed to capacity with crated bombs, when a Russian fighter plane riddled the vehicle with over 2,000 bullets. Kaija, underneath the truck immediately after the attack started, was wounded in the leg by a stray bullet. While transporting food by truck to troops in the front lines, she encountered a Russian parachutist. He landed a short distance away and trained his Sten gun on her. She whipped out a revolver and with one shot, felled him.

Kaija was also a stunt driver for a short picture made by a Finnish film company. She rolled cars over steep embankments, produced realistic effects by driving a car head-on into a bus, and jack-rabbiting off railway tracks before a train passed over the same spot.

But she still possesses plenty of female charm – inch-long fingernails, rose cheeks, velvety skin, long, soft hair and that sweet innocent look. To demonstrate that you need to be strong to wheel stock cars around the track, she lifted her 210-pound manager, Joe Stanek, off the ground and carried him almost effortlessly about six feet.

Kaija wishes more women would take up racing. She would like to have the chance of teaching them how, stressing the fact that the woman racer should be practice-perfect before going on the track so that she would not be scoffed at. Kaija has 20 trophies won in homeland races to prove the point that women can compete successfully with men.

Within a post-race report which appeared in the *Victoria Daily Times*, Kaija's appearance was described:

Miss Kalevala won a special race for guest drivers in which she demonstrated the nerve and ability which won her 20 race trophies in Finland and was warmly applauded by the fans as she added her kisses in presenting trophies and awards.

Alyn Edwards, a freelance writer and auto enthusiast in Vancouver, B.C., had the pleasure of interviewing Miss Kalevala in 2011, when she was a sprightly 86-year-old. With his permission, this is the article he authored afterwards:

Kaija Kalevala – A Finnish Hot Rod Granny

Her name is Kaija Kalevala, and she still gets weepy when she recalls being forced to hang up her race car helmet and goggles. It was a combination of pressures that led the superb driver to call it quits.

In 1956, the Burnaby, B.C. resident was blocked from entering the pits to compete in midget car racing as part of the famed Indianapolis 500 race. Officials said it was bad luck to have a woman in the pits.
Pressure put on her sponsor sidelined her stock car during crucial races at Burnaby's Digney Speedway, causing her to slide in the standings. Then, when her mother arrived from Finland to live with her, she could no longer compete at out-of-town race tracks.

Finally, her employer told her she had to choose between racing and driving his auto parts truck. It was at that point that the career of the first woman in Canada to compete head-to-head in male-only stock car races suddenly ended. But Kalevala wasn't done with getting attention for her driving skills. For two days, she led the 1956 B.C. Truck Rodeo in points and only lost on the final day, coming second. All other competitors were men.

Women just didn't drive trucks back then. But she did. And, in the early 1950s, women didn't compete against men in car races. To add insult to injury, this tall Finnish beauty with striking blonde hair was at least as good as the male drivers – and often better.

The road the Finnish immigrant traveled to achieve racing prominence in Canada is like a fairy tale on wheels. Kalevala's fascination with motorized vehicles started early and became all-consuming. "Any time I saw a vehicle with the hood up, I would go over to look and ask questions," she says of her early years in Finland. When her father refused to allow her to take driver training, she used her allowance to buy books on driving.

At 17, Kalevala was ready to take her driving test, even though she had never driven a vehicle. "I drove in my head everywhere I went," she recalls. "I would operate the controls and shift gears just as if I was really behind the wheel."

She camped out at the local driving school and told the owner she wouldn't leave without being tested. The instructor finally agreed to the test just to get rid of her. He was amazed when she passed. The owner made her take a second test, which she also passed.

She used her driving papers to get a position as a volunteer for the Finnish Army Reserve. She initially chauffeured officers and delivered important documents in a red 1939 Chevrolet. One morning, the only vehicle left in the compound was a three-ton Dodge truck. "I always asked the men how they drove trucks and learned how to double-clutch and downshift on hills without ever driving a truck," she recalls. "I had no trouble when I actually got the wheel of that truck." She was soon hauling loads of heavy guns and food for the soldiers, along with hay for army horses. The job she didn't enjoy was carrying dead soldiers back from the front in wooden caskets.

Her racing career started when she joined the Finnish Film Company, driving heavy three-ton trucks and a bus, along with a front-wheel-drive Renault car, racing film around Helsinki between three theatres just in time to change reels – as there was only one original film available and there were no copies.

In 1950, Kalevala attracted the attention of one of Finland's best-known racers and, when he got a new race car, she got his old Ford flathead-powered Formula One car. She received national attention in her first race for being the only woman entered. The only way she could enter stock car races in Finland was in the so-called "powder puff", all-female races. She won every time, and soon there was no other woman willing to race against her.

She immigrated to Canada in 1951 when she discovered she was being taxed more heavily as a taxi driver because she was a female. When a Finnish friend told her about Digney Speedway in Burnaby, British Columbia, she took the train to Vancouver. Through connections, she got a job at a dealership doing everything, including full engine rebuilds. She got sponsorship with a Ford dealer to start racing at Digney Speedway in 1952 as the only female driver.

The first car was a sedan, and it had so much steel bracing inside that it was top-heavy and wouldn't perform, she recalls. The second car was a much lighter coupe, and the young driver started moving up in the pack and making a name for herself. By day, she drove a truck delivering auto parts to service stations and garages. Her spare time was spent preparing her car for the track, or racing it.

"Aurora Speedway in Seattle heard about me and wanted me to race there," she recalls. She asked for a month off to compete in the lead-up races to the 1956 Indianapolis 500, but when her boss's daughter couldn't manage the heavy clutch in her parts truck, her boss took over the driving. But it was too much for him too. "He told me I had to make a choice. Either give up racing or give up my job."

She kept driving the parts van and, at age 86, Kalevala is still driving a van. Her apartment is filled with boxes of trophies, awards and newspaper stories about her pioneering driving efforts. Her most recent recognition is an induction into the Greater Vancouver Motorsports Pioneers Society.

Kajia Kalevala was certainly a pioneer racer in her own right.

(Images courtesy of The Greater Vancouver Motor Sports Society)

TEN

Billy's Friends Remember – Phil Hendry

Serving in the role of Chief Starter at Western Speedway for many years, Phil Hendry had his eyes on many drivers throughout that time. Billy Foster was one of the local stand-outs.

Phil grew up in Victoria but traveled with his father – a photographer – to Langford Speedway every Saturday night to take in the action. In 1952 he became a member of the Vancouver Island Track Racing Association (VITRA). A year or so later, Phil was one of the many volunteers who were helping Andy Cottyn build Western Speedway, which opened in 1954. Hendry first served there as an assistant Pit Boss, and within the next few years moved up to the starter's stand.

"I first met Billy at his dad's garage," Phil recalls. "His entire family was into cars. We'd chum around at the race track – and he was always a lot of fun to be with. Billy was such an easy-going guy."

And a talented driver to boot, as proven by one of Phil's many tales.

"One night after the time trials I overheard driver Bill Crow ('Kissin' Crow from Idaho') talking to Grant King and asking 'What the hell's the matter with me? Look at my muscles, and that skinny little bastard beats me every time!' And Grant replied, 'Very simple – he uses his head.' Billy would set those guys up one or two laps before he passed them."

In his position as Chief Starter, Hendry explained he had full control over the drivers, and got along with most. Phil always displayed a certain class that earned him the respect of the drivers, and his flamboyant style of flagging always added to the show.

Billy clowning around with Phil Hendry.

(Victoria Auto Racing Hall of Fame)

Years later, when Billy was racing on the national schedule, he'd come home when he could to catch up with his family and Victoria buddies. In keeping with his 'Let's have fun' nature, Phil shared this story:

"Billy comes to town and picks me up. We were going to the fish and chips shop on Cook Street. Billy's driving a Camaro rental car. He asks me, 'Do you know what I can do with this car? I can put it into reverse at 40 mph.' He shoves the gas to full power and throws it into reverse. The car does a 180-degree turn just like that. I said, 'let's get out of here before we go to jail!'"

Phil was a participant in many club and track activities, including the Victoria May Day parades and fireworks displays at Western Speedway. Over the years, Hendry held several key positions for VITRA.

The many faces of Western Speedway starter Phil Hendry.

(Photos courtesy of the collections of Phil Hendry, Ray Pottinger and the Victoria Auto Racing Hall of Fame)

ELEVEN

Billy's Friends Remember – Harvey Chipper

Harvey Chipper's long career in racing began when he became a young crew member for Jim Haslam's team cars, which were driven in 1961 and 1962 by Billy Foster.

"In 1960, my interest in car racing started with me delivering the morning newspaper to local stock car racer Jimmy Haslam," Harvey remembers. "He lived on Millstream Road, which was close to Western Speedway."

(Victoria Auto Racing Hall of Fame)

Haslam operated an auto wrecking and towing business, and the two became acquainted. "Jimmy asked me to stay at his business to look after things when he was away racing," says Harvey. "I knew he currently owned a stock car, and one night he asked me to come with him to the Fernwood Esso, where his race car was located. That was when I first met Billy."

Chipper recalled that he and Haslam were invited to Foster's home on Regina Avenue, and quickly learned of Billy's affinity for speed. "We left in our truck and Billy followed," Chipper explained. "We noticed the wrecker truck he was driving was speeding up - he was pushing us! We eventually arrived at his house and met Billy's wife Bev. She wasn't prepared for us staying for dinner, as Billy hadn't told her in advance. As usual, Billy smoothed things out and we had a nice supper."

During the racing season at Western Speedway, the Saturday morning ritual at Haslam Auto Wrecking was preparing the race car. Bob Vantreight would work on the engine while John Woods would take care of the tires and other maintenance items. Harvey Chipper's job was to keep the car clean and tidy.

Chipper earned an opportunity to try his hand at driving a race car, thanks to Foster. As Harvey explained, "On a practice night at Western Speedway, Billy wanted me to drive his roadster. The engine has six carburetors that we had not covered with an air cleaner, so they would spit out raw fuel that would hit my eye goggles. My driving race cars ended then and there, and I decided to simply become a mechanic."

On the other hand, Billy would let the young Chipper drive his street cars, such as Chevy El Caminos or Ford Mustangs.

Of the many racing events that Harvey helped crew for Billy, several now come to mind. One of them was the annual Mt. Douglas Hill Climb, where Chipper recalls, "Billy ran against several vehicles that were designed for that specific form of racing. He was driving Jimmy Haslam's Ford-powered modified, which was built strictly for an oval track." When everything was said and done, Foster set the fastest overall time up the hill.

Chipper continued, "On our first trip to Edmonton, Alberta with the '34 Chev race car, we used a loaner tow vehicle and trailer. It was a 1957 Chevy half-ton pickup with a home-made canopy, but no back door. There were three crew members in the front seat and two back in the pickup bed. It was I, Billy, Jimmy, Bob Vantreight and Eddie MacDonald. The 200-lap race was won by Eldon Rasmussen in a far superior car to ours. Billy was the real underdog, but he ended up finishing third."

"At the 1963 Daffodil Cup race at Western Speedway, Billy ran his first upright race car," Harvey noted. "During practice, John Feuz was concerned about the engine's condition, so decided to add two cans of STP to the crankcase. During the race itself, John and I were praying the engine would last. It did, and Billy won the race."

Along with these memories, Harvey Chipper reminisced about other times while on the road with Billy Foster – or by towing the race car between Victoria and John Feuz's shop Portland, Oregon.

"With my 1961 Chev Impala, I would drive down to Portland to pick up the race car and trailer," says Harvey. "Arriving at John Feuz's garage, I would load up the car, tires, and spare parts. Heading back north, I would stop in Lynnwood, Washington, and contact an American friend of Billy's. He would then take everything up to and across the border. Once the race was over, I would return the car to Feuz's shop in Portland for any needed repairs."

When Foster made his way to Indianapolis in 1965, he called Chipper and invited him to come along to work on the race car. "After a lot of thinking and fretting, I decided not to go," says Chipper. "In 1965 I decided to get married and asked both Billy and Bev to be in our wedding party. As it turned out, Billy was in Indy at the time and couldn't attend, but Bev flew back to Victoria for the wedding."

As the years passed, Harvey and his wife Jean developed a close relationship with the Foster family. "As time went on with Billy away racing, Jean and I spent many a night with Bev and their three children," Harvey recalls. "Most nights we would have takeout food, or Bev would make grilled cheese and raw onion sandwiches. We spent lots of time in front of their big-screen television. Those nights were good times and will forever be etched in our minds." Harvey learned of Billy's fatal accident on the radio, noting that, "I was completely devastated that we had lost a good friend and my hero!"

(Victoria Auto Racing Hall of Fame)

In the years following Billy's death, Chipper continued his talents as a race car builder and mechanic. In 1967, he built a 1955 Chevrolet stock car with a modified six-cylinder engine. With Roy Haslam behind the wheel, the pair captured the Western Speedway championship that year.

In 1968, Gary Kershaw bought the Chevy engine for his own car and won that year's championship. In the meantime, Chipper and Haslam moved up to the Super Stock class and added to their championship wins.

Continuing in the stock car arena, Harvey built a new car to challenge the NASCAR venues throughout the Pacific Northwest. Teamed with Kershaw, the effort once again proved successful. In January 1970, with Chipper serving as crew chief, they entered their 1965 Chevelle in the Permatex 200 NASCAR Late Model Sportsman race at Riverside International Raceway. "Ironically, I was at the track where Billy had lost his life," Harvey recalls.

After qualifying 16th in the field, the car completed just 21 laps when it suffered a fire. At the 1971 running of the Permatex 200, the combination of Chipper and Kershaw came home the winners – the first Canadians to do so.

For the 1972 stock car season Chipper built two new cars – one for Kershaw and the other for veteran Hershel McGriff that was labeled the "Olympia Express" – in reference to its sponsor, Olympia Beer.

The legendary Hershel McGriff

Again, for 1973 and 1974, Gary Kershaw was racing Chipper-built stock cars. 1974 was a banner year for the team, winning virtually every event they entered. Accolades included the Sponsor's Cup, the Billy Foster Stock Car Trophy, the July Cup, the Corby Cup, and the season championship.

In 1981, Chipper received the NASCAR Mechanic of the Year Award – another first for a Canadian. Harvey was inducted into the Victoria Auto Racing Hall of Fame in 1993.

(Victoria Auto Racing Hall of Fame)

TWELVE

Victoria's Auto Racing Heritage – Western Speedway

As a young man, Andre "A.J." Cottyn relocated from Manitoba, Canada to Langford, British Columbia in 1938. He fit into his new surroundings well, as he held a deep and abiding love for auto racing.

In the fall of 1952, Cottyn purchased a 62-acre parcel of wilderness in Langford on Millstream Road. He held a desire to provide a local racetrack. With no significant assets, 'Andy' sold his logging equipment and borrowed money from the bank and from his brother George to finance his dream. Along with the assistance of his son George and many others, the group carved out the 3/8ths-mile dirt track.

The *Victoria Daily Colonist* provided details about Cottyn's new venture on September 12th, 1953:

Auto Races Slated at Victoria Again After Long Absence

Auto racing will move back close to Victoria next year after several seasons during which the closest racing was at Shearing's Speedway near Cowichan Bay. A new racetrack now being constructed along Millstream Road will provide Victoria racing fans with a type of competition never seen before on Vancouver Island. It will be a clay-dirt track. "Paved tracks are on the way out in the States," owner Andy Cottyn remarked. "They are tearing out the paved tracks and putting in clay."

The track is four-tenths of a mile in circumference, the largest yet constructed on the island. It is 50-feet in width in the straightaways and 70-feet on the turns. The straightaways are close to 200-yards in length. The bleachers will consist of one main stand, and two small stands with a total seating capacity of between 4,000 and 5,000. Mr. Cottyn, who has been working on the track for the past three months, reported it would be ready by the good weather next spring, around the first of May. At present the clearing is covered with a thick layer of dust with a vague impression of a track but this will be all changed by the spring, according to Cottyn.

The parking lots, which will hold an estimated 3,000 cars, will be put in grass by next year, and the road leading to the property off Millstream Road will be graded and covered with gravel. Spectators will not be bothered by dust, he explained. There are several types of chemicals which are sprinkled on the track which keeps the dust down.

Mr. Cottyn reports he hasn't heard one complaint from the neighbors. The track is situated in the middle of his 60 acres about a mile and a half from the Island Highway.

A logger by trade, Mr. Cottyn says he has been thinking of building a race track for some time, but he was finally pushed into making a start this spring when someone was trying to buy the property for a subdivision. With the large stands and the expected big crowds, Mr. Cottyn hopes to be able to draw many drivers from below the border. His plans now call for big car and stock car events with an occasional midget race. An added novelty would be motorcycle races, he said.

He has applied to the B.C. Automobile Sports Association for sanction but hasn't had any reply so far. The track will be called the Western Speedway. Jack Spaulding, veteran race car driver, will be the track organizer and will look after all the promotion.

Western Speedway's grand opening took place on Saturday, May 22nd, 1954. Over 3,000 expectant racing fans filled the grandstands to watch the fast Indy-style race cars take to the track. As the night's activities played out Del Fanning of Seattle – one of the era's most successful drivers – took home most of the laurels. The Sunday edition of *The Daily Colonist* summarized the highly successful opener:

Del Fanning Top Driver as New Speedway Opens

Del Fanning of Seattle, a favorite of Victoria car racing fans, grabbed off the major share of trophies last night in the opening big car meet at Andy Cottyn's new Western Speedway on the Millstream Road. Piloting Dick Barber's U.S. No. 1 car, Fanning held off continued challenges by Bob Simpson to win the featured A-Main event, took first place in the first heat race and missed in his bid for a sweep when Simpson won in the helmet dash.

Andre Cottyn's dream of establishing a new racing venue for Victoria-area racers and fans thus became an instant sensation during its first season. His media campaign was kept simple, and his track had no advertisements on the premises. The facility was just a track – a place for drivers to race and for fans to cheer. Over the next 13 years Cottyn owned and managed the speedway, running his domain with an iron hand – but also with a large dose of fairness.

(Brian Pratt Collection)

Del Fanning continued his winning ways at Western in 1954, right down to the final night of competition at the end of the first season. *The Daily Colonist* wrapped things up with this article on September 9th, 1954:

Seattle Driver Declared Western Speedway King

Del Fanning of Seattle won the Western Canada championship with a victory in the main event of the racing meet at Western Speedway Saturday night. The popular Fanning, who this year won the Pacific Northwest points championship for the second successive season, started in the pole position and held the lead all the way in Saturday's 50-lap title race.

Bob Simpson gave Fanning a tough battle in the early stages until forced out of action with a broken radiator connection. Ed Kostenuk moved up to finish in second place while Corky Thomas took the third position. Simpson got by Fanning on his way to a victory in the trophy dash and scored his second victory in the first heat race as he held off a late challenge from Fanning.

Bill Heller took the checkered flag in the second heat with Chub Filton grabbing second place and Thomas finishing third.

Simpson, who won the Rose's Jeweler Trophy for his win in the trophy dash, also received two other awards. He was presented with the Bardahl Trophy and the Bert Sutton Memorial Trophy for winning the track point championship this season.

Western Speedway in 1955 (top) and 1956 (bottom).

(Barrie Goodwin photos)

During the 1957 racing season, major improvements were made as the track was paved to a flat oval with the size reduced to 4/10ths of a mile. The facility continued to thrive, as illustrated in these articles from *The Nanaimo Daily Free Press* during July 1959:

Willoughby Tops Lambrick After Thirteen Laps

Dick Willoughby finally broke Phil Lambrick's hold on the main event at the Western Speedway Saturday night and won the 25-lap feature race. After being successful in the last two main events, Lambrick failed to place in Saturday's race and lost all hope of winning on the 13th lap when Willoughby took over. Red Burke placed third.

Veteran Al Smith survived a five-car crash that momentarily halted the race and then roared from behind to win the main event of Saturday night's weekly stock car races held at Western Speedway.

Gordon Alberg's first race, where he climbed into the engine compartment of Dave McClelland's car – trying to go through a hole that wasn't big enough.

(Ray Pottinger Collection)

Local Stockers Capture Four Heats at Speedway

The smash-up happened in the fifth lap. Only Doug Bowell was forced to the sidelines as a result of the accident when the race was stopped with Ray Pottinger holding the lead.

Oddly enough, neither Smith nor Pottinger crashed but when five cars banged together it forced track officials to halt the race to untangle the cars. Smith came on strongly after the second start to quickly take the lead and hold off a strong bid by Dick Varley.

Varley held the number two position for approximately 20 of the 30-lap race but couldn't close the distance after losing valuable time due to motor trouble earlier in the race. Although Varley lost out in the July Cup competition, he did win two events. He won the time trials and also the trophy dash. Red Burke, Hank Nielsen, Bob Mawle and Harry Roberts won the four heat races in that order.

Dick Willoughby Killed Sunday

Dick Willoughby, well-known stock car driver of Victoria, died of an electric shock and drowning in a skin-diving accident Sunday. Willoughby grabbed a 110-volt electric conduit as he surfaced after diving in Shoal Harbor, Sydney. The shock threw him back in the water. His wife and others pulled him out in seconds but attempts by ambulance crews and doctors to revive him failed.
Dick was a local favorite who had begun his racing career in the early 1950s in Victoria. His initial ride was a 1934 Ford which he raced in the stock car class at Western Speedway. His debut that year was not what one would call promising, as he demolished three race cars during his rookie season.

Amusingly, his crew fastened a pair of roller skates to the roof of his car at the beginning of the 1955 season. That year he did much better, and he ended the year placing sixth in the points championship.

1956 proved to be a notable year for Willoughby. He recorded six main event wins, three of which were consecutive. At years' end he was named the points champion. His success continued in 1958, placing third in the championship along with taking home the Most Popular Driver award.

Upon his death, his family initiated the Dick Willoughby Sportsmanship Trophy, which continues to this day. But as motorsports history has so often proven, in spite of the sudden loss of a competitor, the racing at Western Speedway continued. 1960 was another big year, especially for the up-and-coming driver by the name of Billy Foster.

(Victoria Auto Racing Hall of Fame)

The following articles are from *The Nanaimo Free Press* during the 1960 racing season:

Dick Varley Still Rolling; Sweeps Vic Stock Events

Still the hottest thing at Western Speedway, Dick Varley piloted his GMC-powered stock car to a sweep of Saturday night's main events. After winning the time trials, Varley then took the trophy dash, the second heat, and came from well behind to win the main event. Bill Foster led the first 15 laps of the main event, a 25-lap race, but Varley took over on the 16th lap and held the lead the rest of the way. Foster finished second, ahead of Hank Nielson.

Doug Bowell's car lost a wheel on the eighth lap of the main event and sent up a shower of sparks, but little damage was done. Five cars were banged out of contention in earlier heats, leaving 11 for the main event.

Victoria Drivers Collect Major Race Awards

Al Smith, top racing driver on Vancouver Island this year, won the 25-lap feature race at Western Speedway last night. Smith beat out Dave Cooper and Bob Mawle and snapped Dick Varley's record of seven wins in seven main events. The race was delayed to let Varley repair his car, which Grant King spun into the infield in the mechanics' race. Varley was challenging Smith for the lead when he spun out along with three other cars late in the race.

Driver Bill Foster won the second heat.

Nielson Thrills Stockers at Victoria Oval

Nanaimo's Ray Pottinger placed third in the main event of the Saturday night stock car races in Victoria, behind winner Al Smith and second place driver Bill Foster. The evening's card featured a spectacular crash in the second heat when Hank Nielson's car did a complete roll in mid-air and a couple more on the ground before coming to a stop on his side. Nielson crawled out of the car hurriedly, as gas was covering the area, and in his rush to get to the side of the track, he tripped and decided to rest there for a spell. Fortunately, Hank came out of the accident with minor cuts and bruises.

Dick Varley was stopped cold, spinning out in three events. Al Smith won the trophy dash with the first heat an all-Nanaimo affair, Red Burke winning it with Doug Bowell and Ray Pottinger runners-up.

In 1961, Western Speedway inaugurated a big, prestigious annual event named the Daffodil Cup, which beckoned big car drivers from around the Pacific Northwest. The first year the race victory went to Eldon Rasmussen from Edmonton, Alberta.

Lo and behold, Billy Foster came home the Daffodil Cup champion in 1962 and '63. Denver's Jim Malloy grabbed the win in 1964, followed by Eldon Rasmussen in 1965. The next repeat champion was Spokane's Norm Ellefson, driving to victory in 1966 and '67. After wins by Roy Smith (1968 and 1971) and Bud Gorder (1969), Ellefson secured his Daffodil Cup third title in 1972.

Another example of the rough-and-tumble competition at Western was described in this Victoria Daily Times report on July 10th, 1961:

Rides Were Rough at Speedway

An engine switch proved totally satisfactory to Al Smith Saturday night, but his victory in the main event for stock cars at Western Speedway proved somewhat anti-climactic to all the action that had preceded it. Practically all of Smith's competition was put out of action by a series of spectacular crashes as about 1,800 fans sat in on one of the wildest nights of racing ever seen at the Speedway.

It started in the second heat when Bill Smith, driving his new machine in only its second race, rolled the car several times in the second lap. Dave Cooper, driving a new Dodge stocker, demolished it on the third lap when an axle sheared, snapping his brake lines and sending him rolling out of control down a bank.

Then came the main event and the biggest – and potentially most dangerous – accident of all. A car spun in front of Dick Varley on the fifth lap and he ran up its wheel and flipped at least five times, ending up smashed against the retaining wall with the fire licking up through the car.

The ambulance and fired truck managed to put out the flames before they reached the unconscious Varley, but he was not freed from the wreck for 10 minutes. Varley was not seriously injured.

Smith, who had gone back to his last year's motor after trying out a new one earlier this year, was driving well and took an early lead. But pretty soon Bill Foster and Ray Pottinger were challenging strongly.

They traded the lead around for a while, but then bad luck caught up with them as well. Pottinger spun out and then half a lap later Foster did the same thing, letting Smith coast home alone for the victory.

The trophy for Billy's second consecutive Daffodil Cup Victory in 1963.

1961 – The combination of Jim Haslam and Billy Foster was hard to beat.

(Harvey Chipper collection)

Birth of the B-Modifieds at Western Speedway

(contributed by Dave Ireland)

Towards the end of the 1963 season, a paragraph appeared in the 'Around the Pits' section of the evening's program which told of a possible switch from the venerable stock cars, which had graced the Speedway since its beginning in 1954, to a new 'B-Modified class.

A number of VITRA officials and stock car owners had put forth the idea, which came on the heels of the start of the 'Modified Sportsman' class which started a year earlier. Unlike the then-current class of Sportsman which largely carried overhead V8 engines and actual racing components, the 'B' class would have overhead six and flathead V8 engines and stock components. They would be similar in appearance to the 'A' class cars but less expensive to build and would "open the door a little easier to the 'A' class modifieds."
This idea came to pass, and the first cars of the new class first took to the track at the inaugural Strawberry Cup race, which was the first modified meet of the 1964 season. This was a CAMRA-sanctioned meet with the 'A' and 'B' class cars running together.

Among the new 'B'-class drivers were ex-stocker pilots Brian Wilson, Bill Smith Sr. and Nanaimo's Harold Sjostrom. These were joined by their fellow stock car competitor Bob Mawle, who brought out his now-obsolete stocker. The 'B'-class car count would grow in subsequent race meets and, along with the jalopy class, would offer the fans a thrilling and memorable 1964 racing season.

(Brian Pratt Collection)

Andy Cottyn eventually sold the facility to a group of local businessmen and racing enthusiasts in the fall of 1966. He continued to retain some shares and served on the track's board of directors.

Moving forward to the late 1970s, Cottyn played a major role in the construction of a new steel and cement-structured grandstand, which would serve as an investment for the future of racing in the area. The $250,000 project made it one of the most ambitious privately-funded undertaking in Vancouver Island's sporting history.

The grandstands were dedicated in Andy's name at the season's opening race in 1979. In 1984, Andre Cottyn was included in the first class of individuals inducted into the Victoria Auto Racing Hall of Fame.

Through its history, Western Speedway has upheld a reputation for producing champions that have furthered their racing careers elsewhere in North America. Billy Foster, of course, heads the list, followed closely by master builder Grant King. And while Western Speedway wasn't his "home" track, Indy Champion Tom Sneva scored victories there when he was running in the CAMRA Series.

A few of the others include stock car driver Gary Kershaw, who began racing at Western in the early 1960s. He went on to team with noted Victoria car builder Harvey Chipper, and during the late 1960s and into the 1970s this duo were perennial champions at tracks throughout the Northwest. In 1971, Kershaw won the prestigious Permatex 200 on the road course at Riverside, California - the first Canadian to win such a race. As crew chief and engine builder, Chipper went home with the NASCAR Crew Chief Award.

In the 1964 racing season Kershaw, driving Chipper's 1965 Chevelle, amassed 16 consecutive main event victories at Western Speedway and another championship.

During this period, Gary was selected the Male Athlete of the Year by the Greater Victoria Sports Hall of Fame.

Roy Smith also developed his driving talents at Western, beginning with stock cars in 1964. In 1967 he graduated to the powerful A-Modified cars and, driving Geoff Vantreight's 'Daffodil Special', captured Pacific Northwest championships. In the following decade Smith switched back to stock cars and, in 1980, became the first Canadian to win NASCAR's Winston West championship. He repeated that title in 1981 and 1982.

In 1982 Smith drove a daffodil-yellow 'The Pride of Victoria' Pontiac, sponsored by the Victoria community, to a tenth-place finish in that year's Daytona 500. In 1998, Smith again captured his fourth Winston West championship. He joined Gary Kershaw by being the second driver hailing from Western Speedway to win the Victoria Sports Hall of Fame Male Athlete of the Year Award.

Another racer who cut his teeth at Western Speedway was Larry Pollard, who began his competition days in 1970 with stock cars. He established himself as one of Victoria's top drivers and later became a crewman for Roy Smith's NASCAR Winston West team.

Due to his mechanical know-how and behind-the-wheel experience, Pollard was hired in 1982 by North Carolina NASCAR Winston Cup team owner Richard Childress, whose driver was Ricky Rudd. The next year, Larry served as a crew chief for Richard Petty's team, and in 1984 he signed with the U.S. Tobacco Company as crew chief for the Skoal team.

Larry Pollard returned to the cockpit in 1985, and in 1987 he became the first Canadian to win a NASCAR Busch Grand National race. In the same time period, he also participated in several Winston Cup events. In 1988, his career came to an end when he was seriously injured in a crash at Dover Downs International Speedway in Delaware.

Today, Western Speedway continues to prosper under the ownership of Darrell Midgley and manager Denise Salmon. The facility hosts races for approximately twelve racing classes on Saturday nights throughout its eight-month season, beginning in April. Drag racing also takes place on selected Friday nights and Sunday afternoons, along a 500-foot strip incorporated into the front straightaway.

A few of the greats that honed their driving talents at Western Speedway (clockwise from left): Tom Sneva, Roy Smith, Gary Kershaw, Bob Gregg and Larry Pollard.

(Victoria Auto Racing Hall of Fame and the Brian Pratt Collection)

THIRTEEN

Ed Kostenuk

Victorian Ed Kostenuk entered the racing arena in 1948 at the Langford Speedway. Upon the opening of Western Speedway in 1954, and through the rest of the decade, he scored numerous main event wins. One of the many trophies he took home was the 1955 Western Canada Big Car Championship.

(Victoria Auto Racing Hall of Fame)

Not stopping there, in 1959 Kostenuk became president of a newly formed Go-Kart association at Island View Beach, where he also competed. In 1961, driving his own Ranger-powered roadster, he won the last Big Car race held at Western Speedway. And then he earned his chance to race at Indianapolis.

During 1959, Rolla Vollstedt built his first upright Indianapolis car, incorporating ideas from Wally Meskowski, a noted race car builder from Indiana. Vollstedt's machine was originally powered by a DeSoto V8 engine.

With Portland driver Ernie Koch at the wheel, they took the car to Sacramento and Phoenix in late 1959 but could never get the engine to fire when it came time to qualify.

For the 1960 season, Vollstedt rented a 270 cubic-inch Offenhauser engine from Guy Weedman.

Continuing with Ernie Koch in the cockpit, they ran the car in many sprint car events in the Pacific Northwest and down in Vacaville, California. Following that run, Vollstedt and Koch headed back east to run in Springfield and DuQuoin, Illinois, Milwaukee, Wisconsin, Trenton, New Jersey and at the Hoosier 100 in Indiana. After these events, they headed back west for races at Sacramento and Phoenix. Vollstedt recalled that:

"During the off-season between 1960-'61, I sold a half interest in this car to Eddie Kostenuk. This sale was conditional upon Eddie making an attempt to qualify for the first three races [for the next season] that we ran. If he was not successful, we would then be allowed to hire a driver of our choice. As Kostenuk was not able to qualify for any of those first races, we were fortunate enough to hire Len Sutton, who finished out the season for us in a very successful fashion."

Apparently that car went on to have a fine history, as Vollstedt explained.:

"That upright car was one helluva' race car. After he bought my interest, Eddie Kostenuk had all kinds of guys driving it. Johnny Rutherford ran it at Langhorne and Trenton in '63, Len ran DuQuoin, Bobby Grim on the dirt at the Hoosier 100 and at Sacramento. In '64 Bobby Grim ran it - with "Konstant Hot" sponsorship - all over the place. Bruce Jacobi, Bob Harkey, Joe Leonard, Arnie Knepper, everyone drove it."

Eddie Kostenuk at Indy in 1962.

(Victoria Auto Racing Hall of Fame)

In 1962, at the age of 33, Eddie Kostenuk passed his United States Auto Club rookie tests and entered the Indianapolis 500. He became part of the three-car Leader Card team that included veteran drivers Rodger Ward and Len Sutton. Bob Wilke was the team owner, and the cars were Watson/Offenhausers designed by A.J. Watson.

Unfortunately for Eddie, his chances of attempting to qualify were shattered when he was struck by a bird while on a practice run at 140 miles-per-hour. This article describing the incident appeared in the *Daily Colonist* newspaper on May 17th, 1962:

Freak Accident Finishes Kostenuk's '500' Hopes

The hurt and bitter disappointment crackled over the telephone wires yesterday as Ed Kostenuk spoke of the freak accident that wrecked his chance at the Indianapolis 500. "It was a bird, an ordinary bird," he told the Colonist. He didn't sound angry, only terribly puzzled that such a little thing could be the cause of such a calamity.

The Victoria driver was taking a practice run in preparation for an attempt to qualify for the 500. On the second lap, when he was doing 140 miles-per-hour, a bird smashed into his goggles, breaking the plastic and ripping shreds of it back into his left eye. Somehow, Kostenuk kept the car from stacking up. If he hadn't, he was dead. Instead, he was lying in a hotel room yesterday afternoon, unable to see out of either eye, his teeth jarred loose, his outlook bleak.

"The doctor says I may be all right, or I may lose the sight in the eye," he said. "It's hemorrhaging internally. If it stops in three days, it will be fine. Otherwise …" he let it trail off. Doctors said the smashed goggle lens was forced against the eye, scratching the cornea and causing bleeding around the iris. Both eyes are covered by an enormous "mouse." Until the swelling goes down in the other eye, Kostenuk can see only blurred images – as blurred as his recollection of the accident. "Don't ask me how I got the car in," he said. "I just don't know. All I can remember is the crash. Then I dove for the white line to try and stay there for the last mile to the pit. I don't remember driving there."

Kostenuk was given emergency treatment in the pits before taken to a specialist who immediately vetoed any attempt to qualify his Leader Card car on this weekend's final attempts. He didn't know it was a bird until mechanics found feathers in his goggles. "It came just when everything was going so well," said Kostenuk. "That's the part that really hurts. We'd been working the bugs out of the car last night and A.J. Foyt (last year's 500 winner) set it up for us. It was going perfectly."

"I know I could have qualified in it," Kostenuk declared, the anger slipping through for the first time. "I just know it." Kostenuk wasn't sure who will try to qualify the car now, but an attempt will be made. Meanwhile, Kostenuk lay in bed and made his plans. "If the eye is all right, I'm going to drive that same car in a 100-mile race in Milwaukee June 10," he said. "Then I'm coming home."

"But I'm coming back," he added quickly. "I may do quite a bit of racing on the circuit, and I'll be back to try the 500 again next year. If the eye is all right, I'm not through yet," he concluded. "It all depends on the eye."

In an ironic twist of fate, Eddie's teammates Rodger Ward and Len Sutton finished one-two in the Indianapolis 500 that year.

Ed returned to Victoria to make a quick and full recovery. Once he returned to the cockpit, he again ran in local events. At the Centennial 100 modified race in Victoria, he set a new track record in qualifying and won the Saturday race.

Kostenuk didn't give up on his dream to run with the premier division of USAC during 1962 and appeared in three more events in Leader Card cars. He failed to qualify for the Trenton 150 in July and at Milwaukee in August. He was back in New Jersey in late September for the Trenton 200. There, he started 19th and finished 15th. He was running at the end, completing 184 of the 200-lap contest.

Ed returned to Indianapolis in 1963, but a lack of funding forced him to withdraw his self-owned 'City of Victoria' Special before even one qualifying attempt. But a sponsorship deal with U.S. Equipment was put together for his Watson/Offy, and a young driver by the name of Johnny Rutherford was brought on board. The car qualified 26th but was sidelined after just 43 laps with transmission ills and ended in the 29th position.

1963: Kostenuk with his self-owned 'City of Victoria' Special.

(Victoria Auto Racing Hall of Fame)

Kostenuk competed in two more USAC races in 1963, driving his own Kurtis/Offy. At the Tony Bettenhausen 200 at Milwaukee, Wisconsin in August, he started 18th but finished 21st after a water hose let go on the 64th lap. In September he ran in the Trenton 200, starting 22nd and finishing 11th, completing 187 of the 200-lap event.

Eddie's last year on the USAC circuit was in 1965, when he entered four races. The first was at Phoenix International Raceway in March when he again ran his Kurtis/Offy. From the 21st starting spot he was credited with a 19th place finish, spinning out on the 72nd of the 100-lap race.

The next month Kostenuk returned back east for the Trenton 100, qualifying 21st and finishing 12th. At the Rex Mays Classic in June in Milwaukee, he was unable to qualify.

Ed's last USAC race, again at Trenton, took place in July 1965. There, he was running a Vollstedt/Offy, entered by Tassi Vatis. He began the race from the 23rd position on the grid, but the car's rear-end gave out on the 57th lap, recording a 19th-place finish. And that marked the end of Eddie Kostenuks's national driving career.

In summary during those USAC years, he completed a total 649 laps with an average race finish of 16th-place. His total earnings were just $2,349 but, in the end, he was living his dream.

Eddie was inducted into the Victoria Auto Racing Hall of Fame in 2004. He passed away in September 1997.

(Victoria Auto Racing Hall of Fame)

FOURTEEN

Victoria's Auto Racing Heritage – Grandview Bowl

Beginning in 1958 in Nanaimo, British Columbia, a new race track on the Island was opened that would both complement and rival Western Speedway for action. Known as Grandview Bowl, the location was less than 70 miles north of Victoria, allowing an easy commute for both competitors and racing fans.

(Brian Pratt Collection)

The emergence of Grandview Bowl began a friendly rivalry between the cities of Nanaimo and Victoria (home of Western Speedway) for racers and spectators.

Whether true or folklore, one account notes that on some of those inter-city trips the racing cars were driven, rather than towed, to save the added cost of a tow vehicle.

Nanaimo's mayor, Pete Maffeo, first announced the project in March of 1958. The purpose was the creation of an all-purpose sports center, including a racing oval, at the old exhibition grounds in Nanaimo's Northfield district.

The initial cost estimate for the project was $100,000, which was kicked off by a $20,000 grant from the city's recreational fund. The remaining costs were left up to the Exhibition Board, which planned to sell interest-bearing debentures.

The 5/16ths-mile paved track and grandstands came together quickly, and the inaugural racing event took place on Monday, May 19th, 1958, to rave reviews. Sixteen cars, from Canada and the United States, were entered.

The next day, the action was fully described in this review that appeared in the *Nanaimo Free Press* newspaper:

Thousands See Auto Racing

Approximately 4,000 sports fans cheered themselves hoarse last night as Indianapolis-style and stock car racing were introduced at the Grandview Bowl at Exhibition Park. Monday night's events were crowd pleasers from the start of the first dash and much color was loaned to the various heats as American and Canadian demons battled it out for first, place and show money. Drivers were all agreed that once a few of the wrinkles are ironed out that Nanaimo can boast of a speedway second to none in the Pacific Northwest.

The curtain-raiser, Quinn's Jewelers Trophy Dash, of four laps with the four fastest cars entered saw "Big Bill" Hyde, of Portland, cop first place, winning the cup and the right to "buss" the May Queen. Bill, an old hand at the game, was presented with the trophy by the May Queen, who was in attendance with her "Maids of Honor." Taking second money was A.R. Laing, another American driver while Bob Simpson, a down-island driver, placed third.

Breath-catching was the main event, with sixteen cars facing the starter's flag for the grueling 25-lap race. Don Porter, a classy speedster from Portland, Oregon, driving a Ranger, won the event. He was closely followed by Bill Waring of Washington in a GMC, while Del Fanning, of Seattle, had to be content with third. Nanaimo's lone entry in the race, Ray Pottinger, held the lead for about eight laps but made a wide turn cutting into the front stretch and spun out of the race.

Up to this time Pottinger and Porter battled around the track with Pottinger maintaining his slight margin on the inside. Both drivers were out for the big stakes and they had the stands in an uproar from the start. With Pottinger out, Porter took over and was closely pursued by Del Fanning, who in the heats had shown the fans some very fancy driving.

The special event introduced the stock cars, mainly for the purpose of showing fans what they may expect every Friday night, weather permitting, at Grandview Bowl. Red Burk, driving car #71, led the classy field to win the event with Wally Illot and Hank Neilson tied for second place. In this race the stock boys showed as much class as their big brothers in the Indianapolis-style racing.

During the Summer of 1958, the weekly and special events at Grandview Bowl continued their widespread popularity – and attracted more competitors from the region and beyond. The *Nanaimo Free Press* continued with its excellent coverage, as illustrated in these sample news clips:

Stock Feature to Pottinger

Stock car racing came into its own Friday night at the Grandview Bowl, Exhibition Park. The debut was witnessed by some 2,000 sports fans who, in addition, saw Nanaimo's Ray Pottinger lead the pack in the main event – a 25-lap race.

While Pottinger took the lead shortly after the start of the race Hank Nielson, driving car No. 92, challenged for the first few laps and then was content to hold second spot. But he in turn was challenged several times but hung on grimly to the end. Lamont Brooks, in car No. 4, was third in the main event.

Quinn's Jeweler Trophy Dash, a crowd-pleaser right from the green flag until the four-lap finish, was won by Dick Varley of Victoria. Not only did Varley win the Quinn Cup, but in his time trials established a track record. Second in this event was Digger O'Dell. At the conclusion of this, the opening event, Miss Jo-Anne Trembley, presented the winner with the cup and was in turn presented with a corsage, courtesy of Gulliford's Florists.

Mention must be made of the "Special Race" which saw the mechanics give the old heave-ho to the "pro" drivers and take the wheel in the chariots themselves. This three-car event gave the fans a thrill as the mechanics appeared determined to show their skill and not be regulated to a back seat. Ted Melzer, in car No. 92, was the winner in the four-lap show with Al King and Roy Erickson coming in second and third respectively.

Next Friday night the association has lined up a star-studded card of events which will make stock car racing a must for the fans.

Track Record Set at Big Car Races

Fourteen Indianapolis-type cars braved Friday the 13th to put on the second big-car event of the season at Grandview Bowl last night. Despite the unlucky day, no accidents occurred, although they came close in the main event when Ray Laing, in an attempt to forge in front bumped Del Fanning, who had led the field for 18 laps. Fanning was forced out of the race. Laing almost rolled over, but some quick thinking and expert driving kept him upright and he carried on to take third place.

The main event was won by Ernie Koch, who clocked in at 6:28, followed by Gordy Youngstrom.
In the trophy dash, Ray Laing easily won over Bill Hyde with a time of 54:12. Local driver Ray Pottinger had trouble throughout the night but still managed to place third in two events.

The second big car race of the season has been billed for Western Speedway in Victoria this Saturday, and the names and numbers of the U.S. field is such that track officials are predicting "the speediest meet" ever to be held on the Island.

Two Victoria drivers – veteran Bob Simpson and popular Carmen Pascoe -- both scored victories to surprise many of the 3,672 fans that expected domination by cars from Washington and Portland. Pascoe captured the third heat while Simpson, behind the wheel of Grant King's sleek fuel-injected GMC, captured the trophy dash, placed third in the opening heat and was running right on the leader's exhaust pipe before he spun out of contention in a weird main event.

Simpson, holder of the old track record at Nanaimo, also was one of four drivers who cracked the former Western Speedway record set by Frankie McGowan of Portland. King's machine, perhaps one of the finest ever assembled on the island, has been a consistent threat in Northwestern meets. In Portland's big Memorial Day races, for example, Simpson handled the car to a fourth-place windup in the day's overall standing.

Nanaimo's Ray Pottinger, veteran Corky Thomas, who finished third in two dashes, and Dave Cooper, the Island's top stock car ace last year, also finished "in the money." There was an Island car finishing in the first three in each of the six races last month.

With one or two exceptions, big-car drivers and owners rarely manage to earn more than expenses at any single meet. Now that they can look forward to a "double date" on the Island, their chances of picking up extra expense money is that much better.

(Brian Pratt Collection)

Seattle's Ray Laing Captures Main Event

Ray Laing seems to have taken a liking for Nanaimo's Grandview Bowl. Either that, or else the track is playing favorite to him. The Seattle driver copped the 25-lap main event at the third meeting of the "Indianapolis-style" big-car races Friday night before nearly 2,000 fans.

He was also just a fraction of a second off the track record, held by himself, in the time trials. Laing probably could have lowered the mark if the track wasn't slower than usual because of the recent hot weather. Despite chalking up the fastest time trial, he slipped to second in the Quinn's Trophy Dash. Del Fanning won the three-lap event and Digger Caldwell was third. Laing also placed third in the eight-lap first heat, which featured the six fastest cars in the time trials. The winner was "Wild Bill" Hyde.

Bob Burgess took the second heat while Gordy Youngstrom captured the third. Nanaimo's Ray Pottinger followed Youngstrom across the line in second place.

Miss Comox Valley, 18-year-old Myrna Holt, presented the trophy to winner Del Fanning in the Quinn's Trophy Dash. Fanning was also in a good position to capture the second heat before he went into a spin-out in the early laps. Fanning was pressing leader Bob Burgess at the time. He slipped into third place and although he stayed far back, he managed to keep the position at the checkered flag. Digger Caldwell passed him at the spin-out and streaked home second.

It was an all-American finish in the main event. Hyde took an early lead from Corky Thomas in the first lap, but after a few laps was passed by Laing, who stayed out in front to win easily. Hyde managed to come in third, while Youngstrom roared across in second.

Harry's Green on Thirteen

Harry Roberts will never learn. He drives the jinx car on Island stock car tracks and, no matter how many people tell him to erase the jinx, he still carries on. To get rid of the jinx, all he has to do is open a can of paint and dip in a brush.

The jinx? For one, his wagon carries number 13. For two, his car is painted green, a hex that has plagued racing drivers since the start of Indianapolis. Briefly, it's just murder to combine 13 and green. So far this year it's cost Roberts several blown motors. But something happens every race now. Last Friday he got a hole in his radiator. He fixed that and went to the Victoria races Saturday, only to burn out his bearings. Last night he was the victim of a broken axle. And so, Harry was on the sidelines most of the night at the Grandview Bowl stock car races. He's got a lot of work to do to get that car fixed up for tonight at Victoria, and for two races on Labor Day.

Roberts wasn't the only victim last night though. Bob Mawle, who came within six one-hundreths of setting a new track record in the time trials, was one of three cars involved in a spectacular smashup in the trophy dash. It cost him a broken axle. And later, Herb Veasey suffered a blown motor. Phil Lambrick was an easy winner in the trophy dash – the only driver to finish. The pileup, which occurred in the last lap, took out Dave Cooper and Dick Varley as well as Mawle.

All around, it was an exciting night. There were also little pileups in the first and fourth heats. In the second heat Red Burke had built up a tremendous lead and was winning all the way before he ran into motor trouble and had to drop out. Al Smith won. Bill Temple lost a wheel in the third heat, put on a new one and raced to victory in the fourth, beating out Jim Milner and Bob Smith.

Inability to dress in a hurry cost Larry Van Humbeck the Le Mans start, which was the special event. Drivers had to race on foot to the starting line, sort out their jackets which were in a pile, put them on and race four laps. To make it more difficult the jackets were tied in knots. Van Humbeck got his jacket first, but by the time he got it on, two cars were already gone. Ray Pottinger won easily.

Only 11 of 21 cars survived the 25-lap main event which was won by Digger O'Dell. Dave Cooper finished second and Pottinger third.

(Brian Pratt Collection)

With a first successful season under its belt, Grandview Bowl began its 1959 season with as much enthusiasm – if not more – as the prior year. Heck, even England's Queen Elizabeth II and Prince Phillip paid the facility a visit in July.

The race cars became faster and more sophisticated. The emergence of the Modified Sportsman class featured heated battles by both local competitors and others from around the Pacific Northwest. Several of these drivers would go on to compete in the prestigious CAMRA Series, which began in 1963.

Highlights of the 1959 season are best described in additional newspaper clippings from the *Nanaimo Free Press*:

Cal Walker's Sports Column

The Mid-Island Auto Racing Association (MIARA) held their election of officers the other day and Ray Pottinger turned over the reins to Wally Ilott, newly-elected president. This was their first full season at the new Grandview race track and, as was expected, was a complete success.
Very few people know the work that goes into an organization such as this. Rules are strict, deportment must be excellent, and they are always devising ways to make stock car racing safer. To the fans that watch stock car racing it is a thrill-a-minute. To the men that jockey these powerful "bugs" of dynamite, it is working every spare minute to have to keep the cars in "hair" trigger operation.

New rules are added every year to make it tougher but safer for drivers. This year there were several new rules added to the already long list of five sheets. But as Ray Pottinger puts it, "they are necessary rules and are for the drivers' benefit." Another big year is looked forward to and with the first year more of an experiment in finding out what the fans want most we can look forward to some new events.

I spent some time browsing through the rules and picked out several that I felt racing fans would be interested in. I often asked myself last season why such and such was so. Now with this set of rules I know the answers. One-night last year I was refused entry to the infield. Even showing my press card never got me in. I just wasn't dressed properly. Now that may sound odd but the following rule, which I am told is a must by the insurance company, gave me the answer, and I agree with the pit boss. Any person admitted to the pits must be properly dressed. Dress to consist of clean white trousers and clean shirts and jackets. The infield is not lit up too well on any track and a driver whose car goes out of control into the infield has a better chance of seeing pitmen in the white clothing.

It is interesting to note that one rule states: A fee, to be collected per person, will be paid to the crash fund. This means that the drivers, mechanics and owners are all thinking ahead in case of costly accidents. We think this is a very good rule as stock car racing is an expensive sport.

To show the caliber of drivers and what will happen if they get careless on the highway and lose their license, a rule says: All drivers must have a valid British Columbia driver's license for purpose of identification as necessary. In event of license suspension, track suspension will be reviewed at the next general meeting. One major change is that the rear ends may not be locked, but "torching" the springs, adding sway bars, etc., is permitted. This is something new, and I'm told that it could mean more spectacular driving as it makes the car harder to handle. But the idea of this rule was to put the "jalopy" in the same class as stockers.
In running rules we feel number two is important. It states: Any driver involved in an accident must submit to a check-over by first aid personnel. This is self-explanatory.

There are many running rules that cover drivers, using common sense and respect for other drivers and personnel. Cars must be coupe, tudor or four-door bodies, with no cutting or chopping except windows for vision. This does away with "soft tops" or convertibles. There are several rules that cover suspensions and club discipline, and take it from me, they are plenty stern. It all boils down to the fact that this association is a close-knit group and go all out to give racing fans their money's worth.

Now you are probably saying, "when is he going to tell us just what the definition of a stock car is?" According to the rules, stock shall be construed to mean, unaltered Canadian and U.S.A. passenger and truck parts, up to and including 1950, except where otherwise permitted in these rules, made by original manufacturers to the original design and specifications and to be considered by the trade to be stock.

Here's hoping the above few paragraphs help clarify a few points on stock car racing, a new sport brought to Nanaimo last year. So, come May 1, the roar of cars on the Grandview Bowl will be ringing in the air, and it's off to the races for us every Friday night.

Oh yes, they will have several big car events carded for the season. These went over pretty good last year, and at present Ray Pottinger, who not only drives stock cars, is the only Nanaimo driver who owns a big car.

(Brian Pratt Collection)

Father, Son Race Rivalry at Grandview Bowl Monday

The first big car racing card of the season takes place at Grandview Bowl Monday night, weather permitting. This is the curtain-raiser in what the Exhibition Board hopes to repeat along with some newcomers, who have yet to get their cars ready, several times before the racing season ends.

Twenty-five cars were originally slated for Monday's event, but if you notice some missing it is because they either had engine trouble in Victoria or cracked up. This is something local officials have no control over, but the drivers have promised to go all out to make it an enjoyable evening.

Most of the old-timers are back, either with their old cars overhauled or driving new jobs. Victoria is well represented either with their own cars or driving for someone else. Del Fanning Sr., who at present is the top big car driver in the Pacific Northwest, is back again with his fuel-injected Ranger. Del Fanning Jr. is out to make a name for himself, like father, and it will probably be a father-son duel this season. With Sr.'s experience and Jr.'s daring this should be something to watch this year. Del Jr. is driving a fuel-injected V8 and, according to reports from Bob Simpson, who makes the arrangements for the American drivers, this young fellow will be the driver to watch.

But don't forget the seasoned pros who have no intentions of letting the novices push them out of the limelight. Chaps like Ray Waring, Bob Burgess, Bull Thomas, Bob Simpson, Smokey Blake, Bill Hyde and Ernie Koch, last year's No. 1 driver, to name a few, will be out to pick up some of the loot and they don't like sharing too much of it.

Victoria is well represented with seven drivers who include popular Dick Varley, who had decided to drive both stocks as well as a big car. Dick will be driving Grant King's car, a Wayne GMC. Other Victoria drivers are Ray Barren, driving Chub Flitton's Ford V8, Corky Thomas driving his own Ranger, Ron Douglas in Fred Carson's Gypsy Aircraft, Bob Mawle in his Ford V8, Al Coutts with a GMC and Bill Chester with a Ranger. Nanaimo has two big cars this year - Ray Pottinger with his Ford V8 and Bobby Clarke in Herb McNulty's Chev V8.

Island Car Drivers Cop Prize Money in Dashes

Indianapolis-style cars made their first appearance of the season at Grandview Bowl on Monday night, and although there was a small entry, the races were good and approximately 1,000 fans enjoyed every minute of it. Del Fanning, who was expected to feature the night's activities, broke an axle while warming up and dropped out, as did Wild Bill Hyde.

Four heat races and the main event were run off with veteran Ray Waring coming from behind on the 18th lap to win the main event. Bob Simpson was on his heels with Victoria's Dick Varley nosing out Bob Burgess, who led the field for 17 laps.

The main event was probably the best race the big cars put on since Grandview Bowl opened last year for car racing. Twelve cars entered the main event and they held their position for 17 laps tail to tail. Paul Pold, who timed in with the fastest lap in the time trials, spun, and this opened the field.

Quinn's Trophy Dash winner was the fast car of Paul Pold of Seattle. Pold also drives in Indianapolis competition and put on a wonderful display of driving. He also came second in the third heat. Runners-up to Pold in the Trophy Dash was Ray Waring and Dick Varley.

Dave Cooper Wins Main at Grandview

Dave Cooper, Vancouver Island's number one stock car driver, tucked another main event to his belt at Grandview Bowl last night. Cooper went into an early lead and widened it to get the flag with plenty to spare. Dick Willoughby took second money. Willoughby made a good account himself beating out clubmate Cooper to cop the trophy dash and they reversed positions in the first heat race.

Bobby Clarke, Wally Illot and Oscar Taylor, all of Nanaimo, won the next three events. Clarke beat out Red Burke and Larry Van Humbeck.

Local Stockers Provide All Main Event Thrills

Dave Cooper ended his streak of three wins in the main event at Grandview Bowl last night as the "flying plumber" from Victoria blew his motor on the fifth lap of the main event of the weekly stock car racing last night. Cooper was running third after starting in the top position of the reverse start and sporting a consecutive streak of three main event victories here. But Cooper picked up his usual share of the money by copping the Trophy Dash and a heat race.

Big honors go to Fred Rummings, driving his first full card. He won the third heat race and led the main event for 12 laps until the veterans moved in.

The main event was a home town affair as Cooper pulled into the pits early in the race leaving Nielson, Roberts and Burke to battle it out. Nielson finally got the flag over clubmate Harry Roberts and Red Burke. Bobby Clarke started off on the tough side of the ledger when he threw a wheel in the first lap of his time trial. He was set back and unable to time in, thereby given the last place in any heats.

Clarke, driving a GM "buzzer", came back to win the fourth heat working his way through the pack and hitting the flag three feet ahead of clubmate Red Burke. Hank Nielson, Harry Roberts and Red Burke ran in that order in the main event. The lead changed hands on at least five occasions as Hank Nielson and Harry Roberts battled it out for the cream of the card.

Pottinger Cops Racing Moola

Ray Pottinger's doctoring job paid big dividends as the popular Nanaimo driver had his number six away and winging last night to take the 25-lap main event before a crowd of 1,250 race fans at the Grandview Bowl. Pottinger also won the first heat by a good margin. Taking the lead on the 15th lap, Pottinger drove a heady race to finish in the clear. In a rousing duel for second place, Dick Willoughby of Victoria nudged out Harry Roberts.

Bad luck continued to dog the footsteps of Bobby Clarke when he got into another pileup and was forced to retire from the race.

Gil Falardi of Victoria jumped into a big lead in the second lap of the main event, with Ted Eastholm second and Bob Smith third. The rest of the field were strung out, well back of the leaders. By the seventh lap, Falardi still held the lead and Pottinger had moved up into fourth position with a fine bit of driving. Nanaimo's Hank Nielson and Bob Smith were in second and third spots.

On the twelfth lap Nielson spun out. Pottinger was moving into second spot as the cars began to pileup on the back stretch. In the center of the muddle were Bobby Clarke, Jack Milner, Ted Eastholm and Glen Krause. The drivers slowed right down when given the caution flag and then came to a halt on a red flag as attendants cleared the track of debris.

When the race resumed the cars were lined up in the following order: Falardi, Pottinger, Humbeck, Milner, Krause, Smith, Roberts and Mawle. Pottinger took the lead from Falardi and by the seventeenth lap, Roberts had moved into second place with Willoughby a close third.

The race turned into a duel for second place as Pottinger widened on the field by the 23rd lap and won going away. Willoughby got the nod over Roberts for the runner-up spot. Bobby Clarke had little trouble in winning the Quinn's Jewelers Trophy Dash, besting Harry Roberts and Dick Willoughby.

Red Burke Provides Extra Racing Thrill

Through no fault of his own, Red Burke left his trademark on the cars of two racing fans last night at Grandview Bowl in an unscheduled added attraction for 1,350 stock car fans. Wheeling into the south turn on the first lap of the time trials, Burke lost his right rear wheel and came to a sudden stop. But the wheel kept right on going, jumped the fence in a tremendous arc, to land against two cars in the parking lot. Chrome flew in all directions from the cars, but fortunately they were empty, and no one was injured by the runaway wheel.

Another new item for the fans came when Dave Cooper appeared on the track and announced a new motor, new paint job, new sponsor, but the same old driver. Cooper's car now sports a bright yellow coat, making it easier for the rest of the drivers to keep an eye on him.

Harry Roberts won the 25-lap main event in addition to the second heat, while Bobby Clarke crossed the finish line first in the Trophy Dash. Clarke also turned in the fastest time in the time trials. Lyle Gallia proved the best driver in the special event race for mechanics, winning from wire to wire. Other entries in the race were Ross Webster, Hector Caillett, Tom Simpson, Jim Berry, Bill Chipman, Tony Slogar and Bill Smith. Jim Berry lost a wheel on the first-round while cars were lining up for positions.

The best heat race of the night saw Dave Cooper edge Ray Pottinger in the last 50-yards in an exciting finish. Pottinger jumped into the lead from the opening gun and held off the ever-pressing Cooper for nine and a half laps before losing out in a photo finish.

The main event had its tense moments. Ray Decock and Al Smith dueled for the lead with Smith taking over on the fourth lap. Glen Krause moved up ahead of Smith but fell back before another lap had finished. Jack Milner started a drive on the leaders, Smith and Krause, on lap number eight, but couldn't get past Harry Roberts who held the third slot.

By the 12th lap Harry Roberts took over the head-end and Glen Krause held second with Dick Varley third. As Roberts started widening on the field, Dave Cooper, who had been boxed in up to this point, started to move, taking over fourth position on the 15th lap. On the 18th lap it was Roberts, Nielson, Krause and Varley, with the field strung out well behind the four leading cars.

Cooper pulled out of the race after swinging into the infield and it became a two-car affair between Roberts and Nielson, with the rest of the field well back. When Roberts crossed the finish line followed by Nielson, the two cars had a half-lap lead.

Red Burke Tops Stocker Rivals

Bobby Clarke of Nanaimo turned in the fastest clocking in the time trials, won the Quinn's Jewelers Trophy Dash and the second heat race, then finished down the track in the 25-lap main event at the Grandview Bowl which went to another Nanaimo driver, Red Burke. Thirteen hundred stock car fans attended the weekly meet.

Harry Roberts, last week's main event winner, could do no better than third in the big race after holding second position behind Burke from the eighth to the 18th lap before dropping back into the third slot. Red Burke also won the first heat in addition to the main event.

The third heat was a nip and tuck affair between Ray Pottinger and Larry Rose, who staged a thrilling duel with Pottinger winning by a whisker. Rose got the jump at the gun and drove into the lead, with Pottinger in fourth position trying to get through on the rail. When this move failed, Pottinger took the outside lane and with some heady driving, quickly moved up into second position. Still driving on the outside, Pottinger finally took over on the last turn, and in a driving finish with Rose, crossed the white line with inches to spare.

The pit crews got the hardest workout in the special event. Known as a Le Mans start, the boys who do a lot of work while the drivers get all the glory, had to run a fifty-yard dash to touch the boss's hand before the cars took off.

After a false start that called for a second run, the race was on and Ray Pottinger won the bacon, beating Hank Nielson and Glen Krause to the wire.

Eighteen cars started in the main event with Jingles Wheatley and Norm Wilton at the lead of the lineup. Bobby Clarke and Oscar Taylor were the rear-guard. With gasoline for blood, Taylor makes the trip from Indian River every week to wheel around the Grandview Bowl.

The race got away to a good start with Norm Wilton taking a good lead. Bob Smith was second, Dave McCelland third and Glen Krause fourth. By the fifth lap, Smith took over followed by Krause and McCelland. Ray Pottinger, failing to find racing room, held sixth place. Smith and Krause drove head and head until the eighth lap when Red Burke forged to the front. Harry Roberts moved into second as Smith fell back to third place. The cars held these positions until the 10th lap when Al Smith took over third place as the cars were starting to string out around the oval.

Ray Pottinger spun out on the 12th lap but got back into the race, losing all chance to finish in the money. By the 14th turn, Burke moved into a long lead followed by Roberts, Al Smith and Hank Nielson in that order. The four lead cars were lapping rivals on every turn and held their positions until the 18th lap, when Al Smith moved ahead of Roberts to second place. Bob Smith lost any chance at prize money by spinning out on the 19th lap. The lead cars continued to widen on the field for the balance of the race and Hank Nielson moved up to finish fourth.

Cooper Rolls Car Over in Thrilling Main Event

For 1,500 stock car racing fans at Grandview Bowl last night it was a thrilling evening, at least in the main event. Dave Cooper, the Island's top driver, came up with the biggest thrill when he got tangled with another car in the north turn on the 12th lap and rolled over, skidding on his roof for over 50 feet.

This wrote an end to Cooper's car as the roof was crushed in beyond repair. The plucky Victoria driver walked away from the crash with a bruised eye. When the checkered flag came down in the main, Harry Roberts ended up against the north turn guard rail and Al Smith plowed into a light pole midway on the far stretch. Winner of the main event was Bobby Clarke who forged ahead after the restart and put distance between himself and the rest of the pack. Hank Nielson led the race for 12 laps but fell back of Al Smith, who in turn gave way to Clarke.

Clarke had a big night after timing in as the fastest. He picked up a second in the trophy dash won by Al Smith, with Red Burke third. The first heat was won by Hank Nielson with Dave Cooper second and Al Smith third. Bobby Clarke captured the second heat over Doug Bowell and Doug Rose. The third heat went to Dave McLelland with Jim Milner and Glen Krause, runners-up.

Bob Smith beat out Dick Varley who was driving the Fanny Bay car for Larry Van Humbeck, who has left the district. Jimmy Raeburn from Bellingham, making his first appearance here in a Hudson Six, was third. The special event saw the mechanics go at it and Jim Berry won handily over Jack Robbins and Dick Midgely.

Six Nanaimo Stock Car Drivers Among Top 10

Stock car racing will be at its peak tonight in the weekly card at Grandview Bowl, weather permitting. The time of the season has come when all drivers will be fighting for point positions for the coming year.

Dave Cooper of Victoria piled up last week, but he was back racing the following night in Victoria and the number one driver on the Island will be out again to defend his stand and, if possible, increase his present lead.

Dick Varley, who was banned from driving his "Peanut Butter" car on the Nanaimo oval, has been picked up by the Fanny Bay club a few weeks back to replace Larry Van Humbeck, who left town to work.

Last year only two Nanaimo drivers placed in the top 10., Ray Pottinger and Hank Nielson. This year the local drivers are making their presence known in the standings both here and in Victoria. Nanaimo drivers now hold down six of the top 10 spots.

Cooper leads with 224.5 points, 21 more than Dave McLellan. Bob Clarke, Nanaimo, holds down third place with 195.75, followed by Hank Nielson with 179. Victoria's Al Smith is fifth with 163.5 and the next four places go to Nanaimo drivers Harry Roberts, Doug Bowell, Red Burke and Ray Pottinger. The tenth spot is held by Dick Varley who was the number two-man last year.

Cooper Again Rolls Over at Grandview Bowl Races

For the second straight Friday Dave Cooper has halted the main event of the stock car races at Grandview Bowl by rolling over. Last night, the Island's number one driver, after taking the lead in the main from clubmate Dick Varley on the 10th lap, went into number three turn and Al Smith, who also passed Varley, skidded into Cooper on the 21st lap, forcing him into a slow roll. Cooper came out of the flip unharmed. On the restart Al Smith was in the number one position and went on to win the feature with Hank Nielson and Bob Clarke second and third in that order.

It was a good night for Victoria's Al Smith; he clocked in with the fastest time, won the trophy dash, came second in the first heat and won the main.

Bud Hopkins beat out Al Smith and Dave Cooper to win the first heat. Oscar Taylor led Jack Milner and Harry Roberts in the second heat. Ray Pottinger edged Dick Varley in the third heat with Bob Smith third.
The fourth heat saw Hank Nielson, Bobby Clarke and Gil Falardi put on a neck-and-neck battle, with Nielson getting the flag and Bobby Clarke squeezing past Falardi.

Despite the cool weather, 19 cars showed up and 1,100 fans were on hand as the drivers gave a good account of themselves. In place of the special event, two sports cars from the Alberni Valley were on display and made a couple of turns around the oval. One was a shiny 1932 roadster owned by Ray Bowerman and powered by a 350 hp Buick engine. The other was a cut-down 1940 Ford owned by Benny Cawthorne and powered with a 225 hp Oldsmobile.

Cooper Back in Form; Wins Stock Car Feature

Dave Cooper of Victoria, who has been plagued with tough luck for the last three Friday's at Grandview Bowl, wheeled his stock car in true fashion last night to capture the feature event.

Nanaimo's Doug Bowell, last week's main event winner, poked away at the leaders and finally wormed his way to second spot but Cooper's lead was too much for him and he had to settle for a second. Hank Nielson got third. Fast car for the night was Al Smith of Victoria. He also won the Quinn's Trophy Dash nosing out Hank Nielson and Harry Roberts.

The third heat went to Dave Cooper over Hank Nielson and Doug Bowell. Bob Clarke, who seemed to have engine trouble, came through in the second heat to win out over clubmates Ray Pottinger and Oscar Taylor. The next two races went to Victoria drivers Bud Hopkins and Dave McLellan. Hopkins won over Harry Roberts and Bob Mawle, who was driving the Fanny Bay car, was third. In a special feature, five-year-old Guy Lynn drove a micro-midget, a perfect replica of an Indianapolis racer, around the track to the pleasure of the fans.

Smith Captures Marathon Race

The weatherman was good to stock car racing at Grandview Bowl last night, giving the 1,000 fans clear skies for the big race of the season. After two rainouts both here and in Victoria, drivers were well prepared for the marathon 40-lap main event and the winner Al Smith of Victoria was deserving of the victory.

Al had transmission trouble all day and just made it to the track from Victoria but still had work to do on his car. He was unable to time in and missed all the preliminary races. Just before the main event he asked and was given permission to time in for the feature. His time was not to count for the fast time, which was won by Bob Clarke, but it qualified him for the main.

Smith actually timed in faster than Clark, but it never counted. He was given the last spot and most of the fans never gave him a chance. But they never reckoned with the plucky Smith and he threw all caution to the wind. He vacated his last spot early in the race and worked his way up the route and took over at the 17th lap. From then on it was just a matter of widening his lead. It was no contest as Al came home in a breeze with almost a lap to spare.

Second and third place was a battle most of the way between Doug Bowell and Hank Nielson with Hank edging Bowell out for the runner-up spot. Bobby Clarke won the trophy dash over Dave Cooper and Harry Roberts.

Clarke came back to add to his winnings by capturing the second event over Doug Bowell and Bob Smith. Bob Mawle, driving for the Drifter's club of Fanny Bay, gave them a win in the third heat. Glen Krause and Oscar Taylor were runners-up. The fourth heat went to Hank Nielson with Jack Milner and Don Browne ending in that order.

Next week, trophies for the season will be presented before the main event and if the weather holds out, there will be another race the following Friday.

Four-Way Race for Stockers

Vancouver Island stockers are looking to the weatherman to shine on them this weekend both in Nanaimo and Victoria. With previous races cancelled by rain, they are carded for tonight at Grandview Bowl and Saturday in Victoria. For both cities it is the most important race of the season as it is the last chance for drivers to gain points for the season. At present, Nanaimo's Bobby Clarke is leading the pack, with Dave Cooper, who has been the number one driver for the last two years, right on his bumper with only a couple of points separating them. Following tonight's meet the drivers go to Victoria where the final race of the season takes place for the coveted Island Trophy, now held by Dave Cooper.

Another private battle shapes up between Nanaimo's Hank Nielson and Victoria's Al Smith for second and third spots. Hank leads Smith by three-quarters of a point. Harry Roberts and Doug Bowell, two Nanaimo hotshots, are sixth and seventh respectively, and this should be a race to the wire. Roberts is sitting with 217.0 and Bowell has 215.25.

But, and this is an important word in stock car racing, if Clarke and Cooper break up or if either one has a non-productive night tonight, and Hank Nielson and Al Smith come through with an upset, gaining maximum points, the entire picture could be changed. Certainly, anything is possible in stock car racing and no matter which way you look at it, Nanaimo drivers are in the best position to take home top honors. This has been their best year and, as one top driver said, "It is not a case of the top drivers having poor cars, but it is the so-called poorer drivers getting better."

Bobby Clarke No. 1 Stocker

Al Smith, veteran Victoria driver, won the Vancouver Island stock car racing championship at Western Speedway, Victoria, Saturday. The victory was the first in three years of trying for the Victoria man. Doug Bowell of Nanaimo ran second, and Dave McLelland finished third. Dick Varley led the 50-lap main event for 35 laps, but engine trouble forced him to give way to Smith, who made no mistakes when he got into the lead. Final standings gave Nanaimo's Bobby Clarke the coveted number one position for next season. Al Smith was second in the standings.

Going into the 1960 season of competition, officials of the Mid-Island Auto Racing Association announced that Victoria and Nanaimo agreed on two new changes for the year. They were hopeful the changes would further enhance competition at both Grandview Bowl and Western Speedway.

A new payoff system was worked out which would give a novice driver an equal chance to make the same money as the seasoned drivers – an added incentive for bringing in more competitors.

Secondly, the clubs agreed that all camshafts would be sealed, in hopes of ending the controversy which marred some of the events in 1959. Both clubs would use the same method and a three-man committee would make inspections prior to each meet.

The season at Nanaimo began on Friday, May 13, 1960. The *Nanaimo Free Press* issued this preview, followed by a post-race recap the next day:

Stockers Open Season at Grandview Tonight

Stock car drivers are hoping Mr. Sol smiles his best this afternoon to keep Grandview Bowl nice and dry for the opening of the 1960 stock car racing season tonight. The official opening date was postponed last Friday due to the weather and some cars not being ready. At press time every Nanaimo driver has signified his readiness for tonight's opening. Victoria, led by Dick Varley and Dave Cooper, will bring a large contingent of cars and tonight's opening should be the biggest in the three-year history of Grandview Bowl.

Nanaimo's Bobby Clarke, the island's number one driver, who was unable to race in Victoria last week, has his "Jimmy" ready for tonight and will be out to build up points in defense of his crown. Doug Bowell, sporting a new car, same color, made the veteran drivers in Victoria sit up and take notice last Saturday. He proved that it's driving, as well as the car, that wins races. Doug drove a Ford sedan last year and switched to a 6-cylinder Chrysler coupe. He was second in the fast heat and placed well in the main event with some surprise driving. Novice driver Jim Berry showed he was ready for the big time Saturday. Taking part in his first race as a driver, Berry kicked up his heels in every race he entered and placed well in the main event.

Bob Smith deserves some credit with his driving in the third heat in Victoria. Bob took command from the start and never looked back. He led clubmate Red Burke by a quarter of a lap at the flag. Red came up with his usual good showing, posting a second in the trophy dash, second in the third heat and third in the main event. Red has taken over Doug Bowell's blue sedan from last season.

Hank Nielson won the honor of being the first car of the season to roll over. He took to his roof on the first lap of the first heat race. Hank will be out tonight despite the rollover. The special event for tonight is the "Mechanic's Race." In this event mechanics draw for position and they must not have driven more than two races at any time.

Victoria Driver Wins Feature

Honors were split between Victoria and Nanaimo as the 1960 stock car racing season got away to a good start last night at Grandview Bowl before 1,100 fans.

Al Smith, the number three driver from Victoria, easily won the main event taking the lead in the opening lap on the north end and was never threatened. Hank Nielson got the flag for second spot nosing out Bill Foster, both about 10 car lengths behind the winner.

The trophy dash for the four fastest cars saw Red Burke walk away from Ray Pottinger. Burke had the fast car in the time trials. Trial times were slow as expected with new engines still not completely broken-in. Burke led the trials, followed by Ray Pottinger, Al Smith and Bob Mawle.

The first and fourth heat races went to Victorians Bill Foster and Gil Fillardi. The second and third races were taken by Nanaimo's Hank Nielson and Bob Smith.

Following are several more *Nanaimo Free Press* reports during the 1960 season, which happen to mention an up-and-coming driver named Billy Foster:

Victoria Cops Honors in Stock Racing

Victoria drivers carried home the major share of awards in the Nanaimo stock car holiday racing bill held at Grandview Bowl last night. Victoria's Bill Foster, who edged out Ray Pottinger of Nanaimo in the first heat, duplicated the feat in the main event.

Al Smith of Victoria placed first in the trophy dash and the second heat, while Bob Smith and Red Burke of Nanaimo won the other heat events. Hank Neilson came home first in the special event. Harry Roberts was the hard-luck driver of the night, losing a wheel on the third lap of the third heat and then wrecking his car after a spinout in the 14th lap of the main event. Five cars piled up after the spinout.

Pottinger Eyes Place Switch

Ray Pottinger is tired of inhaling carbon monoxide from the exhausts of rival drivers and intends to do something about it tonight at the weekly Mid-Island stock car races at Grandview Bowl. Pottinger scored a sweep of second placings during the holiday card last Monday night and plans to cross the finish line in front for a change. After making a few minor adjustments last night, the Nanaimo driver is ready for all comers.

Victoria racing rivals Bill Foster and Al Smith will be back after a successful invasion last week. These two, along with Pottinger, are strong contenders for the top dog mangle currently resting on the shoulders of Dick Varley.

Both Foster and Smith are main event winners at Nanaimo this year and hope to continue their domination of the racing events.

Oscar Taylor is expected to make his first appearance of the season along with veteran driver Dave Cooper from Victoria. There is a strong possibility that Varley, who has been cleaning up in Victoria, may settle his differences with Nanaimo and race here. While Varley leads the point parade, Bill Foster is a close second. In third place in the points is Victoria's Al Smith, three behind Varley.

Stockers Promise Additional Cars

The Mid-Island Auto Racing Association has reached an agreement with their Victoria counterpart whereby more cars from Victoria will take part in the stock car races at Grandview Bowl. Meanwhile, officials of the Nanaimo organization have announced that some of last year's favorites will be back in competition tonight at the regular weekly racing feature at the local track. Harry Roberts will be out for sure with his new car as will Oscar Taylor, whose overhauling job took far longer than expected. Norm Wilton will also be seen in action tonight.

As predicted last week, Ray Pottinger has finally broken the jinx and managed to pick up a first last week after knocking on the door in other meets. Jim Berry, touted as a strong contender before the season got underway, has finally started to move up. Nanaimo drivers have now started to break the grip that Victoria's Al Smith and Bill Foster have had on the distance event.

#98 – Lamont Brooks; #2 – Dick Varley; #56 – Billy Foster.

(Ted MacKenzie photo)

Two major announcements were made in mid-July of 1960: the introduction of a brand-new car for Billy Foster, along with the news that popular driver Hank Nielson would be out of competition for the rest of the season:

Hank Nielson Out for Season

Taking part for the first time this year in the weekly stock car racing at Grandview Bowl tonight is the most talked about car on the Island. It's the GMC that Bob Vantreight of Victoria has been building for some time and local drivers got a quick look at it in Victoria last week and they admit it's a beauty. Driving it will be veteran Bill Foster of Victoria, and Bill has made no predictions but has issued a warning that he will be out there to capture some top money.

The Fanny Bay Drifters' Club have bought Hank Nielson's engine and it is installed in their car and ready to go and, as usual, Bob Mawle will be at the wheel.

Followers of stock car racing are sorry to hear that Hank Nielson has retired for the season. Hank rolled over in Victoria a couple of weeks ago and his car was too badly damaged to get ready in time. Hank will be missed as he has been racing on the Island for the past seven years and has always been a good contender. He is considered, along with Red Burke and Ray Pottinger, as one of the original Nanaimo drivers. Hank, at one time or another, has helped every driver on the Island to repair their car. All hope that Hank will be back again next year.

Racing at Grandview Bowl continued to thrive over the next three seasons, though it was difficult to locate newspaper coverage for that time. This sample from the *Nanaimo Free Press* previewed the action taking place on July 7-8th, 1961:

Sprint Cars Featured at Grandview Bowl

Although sprint cars take top billing, the glamour cars of the speedway will have to share the spotlight with rugged stock cars, flamboyant jalopies and blindfolded drivers when racing resumes at Grandview Bowl tonight. The Mid-Island Auto Racing Association has lined up one of the best race programs of the year and will feature the ever-popular Indianapolis-type speedsters with Nanaimo driver Ray Pottinger favored to take a top position.

Pottinger will be at the wheel of his low-slung machine with a flathead Ford engine, a car in which he has raced against top Pacific Northwest drivers in Nanaimo and Victoria on Vancouver Island and at Great Falls, Montana and Portland, Oregon, and Chehalis and Seattle across the border in Washington.

Also demonstrating their driving skill in sprint races will be Bob Mawle, Dave Cooper, Bob Simpson, Corky Thomas and probably Al Coutes of Victoria. Ed Kostenuk of Victoria will be at the wheel of his fuel-injected Ranger roadster and is a favorite to take top money. Cooper and Simpson will both drive cars with fuel-injected motors. Cooper's being a V-8 Buick and Simpson's a six-cylinder GMC, while Thomas has a Ranger Aircraft Engine and Mawle a Ford V-8.

Thomas has been scoring many firsts and is expected to keep Pottinger hustling. Coutes has been the hard luck driver of the group, being dogged by rear-end trouble. He has purchased a completely new assembly and is working to put everything together in order to be able to make the starting line tonight.

In the stocker section, action has been rugged and there is no letup in sight. Last Saturday, in Victoria, Nanaimo cars took a pounding. Red Burke and Jack Milner both blew transmissions in the heat races but are ready for action tonight. Don Brown really had it going for a while but halted abruptly when pushed into the wall. His car walked eight feet up the wall before bouncing back on the track. Two late starters in the stock division are Norm Wilton and Ted Eastom. They will be moving up to the starting line tonight. It is reported Chic Milo is building up a 1948 Cadillac for a jalopy with the possibility Bob Clarke will do the driving.

Also in the books is the possibility of a family feud with the news Glen Krause has completely rebuilt the motor of his car and is all set to get even for the beatings handed him by brother-in-law Bob Smith. Special feature of the evening, the boy-and-girl blindfold race, will have at least five entries and is causing plenty of comment along coffee row.

The next day's edition of the newspaper listed the major results of the racing card:

Close Finish Grandview Bowl Race Feature

Ray Pottinger continued to set the pace in the sprint car main events, flashing across the finish line inches ahead of Ed Kostenuk and Bob Simpson at Grandview Bowl last night. Pottinger took over on the second turn of the first lap, then held off all threats for the rest of the 10 laps.

Bob Mawle and Kostenuk were the big winners last night, with the Fanny Bay Drivers' driver taking the stock car trophy dash and main event, and Kostenuk winning the sprint car dash and heat.

Jump ahead to the 1964 season, and we have these *Nanaimo Free Press* clippings beginning in August:

Daffodil Special Guns for Record

The skies may have been cloudy, but everything was sunny for Mel Keen of Vancouver as he wheeled his Chev-powered A-Modified Sportsman around Grandview Bowl last Sunday. "Man, what a track," chirped the mainland driver, after his very profitable day at the exhibition grounds. Keen had reason to be elated. He posted a time of 16:95 seconds in the time trials, fastest of the day, then managed to edge clubmate Ken Wilcox to get the nod in a hard-fought main event. "This track is so smooth, I thought I had gone only two laps instead of four," Keen said. "I would like to see a course like this in Vancouver."

Keen will be back in action Sunday along with 15 other mainland drivers for the all-Modified race card at Grandview Bowl. With cooperation from the weatherman the stands should be packed when drivers of the A and B-Modifieds set their sights on lowering the track records.

An attraction for Nanaimo race fans will be the appearance of Al Smith behind the wheel of Geoff Vantreight's $10,000 Daffodil Special. It is not a secret that Smith will be out to lower Colorado driver Jim Malloy's Canadian-American Modified Racing Association track record of 16:32 set last year.

Among the Nanaimo contingent, Jack Milner will be a crowd favorite as he tries to keep the major honors in the Hub City. Milner started racing eight years ago as a mechanic on his brother's stock car. He built his first car in 1959, starting in the stock car division, then moved up to the A-Modifieds two years later. Milner's car is a Chev V8 with three carburetors, a 283 cubic-inch motor, with a 90-inch wheelbase and a Crosley body.

Milner missed last week's action when he could not be reached when MIARA officials decided to put on the auto show after earlier calling the races off due to inclement weather. In 1962 the Nanaimo driver won the best car award and in 1963 placed second in the point standings. He traveled the CAMRA circuit last year.

Other Nanaimo A-Modified pilots include Nibbs Anderson, Ray Pottinger, Bob Browne and Bob Clarke. However, Clarke and Browne are "between engines" right now, and it is doubtful the pair will see any action Sunday. Browne blew his engine at Boise, Idaho and Clarke pulled off the same caper at Spokane. Another Hub City speedster, Ray Pottinger, also came to grief at Spokane and has been burning the midnight oil making repairs. Pottinger expects to "fire up" tonight, and if trial runs are successful, will be in the lineup Sunday.

Harold Sjostrom, who didn't fare too well against the more powerful cars last week, will try for another repeat in the B-Modified main event and trophy dash.

The Victoria brigade of Brian Wilson, Bill Smithy, Dave Farris and Wally Lum will provide the other island opposition. Vancouver's contingent includes Ken Wilcox, Wayne Willoughby, Barry Chamberlain, Len Jones, Bob Desereaux, Frank McCabe, Don Grey, Len Barcelle, Wes Henham, George Gagnon, Ralph Monhay, Don Bennett, Rhineardt Undra, Gary Destobel and Len Cook.

1,000 on Hand for Auto Races

Nibbs Anderson of Nanaimo, taking to the track for the first time this season, fell one-point shy of a clean sweep in the weekly auto program of the Mid-Island Auto Racing Association at Grandview Bowl Sunday. Anderson won the trophy dash, came second in a heat race, and topped the field in the main event. Jack Milner developed motor trouble during a warm-up and had to sit on the sidelines.

Motor trouble also forced Ray Pottinger out of the main event after the Nanaimo speedster had won a heat race in his first time out. Pottinger was leading when he had to pull out of the final event. Jim Steen spun out in the trophy dash and took out Harold Sjostrom, but Sjostrom repaired the damage in time to win the B-Modified main event.

Over 1,000 race fans took in the show provided by 32 cars.

(Brian Pratt Collection)

Sjostrom Eyes Racing Points

Auto race fans can look forward to another exciting afternoon Sunday as more modifieds are expected to be entered by Vancouver and Island drivers. Last week, 20 of the 29 modifieds came from the mainland, and more are promised for this week's show.

Jack Milner, who sat it out because of motor trouble last week, is ready to roll as is Nanaimo drivers Lloyd Mullaly and Jack McLellan. Mullaly's B-Modified has recently been completed and is the first car with independent suspension to be raced on Island tracks. Another innovation is the use of sports car tires instead of the usual "slicks".

Nibbs Anderson, last week's big winner, will be missing from the starting grid due to commitments with race tracks across the border. However, Harold Sjostrom, a fan favorite, will be out after first place in the point standings. Sjostrom is currently in second place, but with a little luck and good driving could move up to the lead on Sunday. Sjostrom started racing four years ago when he bought a jalopy, then moved up to stock cars a year later, and this season he took up with the modifieds. He drives a six-cylinder Chrysler with one carburetor and a 264 cubic-inch motor. The car has a Morris Minor body and a 92-inch wheelbase.

So far this year Sjostrom, who is a welder by trade, has won four trophy dashes and five main events. He placed fifth in the point standings last season.

Flying Wheel Causes Chilling Racing Spill

Harold Sjostrom, who holds first place in point standings and is currently front runner in the most popular driver balloting, suffered face lacerations when he hit the cement wall at Grandview Bowl in a spectacular spill Sunday.

Sjostrom's car was totally wrecked when his B-Modified hit a wheel dropped by Brian Wilson as the pair were coming into the final lap during one of the exciting Mid-Island Auto Racing Association races. After climbing the wall, the Nanaimo driver's car came to rest on its end with the front wheels high in the air. The track had just been cleared of wreckage from Norm Edgar's pileup after Edgar was hit and rolled his jalopy twice in front of the grandstand. Edgar did a fast repair job and was back running in the main event.

Jack Milner of Nanaimo won the A-Modified trophy dash and main event with Sjostrom picking up a win in the B- Modified trophy dash. Wally Lum of Victoria picked up the winning purse in the B-Modified main and a first in a heat race.

Auto race fans got a preview of next week's "Tony Slogar Memorial" when Super A-Modifieds put on a special show at Grandview Bowl oval Sunday. Tom Fox, of Bremerton, Wash., appeared along with Jack Milner and Bob Clarke of Nanaimo. Nineteen modifieds lined up for the main event but had to restart before the first lap was completed due to a six-car pileup on the backstretch. No one was injured but two cars failed to make the starter's flag.

Mel Keen and Ralph Monhay battled for first place with Keen making it across the finish line first in the British Columbia Track Racing championship. Dave Farris of Victoria beat out Harold Sjostrom of Nanaimo to take the "B" championship. Doug Thompson of Vancouver won the stock car title.

Jalopies proved to be exciting as ever when Ron Crawford rolled over during time trials. In the main event, Dick Miller and John Litvak carried on a personal battle which ended with Miller being disqualified for dangerous driving.

Thrill-a-Minute Racing at Grandview Bowl

The Tony Slogar Memorial Trophy, Jim Malloy's track record of 16:31 and the winner's share of the purse, will be the targets for 24 of the driving aces in the Canadian-American Modified Racing Association's spectacular at Grandview Bowl Sunday, September 6. Sports fans will be able to get a first-hand look at the fastest racing machines in the country, one-step below United States Auto Club specifications. USAC is the top racing circuit in North America. For the average racing driver, gaining admittance to USAC is quite a distinction. Only the most experienced are allowed to latch onto the coveted cards.

Billy Foster, currently leading the CAMRA point standings, will head the elite lineup of he can get back from the U.S. in time. The Victoria driver is presently testing tires for Allstate and Mid-Island Auto Racing officials hope he can make plane connections in order to make the Grandview Bowl show. If Foster makes it, main interest should center around this speedster, but he will be pressed by many other speedway stars, including present track record holder Malloy. The Denver driver is one of the few full-time drivers on the CAMRA circuit and is second behind Foster in the standings.

Nanaimo colors will be carried by Bob Clarke, Jack Milner, Bob Browne, Nibbs Anderson and Ray Pottinger. All have raced in top company and of the quintet, only Pottinger may have trouble getting to the starting line. Pottinger has been plagued with engine trouble most of the season and has been working around the clock in an attempt to be in the Labor Day lineup.

Browne moved up from stock cars to modifieds this year and placed third in the Edmonton Matan Memorial Cup last month. He is credited with making one of the most spectacular winning finishes, when he crossed the line backwards while airborne at Ontario, Oregon. Browne's Grandview Bowl appearances have been few this season because of damage to his car while touring the CAMRA circuit.

Milner is another Nanaimo product making a name on the blacktop ovals. Winner of two consecutive main events recently, he will be shooting for the top prize money. Another returnee from the CAMRA circuit is Bob Clarke. Clarke drives a DeSoto-powered roadster, with a 276 cubic-inch motor, one of the smaller engines on the circuit. However, he was good enough to wind up fourth at Edmonton.

Anderson, in his Ford-powered modified, rounds out the local brigade. Eldon Rasmussen of Edmonton, first Daffodil Cup winner at Victoria, will be back to try for another repeat at the Western Speedway and will be among the Grandview Bowl competitors, as will Bob Gregg of Portland, one of the veterans of racing. Gregg has tried his hand with midgets, sprint cars, stocks and modifieds throughout his racing career.

Other leaders of their field taking bows during the big event include Norm Ellefson, Edmonton; Red Hayes, Eugene, Ore.; Al Smith, Victoria; Ken Wilcox and Mel Keen, Vancouver; Jack Eckman, Ontario, Ore.; Tom Fox, Bremerton, Wash.; Jim Roberts, Eugene, Ore.; George Robertson, Medford, Ore.; Ray Peets, Edmonton; Wes Henham, Vancouver and ace of former days, Dave Cooper of Victoria.

Billy Foster

Slogar Memorial Trophy to Denver Auto Ace

Billy Foster of Victoria sneaked into the lead 100 yards from the finish line to win the 60-lap main event of the Canadian-American Modified Racing Association windup event at Grandview Bowl Sunday. Nearly 3,000 fans watched as Foster moved into the lead when Jim Malloy of Denver, Colo., spun out on the last turn. Malloy finished second and piled up enough points to win the Tony Slogar Memorial Trophy.

Al Smith of Victoria led for about 49 laps then had to pull out after his motor overheated. Smith's car started to smoke at about 30 laps, and it was obvious to the fans that it was only a matter of a few circuits before the motor would conk out. Ken Wilcox of Vancouver supplied the excitement of the afternoon when he spun out in the second trophy dash and sheared off a front wheel after hitting a light pole in the infield.

Packed Stands Expected for Big Holiday Event

Jim Malloy is under the gun, and strange as it may seem, the Denver, Colorado speedster is more than happy with the situation. If you happen to be an auto racing buff, Malloy's accomplishments are old hat, but for those planning their first trip to Grandview Bowl Sunday for the final race on the Canadian American Modified Racing Association circuit, a few statistics may be in order.

Malloy has a collection of over 90 trophies including 100 percent attendance, best dressed driver and crew, best looking car, mechanic of the year and another list of awards as long as a fisherman's arm.
The Denver flash, whose red car with the big 5 will be the cynosure of all eyes Sunday, started racing 11 years ago driving jalopies and the updated list of Malloy's accomplishments makes interesting reading. Listed in order, they are:

1959-60: Track champion for two years; 1959-63: Moved into midget car class; 1960: Won the Colorado State championship; 1962: Won the Copper Cup at Salt Lake City; 1963: July 4th set a one-lap track record at Lakeside Speedway in Denver that still stands. The time of 12.92 is a USAC record. Joined the CAMRA circuit and won the Tater Cup championship; 1964: Nosed out Victoria's Billy Foster in points to win the CAMRA championship. Won the Tony Slogar Memorial trophy at Grandview Bowl.

This will probably be Malloy's last year with CAMRA, as he plans to hit the USAC championship trail next year.

The Grandview Bowl infield will hold some of the fastest racing machines in the country which, according to Mid-Island Auto Racing Association officials are only just a step below USAC specifications.

Although Malloy has been burning up the tracks, he has not been too far ahead of a bevy of a few other racing veterans, and track scuttlebutt has it that Bob Gregg of Portland, Ore., will be shooting the works in order to pack home the coveted Tony Slogar Award. Gregg, who travels with two complete engines, one in his number 25 car and one in the tow truck, also packs an enviable record. After campaigning in the midget division, Gregg started racing modifieds in 1962. Last year he wound up third in the CAMRA points standings. He is the vice-president of CAMRA and director of competition.

Other leaders in their field who will be on the starting grid when the time trials begin at 2 p.m. Sunday include Al Smith of Victoria, who won the first race he entered and has been bitten by the racing bug ever since. Bothered by bugs and gremlins in 1964, a hazard all drivers with new cars face, Smith is confident he will make a good showing when the checkered flag signals the end of the 75-lap main event Sunday.

The City of Edmonton, Alberta, will be represented by three veterans of the racing game in the persons of Norm Ellefson, Ray Peets and Eldon Rasmussen. Ellefson, who is a seed analyst in the off-season, is a steady competitor who prefers the long races and figures the 75-lapper at Grandview Bowl will be his cup of tea. Rasmussen, an Edmonton race fan favorite, finished 12th in CAMRA points last year and would like to add the Slogar Memorial to his well-filled trophy case.

Peets, known as the experimenter around the CAMRA circuit, appears to have taken care of the underpowered problem in his number 1 car.

A fifth-place finish last season made George Robertson of Lewiston, Idaho, unhappy and he set out to make an improvement this year. Dogged with mechanical troubles, Robertson competed in the last nine Gold Cup races at Edmonton and has finished in only two. Next Sunday, he hopes to be on the head-end in the 75-lap main when flagman Wally Ilott drops the checkered flag.

Making their first appearance before a Nanaimo audience are Max Dudley, Bud Gorder, Frank Janett, Gene Milo, Mel Andrus, Dick Card and Terry Nish.

(Brian Pratt Collection)

Portland Star Wins Trophy

Bob Gregg of Portland, Ore., took control on the eighth lap then held off the charge of Jim Malloy of Denver to win the action-packed 75-lap main event of the Canadian-American Modified Racing show at Grandview Bowl Sunday.

Gregg, a favorite of the 2,000 fans who sat in on the show, demonstrated his driving skill. He coolly held off successive challenges of Malloy and Eldon Rasmussen after taking over the lead from Al Smith of Victoria. Gregg just made it to the finish line a whisker ahead of Malloy, who roared wide open down the final straightaway in an attempt to steal the honors. The victory gave Gregg the Tony Slogar Memorial Trophy.

Spills and thrills highlighted the day as cars spun out and crashed, but the most spectacular crash came in the first lap of the main event which sent Nibbs Anderson of Nanaimo to the hospital with a broken arm and other injuries. Anderson's car ran up on the wheel of another and spun four times in the air before coming to rest just off the north end of the track. Hospital authorities reported today that the Nanaimo driver was resting comfortably.

Anderson's roll-over was one of several happening which gave MIARA officials the heebie jeebies during the day. Dave Cooper, driving Ray Pottinger's car, and Bob Browne wound up in a hole at the south ed of the track when the two cars collided on the south turn.

Browne, Ralph Monhay of Vancouver, Jack Milner of Nanaimo and Al Smith of Victoria were the hard luck drivers of the day. Browne was unable to continue after his racing troubles while Monhay, who won the first section of the Daffodil Cup at Victoria Saturday, blew his motor while warming up at Grandview Bowl. He left for Vancouver immediately but could not make the necessary repairs in time to compete in the second section yesterday.

Monhay had to sit on the sidelines at Victoria while Eldon Rasmussen won the Daffodil Cup. Jack Milner lost the rear end of his car and Smith had to pull out of the main event when his oil pressure fell. Smith held the lead for eight laps.

The main event was one of the most hotly-contested ever seen at Grandview Bowl. Gregg, who started out in the pole position, quickly lost the lead to hard-driving Smith. The two were closely followed by Malloy and after Smith dropped out, Gregg had to use all his driving skill to stay on the head end. He held off the challenge of Rasmussen for quite a number of laps and had to be alert in the final 100 yards to beat out Malloy.

A premature announcement had Gregg and Malloy as co-holders of the Tony Slogar Memorial Trophy, awarded for the most points in the meet, but a re-check gave Gregg the award by two points.

(Brian Pratt Collection)

FIFTEEN

Billy and the Mt. Douglas Hillclimb

There was a Mt. Douglas hillclimb in Victoria in 1962 – featuring true sports cars such as Porsches, Austin-Healeys, Triumphs and other similar makes of that era.

Jimmy Haslam had a modified roadster and said to Foster, "Hell, let's take that thing up to the hillclimb." Though the car just had an in-and-out gearbox, they decided not to install a traditional four-speed unit.

Billy conquering Mt. Douglas in Jimmy Haslam's roadster.

"I watched him at the line," said Gordon Alberg. "Billy wound it up, lit the tires, and away he went. At the hairpin, he just nailed the binders with lots of rear brake. He grabbed the hand clutch and it slid through the turn. When he wound it back up, that old Ford engine went up to full song and he'd just let go of the clutch. It went like a dragster up that hill. He beat everybody."

"I won a lot of sports car races with my TVR", said Dave Cooper. "But Billy beat my time at the hillclimb. That was a real deal. Jim Haslam had told me that Bill didn't want to drive on that hill and both wanted me to drive it. I said no, Bill knows that car better than I do, and I planned on driving my sports car in a different class. Bill and Haslam and another mechanic worked on their car to set it up special for the hillclimb".

This article from the *Victoria Daily Times* newspaper, dated May 12th, 1962, summarized that special event:

Ace Stock Car Driver Fastest Up Mt. Douglas

A lone stock car driver made fastest time of the day Sunday at the Victoria International Hill Climb. A crowd estimated at 4,000 watched 35 sports cars, sedans, and coupes as they flashed up the mile-long climb at Mount Douglas.

Bill Foster,, currently the Island's hottest car pilot and winner of Saturday's trophy dash at Western Speedway, drove a Ford Special up the hill in 56.72 seconds on his second run. It was good enough to beat runner-up John Hall's time of 57.50. Hall, driving a Porsche Carrera, set a time of 57.53, jumped to 58.01, and then down to 57.50 but despite his usual skilled driving, the Vancouver man did not have the "inches."

It was the first time a hillclimb had been held at Mount Douglas and little was known about which cars would perform best. It soon developed that it was like most climbs and in the future the cars most likely to succeed will be Specials with loads of power at the rear wheels.

Although Foster set fastest time, the event was actually won by Hall, since it is restricted to sports cars and sports racers of the Northwest Conference. Foster was the only outside entrant to take advantage of the climb, although anyone whose car passed a technical inspection could have entered.

A few days after this report, an additional article appeared in the *Victoria Colonist*:

At Centennial Hillclimb – Foster, Hall Share Honors

A powerful speedway car and a screaming Porsche sports car shared top honors in Sunday's Centennial Hillclimb at Mount Douglas. Billy Foster, in a Ford V8-powered modified stocker, set fastest time overall at 56.72 seconds to win the "formula libre" trophy. John Hall of Vancouver took his Porsche Carrera up in 57.50 seconds to capture the sports car trophy for the day.

A crowd estimated at 5,500 saw close to six hours of competition on the 9/10ths-mile course. The drivers, many from Vancouver and the U.S., were unanimous in praise of the course. "It's got everything," said Arleigh Pilkey, whose tiny Lotus 11 placed third among sports cars. Did the spectators who frequently strayed onto the course bother him? "No," he replied. "I figure they know I'm coming."

Early in the afternoon, the problem of straying people was acute, and the event had to be held up repeatedly. Later it worked into a system. Announcers Roy Shadbolt and Bing Foster would say which car was on its way, whistles would shrill from marshal to marshal along the course, and anyone close to the road took to the high grass. There were no untoward incidents reported.

Vandalism held up the contest several times, in one case destroying a car's chances for a trophy. Karen Hall, wife of the Porsche pilot, was waiting at the starting line when someone cut the wires leading to the timing equipment at the finish. In the resulting delay her Sprite's sparkplugs fouled and her engine, with one trouble or another, was sick for the rest of the afternoon.

Jerry Barber of Vancouver, in a Mercedes 300SL, and Bob Walker of Victoria, in an Austin 850, had a different kind of trouble. They made run after run without being timed because someone would break the light beam of the electric-eye timer at the finish while they were coming up.

"I was beginning to think somebody had it in for me," said Barber later – after accepting the Class B production trophy. Walker grinned it off, as he did the loss of a wheel in the hairpin turn on one of his early runs.
In the overall standings, after Foster and Hall, were John Razzelle of Vancouver in a Jaguar XKE at 58.75 seconds and Pilkey at 58.56.

A few of the many competitors at the Mt. Douglas Hillclimb in 1962.

SIXTEEN

Billy's Friends Remember – Dick Varley

Dick Varley began racing at Shearing Speedway in 1952 at the age of 19, so he held several years of experience before Billy Foster got into the game. Success came early for Dick, who attributed his knack for winning for having a very good crew, which included Bob Vantreight.

"At Shearing we had a very good car, but it takes everyone involved," Dick noted. "That first year or so I happened to make good money. I was winning a lot. I told my dad I was going to make enough to buy a house", he chuckles. "We all lived out in the sticks – in Elk Lake up on the hill – so we had to race all the town boys."

In 1957, the same year Varley got married, he began an association with Grant King, who then had a Ford-powered racer. "I called him and asked if I could drive his car," recalls Dick. "At that time sprint car and stock car drivers didn't get along very good. Since I was a stock car driver, he told me to get lost. Three weeks later though, Grant said, 'you can drive my car, but you will have to maintain it.'"

Since Dick still had a good crew, they further tuned the car for success. One item was to replace the Ford wheels with those from a Mercury, which were much stronger.

I asked Dick what his wife felt about his racing. "She must have liked it," he replied. "She's still with me!"

Dick Varley

(Victoria Auto Racing Hall of Fame)

Like other drivers, Varley had his share of mishaps. The worst one was when he rolled his car about five times down the straightaway at Western Speedway. "I came about a foot from going into the grandstands and destroyed the car," he described. "I found out years later, when I injured my shoulder, that I had suffered a broken arm."

"In 1958, I won something like nine trophy dashes," he remembers. "I just wanted to drive the car. The main trouble with Grant was that I had a lot of good crew members and at first, he was giving them shit for anything. But then we did so well he didn't argue with us anymore. I just went along with it. Since I was somewhat dyslectic, I never felt equal to anyone until I got into the race car."

In 1959 King built Varley another car, which became well-known as 'The Kersey Peanut Butter Special.' As Dick described, "That car was so much faster than anything else. It was actually a Rolla Vollstedt car with a Jimmy engine and big Oldsmobile brakes. It had so much power it was like a Sunday drive – it was that good. I was the only one in 1959 to have that type of motor – I was fortunate. I think I won something like 42 trophies with it."

When his name is mentioned, most people remember Dick for the many thrilling racing demonstrations he provided for the fans while driving Grant King's car.

The very successful Grant King/Dick Varley 'Kersey's Peanut Butter Special'

(Victoria Auto Racing Hall of Fame)

As far as tough competitors go, Dick brought up Dave Cooper's name. "Cooper was older, so he had ten years more experience on us. He was the favorite, and you had to first pass his buddies to get by him. And Billy Foster was tremendous." Dick brought up one off-track memory of Billy: "He had a 1952 Olds 98 convertible. He and his buddies had gotten together, down by the roundabout on Douglas Street. There was another fellow that had a Buick. They more or less raced up to that roundabout – right in the middle of Victoria!"

Varley's last year with Grant King was in 1961 and then he moved on. "Bob Vantreight started up a car and it was so slow," Dick reported. "I ran about five or six races with it, but it was just terrible. Grant said to me that if I couldn't find a better ride I should quit [racing], and so I did."

Dick's primary occupation during his racing years was as a mechanic at "a regular old service station." After he left competition, he and his family moved to England for several years. Upon their return to British Columbia, he started an excavating company and worked on heavy machinery for the next 18 years or so. He was inducted into the Victoria Auto Racing Hall of Fame in 1985.

SEVENTEEN

Billy's Friends Remember – Gordon Alberg

Billy Foster was three years older than Gordon Alberg, so the two didn't meet until Gordon was seventeen and in high school.

"I wasn't racing then", Gordon remembers. "I worked at the Cedar Hill Esso station after school. Billy worked for Gordy Fish and they bonded brake linings. They had an Austin A40 delivery truck."

Gordon continues, "So I'm standing in the front office, waiting to pump gas, and the station is on a hill. Suddenly this little Austin pickup comes flying down the hill and into the gas station. I thought it would come all the way into the office! The thing is sliding sideways - I mean in a four-wheel drift - nearly up to the station door. Before the Austin stopped, its door flew open and Billy steps out with a box under his arm - it was brake shoes he was delivering. That's when I first met him.

(Victoria Auto Racing Hall of Fame)

I was 19 years-old when I started racing in my 1934 Ford, and we raced together. He was just the most fun guy – until he climbed into a race car. His whole demeanor changed. While waiting to get underway for a race, he'd just sit in the cockpit and tap his wedding ring against the side of the car.

I knew nothing about circle track racing when I first started, so the first six to eight weeks I was replacing the radiator nearly every week. And then I got dumped really hard and rolled over about five times. I broke three or four ribs, so I asked Billy if he would drive for me. We threw the car back together. The chassis was never set up good before but – low and behold – when I flipped that car we bent the frame pretty bad, but it was twisted just the right way. It made lots of wedge. Both Billy and I were late getting to the track, so Jimmy Steen qualified the car. Jimmy said, 'we're in the dash because I qualified fourth-fastest.'

Gordy Alberg raced this car that he purchased from Jim Gallagher.

(Ray Pottinger Collection)

So here comes Billy, swinging his helmet as he walks across the pits. He raced the car that night and had a clean sweep – the dash, the fast heat, and the main event."

Once Gordon recovered from his injuries, he returned to the track with the same car. "It was a dream to drive. I ran the rest of that season and got Rookie of the Year and fifth or sixth in the points.

We ran about 22-24 cars in those days and we had reverse starts for the feature race. Somebody asked Billy to drive their car in the stock car championship race. Billy lined up just ahead of me in the feature. Well, that was a piece of cake because all I did was follow him.

To this day I can still see it – it was just like the sea parted. I just looked at the back of Billy's car. It was inside, outside, and we went from the back to the front by about 2/3rds of the race. He's running fourth and I'm fifth, and I know by then he's not going to go farther forward. I'm thinking I'll never get by him."

Gordon continues, "We got up on the main straight and he pulled up high to let me go underneath him. On the last lap I passed the second-place car – I used a lapped car as a pick. On that last lap he nailed me in the back bumper and put me sideways. The car stalled and another guy T-boned me, and that finished the car.

In my first race in 1963 I got hurt really bad. I was in the hospital for about four to five weeks. When I came out, I was still on crutches. That's when a Ford dealership had given Billy a brand-new station wagon – the one with all the wood grain. Billy said, 'Well, you come along with me.'

I was with him for the first half of the CAMRA season, and that's when he won something like 28 out of 33 races."

We rolled up and down the highway during 1963 with CAMRA. Billy had a mattress in the back of that station wagon. He would drive for a while, and then I would drive. We would go from Victoria to Boise, Pocatello, Salt Lake City, Denver, then back to Boise, Pocatello and Edmonton.

Usually it was just Billy and I, though John Feuz, who had built the Chevy V8, would sometimes come along. We would roll that race car off the trailer – it was filthy dirty – but we'd get a clean sweep at the track. Billy was so smooth and very savvy – he was just a natural."

That year I went with him on the CAMRA tour we became really close. We'd sometimes be gone for five to six weeks at a time. Every second night we'd get a motel, but I ran out of money. Billy would say, 'don't worry about it.'

Through Grant King, Billy hooked up with Rudy Hoerr to drive Hoerr's USAC stock car. Rudy had asked King if Billy had run any sports car races and Grant said he had – in Victoria. It was just a little bit of a white lie."

"Billy raced in three Champ Car races in the latter part of 1964. Gordon recalled. "All that was kept pretty quiet. Billy told me, but he hardly told anyone else. He wasn't driving for Vollstedt and that kind of surprised me. The guys on the CAMRA circuit were really impressed. He and Art Pollard were good friends – Art had been winning everything until Billy came along."

When Billy went to Indianapolis for the first time in 1965, Gordon was invited along as both a friend and helper. "I didn't even have a uniform," he says. "I had purchased a brand new Chevelle Super Sport that I picked up at the factory and drove it down to Indy. When I got there Billy asked me where I was staying. I told him I did not have a room."

Billy told Gordon he wouldn't have any luck finding a place, "so he took me around, introduced me to people, and asked about an available room. It turns out the President of D-A Oil took me in, and here I am staying in his personal home! I'm living in a mansion while Billy is staying in a 23-foot trailer."

Gordon recalls Billy's first performance at Indianapolis. "Everyone was astonished. His corner speeds were good, and he just passed everyone in the turns. He was running in ninth place when his car broke."

That was the only '500' that Gordon attended. Following Indianapolis, Billy asked if he'd come to the next race at Milwaukee, but Gordon turned him down. "I said if I went, I would become a race car bum.

In 1965 he was in different cars and was starting to make good money. He always had the best. He bought a brand-new Buick Riviera and built a nice new house."

Billy was known to do a little drag racing with this '32 Ford. Friends remember that he traded street machines often.

(Bob Glenny collection)

Another 'Billy' story Gordon recalls dates back to the late '50s, and centers around a '32 Ford hot rod Bill had for a short time. "Billy would go drag racing in his beautiful '32 Ford back in the day. The drag strip was a private two-lane road up to a quarry.

What car did Billy have for very long? He always kept up with having the fastest car in town, which meant that he traded [cars] quite often. Between he and I we replaced a lot of quarter panels and front-ends of our cars. For a few years there we both seemed to have trouble keeping our cars between the lines and out of the ditches. What a blast! Billy and I were both called up in front of old Bert Pearson, the Saanich Police Chief, a couple of times.

Bob Glenny bought the '32 from Billy around 1960. Bob told me that Billy scared the hell out of him when he took him for a test ride."

Gordon recalls the week before Billy's fatal accident. "I was working in Port Alberni, and on Friday I went into the Tally Ho, where we'd hang out for a beer. It was early in the afternoon and Billy loved to play shuffleboard. He's drinking 7-Up, and said he was leaving for Riverside the next Monday morning. He asked, 'Are you coming?' I said, 'No Bill – I've got a job at Port Alberni starting Monday."

"And that's the last I saw of him."

An avid car collector, Gordie Alberg is the proud caretaker of Foster's Vollstedt/Ford.

(Photo courtesy Goldstream Media)

EIGHTEEN

The Canadian-American Modified Racing Association

In January of 1963 representatives from eight cities in the Pacific Northwest, Utah, and Western Canada met in Spokane, Washington, for the purpose of organizing a regional Super-Modified series. This coalition became known as the Canadian American Modified Racing Association, or CAMRA.

The first President of the organization was Bill Crow of Boise, Idaho. The original eight representative tracks were in Salt Lake City, Utah; Meridian, Idaho; Seattle and Spokane, Washington; Nanaimo, Victoria, and Vancouver, British Columbia and Edmonton, Alberta.

CAMRA's first race was held on May 17th, 1963, in Nanaimo, and the 100-lap feature was won by Bill Crow. The following night at a race in Victoria, Crow repeated as the victor. At the end of the first season, Billy Foster was crowned CAMRA's first Champion, followed by Bill Crow in second and Lewiston, Idaho's George Robertson in the third points position.

The series was an instant hit with race fans throughout the region and gained its fair share of attention within the regional sports pages. One of the premier events on CAMRA's 1963 schedule was the Copper Cup Invitational at the Salt Lake Fairgrounds in early August. The following articles appeared in the *Deseret News*, written by sports writer Hi McDonald:

Top Racers Await Copper Cup Tonight

(August 2, 1963) – With eight of the top ten Canadian-American stock car circuit drivers entered, the two-night Copper Cup Invitational at the Salt Lake Fairgrounds promised to be a humdinger of a race.
Boise's Bill Crow, current leader of the Canadian-American Modified Racing Assn. (CAMRA) loop, will be brewing some of his old racing magic to help boost him farther up the ladder.

Also, among the top ten entered in the rich chase for the $1,500 first place prize is George Robertson, Lewiston, Idaho. In second place: Al Smith, Victoria, B.C. Third: Jim Malloy, Denver. Fourth: Dick Ganoe, Eugene, Ore. Sixth: Bill Foster, Victoria. Seventh: Glen Naylor, Boise. Ninth: Mel Andrus, Salt Lake City. Crow has amassed 570 points for the circuit championship lead while Robertson had 507. Andrus' total is 170. Points in the Copper Cup will count toward the circuit total.

Crow, Malloy and Robertson are frequent visitors to the Fairground's track, while most of the others are new. The top-rated drivers have proven ability, however, for adapting quickly to a new track.
Victoria's Bill Foster is being touted as the toughest racer in the field because of his showing in competition with other circuit leaders.

But don't sell Mel Andrus short. The Intermountain champion put together a heap of luck and some heady driving to win that title this year at the Fairgrounds. And he's fully capable of repeating.
Altogether some 20 out-of-staters are entered. Andrus is top rated among the local drivers, but Dick Card also has a way of coming up with something special when he has the toughest competition.

The circuit drivers move to Edmonton, Alberta, Canada for Gold Cup competition next Wednesday; then to Spokane for the Lilac Cup, Aug. 10-11.

Robertson's Stocker Paces Copper Cuppers

(August 3, 1963) – George Robertson of Lewiston, Idaho, goes into Saturday night's finals of the Copper Cup Invitational stock car races with a comfortable point lead toward the $1,500 first place prize. But after Friday night's harum-scarum anything can happen. Terry Nish proved to be Mel Andrus' nemesis.

The two locked horns early in the A-Main, stalling Nish in the middle of the track. Mel reentered the race, but a few laps later took the turn too fast and slid into Nish's wheel, sending his No. 22 bouncing high in the air and putting Andrus out of the race.

It almost took an electronic brain to figure out the race winner. But after scorekeepers chopped off each of the 20 cars in the A-Main, Robertson came out on top. Dick Card placed second, Pete Cazier third, Bill Starks fourth, Stan Robinson, fifth and Phil Hanson, sixth for the top A-Main finishers. That put Card in second place going into Saturday's finals. Starks and Cazier are tied with 55 points apiece.

Canadian Speedster Annexes Copper Cup

(August 5, 1963) – You don't have to win big as long as you win consistently. Billy Foster of Victoria, B.C., proved Monday. Foster, the pre-race favorite captured the top $1,500 prize in the Salt Lake Fairgrounds biggest stock car race of the season, the Copper Cup, in Saturday night's finale despite the fact:

1. He didn't win the A-Main. Jim Malloy did, but Foster was second.
2. He didn't win the fast-car heat. George Robertson did.
3. He didn't win the fast-dash. Sam Sauer did.
4. He wasn't even the point leader after Friday night's preliminaries – that was George Robertson.

Come to think of it, about the only thing Foster did win outright was Friday night's fast-dash. But he built up valuable points in qualifying and runner-up positions to take home the huge trophy awarded to the Copper Cup winner.

Edmonton's annual Gold Cup was another premier event on CAMRA's summer schedule. On August 27th, 1964 a writer for the *Edmonton Journal* filed this post-race report

Driving Skill Was Obvious

Agreed, the Gold Cup 200 Classic lacked entirely of the spectacular. But stock car drivers and the sport's long-time observers will tell that when the spectacular is missing, the driving skills aren't.

And, the driving skills weren't Wednesday night. Gold Cup champion Billy Foster provided one of the finest exhibitions of driving skills seen in some time on Speedway Park's quarter-mile oval. His path to victory was almost flawless. Art Pollard, Bob Gregg, George Robertson, locals Eldon Rasmussen and Ray Peets ... all ran a clean, outstanding race.

The closest thing to a spectacular incident was a spin-out, if spin-outs can be termed spectacular. There were only two and, in both cases, drivers exhibited outstanding control of their machines to keep the race moving at full pace. Pollard spun coming out of the fourth corner on the 105th lap when jostled by Peets. Rasmussen spun coming out of the third corner on the 193rd lap.

The reason the classic went so well was that only top caliber drivers and mechanically sound machines were competing. Thirteen of the 17 starting cars timed in within nine-tenths of a second in qualifying rounds.
The race was not only a test of driving skill, but a test of the mechanics and pit crews as well. Fourteen of the 17 cars went from the start to finish in a race that took exactly 48 minutes to run for a 60-plus mph average. Indianapolis 500 driver Rodger Ward told all within earshot that the Speedway Park track was "the best I've ever seen in its category."

And he feels a proposed United States Auto Club midget racing circuit extension into Edmonton would be a success. "Midget racing is just holding its own in some centers and losing spectator following in others, mind you. But I think where there is a decrease in interest it is because3 there also is big car racing. The midgets undoubtedly would draw here in Edmonton if for no other reason than that big-name drivers such as Parnelli Jones would be an attraction."

Another interesting report from the CAMRA circuit appeared in the *Victoria Colonist* on September 3rd, 1964, in a lead-up to the annual Daffodil Cup:

Roaring Racers Sooth Ulcers

For fast, fast, fast relief from nervous tension and the pain of ulcers, try car racing. That's the prescription Tom Fox of Bremerton, Wash, will probably give you. Fox, currently in sixth position in the Canadian American Motor Racing Association driver standings, says he enjoys racing because it relaxes his nerves and helps his ulcers.

He first calmed his ulcers in big-time racing in 1961 when he brought a "hopped-up" jalopy to Victoria's Daffodil Cup race. This year he's coming back to the Daffodil Cup Saturday and Monday in a new modified sports car.

Victoria's Billy Foster leads the CAMRA standings at the present and is the favorite in the weekend race. But this Foster's last appearance in the CAMRA circuit, and with five races left in the season, Jim Malloy of Denver, second in the standings, could overtake Foster for the $1,200 first-place bonus.

Malloy is one of the few full-time drivers on the CAMRA circuit. He and his brother Jerry travel the racing circuits six months of the year, earning themselves a good living. They made their first appearance in Victoria at last year's Daffodil Cup, where their car placed third and later set a track record in Nanaimo.

Rated among the top threats to Foster in the two-day event is Art Pollard of Medford, Ore. Pollard ran wheel-to-wheel with Foster for the 150 laps in the 1962 race and finished second by less than a car length. Eldon Rasmussen of Edmonton took the first Daffodil trophy in 1961 and will be back this year to try to break Foster's recent monopoly.

Among the oldest drivers in the race is Bob Gregg of Portland. In his 25 years of competition, Gregg has been involved in nearly every phase of the sport. He has driven in the Indianapolis 500, as well as piloting midgets, sprint cars, stocks and modifieds throughout the CAMRA circuit.

Some of the other top drivers entered in the race are Victoria's Al Smith, who has beaten Foster once this year; George Robertson of Lewiston, Idaho, currently in fifth spot in the CAMRA point standings, and Jim Roberts, a CAMRA director and third in the standings.

More than 30 cars are expected to line up for the time trials on Saturday at 7:30. Saturday's activity has two trophy dashes, four heat races and two main events. Monday time trials begin at 7:30 with a preliminary jalopy trophy dash and main event before the two feature trophy dashes and 100-lap main event. The championship is calculated on a points basis over the two nights.

On Sunday, September 6th, 1964, *The Daily Colonist* followed up with the results of the Daffodil Cup's first night results:

Denver Driver Scores

Jim Malloy of Denver won the first heat of the Daffodil Cup modified sportsman racing classic at Western Speedway last night to take a stranglehold on the Canadian American Modified Racing Association driver championship. If Malloy wins the second heat Monday, he will spoil Billy Foster's bid to win the championship two years in a row.

Malloy raced to an easy win after Foster and fellow Victorian Al Smith put themselves out of contention with a collision in the 27th lap of the 40-lap race.

Foster and Smith had staged a stirring duel in second place as Malloy jumped to an early lead. Smith, who set a new track record in time trials, had been leading Foster until he spun out when Foster nudged him from behind. Foster went on to finish fourth in the race but still has a chance of winning his third-straight Daffodil Cup. Should Foster take the cup, he would clinch the CAMRA driver championship and the $1,200 CAMRA bonus.

Malloy eventually won the race by almost a lap. A crowd of 5,200 watched the mishap-filled program which had two major accidents. Both occurred in the B-Main event, won by Victoria's Dave Ferris. The most spectacular concerned Wes Henham of Vancouver, who flipped end-over-end four times after running up the wheels of another car. Gordy Alberg of Victoria ran into the wall in front of the grandstand in the same heat when his steering locked.

Smith's mishap was particularly disheartening to his pit crew who had worked for seven hours fashioning a water pump from scratch after the original was damaged in the afternoon practice. **They brought the machine to the track late, but still managed to set a track record of 17.17 seconds in time trials.** The unlucky Smith, however, didn't win a race.

Another tough-luck victim was Eldon Rasmussen of Edmonton. His car was badly damaged in a highway accident Saturday on its way to the track. Rasmussen ordered parts flown in from Edmonton and the car was repaired in time to race but failed to place in the top-five in any event.

Second-place was taken by Jim Roberts of Eugene, Ore., and Ray Peets of Edmonton took third. Only the first-place finish of Malloy, however, was official with other results awaiting official scrutiny today.

Despite his first-place finish last night, Malloy must still finish near the top in Monday's main 100-lap race to take the trophy.

Jim Malloy earned back-to-back Championships following the 1964 and 1965 seasons. Second and third in the standings for 1964 were Foster and Portland, Oregon's Bob Gregg.

In some respects, 1965 appeared to be one of the most hotly-contested season for CAMRA drivers and teams, judging by the amount of press stories that were published.

Jim Malloy was the CAMRA Champion in 1964 and 1965.

(Photo courtesy of the Idaho Historical Racing Society)

As the new season began in Victoria, photographer and reporter Barrie Goodwin reported the results for the *Racing Wheels* publication on May 22nd:

Malloy Leads CAMRA Points

Action started fast at the first CAMRA race of the season with Al Smith having the honor of blowing his engine on the newly paved Western Speedway hardtop. Because of the bad weather, this was the first race of the season and "the experts" said the track would be slow and slick because of the lack of rubber on the track, but these so-called experts had to eat crow.

The third car to time in for the night was driven by Jim Malloy, who proved to the 3,400-plus fans that he was the CAMRA champion by turning the 4/10ths-mile oval in the time of 16.96. This is the fastest any car has gone at Western Speedway. The old record was held by Al Smith with the time of 17.17.

Setting the track record was too much for Jim Malloy's car as he pulled out of the pace lap of the trophy dash with a broken U-joint. This gave Ray Pottinger of Nanaimo a spot in the dash. The dash was not one lap old when Bob Etchison of Eugene spun in the first turn causing a restart. The restart was won by George Robertson with Bob Etchison a distant second.

The heat races had only one casualty, that being Earl Veeder of Eugene. Earl put a hole in the pan of his car in the second heat. The intermission also was exciting as John Linder of Seattle went high coming out of the second turn gardening the outside of the track as he went.

Eldon Rasmussen of Edmonton took off like a jackrabbit at the start of the 50-lap main and had a lead of half a lap by the end of the fifth lap. George Robertson took the lead on the 10th lap with Rasmussen and Malloy close behind. Three laps later Malloy was in the lead for good. With 25 laps gone there were still 12 of the 15 starters running. Bob Clarke of Nanaimo did a complete 360-degree spin in the second turn on lap 30, but he didn't drop in the standings.

Norm Ellefson and Robertson gave the fans a good thing to cheer about as they battled for second place, with Ellefson edging Robertson at the line. Robertson made the comment after the race that the traffic was heavy considering the lack of cars and the size of the track.

That same weekend, the series held its second event of the 1965 season at Grandview Bowl in Nanaimo. Once again, Goodwin filed this report for *Racing Wheels* on May 25th, 1965:

Fans Set Record for Racing Show

One of the largest crowds ever to witness a racing program at Grandview Bowl watched Jim Malloy of Denver move out of the pack on the 30th lap then drive to an easy win in the Nanaimo Challenge Cup, 60-lap main event Sunday. It was the second big win on the Canadian American Modified Racing Association circuit for the good-looking American ace, who also picked up the major prize at Western Speedway in Victoria Saturday.

It was standing room only, as over 3,000 sat through the fast-paced show under perfect weather conditions. The Denver driver set the fastest time in the time trials but his 16.56 seconds for the lap failed to break his Grandview Bowl record of 16.31 set last year. Although he has visited Nanaimo for the past three years, it was the first main event win for Malloy. He missed a clean sweep for the weekend when Al Smith of Victoria won the main event at Western Speedway Monday. Malloy was second.

In one of the finest and most exciting trophy dashes seen here, Bob Gregg of Portland won by a width of a wheel over Malloy, with George Robertson third. Two spin-outs on the first lap which caused two false starts failed to deter Joe Bridgeman of Seattle and he wound up winner of the second trophy dash after a duel with Earl Veeder of Woodburn, Oregon and Bob Browne of Nanaimo.

Fourteen cars lined up for the main event with Veeder, Bridgeman and Norm Ellefson leading the pack in that order. After six laps, Ellefson took over the lead with Malloy sitting right on his bumper and Gregg trailing along in third place. The front runners appeared content to hold their positions as they weaved around and through the pack of slower-moving cars. On the 30th lap, Malloy sent his red number 5 to the front and picked a groove in the track to grind out a well-driven victory. Jack Milner of Nanaimo lost all chances midway through the race when he lost a left-rear wheel.

Another big stop on CAMRA's 1965 schedule came in August. The event was the annual Lilac Cup held at the Spokane Fairgrounds. As the *Spokane Daily Chronicle* described on August 30th, 1965:

Malloy is Challenged but Retains Lilac Cup

Portland's Bob Gregg and Al Smith of Victoria gave him a good run, but veteran Jim Malloy successfully defended his Lilac Cup title last night at the Fairgrounds. The hard-charger from Denver, who had trouble earlier in the trophy dash and finished well back in the heat, turned his car loose late in the featured main event to speed home the victor in the Canadian American Modified Racing Association competition.

A chilled but enthusiastic crowd of about 5,000 watched Malloy maneuver his way through the pack to win the A-Main with Ralph Monhay of Vancouver, B.C., second and Gregg third. Gregg, who won the CAMRA Inland Empire Cup here earlier, had won the trophy dash. He finished second in the Lilac Cup on total points over a two-day period. In a separate race in Lewiston Saturday night, Gregg came out the winner.

Smith, who had won the fast heat yesterday, was nearly a lap ahead midway through the 50-lap feature last night when he slid off the south end of the track after hitting an oil slick, and out of the race. Bud Gorder was the top Spokane finisher, getting fifth in the main.

In 1965, behind Malloy in the season standings, were Eldon Rasmussen from Edmonton, Alberta, and Bob Gregg.

Grandview Bowl was again in the spotlight in early September of 1967 when the CAMRA caravan returned for another exciting event, as reported in the *Nanaimo Free Press* by Cal Walker:

Auto Race Double for Victoria Ace

The weather was perfect and the track fast as Al Smith of Victoria turned in a spectacular afternoon of driving at Grandview Bowl Raceway Sunday, to win the Tony Slogar Memorial trophy for the second straight year. Smith piloted his super-modified Indy-type racer to the fastest lap of 16.50 seconds in a day that featured oval track racing at its exciting best.

Coming from last place in the 60-lap CAMRA feature, Smith snatched the lead from Chuck Neitzel on the 55th lap after a brilliant display of driving that saw him pass the remainder of the 20-car field, and finally press hard on Neitzel's heels.

During the 33rd lap, Cal Arnold of North Surrey was burned when a water line in his car broke and sprayed boiling water over his arms and chest. The race was halted to allow the track ambulance to assist Arnold. Reports said later that his injuries were not serious. Arnold was running a strong second at the time of his injury.

As Smith and Neitzel raced neck-and-neck down the back straightaway, the third-place car, driven by Eldon Rasmussen of Edmonton, suddenly spun out of control and crashed through the white fence behind the back straight at full throttle. The race was red-flagged again, and drivers told to hold their positions as track marshals and ambulance men rushed to Rasmussen's assistance. Fortunately, Rasmussen received only minor injuries from his duel with the fence and appeared in the infield shortly after, checking over his battered car.

The race was restarted 20-minutes later, with Smith in second position. The rules of CAMRA stipulate that if a race is stopped for injury or accident that competitors will be started in the position they held one-lap previous to stoppage. Smith and Neitzel dueled feverishly through the last four laps, but Neitzel held his lead and took the checkered flag just yards ahead of Smith.

Mrs. M. Slogar presented Smith with the Tony Slogar Memorial trophy, given in memory of her son, who was killed racing in Eugene, Oregon, in 1962, while a crowd of some 2,500 spectators strained the pit fence to cheer one of British Columbia's most celebrated drivers. Smith won the trophy by gathering most points during the afternoon's competition.

The final year for CAMRA came in 1984 when Jan Sneva of Spokane won his second straight title, followed by his brother Blaine in the runner-up spot. CAMRA then merged with the Washington Racing Association, which became the short-lived USAC-Washington series.

Along with Billy Foster, Jim Malloy, and Jan Sneva, CAMRA's list of champions includes Norm Ellefson, Jim Roberts, Ken Hamilton, Tom, Jerry, and Blaine Sneva, Palmer Crowell, Don Selley, George Robertson, Doug Larson, Bob Cochran, Marc Edson and Marty White.

During its long run, CAMRA served as a memorable chapter in the history of Northwest racing. Through the years the series featured fields of great diversity – such as winged sprints, uprights, roadsters and rear-engine cars. CAMRA was also instrumental in furthering the professional careers of a number of racers, including eight drivers that went on to compete in the Indianapolis 500.

This esteemed group includes Billy Foster, Art Pollard, Jim Malloy, Tom and Jerry Sneva, Dick Simon, Eldon Rasmussen and Cliff Hucul.

CAMRA Season Points Results: 1963-1984

(**First**, Second, Third)

1963: **Billy Foster** (Victoria, British Columbia), Bill Crow, George Robertson
1964: **Jim Malloy** (Denver, Colorado), Billy Foster, Bob Gregg
1965: **Jim Malloy** (Denver, CO.), Eldon Rasmussen, Bob Gregg
1966: **Norm Ellefson** (Edmonton, Alberta), Bob Gregg, George Robertson
1967: **Norm Ellefson**, Bob Gregg, Al Smith
1968: **Jim Roberts** (Eugene, Oregon), Bob Gregg, Ralph Monhay
1969: **Norm Ellefson**, Bob Gregg, Ralph Monhay
1970: **Tom Sneva** (Spokane, Washington), Bob Gregg, Frank Weiss
1971: **Palmer Crowell** (Hillsboro, Oregon), Tom Sneva, Bob Gregg
1972: **Don Selley** (Portland, Oregon), Bob Gregg, George Robertson
1973: **George Robertson** (Lewiston, Idaho), Jerry Sneva, Gerry McLees
1974: **Jerry Sneva** (Spokane, Washington), George Robertson, Ralph Monhay
1975: **Doug Larson** (Quesnel, British Columbia), Cliff Hucul, Ralph Monhay
1976: **Bob Cochran** (Seattle, Washington), Doug Larson, John Tharp
1977: **Doug Larson**, George Robertson, Les May
1978: **Doug Larson**, George Robertson, Marty White
1979: **Doug Larson**, Marty White, Pat Jesmore
1980: **Marc Edson** (Boise, Idaho), Tom Naylor, Marty White
1981: **Blaine Sneva** (Spokane, Washington), Mike Gorder, Mickey Mumua
1982: **Marty White** (Kamloops, British Columbia), Glen Naylor, Mickey Mumua
1983: **Jan Sneva** (Spokane, Washington), Marty White, Mickey Mumua
1984: **Jan Sneva**, Blaine Sneva, Mike Ehlers

NINETEEN

Billy's Friends Remember – Eldon Rasmussen

Like Billy Foster and several others, Eldon Rasmussen was a super-modified driver who graduated to the big time in USAC's Champ Car Series after competing in the Canadian American Modified Racing Association (CAMRA). During the years 1971-1979, Eldon drove in 23 Champ Car events – including the Indianapolis 500 in 1975, 1977, and 1979. His best finish at the Brickyard came in '77 when he finished in 13th place.

Eldon Rasmussen in his younger days.

(Brian Pratt Collection)

Eldon's final race was at Pocono in 1979 when his car struck the wall on the 75th lap. He was unconscious when the track's emergency crew arrived on the scene, but quickly regained consciousness. He was transported to the local hospital where doctors determined he had suffered a broken ankle, possible fractures and a concussion.

Eldon Rasmussen was born in 1936. His parents had moved to Canada from the United States. "I grew up in a grain town called Standard, which was about 50 miles east of Calgary," says Eldon. "Of course, we had a big machinery shop on the farm. I built my first soap box derby car in that shop when I was eight-years-old."

About a year later he fashioned his first go-kart. "I used parts of a Ford Model T frame and used an engine from a grain loader," he remembers. "We had a Wisconsin engine that had a clutch. I modified a rear-end from a Model A, and the whole driveline was off-set to one side. I went on to build four or five more of that same car for the other farm kids. I was a fabricator from the start and worked on my brother Gordon's Model T sprint car."

Eldon began racing seriously in 1952 on the dirt tracks of southern Alberta at age 16. "They didn't care much about age at the time," he says. "A lot of cities had a quarter to half-mile horse racing track that we raced on."

In those early days of his driving career, Eldon was behind the wheel of a race car known as the 'Stedelbauer Special'. "Local rules at the time said you had to run the same body shell as the frame," he says, "so that car started out as a 1931 Ford Model A five-window coupe. We called them modifieds. George Stedelbauer was my boss at the time. He ran his father's auto dealership in London, Ontario - Central Chevrolet. I was building race cars for my competitors in my two-car garage."

Rasmussen maintained a friendly rivalry with Norm Ellefson, another popular pilot from the Edmonton area. This article that appeared in *Racing Wheels* sets the tone:

Rasmussen Keeping Wary Eye on Ellefson's Stock Car Challenge

Who's afraid of the big, bad Norm Ellefson? Certainly not Hinton's Eldon Rasmussen, whose Speedway Park stock car superiority has been sternly challenged by Norm's return to action in a brand-new bomb.

The blonde, stocky Hintonite was at the Park yesterday afternoon, working the kinks out before an appreciative audience of about a dozen little boys who had slipped through the gates when nobody was looking. "Afraid?" Rasmussen looked a little surprised at the suggestion made. "I respect Norm, and I've got to keep looking out for him, but I'm driving to win, you know."

Eldon has been likened, at least in local circles, as stock car's answer to Jackie Parker, the football man made for those overworked words – "terrific, amazing, a star." But perhaps this praise was a little premature. For Eldon's car, through the season, was obviously superior to the others on the track. Then Ken Dawson came up with a dandy. Ellefson returned to competition a few weeks back with another hot rod.

Meanwhile, Ray Peets and Bill Strong and George Stevens and Frank Taylor were always there, waiting in the weeds, willing and able to take over at a moment's notice.

Through the ensuing years, Eldon honed his skills both as a driver and master fabricator – winning many local championships throughout Western Canada and beyond. He won championships in Victoria, B.C., in 1961 and 1965. Naturally, Eldon was a big fan favorite up in his neck of the woods and was dubbed the 'Hinton Hornet.'

Barring a mechanical breakdown, he was always the driver to beat, as illustrated in this post-race report in the *Edmonton Journal* on July 13, 1961:

Spaulding Edges Rasmussen For Matan Victory

Cliff Spaulding of Seattle returned to Speedway Park with a vengeance last night and left with a souped-up opinion of local drivers. Particularly after his fantastic battle – reaching neck-and-neck proportions towards the end – with Eldon Rasmussen in the 100-lap Eddie Matan Memorial stock car race.

A capacity crowd of close to 10,000 fans – most ever in Speedway history – watched as Spaulding, who lost the 1960 Gold Cup race to Norm Ellefson, won by 15 yards over Rasmussen. But the Hinton Hornet later said that at about 54 laps (when he had a runaway lead going for him and was two-thirds of a lap ahead of the Washington State pilot when his front axle broke. Spaulding had his troubles too, although you wouldn't know it. The car, in a race for the first time, didn't act quite the way he wanted it.

They had quite a race, anyway. Frank Taylor moved quickly into the lead. By the fifth lap Rasmussen had moved past 10 other cars to go ahead. There he stayed, until Spaulding began to inch forward after some 60-odd circuits of the quarter-mile track. With 25 rotations left, Spaulding drew dangerously close and worked his way up to Eldon's rear bumper. The Yankee whiz nosed ahead at 80 laps but Rasmussen, holding the inside, made it a neck-and-neck affair and the fans roared.

On the 87th lap, Spaulding had to swing wide on the fourth corner to pass Tom Stoddart's 22, lost three lengths to the Hintonite but edged back up and took the lead on the 90th lap, cruising in to victory. Another American, Lewiston, Idaho's George Robertson, placed third. Fourth was Fort Saskatchewan's Billy Strong, with locals Eric Van Camp and Doug Pescod fifth and sixth.

(Ted MacKenzie photo)

Norm Ellefson, out for the first time this season in a brand-new bomb job, had to drop out after 15 laps after bumping into John Feenstra's 21. The race had earlier been delayed when Ellefson's transmission got sticky. Fourteen cars started the Memorial run and eight finished what turned out to be one of the hardest-driven, fastest races of the year.

After the dust had settled, Spaulding said that "it was a pleasure" to drive against Rasmussen, particularly. He added that the caliber of cars and drivers had lifted considerably since his visit here last season.

One of the most prominent events on the West Coast circuit at the time was the Copper Cup, held in Salt Lake City. In August 1961, Art Pollard and Eldon Rasmussen went head-to-head for the winner's gigantic trophy.

Hi McDonald, sportswriter for the *Deseret News* in Salt Lake City, provided this feature article following the first night of racing on August 19th, 1961:

Pollard Leading Copper Cup Race

It looked like money in the bank Saturday for Art Pollard of Roseburg, Ore., as the Copper Cup invitational moved into the final night at the Salt Lake Fairgrounds. The booming Pollard, winner of Canada's Gold Cup only last week, jumped into a substantial point lead Friday night as a host of out-of-state and local drivers opened a bid for the $1,000 first prize.

Pollard racked up 74 points in a night of sterling performances which saw him:

1 - Set a new track record of 14.67 seconds – substantially below Mel Andrus' best mark set only a week ago.
2 - Win the trophy dash, gunning through a hole left by Andrus on the last lap.
3 - Win the 40-lap A-Main after hasty repairs on a bent axle when he was bumped into the fence during the fast-car heat race.

Another out-of-stater, Eldon Rasmussen of Edmonton, Alberta, Canada, stood second in the Copper Cup battle with 58 points. Eldon put up a stirring battle with Pollard in the A- Main but was forced to settle for second. He captured first-place honors in the fifth heat.

It was a night which saw the out-of-staters dominate most of the races. Besides Pollard and Rasmussen, Boise's Bill Crow showed plenty of skill in winning the fast-car heat race, and George Robertson of Lewiston, Idaho, took the third heat and won the B-Main hands down.

At the end of the two-night Copper Cup event, Pollard swept the meet, taking home the $1,000 prize money and the big trophy. Rasmussen placed second in the final standings, earning $600 for his effort.

Just a few weeks later, at Western Speedway in Victoria, officials of the Vancouver Island Track Racing Association (VITRA) staged their first Western Canada championship car race – the Daffodil Cup.

It was a thrill for the local fans, who wedged themselves into the grandstands. They quickly became familiar with a driver named Eldon Rasmussen. The *Victoria Times* reported the full details on September 5th, 1961:

Edmonton Driver Captures Title in Stocker Race

The crowd that jammed Western Speedway for the 150-lap Daffodil Cup race definitely ranks with the biggest crowds ever attracted to single sporting events in Victoria history. VITRA officials said there were 8,200 people at the track. Cars were parked along Millstream Road back to the highway and fans practically surrounded the track. VITRA officials finally turned people back at the gate and many more turned back when they couldn't get off the highway.

The big winner was an Edmonton driver by the name of Eldon Rasmussen, who led all the way through the 150-laps to post an easy victory. Second was Bill Crow of Boise, Idaho, who never challenged the winner after the first few laps but who, in turn, was hardly challenged himself.

Rasmussen started first in the race, so it was no surprise when he finished there. Crow started fourth. The big surprises came from local driver Ray Pottinger, driving a car resembling a go-cart with sides. After starting sixth in the 30-car field, he moved up fast in the early going and then hung on to finish third, an extremely good showing against the hot American competition. Seven of the fastest nine cars in the field were from the U.S.

Dick Varley, driving a machine that was simply Grant King's sprint car with a roof added, timed in second fastest but could not match the pace and faded early. He finally spun out of the race near the 90th lap.

Local favorite Billy Foster timed in only 12th fastest but quickly moved up into fourth. He lost a wheel on lap 107, but instead of quitting kept on going around for a few more laps, then came in, got another wheel slapped onto his car and went out again to finally finish the race.

Rasmussen won the Saturday night all-comers race by traveling the last 25 laps with no brakes.

Friendly rivals Art Pollard and Eldon Rasmussen both have big eyes on the trophy.

(Brian Pratt Collection)

1961 Daffdil Cup race at Western Speedway when Eldon came home the victor in this inaugural event. Second place went to Idaho driver Bill Crow. Afterwards, they celebrated with their wives.

(Ted MacKenzie photos)

With the advent of the CAMRA Series in 1963, it became a natural career step-ladder for Eldon to become involved in that endeavor. He would join other CAMRA veterans Billy Foster, Art Pollard, Jim Malloy, Tom and Jerry Sneva and Cliff Hucul, who would all go on to compete at Indianapolis.

"I palled around with Billy Foster – he was a great guy," Eldon remembers. "He worked at Ford and always towed his race car with a Ford Country Squire station wagon that was a special order from the dealership that sponsored him. It had a big-block 428 engine – I think only twelve were built with that size motor."

"At that time, I couldn't afford to run all the races because my Dad had cancer and I was busy with the farm – seeding, hauling grain, and maintaining all the trucks and combines."

On July 8th, 1963, the *Edmonton Journal* provided this update on Eldon:

Rasmussen Feels Uneasy; Rebuilds Stock Racer

While the top drivers from western Canada and the northwest United States began arriving today for the Matan Memorial Classic at Speedway Park, Eldon Rasmussen is still keeping a weather eye out for a local rival. Defending champion in the event, Rasmussen arrived back in Edmonton last week after winning the British Columbia championship race in Prince George to learn that Norm Ellefson has set his sights on taking the Matan title away from him.

Today, Rasmussen's garage is a beehive of activity. He and his aides have torn down the speedy Edmonton Motors Special and are rebuilding it from the ground up, adding a little here and there, to make sure that all is ready for the big event Tuesday and Wednesday at Speedway Park. Meanwhile, the outside competition is starting to flow and by Tuesday at least 10 of the top dogs from British Columbia, Washington, Oregon and Colorado are expected to be here, ready to take a run at the gold and the glory.

The two leading point men in the Canadian American Modified Racing Association, which sanctions the Matan event, will be here: Bill Crow of Boise, Idaho and George Robertson of Lewiston, Idaho. In addition, Al Smith and Billy Foster of Victoria will be in from Victoria; Mel Keen and Ralph Monhay of Vancouver; Don Walker of Seattle; Jim Malloy of Denver; Bud Gorder of Spokane, and a few others will be in action, including Ray Pottinger of Nanaimo, B.C.

Though running on a limited budget and schedule, Eldon finished seventh at the end of CAMRA's 1963 season. Billy Foster was the series' first champion, followed in order by Bill Crow and George Robertson.

During Eldon's limited CAMRA season in 1964, there was one controversy involving he and Foster. It occurred during qualifying for the Edmonton Gold Cup. An article written by Gary Cooper of the *Edmonton Journal* explained:

Rasmussen Clocks Fast Time, But Gold Cup Pole Goes to Foster

The name of this piece might be: Was it Fact or Fiction? Or: This May Be The Electronic Age, But Are We Ready For It? The question is: Did Eldon Rasmussen actually turn a time of 13.46 seconds over the quarter-mile Speedway Park oval in Tuesday night's Gold Cup 200 time trials? An expensive electronic time clock said he did.

Race officials said he didn't. Speedway timers looked his times over, determined the round implausibly fast in comparison, and decided the clock mechanism somehow must have been tripped manually by mistake. The time was wiped out. As a result, defending Gold Cup champion Billy Foster of Victoria, B.C., pocketed $300 first prize money in fast time competition.

The Edmonton driver had to settle for $150 second-place money and the distinction of sharing the new Speedway Park track record of 13.64 seconds with Foster.

Both Foster and Rasmussen hit 13.64 seconds, smashing the old mark of 13.75 set just last July 8th by Jim Malloy of Denver, Colo., because he timed the 13.64 before Rasmussen. The rhubarb was the only incident to mar the time trials that saw 13 of the super-modified race cars time within nine-tenths of a second. Third-place money of $50 in the fast time purse went to Malloy, who turned 13.71. Just out of the money was Edmonton's Ray Peets, who wound up his Weldagrind Special for a 13.78.

Rasmussen arrived late for the trials. The gentlemanly little blonde and his mechanic brother, Arnold, had just replaced the head of the 327 cubic-inch Stedelbauer Special after discovering late in the afternoon that a valve had damaged it. As usual, Rasmussen went along without argument on the official time trial ruling, although hard luck and mechanical breakdowns have been plaguing him all season. "I wouldn't want to take something I didn't earn," was his only comment.

Rasmussen and Foster

But he had his champions. Among the loudest in his support was Norm Ellefson, Eldon's number one track rival on the home course. "If it would have been one of the hot dogs from out-of-town, it would have gone down as a record, I'll lay odds," snarled Norman. "Who's to say that 13.46 is impossible? It doesn't take much to be a half-second faster or slower on a round. Eldon simply had a perfect round. His car was hot and he hit each of the corners perfectly," Ellefson expounds.

No stop watches were put officially into play to back up the electronic timer. One interested observer in the pit area, however, clocked Rasmussen in 13.51 on the lap and another had it 13.53. Foster ran five laps after the official qualification to further test the clock, and he pared his best time down to 13.61 seconds.

In an interview with this author, racer Norm Ellefson further explained the incident from his point of view:

"I think it was the second time Billy Foster was there for the Gold Cup. [Promoter] Percy Booth had to pay him appearance money, which made Booth choke a little. Eldon out-qualified Foster, so they wanted Eldon to go out again because they thought there was something wrong with the clocks. He goes out again and goes faster, so then they knew the clocks were wrong. Eldon is ready to go out a third time and I'm standing there thinking, 'what are you doing? You out-qualified the guy, so you get the money. Tell them you're not going out again – tell Foster to go back out and beat you.

But Eldon was going to go back out, so I took his helmet and hid it. He couldn't find it and I said I didn't know where it is. They finally found a screw-up in the clock and they paid Foster, so they wouldn't have to pay the local guy. That's just the way promoters worked – they're just different people.

It shot Eldon down. He goes home that night, takes his whole car apart and works on it all night. I thought, 'keep away from that car' because Eldon was faster than Billy."

In 1965 Eldon's schedule and resources allowed him to take part more successfully in the CAMRA series. That year he finished second overall in the season points championship behind Denver's Jim Malloy, while Bob Gregg of Vancouver, Washington, placed third. "That was my best year," Eldon says. "I ran more, missing only three or four races out of 36 events."

In 1966, Edmonton's Norm Ellefson won the first of his three CAMRA championships, ahead of Bob Gregg and George Robertson of Lewiston, Idaho. That year, Eldon placed sixth overall.

When not racing, Eldon continued to apply his fabrication expertise for many racing teams. He also served on the CAMRA Board of Directors and was President of the Edmonton Auto Racing Association for many years.

In 1967, Eldon was contacted by his friend Grant King, who needed Eldon's assistance at King's race shop in Indianapolis. As he recalls, "Grant King was instrumental in bringing me down to Indy. He called me in October and asked what I was doing. I told him I was building and selling cars. He said he had three sprint cars and a championship dirt car to build for customers before the end of March. Grant had a two-car garage behind his house. He wanted me to come down and help build those four cars."

"I said, 'Well Grant, I've got a pretty good job here.' I was the service manager at George Stedelbauer's auto dealership. He sponsored my car for $200 per race. He paid me even when I was on the CAMRA circuit. No matter where I ran, it didn't do him much good as a dealer because he wasn't located in those areas."

Eldon did move to Indianapolis. He said one of the reasons he didn't start racing himself on the Champ Car circuit sooner was because his engineering talents were much in demand. He was just too busy building, tuning, and repairing wrecked race cars for other teams and drivers.

In a 1975 interview with Ray Turchansky of the *Edmonton Journal*, Eldon spoke of that era: "The first few years in USAC were demoralizing. You'd work on Mario's [Andretti] car until 3 a.m. after he'd banged it up. When it did well, the chief mechanic got the credit and glory, so you ate a lot of crow."

Rasmussen updated cars for various teams while designing and building his own race cars. A visionary, Eldon built some of the first wings found on Championship Series cars. He designed the wing for Gary Beck's top-fuel dragster in 1972 that led to Beck's first Top Fuel U.S. Nationals victory. Eldon also engineered the first tall wing used by Top Fuel Champion Joe Amato. He designed and built the North American Ice Racing car for Hall of Fame member Tom Jones of Thunder Bay, not to mention the racing motorcycle and sidecar he built for Greg Cox and Bill Davidson of Ottawa in 1975.

According to records, Eldon's first USAC race as a driver took place at Trenton, New Jersey, in 1971. At age 34 he was behind the wheel of a Gerhardt/Offy. Suffering a crash on lap 134, he earned an 18th-place finish. Two years later, his second drive was at Texas World Speedway. In a Rascar/Foyt machine – a chassis of his own design powered by an A.J. Foyt-built Ford Indy V8 – he finished 13th.

Continuing with his Rascar/Foyt, Eldon took part in three USAC Champ Car events in 1974 – once at Pocono and twice at Michigan. His best finish was at Pocono, where he placed ninth.

Eldon's most active year in USAC was 1975 with seven races, including his first stab at the Indianapolis 500. He started the race from the 32nd position, but his run ended on the 125th lap as he was being lapped by Tom Sneva. At the time, Eldon was running in the 12th position.

As their cars went side-by-side in Turn Two, they touched wheels. Sneva did a barrel-roll over the nose of Rasmussen's car, becoming airborne and upside-down. Sneva's racer then rolled upright, hitting the outside wall and catch fence with the rear of the car.

Sneva's engine, gearbox, and rear-end were ripped from the chassis, leaving a huge flash of fire as the fuel and oil ignited in front of the spectator suites. The cockpit section continued down the track – flipping at least twice – and came to rest on the track right side up, then spun for several yards before coming to a rest facing backward.

Eldon stopped the next lap around, giving up a potential gain in prize money. "As it turned out, it was fruitless to stop," Eldon stated in a later interview. "I don't know whether it did Tom any good psychologically, but I just hoped most of the guys would do the same for me."

Miraculously, Sneva did not suffer serious injuries, except for burns to his face and hands. One month later, Tom Sneva was back racing.

Between 1975 and 1980, Eldon designed and built about 180 Ras-Car rent-a-racer cars for the Mario Andretti Grand Prix International tracks. "I sent the first 33 cars to Sydney, Australia," he remembers, "and another half-dozen to New Zealand. I was able to go over there a couple of times."

For many years Eldon maintained Rasmussen Racing Products in Indianapolis. He continued to be involved with – as he puts it – "anything on wheels." Among his many projects was building exhaust header systems for Indy cars and various types of pit equipment.

Eldon also knew Rudy Hoerr, whose USAC stock cars were driven by Billy Foster during 1965 and 1966. Reflecting on those days, Eldon recalled when Billy was named Rookie of the Year for that series at the end of the 1965 season.

"Billy had me come down for the end of the year banquet in Chicago," recalls Eldon. "It was a brand-new hotel. At the end of the night, Billy said, 'let's go to Indianapolis.' I had gone to Lansing, Michigan, to pick up a new Oldsmobile 98 for a customer in Edmonton. I had driven it to the banquet, so he and I jumped in for the trip."

"I'm driving, and we had gotten to Lebanon, Indiana, doing 90-95 mph most of the way – but I was getting too tired to continue. I pulled into this restaurant parking lot and Billy was sleeping in the back seat. I told him it was his turn to drive, so we swapped places. Next thing I knew he was driving by the Indianapolis Speedway and he says, 'here's the number one turn.'"

"There was a brand-new hotel that had just opened a few weeks before. We checked in and then went to this place about a block away. There was a guy who played both the piano and organ at the same time. His name was 'Dirty George'. He was fantastic and could really tell good jokes."

Eldon has been married to his wife Diane since 1959. They have four grown children – Michael, Marcene, Melanie, and Jeanine – along with several grandchildren.

(Photos courtesy of the Indianapolis Motor Speedway and Eldon Rasmussen Collection.)

Fittingly, Eldon was inducted into the Canadian Motorsports Hall of Fame in 2001.

TWENTY

Billy's Friends Remember – Norm Ellefson

Like many other Canadians born during the 1930s, Norm Ellefson became smitten with cars and speed at an early age. A native of Edmonton, Alberta, he remembered in one interview that: "When I was asked at five years of age what I wanted to be, I said 'I want to be a race car driver.' Where I came up with that idea in 1937 is a good question."

(Norm Ellefson Collection)

In the following decades, Norm Ellefson more than filled that boyhood dream. His competitive career began in 1954 at Calgary's Springbank Speedway and he raced sprint cars, super-modifieds, and NASCAR stock cars until 1980.

His many accomplishments as a driver of open-wheel racers include the Copper Cup in Edmonton and a win at the Minnesota State Fairgrounds. His biggest claim to fame, though, must be winning the

Canadian-American Modified Racing Association (CAMRA) title in 1966, 1967 and 1969. The only other driver to top Norm in that category was Doug Larson, who captured the CAMRA championship in 1975, 1977, 1978 and 1979.

Today a resident of Spokane, Washington, Norm Ellefson is still enjoying life at age 86. In recognition of a long and successful motorsports career, he was inducted into the Canadian Motorsports Hall of Fame in 2011, and the Inland Empire Motorsports Hall of Fame.

Norm enjoys telling the story of when it all began for him on a Saturday night in Calgary, Alberta, in August of 1954. "I was walking a girl home from a movie date and we stopped at the Whitespot restaurant for pie and coffee. I noticed a guy in white overalls walk to the middle of the intersection outside. He held up his hands to stop traffic and suddenly – like a bat out of hell – a couple of sprint cars went speeding by. I paid for the treats and ran outside, thinking 'where the hell did those cars go?'

Down at the other corner, there's another guy standing out there in the middle of the street also blocking traffic and 'zoom-zoom', the cars go by him. They're getting the cars ready for a race at Medicine Hat the next day – just running up and down the street, through a hospital zone, right across the street from a service station. Two blocks this way and two blocks that way, and a block north and south – that's about a half-mile.

So that night, I got to meet some of the 'boys'. By the way, I never saw the gal after that and don't even know how she got home", Norm chuckles.

Not long after, Norm noticed a local newspaper advertisement looking for race car drivers, as there was a speedway being built south of Calgary. "That was the break I was looking for," he says. At the time I worked for 'The Magic Shop' in Calgary and Sam Klein was my boss. It was a front for a bookmaking joint, and Sam was the head bookmaker. I said to him, 'We've got to get a car and put in on the race track. We'll have The Magic Shop race car.'"

Sam thought that was a great idea and asked Norm what kind of car he needed. "A 1935, '36 or '37 Ford," Norm said to his boss. "I don't care."

Norm continues, "Sam called a used car dealer down the street who was his buddy. This friend mentioned he had a '37 Ford sedan we could have for $100. Sammy says, 'Let's flip for it over the phone. If you win, I'll give you $200, and if I win, I get the car for free.' So they flipped, and Sam won – we got the car for nothing.

"My folks were both deceased, and I was on my own since I was 14 years-old. My sister and brother-in-law, Ray Basset, lived in Calgary and he was a boilermaker. I said to him, 'Ray, we're going to go racing'. He was a hell of a welder. I told him we've got to have a grille guard and roll bar put in this car by Labor Day, so he said to bring it over on Sunday morning to the shop he worked at. About three hours later, he had the crash guard and roll bar installed."

In Gerald Hodges' book *Early Supermodifieds, Volume IV*, Norm described his first race at Springbank Speedway on Labor Day weekend in 1954:

"It was a real zoo. No one knew what was going on. We just went out and raced whenever they called our number (5). At the end of the day, we were standing around BS'ing and I asked the guy who was pitted next to us whether we got any money for this. His name was Phil Kurley and he said, 'Let's go see.'

Down by the start-finish line was a group standing around yelling out car numbers. I hollered out '5'. The guy took a minute figuring and said, 'You won $75.' WOW! Here I've got a $100 car and just won $75. How easy was that? Little did I know how tough the road would be to become a racer."

Ellefson letting it all hang out, circa' 1956.

(Barrie Goodwin photo)

"We raced Tuesday and Friday nights that fall until Thanksgiving Day, October 12th, in Canada and I did all right," Norm recalled. I was lucky though, because by that time, George LeMay returned from the IMCA (International Motor Contest Association) circuit and I was running his number 5. He watched me and then decided to take me under his wing and 'shape me up' – as he put it. He taught me the basics of being a racer, about engines, and most importantly, about chassis set-ups."

From that point forward Norm Ellefson drove cars for several owners, achieving many wins and local championships. In the late 1950s he hooked up with Zane Feldman from Crosstown Motors in Edmonton. Feldman was losing his driver, Richard 'Kid' Klatt, who was moving to the United States. Norm's good racing buddy, Eddie 'Tiger' Matan, gave Norm the nickname 'The Crosstown Cowboy.'

The combination of Ellefson and Feldman proved successful and the pair won many races together. Their first notable victory was 'The Matan 100', a race honoring Tiger Matan who had recently lost his life in a boating accident. "I still have the gold ring from that win," Norm told Gerald Hodges. "I also won it twice more in my career."

Another big win for Ellefson and Feldman came in 1960 at the Edmonton Gold Cup race in their car which was powered by a 292 cubic-inch Ford V8. During the race the engine dropped not one, but two cylinders. Norm soldiered on for the win on just six cylinders in front of the largest crowd ever seen at the track.

1960 - Norm and his crew celebrating a big win at the Edmonton Gold Cup race.

(Brian Pratt Collection)

Ellefson Comes Up Strong; Threatens Hornet's Hold

Norm Ellefson served notice before 2,000 fans last night that he wasn't to be fooled with at Speedway Park stock car battles. He had his brand-new Number 5A out at last week's 100-lap Matan Memorial run, but didn't get a chance to show, leaving after 17 laps with mechanical troubles.

But last night he was out – and running – and stopped previous runaway driver Eldon Rasmussen of Hinton without, it seemed, pushing the limit. He won the two A-Class races he entered and came up against Rasmussen – late in arriving – the second time out.

With only John McEachern, filling in admirably for George Stevens, and Doug Pescod filling the rest of the lineup, Rasmussen and Ellefson made it a two-way thing for all the nine laps, McEachern hanging to third until dropping back half-way through. With Ellefson quickly grabbing the lead, Rasmussen bit into second, making a frantic bid on the last lap but wiggling wide on the fourth corner and coming across the line three lengths back.

In the feature, brother Arnold Rasmussen, mechanic and co-sponsor of Eldon's Hornet, turned all the way to victory with Shell serviceman Jim Baker coming in second.

In 1961, for an Edmonton publication, Norm wrote a personal perspective on what it was like winning the Gold Cup in 1960:

First of all, for the record, let me say it was a pleasure – as it has been this year – driving in front of the wonderful turnouts we've been getting from you fans.

Now, back to last year's Gold Cup. You'll remember, of course, how it went? How Cliff Spaulding, the little guy from Seattle, came up here, was touted the favorite, but didn't make it because his machine gave out. I was lucky to limp home.

And I've never had the sensations I had in that race. If you think pushing a stocker is easy, brother, try it for 200 laps – 50 miles around and around, with 800 corners straining at your machine and a number of other drivers straining at your skill. You hit this "highway hypnosis" where suddenly you just don't care. You get giddy, and you have to mentally slap yourself to snap out of it.

I know that, by the time the race was half over, my face was grimy, my eyes stung, my lungs were full of exhaust fumes and my hearing was all but gone from the constant roaring. I was singing as loud as I could to keep my brain active – or as much of it as ever is active, anyway. If any of my friends had seen me, they would have sworn I was drunk.

And, all the time, that pest Spaulding was on my heels. For a while, I pretended I was a fighter pilot in the war, screaming back to base, and Spaulding was my enemy, on my tail all the time and I had to keep him off. But this pretending has dangers – my mind started to wander so I began singing once again.

Then, suddenly, so suddenly it couldn't have happened, the race was over, and I had won. All I knew was that people were tugging me and I could feel a goofy grin. Then somebody handed me a trophy. The idea that I had won still hadn't sunk in.

As a matter of fact, that night I went right home and slept for hours. Then, half-way through the next day's activities, I suddenly realized I had won the Gold Cup. I realized that this was real, not a dream or a daze. It was a nice feeling and, by gol-dang, I'm not going to give up the trophy this year, no matter how many imports are brought in to run.

It looks too nice on the mantle.

Shortly thereafter, the team concluded they needed a better car to be more competitive with the racers traveling up from the Pacific Northwest region of the United States. Together with Bob Hissett, Norm traveled down to Portland, Oregon and bought a Mopar-powered, off-set modified racer from Benny Zackett.

Back in Edmonton the car performed well but was still lacking an edge in the big races. At the Gold Cup race in 1961, Ellefson started alongside pole-qualifier Art Pollard, but just couldn't keep up with the Roseburg, Oregon driver. Pollard's GMC-powered car, built by Rolla Vollstedt, won three Edmonton Gold Cup races – the first with Portland's Ernie Koch behind the wheel and then twice by Pollard.

When Vollstedt decided to sell the car, Ellefson and Feldman purchased it. "I wound up with that car after Art got tired of it – it was heavy and getting old," said Norm.

(Brian Pratt Collection)

"In Edmonton, it had ran our pants off. The mistake we made was putting a DeSoto Hemi in it – a good motor and good power – but it was like driving around with a huge rock in your pocket. It weighed about 250-pounds more than a Chevy small block. We bought the motor from Vollstedt, who was a shrewd dude. Every time you dealt with Rolla, you'd better have your hand over your wallet! We took the car to Portland and Ernie Koch and Keith Randol dropped in the engine and exhaust. We ran the car for about a year and a half, and then the engine blew."

Norm recalled that he first crossed paths with Billy Foster in Edmonton. "This kid comes up and hell, we'd never heard of him. He was out there smoking around in this white roadster he had. I thought the car was weird because every time he accelerated, the front of the car would lift in the air 3 or 4-inches. When he dropped off the throttle for a corner the car would settle down. I was so amazed at the movement in the car and how smooth he was – it was unbelievable!

My first year in the CAMRA series was 1963. It was a great training ground since we went to so many different races: Edmonton, Alberta to Salt Lake City, Washington, Oregon, Idaho and Vancouver Island. The miles we put in! The first time I went out of town to race was to Meridian, Idaho. It was like driving on an egg at that place, and Billy Foster drove around everyone. Everywhere he went, Billy opened eyes."

Ellefson has another recollection of Foster when, in 1966, about 30 Championship car teams and drivers traveled to the Mt. Fuji circuit outside of Tokyo, Japan for an exhibition race.

"Billy blew everybody off the track there, but then the vibration damper came off the front of the engine when he was in the lead – that's what ended his day. He would've won that thing hands down. With that failure, Jackie Stewart took over the lead and won the event."

Though he had been competing in the series for several years, Ellefson's breakthrough year came in 1966 when he captured his first CAMRA championship. He had teamed up with car owner Bob Morgan, who had purchased a new Jim Tipke-built roadster over the winter. They based their operation in Boise, Idaho because it was central to most of the tracks they would compete at.

Jim Tipke, who passed away in 2015 at the age of 77, was well known throughout the Pacific Northwest and beyond as one of the premier race car builders for more than 40 years.

Never advancing beyond a high school education, Jim learned basic car design by reading books on Formula One cars. Early in his racing career he drove one of his sprint cars, which was labeled a '12-cylinder beast' and boasted that he held the records for the highest flip and longest barrel-roll at the track in Monroe, Washington when a torsion-stop broke.

In 1965, in his home town of Spokane, Washington, he opened his own shop (Tipke Manufacturing) and began building sprint cars for customers. It was a full-service operation, which meant that he could fabricate, bend, weld, or cut just about anything a racer would need. His specialty was building super-modifieds that were raced around the country. He was noted for his rear-engine machines powered by off-set big block, fuel-injected Chevy engines. Among Tipke's notable customers in the early 1970s was the Sneva family of Spokane. Jim lent a helping hand on Tom Sneva's first Indy car in 1972.

Jim Tipke's imagination and skills went beyond just race cars. When Spokane held its World's Fair in 1974, he used his Chinese Pedi Cab as the prototype for an upgraded line of people-powered taxis that were featured at the Fair. They later used these innovative Pedi cabs in Seattle, Washington.

"Pretty soon I was getting orders from all over the country," Jim stated in an interview with Spokane's *Spokesman-Review* newspaper in 2015. "We built hundreds and hundreds of them, and I became the Pedi Cab king."

Jim Tipke 1938 – 2015

(Photos courtesy of the Tipke Family)

Tipke Manufacturing also created the unique 'Fold it' cart, which he described in the same interview. "My wife wanted me to build her a wooden cart for the garden. I said, 'I'll make a metal one that you can fold up, so you can store it in the garage.' That was in 1987 and today they're hotter than ever. We'll sell 4,000 of those this year."

Before his passing, Tipke enjoyed restoring old cars and had quite a collection which included two 1922 tour busses from Glacier National Park - one of which he purchased when he was just 18 years-old.

"The car that got me the break belonged to Bob Morgan," Norm Ellefson recalls. "I got a ride with Morgan in Salt Lake City. My first drive in the car and I won that night. From then on we did some pretty good stuff with that car. But at a later race in Salt Lake, Dick Simon put me into the fence. I hit the fence, came off the Armco barrier and I still had my leg in it and went back into the fence again. They said my head came out the front of the car – I hit that hard! I was really messed up, my head and my back. I went home to Edmonton after that."

After a winning season for Ellefson and Morgan, the big event on the 1966 calendar was at Meridian, Idaho. Norm was locked in a tight point battle with Bob Gregg, George Robertson and Ralph Monhay. In the end, Norm came home the victor in the main event to capture the season title.

Ellefson duplicated his CAMRA championship in 1967 and 1969. An article that appeared in the *Edmonton Journal* newspaper during that time did a nice job in summing up a few of Norm's accomplishments:

A former Edmonton stock car racing driver, Norm Ellefson, made a shambles of the Edmonton International Speedway oval records during the 1968 season. Stormin' Norman breezed to victories in both Edmonton dates – the Matan and Gold Cups – in the Canadian American Modified Racing Association calendar. Ellefson, who holds the hope of someday driving in the USAC Indy 500, accomplished both victories with unprecedented class. He races out of Spokane, Wash.

In both events, he qualified first with record times. In the July Matan Memorial, Ellefson knocked the track record of three years for a loop, lowering it from 13.56 seconds to 13.27. Then, in the August Gold Cup, Stormin' Norman drove his Chevy-powered roadster around the quarter-mile banked oval in 13.18, which worked out to a fantastic 84-mph average speed. The second fastest qualifier in the Gold Cup was Tony Mortel of Victoria, B.C., in 13.33 seconds.

For Ellefson, it was his third Matan and second Gold Cup victories, and he became only the fourth driver in the 16-year history of the events to win both in one season. Two other double winners, the late Billy Foster of Victoria and Jim Malloy of Denver, made it into the big-time USAC circuit. Ellefson went on to win his third CAMRA driving championship.

It was in that era that Norm had a faint opportunity to attempt a try at the Indianapolis Motor Speedway. "We were in Victoria for the Labor Day CAMRA show – the Daffodil Cup," he told author Gerald Hodges. "Eldon Rasmussen had invited Jim Hayhoe, a Championship car owner, up to watch him drive. Unfortunately for Eldon, I won the races in Victoria and Nanaimo that weekend. Hayhoe congratulated me and told me he would give Rolla Vollstedt a holler about me, since he (Hayhoe) already had a driver who was Bruce Walkup. That fall, I got a call from Vollstedt, who would be in Spokane on business and wanted to talk."

When Vollstedt arrived, he met with Ellefson and his wife, along with Don Wilbur. Wilbur was a local friend of Norm's, and an associate sponsor for his car.

The hitch was that in offering Norm a ride in Vollstedt's Championship Car, Ellefson would have to pony up $2,000 every time he jumped into the cockpit. Lacking those funds, Norm and Wilbur tried to raise the money in Spokane, but there was no support. That ended that deal.

Norm had an opportunity, though not as a driver, to take part in the 1968 running of the Indy 500. As he explained, "One day I was down in Portland and I stopped by Jim Hayhoe's shop in Vancouver, Washington, to see what the heck he was doing. Sure enough, he was there and had race cars, but everything was at a standstill. I asked him what he needed, and he said he needed a metal man."

"I told Hayhoe to call Jim Tipke, and Hayhoe asked who the hell was Jim Tipke? I talked to Jim and they put together a deal. Tipke came over and finished the cars, and then we went to the Speedway at Indy. Because I got him a connection, Hayhoe said he'd take me along, but I wouldn't be on the crew. He said I'd just be there, and he'd pay me a dollar a day. The reason he had to do that was in case there was an accident or something, I'd be covered by insurance."

Ellefson added, "I was just a gopher for the crew and that was fine by me. It opened my eyes. We were garaged right next door to STP (Andy Granatelli's team) and the Lotus cars with Art Pollard. It was just like home."

Following Indianapolis, Norm went on to Trenton, New Jersey with the team, but during that time Tipke went back home to Spokane.

"They pissed him off," says Norm. "The Brabbhams they had were just falling over in the corners. They had cameras on the car which were showing the body roll that was going on. Jim's in a meeting and said, 'why the hell don't you put springs in it, which is obvious. Also, an anti-roll bar.'

Hayhoe got a hold of him and said, 'don't you ever say anything like that – you're just a monkey here. You do what you're supposed to do – we don't want any input from you.' All Jim was trying to do was help, because he was a good chassis man – but they weren't listening."

A successful real estate developer, Jim Hayhoe loved racing and attended his first race in 1951. In 1967, at age 32, Hayhoe entered his first car in the Indianapolis 500. One year later, his Hayhoe/Offy finished the race in the sixth position in the hands of driver Ronnie Duman. In the following years, the Hayhoe Racing Enterprises team fielded cars for a number of drivers, including Art Pollard, Roger McCluskey and Bruce Walkup.

In the 1990's Hayhoe joined forces with the Target/Chip Ganassi Racing enterprise, which won the Indy Car championship with driver Jimmy Vasser. After a long bout with cancer, Jim Hayhoe passed away in 2010.

The Minnesota State Fairgrounds was holding an event in 1969 which was big, with 143 sprint cars vying to make the 44-car field. The event was held in four races – three 50-lap features and then the most important 200-lap main event.

Ellefson won the first and second heats, placed fourth in the third race, and captured the win in the Golden State 200. Ellefson and Tipke certainly opened a lot of eyes with this success! They accomplished this with a traditional roadster.

One light-hearted perspective of Norm was offered by Tom Burnett, a staff writer for the *Spokane Spokesman-Review* in the late 1960s:

Norm Ellefson and Racing: He Knows What It's About

Norm Ellefson comes on like, say, a small-town grocery store owner or maybe the guy you would want on the other end of a telephone for advice on the best way to water a lawn or change a spark plug. He is personable, genial, and, where some of the big names in racing do not know one end of a wrench from another, Ellefson knows the inner workings of a race car. The grease under his fingernails came from fabricating parts and not from scratching the top of the work bench.

It all changes when he pulls tight his shoulder harness and squeezes into the cockpit of a race car. In a race car, he is far from a grocer, the nice guy next door; he is a professional race driver – probably the only one in the Spokane area.

When Ellefson is racing, he is paying his bills. If he doesn't win, he doesn't eat. He knows that. "Yes, I remember one time when we were racing at Phoenix, Arizona, a time that if I didn't win that day, I couldn't pay the motel bill. "Oh yes, I won so we came out of that situation in good shape."

Also, in a race car, Ellefson is fulfilling a dream he has had since childhood, since he was five years old. "At home in Calgary, Alberta, there were no race tracks, no cars, nobody that knew much about racing. Yet I wanted to race.

"My first race, now there's a story. Saw an ad in the newspaper for race drivers. That ad said something to the effect that some outfit was planning a race track in Calgary and wanted race drivers to run the track." At the time, Ellefson had just turned 18. "Anyway, I saw a shot at racing. I showed up at the track, showed up in my 'flying' 1937 Ford. Couldn't be too choosy in those days – any car was a race car. You just kicked out the glass and put on a helmet."

"After the races, there were a bunch of us drivers standing over a car when somebody said that a track official was asking the names of the various drivers. Well sure, I hollered out my name and this fellow walked over to me with $75, my winnings for the day. First money I'd ever won!"

"That was it. I was sold on racing. It's been my bag, my thing ever since. I'm just not happy doing anything else. I've had to quit a couple of real good jobs because they did not allow my time for racing." Ellefson remained at Calgary for years, until the track was sold and turned into a gravel pit.

He next raced at Edmonton from 1957 until 1964. In 1964, he joined the CAMRA (Canadian American Modified Racing Association) tour. He finished tenth overall in 1964, fifth in 1965 and first in 1966 and 1967. In 1968, Ellefson made his first trip to Indianapolis as a pit crew member along with Jimmy Tipke. The two have worked together since.

Just last week, Tipke completed the $16,000 race car that Ellefson will drive in upcoming races at the Spokane Interstate Fairgrounds as well as tracks throughout the western United States. The modified is a one of its kind, by virtue of being almost hand-built by Tipke. Ellefson, like the growing number of drivers who run Tipke creations, has only praise for the winning car builder. "When you're out there at 110 miles-per-hour down a straight or hanging around a turn, you want to be in the best of equipment," he said.

Before the new car, yet within the confines of this racing season, Ellefson has finished either first or second in 90 percent of the races he's entered. Ellefson wants only one additional satisfaction out of motor racing – a shot at Indianapolis. This trip, he wants to go as a driver; a driver of a Tipke race car.

Beware of Norm Ellefson!

Watch out for Norm Ellefson Friday and Saturday night at the Canadian American Modified Racing Association Intermountain Championships at Salt Lake Fairgrounds Speedway! "We've had some great drivers such as the late Billy Foster, Art Pollard and Jim Malloy graduate from our circuit to the Indianapolis 500, but all things being equal I think Norm could out-drive any of them," CAMRA president Bob Morgan says.

Ellefson and 12 other drivers from the CAMRA circuit will be competing against some 40-50 local pilots in the two-night event this weekend. Ellefson is the third-leading point winner so far this season on the CAMRA circuit, despite the fact that he hasn't been able to race in all the CAMRA events due to other commitments. "He has a comparatively small (318 cubic-inch) engine in his car, but just watch him get the most of it," Morgan continues.

At a CAMRA race in Boise last weekend, Ellefson started next to last in a field of 16 as a handicap for his good qualifying time. In the first four laps on a one-third mile track, he passed 11 cars. "He was passing them so fast it was hard to keep track," Morgan opined. Ellefson's top win so far this season was a victory in the Billy Foster Championship 100 race last month in Victoria, British Columbia.

Foster, mentioned above as one of the top driving prospects to ever come out of the CAMRA circuit, was killed three years ago in a stock car in California.

Top CAMRA drivers (in addition to Ellefson) who will be in town for the Intermountain Championships include: Bob Gregg, Ralph Monhay, Bud Gorder, Chuck Neitzel, Brent Nyborg, Tony Mortel, Glen Naylor, George Robertson, Bill Schornhurst, Errol DeBock, Frank Weiss and Dusty Nelson.

Top point winner on the circuit is Monhay of Vancouver, B.C., with 520 points. Portland's Gregg, Salt Lake Intermountain Championship winner last year, is second with 465 points. Ellefson has 416 points.

The CAMRA circuit returned to Salt Lake for a second showing the following August, with Ellefson scoring a close victory over Portland's Bob Gregg. On August 11th, 1969, this article was published in the *Desert News*:

Copper King: Ellefson!

You can't blame Canadian American Modified Racing Assn. driver Bob Gregg if he's just a little bit disappointed today. Gregg, a veteran racer who drove at Indianapolis in 1956, was presented his second consecutive Copper Cup championship trophy Saturday night at the Fairgrounds Speedway amid an impressive ceremony.

Only thing is, Gregg didn't end up being the winner. Eight points garnered in qualifying by current CAMRA points leader Norm Ellefson turned up at the very last minute, giving the Spokane racer a paper-thin, six-point victory margin over Gregg.

The victory was worth $750 to Ellefson, while Gregg's second-place money ended up being $643.90 He turned in a record-tying 13:91 qualifying time and then came from the back of the pact in the A-Main to capture the lead on the 39th lap and win the 50-lap event going away.

Brent Nyborg finished second in Saturday night's action, with Tony Mortel third and Gregg fourth. Gregg had finished first in Friday night's half of the action.

In 1971, Ellefson returned to the Minnesota fairgrounds with an unconventional, rear-engine car with a small block Chevrolet V8 built by Jim Tipke. In a 2006 interview with the *Spokane Spokesman-Review*, Ellefson said, "Because we had such a small engine, I talked Tipke into taking the clutch and starter out. 'Throw all that crap away,' I told him."

"In those days that was the biggest sprint car race in the nation, before the World of Outlaws", Ellefson continued. "Anybody who was anybody was there. We had been back there in 1969 and blew 'em away with our roadster. The first three days of the 1971 event, and driving the only rear-engine entry, the Ellefson and Tipke car was so dominant, "We turned into a target," Ellefson said.

In the big race on the half-mile oval, Norm encountered "a big, bloody oil slick", spun the car and stalled the engine.

Lacking a starter, he had to wait for a push truck to get back underway but lost five laps. His right rear tire was flat, which demanded a pit stop.

"When I came back out, I'm on a mission", he stated in the newspaper's interview. "By the 100th lap, we were back in the third spot after being down seven laps."

Following another caution flag period, Norm saw his chance to take the lead. As he was trying to pass the first and second-place drivers, he tangled with another car and stalled again. "They left me sitting there for 11 laps that time."

When the checkered flag flew, Ellefson was credited with a third-place finish after gaining back 18 laps of the 100-lap race. "It was unbelievable how fast we were."

Following the Minnesota event, they brought the Tipke car back to the Northwest for further successes.

Ellefson and crew at the 1972 CAMRA Daffodil Cup with Jim Tipke's Super Modified.

In the *Spokane Spokesman-Review* interview, Norm stated, "We won quite a few races with it. It was just an awesome car. The last race Tom and I had together, I beat him in it."

While they were in Minnesota, Norm and his friend and sponsor, Don Wilbur, were spectators at the local stock car race. "We went to the race there and what I noticed was that the grandstands were packed, but during the sprint car races the stands were about half-full. I thought, 'the super-modifieds are done – there's no way to go.' I didn't think there was any way they (the modifieds) had any future."

"So I told Wilbur, 'if you want to go racing, you have to have a stock car.' When we got back to the Northwest, he came up with a stock car and he and I went racing with that – I quit driving the modifieds."

Don Wilbur built a 1971 Chevrolet Monte Carlo for local and Winston West competition, of which Norm said, "We thrashed with that thing all year, but it was never where I wanted it to be. We got a couple of third-place finishes with it in Winston West, but nothing outstanding. I only remember winning one main event with it."

In an article that appeared in the *Spokane Daily Chronicle* in early April of 1973, Norm talked about his move into the stock car ranks:

Norm Ellefson figures he just "was never in the right place at the right time." Tom Sneva hopes to be.

Ellefson, who was never able to parlay his virtual domination of sprint car racing in the Inland Northwest into a shot at the big time, has forgone that area this year to concentrate on the late-model super stock circuit in hopes of "moving up," so to speak. The transplanted Canadian, who has divided his time between the modified open-wheeled cars and super stocks the last couple of years, and enjoyed success in both, will handle only a super stock this season – a 1971 Chevrolet Monte Carlo for Don Wilbur and the "Mr. Midas" team. They'll debut tomorrow afternoon when the 1973 stock car racing season gets underway at the Interstate Fairgrounds.

By that time young Sneva, a school teacher who has risen to driving on the United States Auto Club's championship car circuit, should have an indication of what 1973 has in store for him and the Tipke Offenhauser. The Spokane racer is in College Station, Texas, for today's running of a 200-mile USAC championship race. Sneva qualified the big orange machine in 18th spot among the 26 starters at an average speed of 188 miles per hour.

Ellefson agrees there's no comparison between driving a sprint car and a super stock. "Sprint cars are so much faster," he says. "But I believe I exhausted my avenues in the sprint department," said the fellow who was three-time champion of the Canadian American Modified Racing Association circuit. "I won all the big races that there were and won CAMRA three times," he notes. "That should be a springboard to something bigger, but it wasn't. I was never in the right place at the right time. So, we'll try this route and see how it goes."

Ellefson, whose Chevy is powered by a 390 cubic-inch engine, said the car "is NASCAR legal" and will be competing on NASCAR's Western Grand National circuit when it is not racing in Spokane. "We'll go over there (to the coast, where NASCAR races are primarily held in the Northwest) and see if Hershel McGriff and some of those guys are as tough as they're supposed to be," he said, confidently. McGriff is one of the Western Grand National "hot dogs," as the top drivers are called.

But Norm admitted it won't be easy establishing himself or the car on that circuit. "Chevys just haven't done that well in the past, especially on the bigger tracks," he noted. "The Dodges had been dominating things until last year, when Bobby Allison won seven races nationally. But I've got a lot of faith in this car and crew," he said. "I think we'll do all right."

Ellefson said it will get a little hectic traveling around for races. "It's going to take some time on our part, but seeing that I just quit my job, I've got a lot of that. I'm ready to go racing."

Norm recalled one race at Yakima running against Hershel McGriff, the West Coast stock car king. "He was the big gun there. He knew Yakima like the back of his hand with that big Mopar he drove – he'd just drive away from everybody!"

Norm continued, "I was sick, so I told Don Wilbur to give Don Dowdy the car and see what he could do with it. He had new Goodyear tires, so he took the tires off his car and put them on ours and ran much quicker. His car was a Mopar and ours was a big-block Chevy, and he wasn't used to that much power – but he got us a new set of tires and we kicked their ass all over everywhere."

"So, we came back two weeks later, and they stopped us outside the gate and said we couldn't come in, because we had a big-block Chev with aluminum heads. We asked, 'where does it say we can't run aluminum heads?' They told us to go home and never come back again – we were essentially banned from Yakima. They said, 'it's OK to come here, but just don't go fast.'"

Ellison's final season of racing was in 1980 when he won the Northwest Super Stock Championship. He retired and never got back in a car until 19 years later.

"Just for a lark, I ran Tom Dory's 'Fever Four' Mustang for five races at Spokane Raceway Park," he told author Gerald Hodges. "I made the trophy dash every night, had fast time a couple of nights, and won the fast heat three times.

The last night I swept the program with fast time, won the trophy dash, fast heat, and the main event. Then I retired again."

Prepping for the 1971 Permatex 200 at Riverside International Raceway. Norm and his crew with Dick Midgely's Chevy Beaumont (a Canadian Chevelle). Ellefson managed 7 laps before falling out of the race. Victoria's Gary Kershaw won the event.

(Ted MacKenzie photo)

TWENTY-ONE

1964 – Billy's Debut in the Champ Car Series

Billy Foster's first taste of the big leagues of the USAC Championship Car Series came on August 23rd, 1964 at the Milwaukee Mile in West Allis, Wisconsin. He was drafted to be behind the wheel of the #27 Flynn/Offy, entered by Walt Flynn.

Flynn was the owner and operator of the Enterprise Machine Company in Indianapolis. An Army veteran of World War Two, he built and maintained race cars that participated in the Champ Car series, including the Indy 500. He had invented the Flynn racing carburetor and became a life-long member of the Old Timers 500 Club. Walt passed away in 2002 at age 86.

Credit Rolla Vollstedt for providing Billy the opportunity to "mix it up" with the outstanding drivers of that era. In his autobiography Rolla observed:

"I had another stroke of brilliance in '64. I hired Billy Foster! Grant King, my mechanic who came from Victoria, B.C., got Billy to drive an upright car in Milwaukee and Trenton for a fellow named Walt Flynn. That got Billy used to the Championship circuit."

The 'Tony Bettenhausen 200' at Milwaukee drew 26 entries, driven by the likes of A.J. Foyt, Mario Andretti, Parnelli Jones, Rodger Ward and the Unser brothers. Qualifying found Jones on the pole with his rear-engine Lotus/Ford, followed by Ward and Foyt. Billy would start the race from the 18th position.

Once the race began, Jones led the first 14 laps and then turned over the lead to Bobby Marshman. But then Marshman's Lotus/Ford went out on the 37th lap due to engine issues. Foyt made only one lap, dropping out with transmission woes.

From that point on to the checkered flag, Jones dominated for the win in the caution-free race. Ward finished second, two laps down to Jones, and Andretti completed 196 laps to finish third.

Foster was running at the end, credited with a 16th place finish after completing 181 laps. It would prove to be a good debut for the young Canadian driver. He had held his own against the "Big Guns".

The next opportunity for Billy and the Flynn/Offy took place on September 27th, a 200-lap tour of the one-mile paved oval at Trenton Speedway in New Jersey. He would again compete against the same crop of cars and drivers he first encountered at Milwaukee. Once again, the field was led by Parnelli Jones in the Team Lotus/Ford, who would start from the pole alongside Jim McElreath's Brabham/Offy entered by John Zink. Foster qualified 21st in the 26-car field but was optimistic about his chances.

Billy in Walt Flynn's Offy

(Photo courtesy of The Jalopy Journal)

By the end of the event, which averaged 96.415 mph, Jones was once again unapproachable and led 190 laps in gaining the win. Several spins and crashes during the race accounted for five caution flag periods, or 34 laps under the yellow. Finishing one lap down behind Jones was Don Branson in second place, while Bud Tingelstad finished third. Billy worked his way through the field during the afternoon, completing 193 laps, and crossed the finish line with a seventh-place result.

"I had another stroke of brilliance in 1964. I hired Billy Foster!" – Rolla Vollstedt.

(Author photo)

Foster's third race on the 1964 Champ Car calendar was the season's finale at Phoenix International Raceway. He qualified the Flynn/Offy in the 22nd position, but spun out of the race on the 32nd lap to only realize a 21st-place finish. A.J. Foyt started from the pole position but could only lead the first six laps. Parnelli Jones then led through the 39th lap but was sidelined by a faulty injector. Lloyd Ruby took over the lead in his Halibrand/Offy and held the position to the checkered flag.

When all the driver points were totaled up, A.J. Foyt claimed the 1964 Championship, 772 points ahead of Rodger Ward, who placed second. In thirteen races, Foyt won an astonishing ten events and earned $220,271 in prize money.

Foster raced in just three events, placing 31st on the season. Victoria's Eddie Kostenuk also raced in three events during 1964 - twice at Trenton and once at Phoenix - but scored no points.

There was one more story in Vollstedt's memoirs regarding Billy's first year in the Champ Cars:

"In the fall of '64, Goodyear was having a tire test at Phoenix. Len Sutton was not available, so with Goodyear's permission I got Billy Foster to drive at the test.

"I'll divert again to tell you a story about Billy. He had never driven in competition a rear-engine car. Lots of drivers had no rear-engine driving experience because there weren't many rear-engine cars around. He was driving during this tire test and there were two Goodyear engineers there at the time. One was Ed Long and the other was Ed Alexander; they were the two who worked with Championship cars.

Grant King and Art Pollard were my two mechanics there. This engineer, Alexander, came up with his pet tire, on which he had done a lot of the development work. He had Billy try this tire out after he had been testing other tires. Billy took one hot lap and then he came in and Alexander ran over, real excited, and wanted a grand report on the tire. He said, 'Billy, how was that?'

Tire testing at Phoenix (left to right): Art Pollard, Billy Foster and Grant King.

(Rolla Vollstedt Collection)

Billy said, 'Ed, those tires could kill me they're so bad!' Alexander said, 'Billy, do you think you're qualified to make a statement like that?'

And Foster says, 'If I'm not qualified to make a statement like that, then why in the hell are you paying me?'"

TWENTY-TWO

The 1965 Champ Car Season – First Half

In just three appearances in late 1964, Billy Foster had raised eyebrows in the Championship Car ranks of his potential entering the 1965 season. It was also clear that the new rear-engine chassis was the wave of the future, and Billy was becoming more acclimated to the nuances of driving this style of chassis.

As early as February 1965, there was a lot of talk in Victoria about Foster and Vollstedt's chances for success at Indianapolis, even though the race was several months down the road. Hal Malone, sports columnist for the *Victoria Daily Times*, addressed the subject in one of his columns:

Rolla Vollstedt walks the edge of a dream. He does not aspire to be president of the United States or chairman of U.S. Steel, or the guy who drew Jayne Mansfield on a blind date. All he wants is to be the designer and the manager of the winning car in the Indianapolis 500, auto racing equivalent of the chariot races Julius Caesar presided over at the Via Appia Speedway.

Vollstedt is a Portland, Ore., lumber operator who builds and races jet age buggies as an avocation. "Sometimes," Vollstedt was saying Monday, "I'm not sure whether cars aren't my job and the lumber business my secondary interest. My boss isn't sure either."

Last year Vollstedt almost had his paws on the 500 hardware, a massive mug stuffed with $153,000 for the winning jockey. A Vollstedt owned and driven car was in third place and humming when a $75 pump casting coughed it up.

"We had stripped the car, every bolt and nut, before the race. Some of the old parts went back in but we decided on a new pump. If we had put the old one in it might have made the difference between third place and 15th. Some difference. They pay $6,000 for 15th, $36,000 for third."

It is almost axiomatic that people who fall off mountains just when the summit is in sight return for another whack. Losing at Indy has had a similar effect on Vollstedt. He has the enthusiasm of a soap-box orator, the confidence of Dr. Norman Vincent Peale when he talks about "this year." This year, Vollstedt was telling a sedentary group of press, radio and TV men at the Pacific Club Monday, he will try with two cars. Len Sutton, a distinguished chauffeur, will pilot a new one. Billy Foster, the pride of Victoria's hit-the-pedal-and-let-'er-rip set, will guide the '64 chariot.

"I had three chances to sell last year's car," Vollstedt said. "But I'm selfish. I believe Foster has the potential to be a great driver and I'd like to share his success. So, I talked to some Victoria people who I thought might be interested in having the first Canadian car and Canadian driver at Indy. We formed Canadian Automobile Racing Enterprises Ltd., a private corporation. The car is valued at $24,000 and we're selling shares in the company." The corporate body (chairman, Reg Midgely) encouraging investments ($1,200 per share) in Foster, will bring Billy's buggy to Esquimalt Arena April 13. Thousands of art lovers who grow dewey-eyed at the aroma of exhaust fumes will likely stroke its pelt. It has been 18 years since the last Indy car, the City of Tacoma, passed through these portals.

Last year, after conducting clinics for drives in the Pacific Northwest, Foster was accepted by USAC (United States Auto Club), the ranking order of ground jet pilots. He was unplaced in three major races, squirting oil and spouting smoke with A.J. Foyt, Rodger Ward, Parnelli Jones, USAC aristocrats with heavy throttle feet and juicy bank accounts.

Rolla Vollstedt watched Foster at Milwaukee and he says: "Billy hadn't been in an Offenhauser before. He was peering into the cockpit as they unloaded it, trying to figure out what the knobs were for."

"As a race it wasn't much. Parnelli Jones won it so easily they called it the Jones' Benefit. The action was provided by Foster. His car came up with a cracked magneto early. Against other cars running properly, if not too fast, Foster would lose ground on the straight-away where you just push the button and hold on. But on every corner Foster would go in last and come out first. He was fantastic."

Foster's credentials appear in order, but what about Vollstedt's? Last year A.J. Foyt won the 500 in an A.J. Watson rear-engined Offenhauser. Watson is widely heralded as a drawing board genius, up there with Colin Chapman, the Britisher who imposed the rear-engined Lotus on the racing world.

Vollstedt knows Watson. "He called me long before the 1964 500," Vollstedt says. "He asked all about my design for a rear-engined Offy. I even sent him my drawings." Traditionally a front-engine Offy proponent, Watson converted to Vollstedt's concept, came up with an exact copy. Picking Vollstedt's brains, Watson and Company collected the gold and glory. Rolla didn't weep. What's $147,000, except money?

But Vollstedt twitched a little when the auto racing people made a post-Indy announcement. "For his rear-engine Offenhauser," they said, "A.J. Watson has been chosen designer of the year."

The first event on USAC's 1965 schedule was the 'Jimmy Bryan Memorial', a 150-lap race on March 28th on the one-mile paved oval at Phoenix International Raceway. For this event Foster was hired to drive an Eisert/Chevy for car owner J. Frank Harrison. Harrison was an early convert to the benefits of the European-style chassis and, with mechanic Jerry Eisert, had debuted their belief at a race in Trenton in 1963 when Lloyd Ruby took the pole in Harrison's 2.7-liter Lotus 18-Climax.

For the 1965 season, Harrison commissioned a brand-new, space-frame design from Eisert, based around a stock-block Chevy V8 engine. In its first appearance at Phoenix, it was listed as the #96 Harrison Special.

Eisert built his first sprint car in the early 1950s to race on the dirt tracks of California but following a bad accident, he gave up driving and focused on building cars. He would prepare sports cars, including Ferrari's, for car owners. Around this time in the early 1960s, Eisert began his long relationship with Dan Gurney when he designed a Lotus 19 that Gurney won the 1962 Daytona Continental race. Jerry was among the first designers to incorporate aerodynamic wings on Champ Cars and, in 1966, he received the Mechanical Achievement Award for his Indianapolis car.

The season-opener at Phoenix drew 24 entries, with the #1 Lotus/Ford of A.J. Foyt taking the pole position with a speed of 117.493 mph. The second and third starting positions went to Rodger Ward's Watson/Ford and Mario Andretti's Blum/Offy. Foster qualified in the eleventh position, sandwiched between Gordon Johncock and Roger McCluskey.

The race turned into an early disappointment for Billy, as he could only complete twelve laps before his engine went south. The remainder of the race was a fight between four drivers: Foyt, Ward, Andretti and Don Branson. Branson's Watson/Offy led the final 26 laps to take the win over Jim McElreath and Ronnie Duman.

It was a much better outing for Foster's Eisert/Chevy on April 25 at the next event on the one-mile paved track in Trenton, New Jersey. He qualified for the seventh position in the 22-car field, while Foyt would again start the race from the pole. Jim McElreath, starting second, led the first three laps before giving up the lead to Foyt over the next 28 laps, who then suffered a broken axle.

The month of May was now approaching, and every team and driver's focus now turned to the 1965 running of the Indianapolis 500 – and Billy Foster's rookie year at the Brickyard.

TWENTY-THREE

Key Members of the Vollstedt Champ Car Team

Grant King played a major role during Billy Foster's racing career. Starting at an early age, King became a master race car designer, fabricator and mechanic, who spent his life custom-building over 250 successful racing machines.

Grant was born in 1933 in Victoria. The son of Chinese parents, his family had relocated to British Columbia from China, in search of a better life during the Depression era. The youngest of nine children, Grant learned to speak both Chinese and English as a child.

His father, who had been a professor in China, worked as a cook on a steamship while his mother maintained the household. Though now living in North America, the family continued to observe many Chinese traditions.

As a teenager, King became obsessed with race cars while working in his older brother Len's garage. In one interview Grant recalled, "He [Len] taught me the trade. One day a customer of Len's brought a sprint car to store in the garage over the winter. The minute the next season opened, I went with them to help run the car. I was still in school at the time and in machine shop class. Instead of making screwdrivers and chisels like everyone else, I was making race car parts."

King became a regular at Victoria-area tracks such as Langford, Shearing, and Western Speedway. He built his first race car at the age of 18, which was raced by a Chinese driver named Bung Eng. That first car led to an ever-evolving succession of racing machines that were driven by renowned drivers from the Pacific Northwest.

Beginning in 1950, King worked with local driver Bob Simpson and the pair collaborated to win many races. In August 1955, this article by Bill Rayner appeared in the *Victoria Daily Times*:

Grant and Bob, They're Partners

Grant King builds them and Bob Simpson drives them. That is the basis for a deep friendship that began in 1950 and that has developed a Victoria combination into one of the most respected big-car racing teams in the Pacific Northwest.

Bob Simpson, who has been race driving since 1947 at the old Langford Speedway, has been catching most of the headlines. He does the winning while King waits between races to do his vital work. The two got together at Langford after Simpson had a bad accident while driving for Gene Fanning of Seattle. The mishap, the worst of his career, put Simpson in the hospital for a month and a half with one ear torn off and a triple skull fracture. Simpson was only out of the hospital two days when he placed second in a championship race. He's been driving with notable success ever since.

Racing as far east as Boise, Idaho and south to San Francisco, Simpson has won numerous heat races and the not infrequent main event. Simpson has raced against such well-known drivers as Eli Vukovich, brother of the late Bill Vukovich of Indianapolis fame, Cal Niday and Shorty Templeman. He beat Niday and Templeman in 1949 by coming in third in a 100-miler at Portland. A main event win against top opposition at Ferndale, California in 1951 is also on Bob's list.

In Canada, where he is regarded as the best sprint-driver in the West, if not the Dominion, Simpson has taken the point championship at Langford in 1950, Shearing's Speedway in 1952 and Western Speedway in 1954.

Bob Simpson

(Victoria Auto Racing Hall of Fame)

In the background, however, is affable Grant King, who has been fashioning racing cars ever since the end of World War II. His present sprint car is the second one tooled for Simpson and was built in 1953. It is of all-aluminum construction, with a full GMC motor. King built every inch of it himself from his own design.

The car, which burns methanol, not gasoline, has never been officially clocked at its top speed, but recently at Yakima, where Simpson was racing and beating 270 Offenhausers and Indianapolis cars, it averaged 120 mph on a 1-1/8th mile track.

And that reasonably rapid speed could be getting too much for 32-year-old Simpson and he may heed the advice of his wife and hang up his helmet. He runs his own logging concern as a more prosaic sideline, and thrills like flipping 12 feet in the air and seeing another racer flash by under him at Langford in 1950 may give way to strictly wrestling with a logging truck.

On the other hand, 25-year-old King, who also owns his own business, an auto repair service, plans to keep on turning out sleek machines. And he will have the GMC ready Saturday night at Western for Simpson when the big car meet gets underway.

Does Grant drive himself? No thank you, says he, he will leave that part up to fellows like Bob Simpson.

After the 1956 season, King purchased the Rolla Vollstedt-built roadster that driver Len Sutton had great success with over several years. That car – a 1925 Model T-bodied track roadster – was powered by a 12-port, Horning-head, GMC engine. This powerplant provided much more horsepower than the iconic flathead Ford V8 that was popular during that time.

Beginning in 1958, King teamed with driver Dick Varley, and this combination won many more races with their 'Kersey Peanut Butter Special.'

In Rolla Vollstedt's autobiography *The Rolla Vollstedt Story*, King recalled:

"When I was a kid, I went to the race tracks and hung around the cars. I figured I could learn something and maybe build a better one. I remember Rolla caught me looking over his car one day. I was making a sketch of the back end. He hollered at me to get out of there. I kept hanging around and eventually he gave me some jobs to do."

In 1961, Grant began designing and building his own 'Kingo' go-karts while still working with Bob Simpson and the sprint car. 1963 found Grant constructing five new super-modified racers at the old Gordon Head Community Hall owned by Geoff Vantreight. The cars were some of the first upright, offset sprint/modifieds that were ever constructed and they had quite illustrious careers throughout the Pacific Northwest. The #7 'Daffodil Special' was campaigned for many years around Victoria by Al and Roy Smith.

King continued to expand his reputation for various roadsters, sprint cars, and modifieds that were both fast and beautiful. One of his achievements was a sprint car he built in the early 1960s for Art Sugai of Ontario, Oregon. This car – known as the 'Pink Lady' – although somewhat modified, was still winning in the 1990s.

King moved to Portland, Oregon in 1963 to work for car owner and builder Rolla Vollstedt. He was part of a small team building Rolla's innovative rear-engine Offenhauser-powered car for Indianapolis – to be driven by Portlander Len Sutton.

While a member of Vollstedt's crew, King could build upon his mechanical skills. In November 1963 the team packed up the car and headed to Indianapolis for a Goodyear tire test. Bob Sowle was part of the crew and tutored Grant on the inner-workings of an Offenhauser engine during an overnight engine rebuild. The following day Sutton ran a fast lap of 154.5 mph around the Speedway.

In an interview years later with Fritz Frommeyer of *Vintage Motorsports Magazine*, King recalled that Sutton was:

"So happy he jumped for joy. A.J. Foyt, Clint Brawner, and everyone else who was there wanted to see our car. I owe a lot to Rolla Vollstedt and to Bob Sowle. They introduced me around and showed me the ropes. Rolla races the same way I have always raced – by working out of his own pocket."

Sutton qualified the #66 Offy eighth on the grid for the 1964 '500' with an average speed of 153.813 mph. By the halfway stage of the race, Len had worked the car up to the fourth position, but then a broken fuel pump sidelined the car on the 140th lap. The result was a 15th-place finish. A week later, at the Milwaukee Mile, Sutton drove the car to a second-place finish behind winner A.J. Foyt.

One year later and piloting the same car, Billy Foster would be a rookie at Indianapolis.

Grant elected to move to Speedway, Indiana and established his first race shop. At the same time, designer/builder A.J. Watson was building his own shop right next door.

During the second half of the 1960s, King also served as a mechanic for Rolla Vollstedt, sponsor Jim Robbins and Andy Granatelli. He was the chief mechanic for fellow Northwesterner Art Pollard's two Championship Car victories in 1969 – at Milwaukee and Dover – in Granatelli's familiar STP-sponsored racers. While the Milwaukee car was Offenhauser-powered, the winning car at Dover was powered by a stock-block Plymouth engine, the one and only time that specific V8 would score a victory.

Many of the contacts King gained working in the Pacific Northwest would prove valuable during his long involvement with the Indianapolis 500. One result was his association with several drivers from the region when they were rookies at the Brickyard – Billy Foster, Art Pollard, Jim Malloy and Tom Sneva.

The *Vintage Motorsports* article added:

Working with each of these rookies was especially rewarding for Grant, but he seems to have the greatest respect for Foster and Sneva. 'They were super personalities,' Grant explains. 'They were fast, and they made no phony excuses. A lot of drivers can go fast but they cannot pass another car in a race. Both of these guys were passers. They were easy to work with and they had no hang-ups. They got in a race car and could squeeze every mile-per-hour out of it."

In 1970 Art Pollard partnered with businessman John Newcomer, President of Race-Go, Inc., to form a new endeavor called 'The Art Pollard Car Wash Systems' team. For this effort, Grant King designed and built an Offenhauser-powered racer for Pollard and would serve as Chief Mechanic. Driver Greg Weld was brought onboard to pilot a second car, though that would be a Gerhardt/Offy.

The first Kingfish/Offy made its debut at the Trenton 200 in late April 1970. Pollard qualified the car 12th but completed only 22 laps before dropping out because of ignition problems. This race was merely a tune-up for the month of May and the Indy 500.

During qualifying for the '500', Pollard had an outstanding run with the #10 car by setting the sixth-fastest time and would start the race on the outside of the second row. Weld's #93 Gerhardt/Offy struggled with speed and placed 28th on the field.

In the race, Weld's car fell out after just twelve laps due to a broken suspension. Meanwhile, Pollard had worked his way up to the third position and was charging hard, but a piston let go on the main straight, cutting short his hopes for a strong finish.

Following Al Unser's first victory at Indy, it turned out to be a disappointing month for the team and Grant King. Pollard finished 30th and Weld 32nd. Their combined earnings amounted to just $28,000.

One week later, it was a one-car effort for the Pollard Car Wash Team at the 'Rex Mays Classic' at Milwaukee, Wisconsin. Pollard qualified the King/Offy 12th-fastest, but in the race he only lasted until lap 119 when an oil leak took him out of the running. It amounted to an 18th-place finish and just $119 in earnings.

Soon after Milwaukee the team disbanded, and the partners went their separate ways. The enterprise was economically starved.

Grant's love of designing and building race cars never faltered, and his Grant King Racers shop in Indianapolis was kept very busy. He and his crew would build hundreds of race cars during the business' lifetime and he left indelible marks in midget, sprint, and championship car racing. It is estimated that King and his small crew produced over 250 complete cars – no 'kits' – and many of his cars were shipped overseas for racing.

Grant once said, "It's enjoyable to create something from a piece of raw material, form it into the shape of a race car, and watch it go around the track. It's a real thrill when you do this yourself."

King-built cars won championships with the United States Auto Club (USAC), the International Motor Contest Association (IMCA), and countless outlaw circuits. These cars were raced by many famous open-wheel drivers including Pollard, Foster, Bob Gregg, Tom and Jerry Sneva, Ken Hamilton, Tom Bigelow, Rich Vogler, Mario Andretti, Al Unser, Sr., A.J. Foyt, Sheldon Kinser, Steve Krisiloff, Greg Weld, Jim Malloy, Billy Vukovich, Gary Bettenhausen, George Snider and Bentley Warren – just to name a few.

1969 – Driver Greg Weld in Grant King's dirt sprint car, powered by a 318 cubic-inch Plymouth stock block V8.

It should be noted that Grant's wife, Doris King, played a major role in his success for many years. In one interview, when asked why she was involved with the sport, she matter-of-factly replied, "I belong here. Auto racing is my life."

Her introduction to racing was through sprint cars. Through mutual friends who were part of the racing scene, she first met Grant. She explained in an interview with Don Hendry:

"I was working as a secretary for a large CPA firm at the time, and Grant needed someone to help with the books. Well, it didn't take us long to discover we had an awful lot in common. We were married a year later and my involvement in auto racing has been full-time ever since."

When asked to describe her role in the business operations of Grant King Racing, she seemed stumped at first.

"I'm not quite sure. I guess you could say I do whatever needs to be done. I run the gambit from chasing parts to showing the California Attorney General and his wife around Ontario Motor Speedway when they were our guests at the California 500"

When one of the Grant King-designed Indy cars would go on display, Doris would invariably accompany it. In the same interview, she explained that people in general were very curious about USAC Championship Cars and felt an informed spokesperson should be on-hand to answer the public's questions.

Grant and Doris King with Tom Sneva at Indianapolis 1974. Tom qualified 8th but dropped out after 94 laps with mechanical woes and was credited with a 20th-place finish.

(Tom Osborne photo)

"I enjoy working with and around public gatherings. I've made speeches on auto racing to clubs and organizations. My goal is to provide my audience with an understanding of auto racing - let them know what they're watching and why. Understanding leads to interest and interest leads to more auto racing fans."

Doris noted that her promotion of the Indy Sprints was one of her proudest achievements. The inaugural event in 1970 was known as the 'Pole Night Sprints.' Later, this annual race card was renamed 'The Indy Sprints'.

Held the first night of qualifications for the Indy 500, this promotion became one of the biggest name-drawing races of the season. Doris pointed out, with pride, that the Indy Sprints was one of only two sprint car races that paid lap money. Since its inception, the event paid the largest purse of the [then] 33 non-televised sprint car races on the USAC schedule.

Grant King ended his long career in racing in the early 1980s, but remained active in other business endeavors, including race car restoration, in his adopted Indiana.

It would be remiss to not mention one event in King's later life when he made a poor business decision. According to an article which appeared in the *LA Times* newspaper on December 21st, 1990:

Former Indy-car owner Grant King received a six-month prison sentence and was ordered to pay $250,000 in restitution for his part in an auto theft ring. U.S. District Judge Sarah Evans Barker also ordered King to forfeit $30,000 to the federal government.

The judge said King's cooperation in a continuing federal investigation was one reason she set his sentence below the 18-to-24-month term called for in federal sentencing guidelines.
King pleaded guilty in November to four federal charges related to auto theft and the sale of stolen automobiles.

King reportedly directed an auto theft operation for up to six years, according to court testimony. King specialized in the theft and sale of stolen Honda and Acura automobiles from Indiana and surrounding states, records show. An FBI agent estimated that King was involved in up to 50 auto thefts.

King owned and served as chief mechanic or car builder on dozens of cars at the Indianapolis 500 from 1964 through the early 1980s. He also built sprint cars, and his drivers won several USAC sprint car championships during the 1970s.

In 1994, Grant King was inducted into the Victoria Auto Racing Hall of Fame and the National Sprint Car Hall of Fame in 1998.

Tragically, on December 18th, 1999, Grant passed away from severe injuries he suffered in a two-vehicle accident near Danville, Indiana. He was 66 years-old.

Grant's old race shop in Indianapolis is today owned by his nephew Bill Throckmorton, whose mother was a sister to King's first wife Doris.

Together with his wife Stephanie, Bill has preserved a huge piece of his uncle's history and the facility is registered as a museum. Among the many artifacts are many of the original jigs and patterns that Grant developed.

"I had been around Grant pretty much all of my life," said Throckmorton. He built my first quarter-midget race car when I was just four-years-old."

Bill and Stephanie Throckmorton are preserving Grant King's legacy.

(www.grantkingraceshops.com)

Over the years, Bill and Grant worked and raced together. "When Grant eventually went to federal prison in later years, I was very upset with him about that," Bill explained. "I was driving for him at the time and we had big hopes that we would get back into the Indy cars. Though he was a smart man, he got in with the wrong people – just got greedy."

A few years following King's death, the Throckmorton's were offered the opportunity to take over the old race shop, which was in a sad state of disrepair. "There was stuff all over the place," Bill recalls, "and lots of barrels to catch the rainwater coming in through the roof.

"This was a very famous place", Bill noted. "Back in the day, it seems like most of the people that became somebody at least worked here or started here. A lot of famous race cars, and a lot of famous race drivers, came through this place – so it has a lot of history."

Besides maintaining the Grant King Race Shop, the Throckmorton's full-time business is Advanced Welding and Engineering, Inc., a large custom fabrication shop. The couple still runs their own team, primarily racing several types of open-wheel cars.

(Photos in this chapter courtesy of the Collections of Ted MacKenzie, Tom Osborne, Rolla Vollstedt, Art Pollard, Scovell, Bill Throckmorton, the Victoria Auto Racing Hall of Fame and the Indianapolis Motor Speedway)

John Feuz was a well-known – and extremely talented – race car mechanic who became a great friend and fabricator for Billy Foster.

Beginning in the late 1940s, John was enamored with cars and racing, learning the trade along the way. Over the next several decades – and throughout the Pacific Northwest – Feuz worked alongside some of the 'best of the best' drivers in the region. His many accomplishments included the two years he was a member of Foster's crew at Indianapolis.

John's mother's family owned the property which is now Gabriel Park in southwest Portland, Oregon. His father owned John's Market in the Multnomah neighborhood, which started out as a meat market in the 1920s and then expanded to offer groceries. "I spent a lot of time working in that darn store, especially during the war," John recalled. "It was my duty to count the food stamps and I hated that."

(John Feuz Collection)

John developed a keen interest in cars at a young age, noting, "I first built a crude soapbox derby racer when I was about ten-years-old, along with building model airplanes. I loved to fly the aircraft and entered competitions. There were many crashes along the way, but I slowly achieved success. I won a Plymouth-sponsored, Oregon state model airplane contest and a trip to the national competitions two years in a row."

While young John was still getting around on a bicycle, noted racer George Amick had a 1946 Ford coupe he raced in the stock car events at the Portland Speedway. "He'd run that thing through the Multnomah area wide open and I used to chase him on my bicycle," John said. "Boy, I thought that was pretty cool!"

Feuz readily admitted that at the time, "My mechanical background was zero. Everything I learned about automobiles was accomplished through my interest in racing."

While attending Lincoln High School in Portland, John and his friends would go out to the Jantzen Beach Arena on Thursday nights to watch the midget car races. Those were exciting times, with drivers such as George Amick, Shorty Templeton, Gordy Youngstrom, Bob Gregg, Frankie McGowan, Len Sutton, Howard Osborn and Bob Donker competing.

"It was the Offys against the Fords," John recalled. "Pat Vidan was the starter, and he put on a show that made racing even more interesting. He would do back-flips and have the cars line up to run pace laps. It was a real professional event, along with some superb racing."

Feuz was a senior in high school in 1949. George Weedman, who owned a gas station in Multnomah, bought a track roadster. John offered to help George rebuild the car, which turned out to be a major project.

"That's how I got started," John explained. "I'd hang around the garage and help them – I was the 'gofer'. I'd go to the races to help out with whatever they needed. George and his old man weren't the greatest mechanics in the world, but they had enough money to put the car together and had quite a few local guys helping them."

"After the first year, they decided they would build a new roadster," John continued. "I salvaged many of the old parts they threw away and took them to a local garage. I had decided to build a track roadster of my own."

With the help of George Amick and George's friend, Bob Erbes, John built his first race car. "Bob was a good mechanic, and he helped me put together the parts I had on hand," John said. "Amick would stop by and give us a little assistance now and then. I bought a flathead V8 engine from Don Walters down in Salem because he was quitting racing."

(John Feuz Collection)

"The night before the opening race of the season, Amick came over and asked if we were going to run the thing. He said he would test it, so he drove it down Multnomah Boulevard and around the area. After a while he came back to the garage and reported that the car wasn't handling well."

It turned out that George Weedman's new car wasn't yet ready, so John gave local racer – 'Wild' Bill Hyde – a call to ask him if he would drive John's car in its first outing. Hyde agreed, and John entered the opening race of the 1950 season at Portland Speedway. The car overheated on that first day.

"I was not a race car driver," John admitted. "I loved to drive the car, but I was terrible – with bad depth perception. I was allergic to running close to guys and crashed the car many times at the Speedway. Rolla Vollstedt said, 'You'd do all of us a favor if you retired as a driver. Just be a mechanic and quit this driving stuff'. The fences weren't strong enough to hold me in."

Following high school, John attended Lewis & Clark College in Portland. Because of his expertise flying model airplanes, he had received a scholarship from a flying organization.

"I loved sports, especially basketball (John stood about 6'-5"), so racing was a summertime endeavor," Feuz said. "I turned down a basketball scholarship for guys who needed it worse than I did. My degree was in Business Administration because my folks wanted me to take over their store,"

John noted, "We built a new grocery store on Multnomah Boulevard and my younger brother David and I ran it. Later, I also had a store in Milwaukie, Oregon, which I eventually sold. I finally left the grocery business and bought a company – Water Metrics – that repaired water meters. I had to make a living, so the racing was a summer job for me. There was no way I had any vision of becoming a full-time racer."

Once George Weedman's new car was ready to go, Bill Hyde returned as George's driver, so John persuaded Palmer Crowell to drive his car. "Palmer and I were close in age," said John. "We ran a bunch of races, and then went down to the Calistoga dirt track in Northern California. There was good money there."

When we left Portland I said to Palmer, 'I hope you have some money.' Palmer replied, 'No, I thought you had some!' By the time we got to Calistoga we were broke. The people down there wouldn't let us in because we weren't 21 years-old, so we sat outside the gate. They let us sleep in the back of a restaurant near the track. Vi Scovell finally came by and said, 'I know these guys and they're OK', so they finally let us in."

According to Feuz, Palmer Crowell was an excellent dirt track racer who didn't mind getting his car sideways, and won a lot of races during his career. "Palmer qualified sixth and was leading the fast heat. He spun going into a turn and wrecked about three other cars. Our car was ruined.

After the race the promoter was very kind and gave us a $100 bill to get us back home. Otherwise, we would've been sitting down there in Calistoga."

1952 – Top Oregon driver Palmer Crowell in John Feuz' racer at the Idaho State Fairgrounds.

(Ralph Hunt Collection)

At the track, Feuz considered everyone who was racing to be a competitor. Back then, the combination of Rolla Vollstedt and Len Sutton were the team to beat.

John recalled, "I would always try to park next to them, so I could see what they were doing. There was no sense in watching the guys who were finishing further down the field. I needed to learn what it took to win, so I became friendly with Vollstedt and kept asking him questions. Soon Rolla started saying, 'figure it out yourself.' He wasn't about to give away all his secrets."

Bob Gregg

(Ralph Hunt Collection)

"I always tried something new with tires, wheels, and jacking the weight," explained John. "I'd ask the driver 'did you like that?' There were a few drivers who could tell me what they wanted. Palmer Crowell could tell me when we're good enough. If the car would go down the race track, it was perfect for a driver like Bill Hyde. So, I kept experimenting with a lot of stuff and soon we got the car very competitive. I'd warm the car up and get it going, then take the best driver that was available. The driver was the easiest change on the car, and that was the way I learned. Each driver would tell me something different."

John figured out that with race car drivers, there were those that spun out many times, while others would rarely spin. Bob Gregg drove numerous races in John's cars and seemingly never lost control. John recalled, "At one time we won twelve races in a row. Gregg would say, 'If the back end is a little loose that's OK, but I want the front-end to stick. I can rarely think of a time when Bob passed somebody on the outside. He would start out running on the outside, and then at the last second, dive to the inside of the track. He figured out how to pass cars that no one else had figured out. Gregg won a lot of races."

Feuz managed his racing expenses by working at the grocery store, and he was good at scrounging parts. "I spent a lot of time at the Boeing junkyard near Seattle. We'd go up there and get buckets of bolts and all kinds of other stuff. One time I got aluminum aircraft brake drums because I thought they would work pretty well. Well, they didn't work at all because they got too hot. Most of things I learned were by trial and error. When I first started, I figured out we had a cooling problem, so I kept putting bigger and bigger radiators on the car. Don Collins told me I was just wasting my time – it just takes longer for the water to boil. We did a lot of experimenting, like slowing down the water pump and things like that. We finally got to the point where the Ford V8 would run cool, and we wouldn't have to run a gigantic radiator. I finally found out how to make the thing go."

John also figured out the best way to make money in racing. "From my experience, they didn't pay anything much for winning heat races. They paid for winning the main event, and the only way you're going to get paid is to finish the race. That's the philosophy I tried to pass along to my drivers. We were always within the first five in qualifying, but we could outlast them in the race. We'd get maybe a couple hundred bucks for a win."

Over the first ten years, John Feuz fielded a variety of race cars and drivers, landing in the top-five in season points championships each year. "I always got the best driver available at the time, such as Bill Hyde, Palmer Crowell, Bob Gregg, Ernie Koch, Harold Sperb and Len Sutton. My most satisfying win was when my good friend Del McClure and I put his DeSoto V8 engine in my big car, and together we won the 100-lap championship race at Portland Meadows. We led for over 80 laps and collected $100 per lap, besides the winner's purse. It was a big payday and we all should have retired."

By 1960, racing in the Portland area consisted primarily of stock cars, modified hardtops, and jalopies – and the winner's purses were small. John and engineer Don Robison decided they could build a rear-engine midget racer they could race in the USAC ranks, following the success of the Volkswagen-powered midgets. The two men surmised they could build a rear-engine car for the Indianapolis 500 using the same basic chassis design.

As John recalled, Don said, "We could build a car to go to Indianapolis for the same amount we would spend on this gall-danged midget. They don't pay much money at the midget races, but they pay a heck of a lot of money at Indianapolis."

Feuz and Robison got in touch with Rolla Vollstedt and, showing him their plans, suggested they build a rear-engine, Offenhauser-powered car for Indy. "Vollstedt was skeptical at first, John said, "but having seen the success of the rear-engine Brabham at Indy in 1961, there was no reason an Offy-powered car could not be competitive."

John continued, "There were a lot of guys that thought an Offy would never work. Smokey Yunick said if you put an Offy in that thing, it's going to go straight into the fence on the first turn. He thought there's no way you can make the car turn left. He was used to running stock cars with all the weight up front. Yunick was a great mechanic, but at the time didn't understand how anti-roll bars worked. But Don Robison was never skeptical – he knew it would work."

With Vollstedt eventually coming on board, the project literally started on the ground floor of the basement of Rolla's home in southwest Portland. It was a slow process for everyone involved, all of whom had daytime jobs. "Harold Sperb and I would work evenings from about seven to ten o'clock," John remembered. "We had to quit at ten because Rolla's wife said there would be no noise after that time. The basement shop was cleaned every night and all the tools were put away."

A heavy metal platform was made to fasten the frame to so it would not warp during the welding process, and accurate measurements would be made along the way. John recalled, "Don Robison's plans were very detailed, and every tube was measured and cut to fit perfectly – the ends were cut and reamed to fit with no gaps. Rolla would do most of the welding. Robison was very particular and everything had to be just perfect, though he didn't do any work on the car. He would just come in and measure everything to make damn sure everything was right. Bill DeVeca was an excellent machinist and made the components. Without him the project could never have been completed. Harold Sperb was an excellent fabricator and could form anything out of aluminum – fuel tanks, body components, brackets – you name it. The people who contributed time making parts or helping financially included a cross-section of racers, equipment suppliers, or craftsmen who were experts in their field," John observed.

"My contribution was to work with Sperb," John said. "I made sure he had coffee and the materials he needed to work with. I would also finish parts and made certain everything would fit. I was working for free. I guess you could say I was an organizer that kept the project moving along, because I felt the sooner we got to Indy, the better chance we had to get a head-start on other builders and put us in a position to win."

Feuz reflected on the effort by saying, "It was a slow process, but the end result was a work of art. The #66 car was the best that Vollstedt ever built, and it ran faster than any other normally aspirated, Offy-powered car in history. As Len Sutton said, 'It felt like driving a Cadillac.'"

John remembered that sometime in 1961, Eddie Kostenuk came to Portland from Victoria with an older Vollstedt racer that had been wrecked, hoping that Rolla would rebuild the car.

Kostenuk owned a trucking company in Victoria. A well-known racer throughout British Columbia, Eddie began racing in the late 1940s and posted many wins and a few championships in the decade that followed.

"The frame of Eddie's car was bent pretty badly," John remembered. "Eddie wanted Vollstedt to fix it up for him so he could practice with it and achieve the speed needed to take his driver's test at Indy. Rolla said he didn't have the time to mess with it but suggested to Kostenuk to bring it to me. I lived just across the street from Rolla."

John took on the project because Kostenuk would pay him by the hour – and John was still working for free for Vollstedt. "Eddie was going to pay me $10 per hour and I thought, 'Wow, that's a hell of a deal!'", John recalled.

"I'd help Rolla until 10 p.m. and then came home and worked until about 1 a.m. on the Kostenuk car." John straightened the frame, created a new front axle, rebuilt the rear-end, and added new bodywork. He also acquired a 327 Chevy block from Vollstedt and assembled a new engine.

"Kostenuk kinda' paid me," John said. "He'd come to Portland with four or five fifths of Crown Royal and say, 'Hi, how are you doing?' That's how he wanted to pay me. He'd drive down in his Cadillac and always had some 'honey' with him. He was quite the character! We got that car all done and Kostenuk said he wanted to take it up to Victoria to race. I said fine, but he paid me about half the money he really owed."

Kostenuk took the finished car back to Victoria. Vollstedt and Sutton went along to observe, intending to sign off on Eddie's racing skills so he could make an attempt at Indianapolis. He won the race in Victoria, was signed off, and then purchased a Watson roadster to make his Brickyard run.

Kostenuk returned to Portland with the Victoria-winning car and told Feuz he was selling it. John informed Eddie that until he was paid the money he was owed, the car could not be sold. Kostenuk eventually came up with the money and told John a guy by the name of Billy Foster would be coming to pick up the car.

In 1961, driving his own Ranger-powered roadster, Kostenuk won the last big car race held at Western Speedway. In 1962 at age 33, and having passed his USAC rookie test, Eddie entered that year's Indianapolis 500, joining the Leader Card team alongside Rodger Ward and Len Sutton. Unfortunately, during a practice run at 140 mph, Kostenuk was struck in the goggles by a bird, nearly losing his eyesight. Ironically, Ward and Sutton finished one-two in the 500.

Now back to the time when Foster traveled to Portland to pick up his new race car, John said, "Well, I didn't know who Foster was. But about a week later Billy showed up with a couple of other guys, loaded the car on the trailer, and I wished them well. I hoped to never see that car again - in order to spend more time on Vollstedt's Indy car.

John went out of town for his annual two-week training period with the Army Reserve. Upon returning, he learned that Foster was racing the car that weekend at the Jantzen Beach Arena. "I thought I would go see how the car was doing," recalled John. "I was shocked that the car was all beat up. Both bumpers were smashed, as was the nose and hood. There were tire marks on both sides. I asked Foster what had happened. He said the car didn't handle, and he had hit many cars trying to keep up or make a pass. I went to work on the car and set it up, so it would handle halfway decent. Billy then goes out to qualify and set fast time and I said to myself, 'this guy can drive a race car!'"

To John's frustration, he found that Billy went back to his old tricks. Instead of waiting for the right opportunity to pass another car, he would run into it to push his competitor out of the way. After the race, Foster asked John to continue helping to set the car up.

As John remembered, "I said, first we must have an understanding. You will drive from now on without banging into other cars, and you will avoid any kind of crash – because I will not rebuild the car after every race. In the early days, he ran into just about every car on the track. I told him this was not a destruction derby. If you're going to drive like that, then you'll have to find another mechanic. I didn't want to have anything to do with this. Billy said, 'OK, I'll just take the car and run it myself.' He and his crew took off and ran some more races, and then ended up back in Victoria. About two weeks later, Billy called to say the engine had gone bad and the car needed some more work. He asked if I could come up there and he would pay my bills."

With that, John agreed and traveled to British Columbia. He discovered that they had put the wrong gear in the car. The engine over-revved and the result was bent pushrods.

"I fixed it the best I could", said John. "I did some straightening of bent parts and set the car up to handle well. There was a big 100-lap race coming up – the Daffodil Cup at Western Speedway. I told Billy that the engine wasn't great and to take it easy. He drove like a gentleman and never ran into another car when passing. He won the race by over a lap on the second-place car. We had a meeting of the minds and a great partnership was born."

At the end of the season, Billy sold that car to Geoff Vantreight, who also served as a crew member for Foster. Subsequently, Vantreight re-sold the car to Bill Crow of Idaho.

Billy then purchased a Ben Zakit racer that Ernie Koch had crashed in the last race of the year. Feuz rebuilt this car from the ground-up.

"Everything was first-class," said John. "I spent hours on the engine alone, picking many stock parts from several dealer's inventories to get the best available. Everything was polished and balanced to fit perfectly – there were no shortcuts. We prepared to race just like one would do to prepare a car for Indy."

The following season, Billy Foster won numerous races with no breakdowns. John recalled, "I would go through the engine, transmission, and rear-end after every three races. I could not go to every event but prepared the car with instructions – in order that Billy's group of friends could run the car without me being there. I would prepare the car, have the fuel mixed, and everything needed for the race car on the trailer. All they had to do is start the thing up, run it, and then bring it back to Portland. I couldn't take the time off from work."

John remarked, "I figured out what it would take for Foster to win. If there was a wreck on the track, we weren't going to be involved. I had a transmission and clutch worked out so that if there was an accident he might be involved in, he could put it into reverse, back it up, and get going again. I built the car so we could win races. That was the important thing, because later on when CAMRA got started, they paid $1,000 for first place. One year that car earned about $54,000."

Meanwhile, work continued on Vollstedt's new Indy car. John still had the grocery business to look after – not to mention his family – so he could not spend every minute of his life maintaining racing cars.

"In late 1963 or early in '64, Grant King showed up to help with the Indy car," remembered John. "I always considered Grant a competitor but did not know him well. Grant was a fast learner, could copy anything and had a great memory."

"At some point," John said, "Vollstedt gave some drawings of the new car to noted Indy car builder A.J. Watson. Watson built two or three cars that were a little different, but used basically the same configuration, and earned the Builder of the Year Award. Don Robison should have won it."

The combination of Feuz' mechanical ability and Foster's driving talent made for a great partnership.

(John Feuz Collection)

Vollstedt's rear-engine Offenhauser made its Indianapolis 500 debut in 1964. Len Sutton qualified the car in the eighth position on the grid. Feuz noted that Vollstedt's cars were meticulously prepared, saying, "After qualifications, the car was stripped down, and the frame was glass-beaded and checked for any cracks or defects. Every part was carefully inspected, and the car was put back together – nothing was left to chance. Grant King was surprised and said we were wasting our time, saying that guys like Watson, who had many winning cars, did nothing like we were doing."

1963 - Feuz burning the midnight oil while helping the Vollstedt team assemble the rear-engine Offy for Indianapolis.

(John Feuz Collection)

"But in racing, as most any other type of competition, you cannot be over-prepared," John noted. "There are no shortcuts to winning – failures usually come from a lack of preparation. You must take the time to do it right, and then double-check it. Grant King always wanted to do things quickly and rarely ever re-checked his work – or at least have someone else double-check."

For his first experience at Indy in 1964, John recalled, "When I first got back there, they had six mechanics I hoped were smarter than I was, but it turned out they probably weren't. Vollstedt would make a list of all the things that had to be done. It made no sense arguing what needed to take place, so I stayed in the background and worked with Bob Sowle and Harold Robinson. We were the actual guys that did the work."

The 1964 running of the Indianapolis 500 began smoothly but on just the second lap, tragedy struck. In his autobiography, *My Road to Indy*, Len Sutton described what took place:

"On the second lap at the end of the backstretch, going into the third turn, Dave MacDonald went whistling by me, jumped on the binders and proceeded across the short chute in front of me. Walt Hansgen was right in front of him and Dave drove it deep under him, but not deep enough for Walt to see him.

When Hansgen came down, as that was his line, Dave had to get his nose out or turn left enough to keep from running into him. Dave's back end got away from him and he headed for the inside guard rail. Anyone watching this unfold – and I was – could feel certain it was going to be tragic.

By the time Dave's car was off the wall and heading back out on the race track, I was just even with him and escaped down the front stretch. Unfortunately for Eddie Sachs, Dave's car collided with him, igniting a second ball of flame and sent a burning tire and wheel high into the air. The two drivers, from in front of me and behind me, were both killed, burned beyond help."

In the aftermath, the race was red-flagged for about 90 minutes. Following the restart, Len was running in the fourth position at the 100-lap mark. But on lap 140 his engine just quit due to a failed fuel pump. It was a disappointing 15th-place finish for the unique Vollstedt/Offy.

For the 1965 Indy car season, Vollstedt built a new rear-engine, turbocharged Ford-powered car for Sutton. Billy Foster came aboard to drive the previous year's Offy, now repainted and re-numbered as the #66. The car was sponsored by Autotronics, gaining support from businessman Jim Robbins.

It was Billy's rookie year at Indianapolis, where he joined a prestigious group of other rookies. These included Mario Andretti, Gordon Johncock, Al Unser, Sr., Jerry Grant, Mickey Rupp, Joe Leonard, Masten Gregory, George Snider, Bobby Johns, and Arnie Knepper. Billy was 28 years-old.

Along with Grant King, John Feuz spent most of his time at Indy in 1965 working on Foster's car. John recalled putting on a front 'splitter' beneath the nose cone to gain a little down-force.

"We started out with a tin piece, but that caused sparks when it met with the racing surface. So, I made a rubber one that was right on the racetrack, but no one noticed – it just wore down."

John added, "The only thing you had to go by back then was what the driver told you. Billy was very good at being able to tell if any adjustments to the chassis, springs, sway bars or tires made any difference. I would ask Billy every time we ran the car in practice, what can we do to make you go faster? We would then make the change and he would go faster."

Foster's biggest concern seemed to be a lack of horsepower with the Offenhauser, especially compared with the Ford-powered competition. The crew did the best they could but had no way of increasing the engine's output. Nevertheless, Foster qualified sixth-fastest with a speed of 158.416 mph – a record time for a non-turbocharged Offy that still stands today.

(John Feuz Collection)

As far as the race itself, Foster had a steady drive until a broken water manifold forced the sole Canadian in the field out on the 85th lap. Jimmy Clark won the race.

In 1966, Foster made his second appearance at Indy. Len Sutton had retired from racing during the 1965 season, so Billy and his crew inherited the Ford-powered chassis previously driven by Len. Once again, it was sponsored by Jim Robbins and now carried the #27.

"We had the entire crew on-board we had in 1965," John explained. "That car had much more horsepower than the Offy. We had a heck of a time getting it up to speed. Ford wouldn't let us work on the engine. If you were not up to power, they'd just give you another engine."

Billy qualified the car in the twelfth position, but barely took the green flag when he was involved in a multi-car crash on the front straight. The team was credited with just a 24th place finish.

In retrospect, John Feuz noted that Billy Foster was the best natural race driver he ever worked with. "You could put him up there with Andretti, Clark and any other of the top drivers of his era," said John. "He could tell you what he needed to go faster. He could have been a champion, because he could drive anything and get the most out of it."

"He was like a son to me," John said in closing. "The years I worked with him were the best years of my life. I miss Billy and I will always remember him."

John Feuz with World Champion Jimmy Clark at Riverside International Raceway, 1967.

(John Feuz Collection)

John Feuz passed away at the age of 86 in Lake Oswego, Oregon, on July 25, 2017. Just three months later – on October 22nd – John's long-time racing buddy, Rolla Vollstedt, died at the age of 99.

John was predeceased by Gwyneth, his wife of 60 years, his brother, David, and his son, Steven. He is survived by his daughters, Sheryl and Anne, along with four grandchildren. John Feuz was blessed with many long-lasting friendships and will always be remembered by those that knew, worked with, and spent time with him.

Two Oregon racing legends: Herschel McGriff and John Feuz in 2017.

(Author photo)

Of all the racing machines that Rolla Vollstedt built during a long career in racing, his most significant creation was the rear-engined Offenhauser that made its first Indianapolis 500 appearance in 1964 at the hands of driver Len Sutton.

While several of Vollstedt's close friends and associates had a hand in the car's construction and development, the man most responsible for the concept and design was **Don Robison** of Portland, Oregon.

Don's interest in racing dates to the first post-war Indy 500. In grade and high school, he was one year behind his good friend and future race car builder John Feuz. As close neighbors, both attended Lincoln High School in Portland and Don recalls getting a ride to school with John, who was driving his family's Hudson. They also shared the hobby of model airplanes.

As free labor, Don worked alongside John in 1953 in building a race car based upon Model T frame rails and components, powered by a modified Ford flathead engine. The following year, they replaced the engine with a DeSoto V8 which was acquired from car owner Del McClure. Both Len Sutton and Palmer Crowell raced that car.

Robison earned an economics degree from the University of Oregon and then spent three years in the Air Force. During this time, as Don recalls, "I read *Road & Track* and *Hot Rod* magazines diligently, learning a lot about European race car design. There was a smoke shop in downtown Portland where I'd go to look at these periodicals."

Don's wife Nancy was working for Jewitt-Cameron lumber company along with Vollstedt, and it was through her that Don and Rolla became acquainted.

It was in 1961 that Formula One World Champion Jack Brabham brought his lightweight and fragile rear-engined Cooper/Climax to Indianapolis and caught Robison's attention. Despite snickers from most of the traditional roadster veterans, Indy rookie Brabham qualified the little car 13th and completed all 200 laps, finishing ninth – and raised a lot of eyebrows. The "British Invasion" of Indianapolis had begun.

Inspired by the Cooper's performance, Don studied and measured the suspension details on a rear-engined race car that Portland racer Monte Shelton had. Don and John Feuz continued to discuss the concept with Vollstedt, who eventually said, "Let's build it."

With a space-frame chassis style in mind, Don designed the basic frame layout and suspension geometry, along with all the various suspension components such as A-arms, bulkheads and other systems. Using those specifications, Don turned to his drafting board. "I didn't have any specific engine or transaxle dimensions," he remembers, "so I designed the chassis with some latitude. I used reams of paper sketching layouts, structures and suspension linkages."

Don Robison – Chief Designer of the Vollstedt/Offy.

(Vollstedt Collection)

In his autobiography *My Road to Indy* Len Sutton recalled:

"Don and John wanted to build a rear-engine car. Lacking all of the essentials to do this, they enlisted Rolla's capabilities and got started on the project. In the beginning it was Don, John and Rolla gathering information on material to purchase (basically tubing), cutting pieces to length, welding them together and away they went. Rolla was the only one spending money up to that point and he was just a working man like the rest of us."

Work on the car began in July of 1962 in Vollstedt's basement shop. The chassis was designed to have an Offenhauser engine, but Vollstedt didn't have one at the time. Dick Martin, who owned Exhaust Specialties in Portland, supplied the funds to purchase one.

It was during the construction period that Victoria builder and mechanic, Grant King, became involved with the project, as Len Sutton described:

"During the winter of 1962/63, in one of the Monroe meetings we held on a regular basis, we were in Boise, Idaho. [Len worked in marketing for the Monroe Auto Equipment Company]. To draw interest for good attendance, we contacted a local racer, Grant King, and asked him to bring his racer to the meeting and show it off. I had met Grant before and knew of his racing craftsmanship capabilities."

After the shock absorber meeting, I spoke with Grant about Vollstedt's project. He knew Rolla and had raced against him in the Northwest. Grant was so intrigued by Rolla's project that he came to Portland to join in."

Robison, working for the Honeywell Corporation at the time, noted that once the car was completed the crew took it to Indianapolis in February of 1963. Prior to that, the car underwent testing at the Portland Speedway.

The Goodyear Tire Company was interested in developing a tire for Indianapolis. Sutton secured Goodyear's permission to be a part of the company's tire test with the Vollstedt team's new creation.

Don recalls one stipulation, which Sutton also mentioned. Goodyear said the team would not be on their payroll until reaching 148 mph during the test. On about his tenth lap, Len hit that mark. As the week went on, Sutton recorded the fastest speed of 153 mph. Until then, the fastest lap by any of the other participants was 151.9 mph.

Tom Nehl was a successful Florida-based GMC dealer with a passion for racing. As a friend of Vollstedt, Nehl became a major stockholder in the new car. Nehl was acquainted with legendary builder Smokey Yunick and described the rear-engined Offy to him. Reportedly Smokey told Nehl to "Grease the wall, because on the first turn he is going to hit the wall and he doesn't want to damage the car too much. The rear-end weighs too much and he will never be able to make it steer." But in this case, they would prove Yunick wrong.

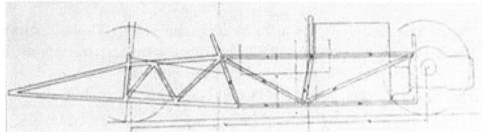

The finished chassis and one of Robison's original schematics.

(Robison Collection)

According to Robison, the Goodyear tire engineers had only driver feedback, tire temperatures, wear patterns and the stop watch with which to evaluate tire performance.

Don says, "I suggested that tire development might be advanced using force and movement sensors in the car, with the data transmitted by telemetry to a stationary recorder for analysis. The engineers were intrigued.

My employer, Honeywell, had the expertise to build such a system and Goodyear's interest was communicated to the Honeywell office in Cleveland. The system I described was subsequently sold to Goodyear."

"We hoped to compete in the 1963 Indianapolis 500," says Don. "We failed because a major out-sourced part arrived three months late."

Don Robison at Indianapolis – 1964

(Vollstedt Collection)

Billy Foster's rookie year at Indy was in 1965, driving the Vollstedt/Offy. But there were handling problems and Billy described the car as being "way loose." Rolla made a call to Robison and asked him to come to Indy to diagnose the problem. Don reports he and John Feuz spent 18 hours on the Bear (alignment) Rack with the car to make sure all the suspension settings were correct. After that, Foster qualified a significant sixth on the grid. Unfortunately, Billy's run ended on the 85th lap of the race due to a broken water manifold.

Don remembers Billy as being "very relaxed and observant." But then he ended with a smile, remembering that Billy "never picked up a wrench."

"After the 1965 race I quelled my interest in racing, fearing my son Matt, then four-years-old, might become involved," Don explains. "I even terminated my subscriptions to automobile magazines. It didn't work out though, as today Matt races a 960-horsepower super-production Mercury in Sports Car Club of America events."

Don continued working for Honeywell until 1966, and during that time was transferred to Los Angeles. Don's wife Nancy passed away several years ago and he continues to reside in Portland.

Robison and Vollstedt.

(Vollstedt Collection)

Len Sutton and Don Robison worked closely together at Indianapolis in 1964.

(Vollstedt Collection)

A master fabricator who played a major role in Rolla Vollstedt's cars and teams for many years, **Harold Sperb** was a racer himself during the early 1950s. He came to be associated with Vollstedt through his friendship with Len Sutton. As Sutton recalled in his autobiography *My Road to Indy*:

"I remember a time in 1952 when the final roadster race of the season was coming up at Portland Speedway and the championship was at stake. The Washington roadsters were there too, and it appeared that both the Oregon and Washington championships were at stake.

I was in Vollstedt's Horning/GMC and we had quick time in qualifying. Ernie Koch and I were probably neck-and-neck for the Oregon championship. In the heat race we 'spun a spool' in the rear-end, putting us out of the race and the championship unless something drastic happened.

One of my close friends but also a competitor, Harold Sperb, came up to me and said, 'How would you like my ride for the rest of the day?' He drove his own car all the time except when something like this would happen. I remembered he had helped me out like this once before.

As you can imagine, I accepted and was now excited all over again. Harold had qualified sixth, but they started me last in the 100-lap feature and I finished third. Shorty Templeman was the winner. With all the points that were scored in that race, Shorty earned the Washington champ title and I was the Oregon champ.

The promoter then believed there should be a Northwest champion and he put the top four Washington-finishing cars and the top four Oregon-finishing cars in a 20-lap runoff. I ended up winning that race and it was about as exciting a finish as you could ask for in one season of racing.

Harold is probably one of the best metal-men and welders I have ever known. You must realize that it takes many hundreds of hours to construct something as complicated as a new racing car. And for the most part, it was done with free labor and a night after everyone got off work. I would say that Vollstedt has less than $15,000 invested when his race car [the rear-engine Vollstedt/Offy] left for Indianapolis. It would have been $50,000 if he had paid wages."

A very early photo of Harold Sperb and Len Sutton at the Portland Speedway.

(Jay Koch Collection)

"I first met Rolla in 1952 when I built a track roadster for myself," Sperb remembered. In 1959, I built the body for his championship dirt car, and then worked on his Indy cars. In 1966, I became an 'employee'. He [Rolla] was real bull-headed (my wife says it takes one to know one) and a real man of his word."

In speaking about Sperb in his own autobiography *The Rolla Vollstedt Story*, Rolla offered these thoughts:

"Hal had been our chief mechanic, fabricator and engine man for over ten years. Whatever we needed, Hal could do it. He fabricated the very long fuel tanks that mounted on each side of the frame of the car, the body, nose, cowling alongside the driver, the engine cover and tail from flat sheets of aluminum. Harold was a master fabricator, second to none in the world. His workmanship was, as was Willy Deveca's machining, a work of art."

Designer Don Robison also spoke highly of Sperb: "Harold was the most skilled fabricator I've known. He worked for a number of teams."

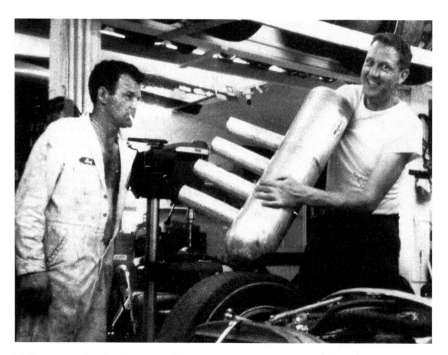

Harold Sperb and John Feuz working together on one of Vollstedt's early Indy cars.

(John Feuz Collection)

In 1971, Vollstedt built a new racer similar to the very successful McLaren Indy car of the time. With little help, Sperb built this car that was designed to receive the turbocharged Offenhauser engine. Unfortunately, the car didn't arrive at Indianapolis in time to qualify. Harold also performed his magic in constructing Vollstedt's monocoque tubs for the 1972 and

1973 cars. Over the next years, Sperb moved on to work on Dick Simon's race cars, but then in 1977 he resigned for personal reasons, wishing to remain living in Indianapolis.

Harold Sperb passed away in April of 2015 in Kaiser, Oregon, at the age 85. He had a bookfull of stories to tell, this one among them:

"I remember when we were at Riverside, California, in 1967. Two of the crew members who were staying in an adjoining room to Rolla and myself unplugged their phone, so Rolla couldn't call and wake them up so early in the morning.

After beating on their door trying to wake them, Rolla set off an M80 firecracker between the doors. That not only woke them up but blew the door jambs to pieces. That cost Rolla a few bucks."

A native of Needham, Massachusetts, **Fred Sewall** is among those who not only spent time crewing for Rolla Vollstedt's team, but also established a personal relationship with Billy Foster. It's an interesting story on how individual lives come together.

Indy 1966 – Grant King, Billy Foster and Fred Sewall.

(Rolla Vollstedt Collection)

Upon graduating from college, Fred spent the next six months in the Navy and then moved to Indianapolis to seek a position on a USAC Championship Car team. While living in the Boston area, Fred had become associated with and worked alongside Richard Carman, who was a mechanical engineer. Carman was a racing enthusiast who built and raced stock cars locally during the 1950s. He designed and built the first Indianapolis-type race car from New England.

It was through this association that Fred became acquainted with Jim McGee, who was also from the Boston area and had worked with Carman. In the years ahead, McGee would go on to become one of the most revered crew chiefs in Indycar history. Over time, more than 40 drivers flourished under his direction, including Mario Andretti, Eddie Sachs, Roger McCluskey, Tom Sneva, Rick Mears and Gordon Johncock, to name a few. With nine national championships and four Indy 500 wins to his credit, McGee was inducted into the Motorsports Hall of Fame in 2007.

When Fred first arrived at Indianapolis in 1966, he worked with famed engine builder Herb Porter as a crewman on driver Bobby Grim's Watson/Offy, sponsored by Racing Associates. But prior to race day, Fred was forced to return home due to "some type of weird arthritic condition," as he recalls. Grim started the race from the 31st position, but was caught up in the big wreck on the first lap and was eliminated.

Upon his return to Indianapolis shortly after the 1966 '500', Fred's friend Jim McGee introduced him to Vollstedt's crew chief, Grant King. In June 1966, King hired Sewall as a crew member for the rest of that season.

"I was paid full-time, working from 7:30 in the morning until 10:00 at night," says Fred. It was during this period he established a close relationship with Billy Foster.

"It was really my first serious year in racing, and I was pretty inexperienced," Fred says. "I lived with Grant for a while, and then with Billy in his trailer. We also roomed together when he nearly won the race over in Fuji, Japan.

1966 – Fred Sewall tending to Billy Foster's car at the Mt. Fuji circuit in Japan. Billy came oh-so-close to winning the event.

(Rolla Vollstedt Collection)

Billy was an absolutely fun guy to be around. Aside from being a great driver, he was also a real prankster – but very kind and charitable. When he won a race, he'd keep some of his prize money in the trailer's freezer. He told me, 'If you ever need some money just help yourself, but just be sure to put it back.' It was probably six to eight thousand dollars, and that was a lot of money back then!"

Fred also recalls, "There was one time, perhaps at the Indianapolis Fairgrounds, where he and Mario [Andretti] both won a small Yamaha motorbike – each a different color. Billy would let me drive his around the garage areas. One time I was doing wheelies and dumped it, scraping the mirrors and what not. I apologized profusely to Billy and said I'd pay for the damages. He simply replied, 'Don't worry about that. But from now on, just treat it as it wasn't your own.'"

Fred eventually moved to California to work for Friedkin Enterprises. Thomas Friedkin, who passed away in 2017 at age 82, was the son of Kenny Friedkin. Kenny was a combat pilot and trainer with the British Royal Air Force during World War Two and founded Pacific Southwest Airlines (PSA) in 1949. In 1962, his son Thomas began working as a commercial pilot for PSA, in addition to holding a seat on the airline's Board of Directors following his parent's death.

At the Indianapolis Fairgrounds, Billy and Mario Andretti both won a Yamaha motorbike.

One of Friedkin's hobbies was racing cars and he was friends with Carroll Shelby, who had turned down an offer to become a distributor for Toyota Motors. Shelby introduced Friedkin to Toyota, which led to Friedkin founding Gulf States Toyota Distributors.

In racing, Friedkin was a NASCAR Grand National car owner from 1965 to 1969 with drivers Jim Paschal and Bobby Allison. For several years, Friedkin also co-owned the multi-championship 'Miss Budweiser' hydroplane with pilot Bernie Little, along with a host of vintage war planes.

"In 1968 we were having the tire wars between Firestone and Goodyear," Fred stated. "Goodyear had Friedkin form an Indycar team, with Jerry Grant as their driver. A.J. Foyt put in a good word for me, because I was running Billy's car while Grant King was always in his shop. Jerry Grant came and talked to me and that's when I gave King my notice. Canadian John Anderson (Eldon Rasmussen's nephew) became part of our team."

With a new Eagle/Ford, the Friedkin team ran just two races (Indianapolis and Indianapolis Raceway Park) in 1968. At Indy, they qualified 15th but finished a disappointing 23rd when an oil leak forced the car out after just 50 laps.

During most of the 1968 season, Fred and the team were involved in the making of the movie "Winning", starring Paul Newman. "We were missing races because our cars were tied up at Indianapolis while they were shooting the movie," explained Fred.

In late 1969, Vollstedt sold one of his Ford-powered race cars to Dick Simon, and Fred was part of the package. In the spring of 1970, Simon first raced the car at Phoenix International Raceway but was sidelined by a magneto failure after just four laps.

Next came Simon's first Indianapolis 500, where he started the race from the 31st position and was running at the end, finishing 14th. At Ontario Motor Speedway that September, Simon captured his career-best finish of third place and finished tenth overall in the 1970 USAC National Championship standings.

In 1972, Fred elected to enter law school back in Massachusetts and embarked on a new career. As Rolla Vollstedt jokingly remarked, "Fred learned the racing business from me and went on to become a crew chief, then he screwed up and went back to school and became a lawyer."

Fred regrets he could not travel to British Columbia for Billy's memorial in 1967, stating that Grant King made him stay back at the shop in Indiana to continue working. "It was so sad for me, but eventually I traveled to Victoria to visit his gravesite."

Today, Fred Sewall is a Vice President and Principal Consultant for Marvin F. Poer and Company in Boston. He continues to follow racing and attends the Indy 500 each year with long-time friends.

Growing up in Indiana, **Bob Sowle** began working at the age of 17 as a mechanic in Trexler's Garage in Indianapolis. While learning the art of auto repair, he also started a life-long love for racing. Sowle progressed to building and owning his own cars and, during the 1950s, became involved with midget car racing and became an expert engine builder.

In 1959, Rolla Vollstedt built an upright Indianapolis-style car that originally had a 330 cubic-inch DeSoto V8. With Portlander Ernie Koch behind the wheel, the car competed at a few races in California and Arizona. For 1960, intending to take the car to the Midwest to run in USAC events in that part of the country, they swapped the DeSoto engine for a 255 cubic-inch Offenhauser. Their first race would be in Springfield, Illinois in August.

Vollstedt's long-time friend and driver, Len Sutton, brought Vollstedt and Sowle together. In his wonderful autobiography *My Road to Indy*, Sutton began by describing how he and Sowle first met:

"I'll never forget the midget race we ran at Detroit one night. A local driver originally from Portland, George Amick, was driving for Bob Sowle of Avon, Indiana. He got a second-place and I finished somewhere behind him in the feature race.

There was a quarter-mile dirt race the next night at Kokomo, Indiana and Amick couldn't make it. He recommended me as a replacement. I usually rode to the races with whomever I was driving for, so I jumped in with Sowle and we headed down the road.

Along the way, he asked me how I was on the dirt. I reminded him that in the Northwest we didn't have too many dirt tracks, so I was just so-so. When we unloaded that night and finished warm-ups, I told him the car felt pretty good, so don't change anything. It ended up I had fast time, won the dash, won my heat and won the feature, starting last in all three events. Bob was flabbergasted."

Bob Sowle and Rolla Vollstedt.

(Rolla Vollstedt Collection)

When Vollstedt arrived in Springfield, Sutton arranged that first meeting with Sowle, whose full-time occupation was managing the boiler house at Bridgeport Brass. He was also the builder and owner of the Avon Motel and Apartments.

Appreciating each other's talents, Vollstedt and Sowle hit it off from the beginning – and that close bonding was to last the rest of their lives. As Rolla described in his autobiography:

"Bob Sowle is my very good friend, the innkeeper for my crew, chief mechanic and Offy engine builder. Bob 'held my hand' from my upright Indy car days with Ernie Koch and through my rear-engine Indy cars from 1964 to 1984."

Another advantage for Vollstedt was that Sowle lived near Indianapolis, so he knew where the machine shops were and "how to get people out of bed, and how to get them to work on Sunday."

When A.J. Foyt fielded four cars in the Indianapolis 500 in 1970, he hired Sowle to change tires on the car driven by George Snider. In 1983, Bob became a member of the Indianapolis 500 Old Timer's Club and in 2005 was inducted into the Hoosier Auto Racing Fans Hall of Fame.

In his later years, rebuilding Porsches and Mercedes and tinkering with engines kept Bob entertained. It was said he never missed an opportunity to enlighten an interested listener in a little bit of racing history and getting together with his close racing cronies.

Bob Sowle passed away in Avon, Indiana in December of 2012 at age 92.

TWENTY-FOUR

The 1965 Indianapolis 500

Racing at Indianapolis in an earlier era differed greatly than it has become in modern times, particularly in the number of entries received by the track's office staff. In the months leading up to May 1965, 57 cars had been registered to vie for a position on the 33-car race grid for the 49th running of the Indy 500.

Following the tragic race in 1964, the United States Auto Club (USAC) implemented several rule changes to avoid the fiery crash that claimed the lives of drivers Eddie Sachs and Dave MacDonald.

For 1965, all cars were required to make a minimum of two pit stops, and the on-board fuel capacity was reduced to 75 gallons. Gasoline was banned in favor of methanol, and a car's fuel tanks were required to incorporate crushable rubber fuel cells to contain their contents in the event of a rupture.

USAC also mandated that the fuel tanks be located behind the driver on the left side of the car. Pressurized fueling rigs were outlawed – fuel could only be delivered to the car via a gravity feed method. A new minimum car weight of 1,250-pounds was established.

The movement to rear-engine cars, which began in 1961 when Jack Brabham showed up at Indianapolis with his modified version of a Cooper Climax Formula One car, had come full-circle by 1965.

In just a few short years, the traditional front-engine roadster was all but gone. A.J. Foyt's victory in 1964 marked the final time a front-engine car would win the '500'. Of the 33 cars that qualified for the 1965 event, only six still had the engine up front – with two of them being Andy Granatelli's Novi-powered machines driven by Bobby Unser and Jim Hurtubise.

For the 1965 season, Rolla Vollstedt and his fabrication friends built a new car for Len Sutton to drive. As Vollstedt described in his autobiography:

"The construction of our second Indianapolis car was again completed in the basement of our Lancaster Road home. My wife, Irene, sometimes accused me of designing the basement shop of that home and then building a house around it. I'm not sure that she wasn't at least partially correct."

By this time, Ford's quad-cam Indy engines were producing about 100 more horsepower than their venerable Offenhauser counterparts. Through Sutton's help, Vollstedt was able to acquire a Ford engine through his friend and sponsor, Jim Robbins. Robbins' company was the world's largest supplier of automotive seatbelts.

Indy 1965: Vollstedt's quad-cam Ford, with Len Sutton in the cockpit.

(Rolla Vollstedt Collection)

The 1965 Rookies

Regardless if you arrive as a driver, crew member or a spectator, an initial visit to the vast arena of speed known as the Indianapolis Motor Speedway can be overwhelming.

Consuming approximately 252 acres of Indiana real estate, the track's infield is so large it could accommodate eight famous landmarks from around the world: The White House, Vatican City, the Taj Mahal, the Roman Coliseum, Yankee Stadium, Rose Bowl Stadium, Liberty Island and Churchill Downs. The Speedway has a permanent seating capacity for over 235,000 spectators, and infield seating that can raise the total capacity to roughly 400,000.

One can only imagine the thoughts that go through the mind of a racing driver making his or her first attempt at competing at Indy for the first time.

Not unlike the youngster playing sandlot baseball while dreaming of becoming the next Babe Ruth, Satchel Paige or Mickey Mantle playing in the World Series, surely aspiring racers share the same imaginations.

Being a Canadian, Billy Foster's youthful avocation was, naturally, becoming a professional hockey player.

Billy is wearing jersey #5 above

Billy standing upper left

Billy was a standout hockey player.

(Foster Family photos)

Upon arriving at Indianapolis in early May of 1965, he said, "I never dreamed I would do it. I always wanted to be a hockey player when I was a kid. I used to get up at 3 a.m. to deliver newspapers, then I played hockey before going to school. As soon as school was over for the day, we used to hurry out and play more hockey. I played hockey 'till I was ready to drop."

Depending on their era, kids could imagine sitting behind the wheel and running alongside racing heroes like A.J. Foyt, Mario Andretti, the Unser Brothers or Rick Mears at the annual "Spectacle of Racing." Racing at Indy was, and remains, the pinnacle of motorsports.

In the book, *Unser – An American Family Portrait* by author Gordon Kirby, Al Unser Sr. spoke of his first appearance at Indy in 1965:

"When you first go to Indianapolis, it's so confusing, being a rookie, because there's so many things going on that I don't know whether it was what I expected or not. It was something that I wanted very badly."

Headline in Victoria' Daily Colonist newspaper in February 1965

(John Feuz Collection)

Another tradition of the Indy 500 experience is that the first time a driver takes to the track, he or she is considered a rookie. There are no exceptions, despite how many years of racing experience one holds. They must prove their ability to safely negotiate the 2.5-mile circuit at a prescribed speed.

It doesn't matter whether the driver is a multi-time Formula One champion, an illustrious star from NASCAR, a sprint car veteran, or a road-racing expert - each "newbie" must pass the rookie orientation program. The program is a phased, speed-controlled, ladder of laps around the 2.5-mile oval, under the scrutiny of Speedway officials and veteran competitors. Oregon's Art Pollard put it this way when he underwent the challenge in 1966: "I really know now why they call us rookies. Until you have driven at Indianapolis, you definitely are one."

In 1965 an unusually large number of rookies were registered at the beginning of May. Joining Billy Foster were: Mario Andretti, Ray Furnal, Jerry Grant, Masten Gregory, Bob Hurt, Gordon Johncock, Bobby Johns, Mel Kenyon, Arnie Knepper, Joe Leonard, Ralph Ligouri, Mike McGreevey, Mickey Rupp, George Snider, Gig Stevens, Al Unser, Sr., Greg Weld and Carl Williams.

In just the first week of practice Billy was already opening eyes while adapting to the nuances of the track. In an article in the May 7th, 1965 edition of *The Indianapolis Times*, reporter Jimmie Angelopolous introduced the Canadian to Indianapolis racing fans:

Billy Foster is no Bill Vukovich. But six-year-old Billy Foster, Jr., Debra, 7, and Kelly, 3, have a 27-year-old pedal-pushin' papa, the likes of which the Indianapolis Speedway rookie rolls have never seen. Today, Beverly – Mrs. Billy Foster – is so happy, things around the house at 274 Regina Ave., aren't the same.

Even the Royal Canadian Mounted Police couldn't summon enough horsepower if they had to catch Bullet Billy. And the most amazing – and nicest thing – about the fastest rookie in the 500-mile race history is that:

- Billy has more bullet-speed and bullets left in him;
- Billy is not brash;
- He is a highly-capable race driver who knows when to "get off it" and when to "get on it."
- And he's not only one of the top rookies to watch this year, but also one of THE drivers to watch in the coming qualifications and Speedway Classic.

Why all this Billy the Kid bit? This relaxed, friendly Canadian cranked up Len Sutton's old 1964 rear-engine Offy yesterday with the fastest laps ever run by a rookie at the Speedway – 155.3 and 155.1 miles-per-hour. And the scholarly-looking Sutton stepped up to the boyish-looking Foster and quipped: "How come you did something like that?"

Billy smiled. And he confessed he got "cross-armed" in the No. 3 turn. "It ran real easy. I stayed near the wall as high as I thought I should. It pushed once in No. 3 and I got 'cross-armed' a little bit too much but I had no trouble. It never did feel it would get away from me." A driver may get "cross-armed" when he is forced to steer excessively and gets his forearms overlapping on the steering wheel.

"I had laps of 154.3 and 154.5," Foster explained. "We've had only about 117 miles on the car this year. That's an 'old' engine. When we break in a new engine and get up to about 430 [horsepower], I think we can get more out of it."

This kid from the Pacific Northwest – Victoria, British Columbia – is no hare-brained kid on the hairy turns. He thinks he can take his Jim Robbins/Rolla Vollstedt Special No. 66 as high as 157 or 158 mph!

The car is the same one Sutton drove for Bryant Heating last year. Sutton qualified the car at 153.813 mph last year with the fastest lap in excess of 154 mph. Sutton started eighth last year and finished 15th, going out with fuel pump casting trouble after 140 laps.

Foster used Goodyear tires. Like Firestone, Goodyear, too, has helped improve speeds today. But most veteran drivers with their 500-horsepower rear engines haven't generated the speed so far that the 400-horsepower Offy fired up yesterday.

Most amazing thing about Foster is that he never saw the Indianapolis track until last week. "I really like this track. The curves are longer than what I've been used to, and I like the straightaway." Foster showed this early. He became the first rookie to pass his final 145 mph test Monday. He says the 87-inch wheelbase on the smaller cars he drove now helped him considerably.

(Rolla Vollstedt Collection)

"I began racing jalopies around home," he said, "then sprints and modifieds." He began driving in the Northwest in 1955.

"These mechanics work real hard [Grant King is the No. 66 chief mechanic] and lose ten pounds," Foster laughed easily. "I weigh around 170-pounds, but when I drive I get down to about 155."

Thanks to Sutton, Foster got a ride in Walt Flynn's championship car last season and he proved his worth. He placed 16th at Milwaukee, 7th at Trenton and 22nd at Phoenix, where he was forced out by mechanical failure. Mechanical trouble isn't new.

"I tire-tested for Goodyear in Phoenix in February," he says, "and I lost my brakes twice. The second time I hit the wall. I hit it only 10-feet from the first time."

He's no fly-by-night. Foster won 28 or 30 sprint races in 1964.

Two other comments:

He played hockey back home where he caught some sticks in his mouth. "And I've got some teeth to prove it," he laughed. He doesn't know Parnelli Jones. "I haven't even met him yet."

Parnelli – Meet Billy the Bullet.

Following the traditional two weekends of qualifying for the '500', A.J. Foyt secured the pole position with an average speed of 161.233 mph in his Sheraton/Thompson Lotus/Ford. Sharing the first row with Foyt was Scotsman Jimmy Clark's Lotus/Ford and Dan Gurney in another Lotus/Ford. An amazing front row indeed!

The fastest rookie was Andretti, driving the Dean Van Lines Hawk/Ford. Those that failed to qualify, or were withdrawn for other reasons, were Furnal, Hudson, Hurt, Kenyon, Ligouri, McGreevey, Stephens and Williams.

Billy's close friend Mario Andretti was the fastest rookie to qualify for the 1965 Indianapolis 500.

(Photo courtesy IMS)

Billy did a masterful job during his run, qualifying the Vollstedt/Offy in the sixth position with a four-lap average speed of 158.416 mph. Not only was this the fastest Offenhauser-powered car in the field, but Billy eclipsed Sutton's 1964 qualifying speed in the same car by 4.6 mph. The next fastest Offenhauser – the MG/Liquid Suspension Special driven by Bob Veith – qualified tenth at a speed of 156.427 mph.

Billy's record still stands at Indianapolis for a normally-aspired Offy. He would be starting the race on the outside of the second row, alongside Andretti and Parnelli Jones' Lotus/Ford.

The hard-luck driver in qualifying had to be two-time Indy champion, Rodger Ward. During the month, he suffered a crash and three blown engines. On Bump Day he made it onto the track in the final 15 minutes, but his qualifying run was still too slow to make the field. Driver Bob Mathouser became he final driver in Indy history to attempt to qualify a front-wheel-drive car but his engine blew, and he did not make the race

Jack Alkire, a reporter for *The Journal and Courier* newspaper in Lafayette, Indiana, conducted an interesting interview with Foster on May 25th, 1965:

"I'm 27, but I look like I'm 19." And he does. He's Billy Foster from Victoria, British Columbia, and one of the hottest rookies to hit the Speedway in many a year. Foster arrived at the Big Plan as a nobody three weeks ago, but before he had finished his driving tests, drivers and car owners were asking, "Who is that guy?"

And well they might. Speedway officials said Foster drove a smoother driving test than anyone in recent memory. And immediately after the test, Foster was on the track winding his rear-engine Offenhauser to speeds of 155.

And if you need more proof that Billy Foster has arrived at Indianapolis, check the car standings on the first day of qualifications. That's Foster in the second row – up there all alone in his little Offy with all those famous guys and their big Ford V-8s.

Who is Billy Foster? Well – he's a Canadian, in case you wonder where British Columbia is, and he has driven just about everything with wheels in the last ten years – mostly on the West Coast. He's cut a lot of rubber in sprint cars, and said he even drove one midget race. He drove in three USAC races last year and two this year. Included were big ones at Trenton, Milwaukee and Phoenix.

Foster never saw the Indianapolis Speedway before this year, but he liked it the minute he hit the asphalt.

"This is smooth. You can really move through those shoots and lazy turns. I really like it. Of course, I might change my mind if I have a few thrills here." (A thrill is when you lose your car and it spins and slides and maybe smacks a wall).

And Foster stands an excellent chance of becoming the first rookie to win the race since George Souders turned the trick back in 1927. These Ford cars can travel, but this year's Ford engine has shown signs of being temperamental. If the Fords fall apart, there sits Billy in the first Offenhauser. And everyone knows that an Offy can finish the race.

Around the track they say Billy is a swift driver, but not a foolish one. He's the Rodger Ward kind. He hangs in there with the hot shots and waits for his opening. If it develops, Billy Foster shows his fangs and goes.
His car is the No. 66 Vollstedt with an Offenhauser mounted at the rear like the Fords. The car has run exceptionally well, and Billy experienced no difficulty in qualifying it at 158.416 – the fastest anyone has ever driven an Offenhauser on the Indianapolis oval.

A week before qualifications, the talk around the track was that Billy blew an engine on his car. That wasn't exactly true. Billy had the car, with its old engine, out for a spin when he felt the engine tighten-up. He shut her off and coasted in, thus saving the Vollstedt outfit major overhaul problems.

This is another sign of a good driver. He didn't let the engine blow up under him. Owners appreciate that. "We were ready to put a new engine in anyway so we could break it in for qualification," Billy explained. "That old engine had over 500 miles on it, and we were expecting it to go at any time. The car and engine had been raced at Trenton.

Even if Billy doesn't win or place high in the race, he stands a good chance at winning "Rookie of the Year" honors. His chief opponent for the title is the lead-footed Italian from Nazareth, Pa., Mario Andretti. Foster appreciates Andretti's skill also. "He's quite a driver from all I can find out," Foster said.
Billy may look only 19, but he has a thriving family to help prove he's really 27. Besides his wife, three small Fosters help fill the Foster home – a boy 6, and two girls, ages 7 and 3.

An Indianapolis tradition: Billy removing his rookie stripes.

(John Feuz Collection)

Pacific Northwest drivers at Indy in 1965: Jerry Grant (Seattle), Billy Foster (Victoria) and Len Sutton (Portland). Grant was driving the Bardahl/MG Liquid Suspension Special for car owner Kjell Qvale.

(Jay Koch Collection)

The 49th 500-Mile Sweepstakes

Pat Vidan, a native of Portland, Oregon, was the Chief Starter at Indianapolis for many years.

(Photo courtesy IMS)

On Monday, May 31st, the cars to beat were clearly the Lotus/Fords. This would also be the first time ABC's *Wide World of Sports* would cover the race, but on a delayed broadcast.

1965 would turn out be Len Sutton's final drive at Indianapolis. In his autobiography *My Road to Indy*, after naming all the rookies that year, Len noted:

"With a line-up like that, a driver at forty years of age ought to think about something else."

On race morning the cars were lined up on the pit apron for warm-ups, but within seconds of firing Sutton's engine, an oil leak was discovered. Vollstedt's crew found that an oil line or coupling had come loose and after a hasty repair, his car was able to join the rest of the field for the pace laps.

Once starter Pat Vidan unfurled the green flag, Clark jumped ahead of Foyt for a lap. Foyt grabbed the lead for the second lap, but then Clark regained the position and quickly pulled away from the remainder of the field.

The first half of the race saw a lot of mechanical attrition, with 17 cars dropping out by the 100th lap. Unfortunately, among them was Billy Foster, who made it to the 85th lap before the water manifold failed.

During the race Billy's teammate Sutton's engine was not performing as it should, so after a series of pit stops the problem was diagnosed as plugged fuel injector nozzles. After a long stop to clean the nozzles, Sutton was able to rejoin the race, noting:

"That seemed to take care of the problem and I went back out. It ran reasonably well," said Len. "I re-entered the race right behind Jimmy Clark and stuck with him until he took the checkered flag. He was the winner. I was down 23 laps with a twelfth-place finish."

Following a continuing duel between Clark and Foyt, Clark took the lead for good on lap 75 and drove the rest of the distance, relatively unchallenged in becoming the victor. Billy came away from his first '500' credited with a 17th place finish and $9,936 in prize money.

Andretti, who ran no lower than sixth all day, finished third behind Jones and was named Rookie of the Year. And though they were, for all practical purposes obsolete, two front-engine roadsters finished in the top ten - Gordon Johncock finished fifth and Eddie Johnson finished tenth, both driving a Watson/Offy.

TWENTY-FIVE

The 1965 Champ Car Season – Second Half

It became apparent in 1965 that the new rear-engine cars had become established, and Billy Foster was becoming confident with this style of driving and handling.

Following Indianapolis, the next event on the Champ Car calendar was a 100-lap race at the Milwaukee Mile on June 6th. Billy did not take part in this race, though Len Sutton and his Vollstedt/Ford were on the grid. The day did not turn out well for him, as he retired after only completing 18 laps due to a suspension failure.

The series traveled to the one-mile paved oval at Langhorne, Pennsylvania, for another 100-lap race on June 20th. This time both Vollstedt cars were entered - Sutton in the #16 Ford and Foster back in the #66 Offy. It would turn out to be a successful day for both drivers but would also mark the end of Sutton's long driving career.

(Jay Koch Collection)

Following qualifications, Mario Andretti would start from the pole alongside second-fastest qualifier Jim McElreath. Billy's Autotron Electronics-sponsored car, owned by Jim Robbins, turned in the 13th quickest time. Sutton would start the race 15th in the 22-car field.

Billy the cowboy relaxing in his 'saddle'.

(John Feuz Collection)

Andretti and McElreath traded the lead over the course of the race. McElreath's Brabham/Offy led the final 24 laps to take the win over Andretti, with Lloyd Ruby finishing third. Eight finishers completed all 100 laps and included Foster in the fifth position and Sutton in the eighth. Their earnings were Foster ($1,764) and Sutton ($1,176), compared to the winner's take of $7,350. It was a good day for the Vollstedt team.

Yes, Langhorne turned out to be Len Sutton's retirement as an active drive – a career that began at the Portland Speedway in 1946 following his naval service during World War Two. In this autobiography, Len explained his final race:

"I was starting 15th (not that good), but during the race things were looking better as I worked my way up to fifth. Midway through the race, a bad accident occurred, and the race was stopped. Mel Kenyon was severely burned and taken to the hospital.

Eventually the race was restarted. With about ten laps to go, I got a muscle cramp in my neck. I could not hold my head up without help. I ended up bracing my head with my right arm and hand, and finished the race driving with just my left hand.

Two cars got by me (one was Billy Foster) and after the race, I was sure I had driven my last race. My real thoughts were focused on watching the fourth driver (Mel Kenyon) get burned in a crash during the last two years. I believed it was time for me to consider my family first and call it quits.

Billy and his good friend, teammate and mentor Len Sutton. Len passed away in 2006 at the age of 81.

(Rolla Vollstedt Collection)

I arrived back home as I had done many times before. Anita (Len's wife) and I had a talk. We talked about the race that I had just driven, and what the kids had been doing. It was probably a week later when, over a cup of coffee, I said 'I think I might just hang it up.' She said, 'hang what up?' and I said, 'driving race cars.' I believe we just stared at each other and nothing else was said."

Following the end of his competitive driving career, Len held a full-time position with Monroe Auto Equipment, as well as representing Raybestos. He also went to work alongside long-time Indianapolis announcer, Tom Carnegie, for a 30-minute local television show in Indianapolis during the month of May. During the years 1970-1972, Len was an expert commentator on the radio broadcast of the Indianapolis 500, working side-by-side with veteran broadcaster Sid Collins.

When Sutton stepped away from the cockpit of the #16 Vollstedt/Ford, Rolla turned the car over to Billy Foster. Billy's first run in the car was the next oval race at Trenton Speedway on July 18th. At the end of qualifying, A.J. Foyt was on the pole. Foster grabbed the eighth-starting position. Popular Texan racer Lloyd Ruby was given the ride of the #66 Vollstedt/Offy for this race and qualified fifth.

At the end of the 150-lap event, it had been an A.J Foyt-type of day. He took home the winner's trophy and prize money by leading every lap in his Sheraton/Thompson Lotus/Ford. Jim Hurtubise finished second, one lap down.

Meanwhile, Foster's car lost a wheel and crashed on the 45th lap, which put him out of the race and he finished in the 20th spot. Ruby made it as far as the 71st lap, but then a Heim joint broke on the right front suspension and he wrecked in turn three.

Trenton Speedway, July 1965. Don Branson in the Watson/Offy roadster dicing with Foster's Vollstedt/Ford.

(Ralph Hunt Collection)

The next race on the USAC trail was on July 25th on the 1.8-mile road course at Indianapolis Raceway Park, but neither Vollstedt car was entered. Andretti and Foyt dueled for the win during the 80-lap contest, with Andretti coming out on top ahead of Bobby Unser, Roger McCluskey and Foyt.

Atlanta International Raceway (now Atlanta Motor Speedway) was first opened in 1960 as a 1.5-mile standard banked oval, and quickly became a favorite venue for NASCAR drivers and fans. The first Atlanta 500 was held in late October of 1960, with Bobby Johns the winner in his Cotton Owens-built 1960 Pontiac.

The Champ Car series held its first event at Atlanta on August 1st, 1965, with 29 cars posting qualifying times. Foyt recorded the fastest lap with a time of 32.430 seconds. Foster timed in just behind with a lap of 32.970 seconds. He would start the race on the front row, alongside Foyt. Behind them, in order, would be Bobby Unser (Huffaker/Offy), Gordon Johncock (Watson/Offy), Johnny

Rutherford (Watson/Ford) and Jim Hurtubise (Kurtis/Novi). The car Rutherford was driving was the same Watson that Rodger Ward was unable to qualify at Indy in May.

Foyt led the first 88 laps of the race and then Rutherford took over the lead for the next nine laps. A.J. then re-passed Rutherford to lead the next ten laps, but a suspension component on Foyt's car broke. The malfunction caused a spin, putting him into the wall and out of the running. He was uninjured.

Rutherford regained the lead and held onto it for the rest of the 167-lap race. The winner's average speed, considering three caution periods, was 141.7 mph. During the day there were several crashes or mechanical failures that eliminated 13 cars.

Just two other drivers finished on the same lap as Rutherford - Andretti in the runner-up spot and Foster, who drove an inspired race and would have finished second had it not been for a late race fuel problem.

"Hard luck," Billy said after the race. "I just ran out of fuel. My pit gave me the 90-lap sign too late to pit as planned on lap 90. They should have given it to me on the 89th so I could have been in on the 90th, but that's racing. I'll win the next one."

Vollstedt and Foster left the track with $5,700 in winnings and an important 350 points towards the driver's championship.

(Jay Koch Collection)

The following week, the Champ Cars traveled to Langhorne, Pennsylvania for the 'Langhorne 125'. For this weekend, Billy was commissioned to drive the #34 Watson/Offy entered by owner Jim Robbins and his Autotron Company.

Gordon Johncock qualified quickest in his Watson/Offy, while Foster would start seventh in the field of 22 cars. Johncock led from the start until lap 42 but was overtaken by Jim McElreath's Brabham/Offy, which led the remainder of the distance to take the checkered flag. A.J. Foyt finished second and Johncock was third in the 125-lap race. Billy completed 98 laps and was running at the end, but only recorded a 17th-place finish.

August 14th, 1965 marked the return of the Champ Cars to the ultra-competitive Milwaukee Mile in West Allis, Wisconsin. At the start of the 150-lap race Parnelli Jones, driving the #98 Lotus/Ford for J.C. Agajanian, jumped from his pole position ahead of number-two qualifier Mario Andretti.

Meanwhile, Billy's Vollstedt/Ford began the race from the 12th position and was working his way through the field when engine problems took him out on the 40th lap. He ended up finishing 20th in the 24-car field. When Jones' car dropped out with electrical issues, Joe Leonard assumed the lead and drove unchallenged all the way to victory. Leonard was driving a Halibrand/Ford for Dan Gurney's All American Racers team. Second and third place, respectively, went to Andretti (Brawner/Ford) and Dan Gurney (Lotus/Ford).

The next race was the 'Tony Bettenhausen Memorial' on the one-mile dirt track at the Illinois State Fairgrounds, but Billy did not have a ride. Winning the 100-lap race was Foyt, driving a Meskowski/Offy sprint car. The next day, though, the Championship Cars returned to Milwaukee for a 200-lap contest.

Gearing up for Milwaukee, Rolla Vollstedt called on Oregon's Art Pollard, a highly successful driver from the Pacific Northwest and a good friend and competitor of Billy's. This would be a two-fold debut for Art – his introduction to USAC's Champ Cars and his first experience driving a rear-engine car in the form of Vollstedt's Offy-powered machine. It was a big leap for Pollard, who would face a field of extraordinary veteran drivers.

Billy making a pass on Tommy Copp's Watson/Offy at Atlanta.

(Jay Koch Collection)

With Foster in his Vollstedt/Ford and Pollard's Vollstedt/Offy, there was an air of optimism going into the race. But after 26 cars had qualified, there was a bit of concern: Foster only managed to score the 15th position on the grid in the Bryant Heating & Cooling-sponsored car, while Pollard would start his Autotron Electronics-sponsored car 25th.

Perhaps the biggest surprise during qualifying was provided by Foyt. After winning the day before on the fairground's dirt track, he learned his new rear-engine Lotus wasn't ready for the Milwaukee event. At the last moment, he decided to unload his dirt car and attempt to qualify it. Well, he did much more than merely qualify – by setting the top time to earn the pole! Dan Gurney would share the front row with Foyt in his familiar Lotus/Ford.

Billy managed to get in just seven laps before a mechanical failure ended his day with a 26th-place finish. Pollard held on for 77 laps before spinning out of the race to finish 22nd. It was a disappointing day for both drivers.

The race itself saw several leaders during the 200-lap afternoon. Joining Foyt and Gurney at the top of the standings were Andretti, Leonard, and Johncock. In the final stages, Johncock led the final 29 laps for the victory. Foyt came home second and Lloyd Ruby was third. Foyt and his sprint car may have won the race if he was not forced to make a stop for fuel. As he described, the car was set-up for a 100-lap run, therefore requiring the extra fuel to accomplish 200 laps.

The next race of the season was another dirt track event at the DuQuoin State Fairgrounds in Illinois, but neither Foster nor Pollard competed. Don Branson was the victor in a Watson/Offy.

On September 18th however, Billy landed a ride for the 'Hoosier Hundred' – a 100-lap race on the one-mile dirt track at the Indiana State Fairgrounds. He was driving a Meskowski/Offy sprint car for owner David McManus and sponsored by Bryant Heating & Cooling.

The legendary A.J. Foyt (#1) fighting off a challenge by Billy Foster.

(Jay Koch Collection)

It came as no surprise that A.J. Foyt won the pole in his Meskowki/Offy, while George Snider was second-quickest in a Watson/Offy. Foster started 16th in the 18-car lineup. From the green flag, Snider led until lap 14 when Foyt took over and drove to victory over Andretti's Kuzma/Offy. Billy finished in the 12th position, three laps down to Foyt, and won $995.

In late September, the Champ Cars returned to the Trenton Speedway for a 200-lap event. This weekend, Foster was behind the wheel of a Kurtis/Offy owned by Tassi Vatis. Billy's buddy Art

Pollard was also entered, driving the Vollstedt/Offy for Jim Robbins. Post-qualifying found Foyt on the pole, while Pollard would start from the 13th position and Foster was two back in 15th.

A.J. Foyt was having a tremendous season thus far, and his winning ways continued this day at Trenton. He wheeled his Lotus/Ford from the head of the field the entire distance, leading all 200 laps in dominating fashion. Foster's car survived only 16 laps before his engine expired, finishing in 24th place. In just his second Champ Car race, Pollard had a heck of a day and finished fifth, behind Foyt, Leonard, McElreath and McCluskey.

There were just two more events on the 1965 schedule: the 'Golden State 100' dirt track race at the California State Fairgrounds in Sacramento, and the 'Bobby Ball Memorial' at Phoenix on November 21st. Billy did not compete at Sacramento, but was in the Vollstedt/Ford at Phoenix. There, he qualified for the tenth position. Pollard was also there with Vollstedt's Offy and qualified 15th. Twenty-six cars would start the race.

Starting from the pole, Andretti led the first half of the 200-lap race with his Dean Van Lines Brawner/Ford. During the second half, he dueled back and forth with Foyt. In the end, it was again Foyt finishing first with Andretti second. One lap down was Bobby Unser's Huffaker/Offy. Foster was still running at the end, credited with a 13th-place finish after completing 188 laps. Pollard suffered a crash on lap 70, finishing 19th.

Despite a very successful season – winning 17 races – A.J. Foyt lost the championship to Mario Andretti in the final standings for the 1965 USAC Champ Car Championship. Andretti won 16 races but gained 610 more points than Foyt. Rounding out the top five drivers were Jim McElreath in third, followed by Don Branson and Gordon Johncock. Carl Williams was named Rookie of the Year.

Billy Foster competed in 12 events, with two top-five finishes and three top-tens. With 520 total points, he finished 16th from a total of 57 drivers who had earned points during the season.

Billy could now go home to Victoria to spend quality time with his family and friends, while making plans for the 1966 season – which was right around the corner.

(Jay Koch Collection)

TWENTY-SIX

Billy's Friends Remember – Mario Andretti

A good friend is like a four-leaf clover – hard to find and lucky to have. – Irish Proverb

(Foster Family Collection)

In the short time they shared together, Billy Foster and Mario Andretti grew so close they could have been brothers. And they shared the same goal – to become champions in the sport they loved.

One came from the east coast, one from the west, and the young contenders first competed against each other in the middle of the country – at the famed Milwaukee Mile in West Allis, Wisconsin.

The event was the 1964 running of the 'Tony Bettenhausen 200' on August 23rd, smack dab in the heat of another busy season for the United States Automobile Club's Champ Car Series.

This had been a transitional year for the series, which was witnessing the slow demise of the traditional front-engine roadsters in favor of the new, lightweight, rear-engine machines.

The standouts in American racing circles were all there: A.J. Foyt, Parnelli Jones, Rodger Ward, Johnny Rutherford and Don Branson, to name a few.

Andretti was driving for Al Dean (Dean Van Lines) and was behind the wheel of an Offenhauser-powered car built by Hank Blum.

Meanwhile, Foster was in a Flynn/Offy upright built and owned by Walt Flynn. Flynn was the owner and operator of the Enterprise Machine Company in Indianapolis and a long-time builder of racing machines. He had also invented the Flynn carburetor that became popular in racing.

Billy's friend Len Sutton had driven a few races for Flynn, and through Len's recommendation, Foster and Flynn hooked up.

There were 26 cars that made up the field for the 200-lap event, with Andretti qualifying ninth and Foster 18th. When all was said and done, Parnelli Jones in his Lotus/Ford was the victor, two laps ahead of Rodger Ward in second. Mario finished third, four laps in arrears of Jones.

Billy was running at the end, finishing 16th after completing 181 laps. Andretti's share of the race purse was $3,200, while Foster pocketed just $700.

It came as no surprise that these two youthful souls bonded during this time period. They were a little over two years apart in age – Billy was 26 and Mario was 24. Though both were small in stature, each had worked their way up to the big time after cutting their teeth and honing their competitive talents in the rough-and-tumble 'little leagues' of racing in their own locales.

Coming from a family that was embedded in Victoria-area racing, Billy began his own time in the cockpit in 1954.

Born in Italy and Formula One racing fans at an early age, Mario and his twin brother Aldo's heroes bore names like Nino Farina, Alberto Ascari and Sterling Moss. In 1955, the Andretti family immigrated to the United States, settling in Nazareth, Pennsylvania.

There, they discovered a half-mile dirt track and several years later acquired a 1948 Hudson that they modified for racing, beginning in 1959. Mario and Aldo took turns driving, but were careful not to let their parents know what they were up to.

Beginning in 1964, the connection that Foster and Andretti developed also included their young families – with the children under the watchful eyes of Billy's wife Bev and Mario's wife Dee Ann, who sadly passed away in July of 2018.

Between the two families at the time, there were five young mouths to feed: Debra (7), Billy Jr. (6) and Kelly (2) Foster; plus Michael (3) and Jeff (1) Andretti

"At Indianapolis, we had a trailer we used to use instead of using apartments for the kids," Mario recalled to this author. "It was a beautiful trailer court that is still there – Lantern Estates. Johnny Rutherford was the other driver that had been staying there and I knew he had good tastes."

"I find myself there and, before you know it, there's Billy – he's my neighbor with his family. That's how we connected, we both had young children and we're coming up to that [racing] level together."

(Foster Family Collection)

Mario went on to say, "Billy was with Rolla Vollstedt, who was the nicest guy and always proud. He brought along this young Canadian hotshot. No question about it – they were immediately a factor, and everything worked. Vollstedt was very intelligent and knew what needed to be done. Billy was in good hands and did his part and, of course, did Grant King."

For young drivers, the 1965 edition of the Indianapolis 500 was noteworthy - as there were eleven rookies that qualified. Beyond Andretti and Foster, the esteemed list included Gordon Johncock, Mickey Rupp, Bobby Johns, Al Unser, Sr., Arnie Knepper, George Snider, Masten Gregory, Jerry Grant and Joe Leonard.

Andretti and Foster both started the race from the second row – Mario on the inside (Hawk/Ford), Billy on the outside (Vollstedt/Offy), with veteran Parnelli Jones in the middle (Lotus/Ford).

The victor was Scotsman Jimmy Clark (Lotus/Ford). Mario had a distinguished run, finishing third and earning the Rookie of the Year Award. Billy was competitive during the early stages of the race, but his Offy suffered a water manifold leak which dropped him from the running on the 85th lap. He placed 17th in the final results.

There were many more races to travel to that season and the friendship between the Foster and Andretti families continued to grow.

"There was much more of a camaraderie among drivers in those times," Mario described. "If we were running in the Midwest, we would stay there for a while and ditto for the west coast. We weren't constantly going back and forth. Airline travel was not like it is today – they did not have as many flights. I was racing sprint cars and everything else, and so was Billy. We were both doing the same thing and had so much in common in that respect. We were both striving to further our careers."

Sharing quality time – Mario and Dee Ann Andretti together with Billy and Bev Foster.

(Foster Family Collection)

Mario continued, "Billy and I really clicked as friends. We bought motorcycles together. I just loved his demeanor – very casual and just took life in stride. We'd take a flight together. I'd ask him, 'where's your bag or your toothbrush?' He'd just reply, 'I'll buy it when I get there.' I loved stuff like that."

1966 - Mario Andretti, Jim Russell, Parnelli Jones and Billy Foster playing with slot cars.

(Jay Koch collection)

In one interview, Andretti was asked how he would define a great friendship. His answer was fitting: "A confidant. Someone you trust completely. Someone who reinforces your best self. A sounding board, a safety net, someone who is there when you go flat out, saying "cliff, waterfall, banana peel, look out!"

Both drivers were progressing nicely during the 1965 and 1966 seasons. "We were making some money of course," stated Mario. "We were looking to the future to protect our families and so forth. And I remember Billy would get on my butt about me still being in sprint cars because it was so dangerous."

When not racing Champ Cars, Billy was busy driving in USAC stock car events for Rudy Hoerr. There were many times when Billy would urge Mario to run more of the supposedly safer sedans over sprints.

"Billy would tell me, 'you're crazy Mario, you should get out of sprint cars.'", Andretti told this author. "Here's a guy who acted so responsibly – thinking about himself and his family. I'll never know how much he got on me about that, and then he loses his life doing exactly that. That's the ironic part about it and it's so sad, sad, sad in so many ways."

"I was connected with Ford and Rudy was fielding a Dodge [in stock cars], Mario remembers. "Billy was doing really well against Parnelli Jones and other tough guys. I did have sporadic rides in the stocks."

Andretti remembered one particular stock car race that took place at Mid-America Raceways in Wentzville, Missouri: "Billy, Parnelli Jones and I were in quite a fight. We were bumping each other, and Billy was really throwing that baby around. He didn't take anything from nobody. He was awesome - showing his talent and his future."

"Billy was a natural race driver, which means a driver who could adapt," as Mario described his friend. "He knew what he needed to do to be up to date. USAC was expanding into road racing, and he wasn't going to be left behind. I was one who was so adamant about getting road racing restored. I lobbied like crazy to get road racing as part of the series, so together we talked about that a lot - those were challenges we wanted to go after."

Billy Foster, Art Pollard and Mario Andretti sharing a light-hearted moment.

(Pollard Family Collection)

Continuing in this vein, Mario explained:

"I wanted to get into Formula One eventually and I needed road racing in order to be proficient - that's why we lobbied. Billy knew that I was involved with the Ford program and I was doing part of the test and development for them, which was golden for me. I'm sure he expressed the same thing.

That's the other thing – he was thinking we could spread our wings outside of racing with a business. Billy was always thinking in those terms – any opportunity to involve himself in business."

With Billy's fatal accident at Riverside, the loss of his close pal devasted Mario Andretti:

"It was the first big race of the season," he notes. "We were rooming together by ourselves - our families were not there. You have to imagine me going back to the room and calling Bev [Billy's wife] while still having to get back into my race car and doing my thing. Those are the moments that we unfortunately experience all too often. I lost several friends, including Jud Larsen and Dick Atkins, in a short time span. Thereafter, that's why I had a tough time getting close to other drivers."

"In the short time we had together we really bonded. It was a natural friendship and I just loved the guy for everything. I loved being with him and our wives and children got on really well when we were on the road."

"We were both coming out of that and we both reached the maximum level in Indy cars. We felt a responsibility, and Billy was doing just the right thing in that respect. That's why he was respected, and everyone that knew him knew he was championship material – no question about it."

In June 2016 Andretti authored an article for *The Players' Tribune* entitled *"Letter to My Younger Self"*, in which he outlined his amazing career in motorsports. Within that excellent recollection, he reflected about Billy: "I don't have any advice for how to cope with the loss of a friend, Mario. There's nothing that can prepare you for something like that. All I can say is that it's something you never get used to. Nothing is ever the same after you lose a buddy – someone who has touched your life."

"Billy will be one of those guys."

TWENTY-SEVEN

1965 – Billy's Start in the USAC Stock Car Series

Just after the turn of the 20th century, the American Automobile Association (AAA) created an organization called the Racing Board, which later became known at the Contest Board. The original intent of this committee was to officiate at the 1904 Vanderbilt Cup international automobile race in Long Island, New York.

At first, the association used the rules of the Automobile Club of America (ACA), but then formed its own set of rules in 1903. The AAA introduced the first track season championship for racing cars in 1905, and the legendary driver Barney Oldfield was the first champion. Over the course of many years thereafter, the AAA was perhaps best recognized as the sanctioning body of the Indianapolis 500.

Two tragic incidences took place during 1955 that prompted the AAA to end its long-standing oversight of auto racing in the United States, beginning with the death of popular driver Billy Vukovich at the Indianapolis 500. Soon thereafter was the disastrous accident during France's 24 Hours of LeMans that claimed the life of driver Pierre Levegh, along with 83 spectators who were killed when both his car and debris flew into the closely-packed crowd.

Upon AAA's withdrawal from racing, the United States Auto Club (USAC) began sanctioning professional auto racing in the United States in 1956 with two primary series – Champ Cars and Stock Cars. Many drivers of that era competed in both divisions on paved and dirt tracks around the country, including the Indianapolis 500.

At the end of the first season, Jimmy Bryan was named the Champ Car Champion, while Johnny Mantz became the Stock Car Champion. USAC also featured a National Midget Car Series, where Shorty Templeman drove to the Championship in 1956. From 1958 to 1962, USAC included a road racing championship.

USAC's Stock Car series during the late 1950s and throughout the 1960s proved popular, particularly in the Midwestern and Northeastern areas of the country, where many smaller tracks were located. The cars were nearly identical to those competing at the time in NASCAR's Grand National ranks.

1956: USAC Stock Cars at Paramount Ranch in Agoura, California.

(Ford Total Performance Photo)

Tracks such as the Milwaukee Mile, DuQuoin State Fairgrounds, Indianapolis Raceway Park, Langhorne Speedway and the annual Pikes Peak International Hill Climb in Colorado played host to the stock car events. Later, USAC found its way to larger tracks such as Michigan International Raceway, Texas World Speedway, Ontario Motor Speedway in California, and Pocono Raceway in Pennsylvania.

The stock car events at these larger tracks were sometimes held in conjunction with the Championship Cars, with several drivers competing in both series on the same weekend. Those that drove the stock cars included stand-outs such as Fred Lorenzen, Paul Goldsmith, Norm Nelson, Jerry and Al Unser Sr., A.J. Foyt, Parnelli Jones, Joe Leonard and Roger McCluskey.

And we can add to that list - Billy Foster.

Billy's first race in a USAC stock car took place on November 14th, 1964, at Ascot Park near Los Angeles. Ascot was a half-mile dirt oval that opened in 1957 and hosted racing until the end of 1990. Though the car's owner is unknown, Billy's 1963 Mercury qualified 10th and finished 5th. Parnelli Jones drove his Bill Stroppe-prepared '64 Mercury to victory.

Two weeks later Billy competed in his second USAC stock car race at Hanford Motor Speedway in California, but again no car owner or make of car was identified in the record books. The 200-mile event on Hanford's 1.5-mile paved oval was labeled the 'Billy Vukovich Memorial', with a field of 25 cars. The race drew 6,500 spectators and was televised on ABC television's *Wide World of Sports*.

A number of notable USAC Champ Car drivers of the time participated, such as A.J. Foyt, Parnelli Jones, Joe Leonard, Bobby Unser and Lloyd Ruby. The 134-lap race was won by Foyt, driving a 1964 Dodge, followed by Jones' '64 Mercury and Leonard's '64 Dodge. Foster was credited with a 13th-place finish.

The stock cars returned to Ascot Park on December 6th, 1964 when Billy qualified a 1964 Plymouth in the 13th grid position. His drive ended after just 13 laps and resulted in a 24th-place finish.

DuQuoin, Illinois, 1963: Gary Bettenhausen (#99) and Mario Andretti (#4) lead the field to the green flag.

(Midwest Racing Archives – Doug Dempsey Collection)

It was about this time that Billy became acquainted with car owner and builder Rudy Hoerr of Peoria, Illinois. Together, this pairing would realize success during the 1965 and 1966 USAC stock car seasons.

TWENTY-EIGHT

The Rudy Hoerr Family

Rudy Hoerr was born in 1921 in Milford, Indiana, and married his wife Ann in December of 1941 in Peoria, Illinois. During World War Two, Rudy served in the U.S. Army Air Corp as a B-24 bomber pilot in the European Theatre.

Given the rate of airmen killed, wounded, missing in action or taken captive during those years, Rudy was extremely fortunate to survive nearly 40 missions. It is generally accepted that the crews of the bomber command had the highest attrition race – roughly 45.5 percent – among all the Allied services during the war. Manned by a crew of eleven airmen, they often referred to the B-24 as the 'Flying Coffin'.

Upon his return to the United States, Rudy trained to pilot a B-29 bomber in anticipation of a transfer to the war in the Pacific. Japan surrendered prior to his being dispatched. In later years, Rudy Hoerr was a Charter Member of the Illinois Air National Guard, 169th Fighter Squadron, ultimately retiring as a Lieutenant Colonel.

With a strong interest in auto racing, Rudy and Ann Hoerr became active as car owners and builders when the old Mt. Hawley Speedway was operating in Peoria, Illinois. As time went by, they advanced from the local scene to become regulars on the USAC Stock Car circuit. During those years, several big-name competitors drove for Rudy, including Herb Shannon, Bill Cheesbourg, Bob Christie, Billy Foster and Al Unser, Sr. During the 1970s and 1980s, with their sons Irv and Scott as drivers, the Hoerr family competed in both the International Motor Sports Association (IMSA) and the Sports Car Club of America (SCCA) racing series.

How did Billy first become associated with Rudy Hoerr?

Both Irv and Scott Hoerr believe it was through Grant King. "I was a teenager in 1964," Irv says. "Dad was working with Bill Cheesbourg (Tucson, Arizona) and then

Rudy and Ann Hoerr.

(Hoerr Family Collection)

Bob Christie (Grants Pass, Oregon), but the team didn't do real well. At the time we became acquainted with Grant King and Rolla Vollstedt."

Scott, five years younger than Irv, said, "To be honest I don't really have a lot of memories because I was very young at that time. I do remember that when Billy came along for Dad the whole family was happy, because the success level definitely was raised from what Dad had before. I can't tell you how Dad met Grant. The only connections he or his team had with open-wheel cars was through his drivers, Cheesbourg and Christie. Dad went to Indy just as a friend to those guys, so I'm sure that's how he met Grant. Billy was definitely a step-up with his driving ability."

When Billy tragically lost his live at Riverside in January of 1967, Rudy Hoerr brought on Al Unser, Sr. as his driver. Al won USAC's stock car Rookie of the Year Award at the end of the season. Hoerr and Unser continued to work together over the next several seasons in the stock cars, switching from Dodge to Ford products in the early 1970s.

As a teenager, Irv Hoerr raced motorcycles and auto-crossed whenever he was not working as a mechanic for his Dad's race team. Al Unser, Sr., who had befriended the Hoerr family, had an early hand in igniting Irv's further interest in racing.

One time, the team was conducting a tire test at Indianapolis Raceway Park and the tires needed to be warmed-up before testing. On a whim, Al invited Irv to go out on the track with him and gave tips on how to drive on a road course. Irv's future driving style was influenced by Unser on those cold mornings.

Rudy Hoerr and Al Unser, Sr.

(Hoerr Family Collection)

"In 1975, I drove my first race in our (race-prepared) Ford Pinto," says Irv. He and his brother Scott proved very successful in their first season racing in the International Motor Sports Association (IMSA) Series. Their results helped to land a factory deal with Datsun at the end of the season.

Following their association with Datsun, the Hoerr Racing Team moved forward with another independent chassis for an American Motors Corporation (AMC) Spirit running in IMSA's Champion Spark Plug Series. Despite being independently-funded and having a home-built car, more success continued.

Hoerr's next custom chassis was underneath a Pontiac Firebird, where they moved up to IMSA's American Challenge Series. They gained the sponsorship of American Technical Services (ATS) in 1982. With that additional support, Hoerr Racing experienced even greater results with a Chevrolet Camaro, nearly winning the championship in 1984. Impressed by their winnings, Chevrolet offered Hoerr a deal that would lead to an eleven-year partnership with General Motors.

Together, Rudy, Irv and Scott proved to everyone what a grassroots team with a great chassis could do. It was a time when each of the General Motors divisions had their own individual racing departments. After two seasons racing a Chevrolet, Irv was spotted by an Oldsmobile representative, Dick Haas, during a race on a very wet Meadowlands (New Jersey) track in 1985. At the time Oldsmobile acted as GM's representative in both the IMSA and Trans-Am Series. Having learned years earlier how to drive fast in the rain by Al Unser, Irv was offered a deal by Haas. The first model he raced for Oldsmobile was a Toronado in IMSA's American Challenge Series.

Irv spent the years 1988-1990 racing his own team, Hoerr Racing, in the Sports Car Club of America's (SCCA) Trans-Am Series. Using Oldsmobile Cutlass-bodied racers, Irv narrowly lost the championship to Audi in 1988 and to Ford in 1989.

In 1991, Irv was brought on as a driver for the Rocketsports racing team. Still driving Oldsmobiles, he won the IMSA GTO championship in 1992. From 1993 to 1996, he drove for Harry Brix's IMSA GTS team, winning that championship in 1995 and 1996. Irv retired from full-time racing at the end of 2006 but continued driving on a part-time basis until 2002.

"I had no desire to run at Indianapolis," recalls Irv. "I had one offer but turned it down because I was too old. One year I co-drove with Buddy Lazier (winner of the 1996 Indianapolis 500 and the 2000 Indy Racing League Champion) in the Daytona 24 Hour race, and we became good friends. He felt I had the driving style that would work well, particularly at Indy."

Scott and Irv were still building custom chassis when Irv was still competing in the Trans-Am series. When Irv's driving career became much busier, Scott and a family friend, Mike Koeppel, continued to build turn-key race cars.

When Irv retired from full-time racing, he and friend Harry Brix entered the new NASCAR Truck Series with a new team but elected to sell the operation midway through the 1997 season. As general manager, Irv could sell the team and most of the equipment in one lump sum deal, but there were still many items that were leftovers.

With this large number parts and no real use for them, Brix asked Hoerr to transport the parts to his shop in Peoria and sell them. Irv came to enjoy selling these parts and soon realized that the venture could prove to be a lucrative business enterprise.

After six months of car building and selling parts, Irv sent out the first Hoerr Racing Products (HRP) catalog to several SCCA teams. As the company continued to expand, it quickly became a full-time exercise. Today, HRP's multi-level expertise and development services allow the company to service every racing need.

"We sell parts to virtually all of the professional road race teams, including the Indy Car Series," Irv explained. "We are the suppliers for all the brake rotors. A number of NASCAR teams also purchase parts from us.

"My son-in-law runs the business now, while I'm down in Florida enjoying retirement. I go to a race now and then to visit with some of our customers."

Rudy Hoerr passed away in November 2012 at age 91. Rudy's wife, Ann, preceded him in death in 2001. They were survived by children Linda, Irvan, and Scott, along with six grandchildren and 18 great-grandchildren. Rudy and Ann were both inducted into the Greater Peoria Sports Hall of Fame.

Sadly, Scott Hoerr passed away in late January of 2019.

Hoerr Family racing through the years.

(Hoerr Family Collection)

TWENTY-NINE

The 1965 USAC Stock Car Season

Billy's first stock car race of the 1965 season was back at Ascot Park in California on March 27th. This was a 200-lap event for NASCAR's Pacific Coast Late Model Division, with Billy driving Rudy Hoerr's 1963 Plymouth. He qualified fourth in the 23-car field, but the day ended poorly with an 18th-place finish. California's Marvin Porter was the victor in his 1964 Ford.

Through the next several months, Billy's schedule was consumed by four major USAC Champ Car races, including the all-important Indianapolis 500, where he started as a rookie.

His return to the stock car circuit began on the Fourth of July weekend on the one-half mile paved oval at Illiana Speedway in Schereville, Indiana. Driving Hoerr's 1965 Dodge, Billy started sixth and finished sixth in a rather small field of just 15 cars. USAC stock car standout Norm Nelson was the winner, followed across the line by Bobby Isaac and Jim Hurtubise.

On July 11th, the USAC stock cars traveled to the Milwaukee Mile paved oval in West Allis, Wisconsin. This historic track began hosting racing in 1903. The facility became one of USAC's crown jewels and winning a race here would be a major highlight in any driver's career.

(Stock Car Racing Magazine)

Thirty-nine drivers qualified for the 200-lap race, led by the 1965 Plymouth driven by Jim Hurtubise. Billy's qualifying position is not listed in the results, but he had a satisfying run by finishing in the eighth position in Hoerr's '65 Dodge. Norm Nelson was again the winner, followed across the line by Hurtubise and A.J. Foyt.

(Harvey Chipper Collection)

The weekend of August 14-15th was a busy weekend for Foster upon returning to the Milwaukee Mile. On Saturday the USAC Champ Car series held a 150-lap race in which Billy was in the cockpit of Rolla Vollstedt's #16 Vollstedt/Ford. He qualified 12th in a field of 24 cars, but his engine went south on the 40th lap and Foster was credited with a 20th place finish. Joe Leonard drove Dan Gurney's Halibrand/Ford to victory lane.

That race was followed the next day by a 150-lap USAC stock car event that witnessed 38 cars take the green flag. Billy's #22 Dodge completed 146 laps and was running at the finish in the 13th position. The top-three finishers were Paul Goldsmith, Parnelli Jones, and Sal Tovella.

Four days later, August 19th, it was a 200-lapper for the stock cars again at Milwaukee. Once again Norm Nelson took the win over A.J. Foyt. Billy completed 192 laps to place 10th at the finish, earning his team just $454 in prize money.

Now in the heart of the summer racing season, USAC's stock cars traveled to the Illinois State Fairgrounds in Springfield the following day. The race would be 100 laps on the fairgrounds' one-mile dirt oval, and 22 cars were entered. Billy started the race in the fifth position but only completed 55 laps before dropping out, recording a 17th place result. Bobby Isaac's '65 Dodge was the winner, followed by Paul Goldsmith and Norm Nelson.

The next event on the 1965 stock car schedule took place on September 5th at the one-mile dirt oval at the DuQuoin State Fairgrounds in Illinois. Paul Goldsmith won the event, while Foster earned another 10th place finish and $704 in prize money. Fairground racing in the Midwest at the time was extremely popular and this event drew an estimated 22,000 spectators!

Just two days later, the race teams again assembled at the Indiana State Fairground's one-mile dirt oval in Indianapolis. There were 29 entries, and Parnelli Jones grabbed the pole during qualifying in his Holman-Moody-prepared 1965 Ford. Billy's qualifying position is not recorded, but at the end of the 100-lap race, he finished a fine third in Rudy Hoerr's Dodge. The winner was A.J. Foyt, with Norm Nelson finishing second. Jones' race ended on the 65th lap due to an overheating issue. The average speed of the race was 83.41 mph and Foster's winnings totaled $1,600.

(Harvey Chipper Collection)

The stock cars moved on to the one-mile paved oval at Langhorne Speedway in Pennsylvania for a planned 100-lap race on September 12th. Billy qualified his Dodge second on the grid, sharing the front row with Bobby Isaac's Dodge. This promising event was rained out and rescheduled for October 24th when a new qualifying session would be held.

(Harvey Chipper Collection)

On September 19th, everyone headed back to the Milwaukee Mile for a 250-lap event which drew a large field of 40 cars. This time, Billy was driving Hoerr's 1964 Dodge. At the finish of the race, Jim Hurtubise was the winner in a '65 Plymouth owned by Norm Nelson. In his other Plymouth, Nelson finished second, followed by the Plymouth of Paul Goldsmith. Billy came home in the seventh position after completing 244 laps, earning $818 for his effort.

Fall was in the air and the 1965 season was grinding to an end. On October 10th, 21 cars were entered for a 71-lap race on the 2.75-mile road course at Mid-America Raceways in Wentzville, Missouri. Fast qualifier Norm Nelson's '65 Plymouth dominated the race for the first 46 laps before his engine expired. Taking over the lead for the rest of the race was Don White's '64 Ford. Jim Hurtubise finished in second place, one lap down to White. Foster was credited with an eighth-place finish after an accident on the 52nd lap. Twelve cars could not make it to the end.

The rescheduled race at Langhorne Speedway ran on October 24th. Just like in September, Billy qualified his '64 Dodge in second and would share the front row with Paul Goldsmith, who was driving a Ray Nichels-prepared 1965 Plymouth. The 250-lap contest was completed in two hours and 25 minutes at an average speed of 102.9 mph. During the race, Billy was in front for 63 laps, but Goldsmith dominated by leading 179 circuits. Behind winner Goldsmith, the finishing order was Hurtubise, Isaac, Foster and Nelson.

The final stock car event of the season for the Hoerr and Foster combination was at Hanford Motor Speedway in Southern California. Thirty-one cars were entered and some notable West Coast drivers were competing, such as Hershel McGriff, Kuzie Kuzmanich, Carl Joiner, Bill Amick, Dick Bown, Scotty Cain, Ron Hornaday, Sr. and Jack McCoy. There were also several drivers known primarily in USAC's Champ Car ranks, namely Mario Andretti, Gary Bettenhausen, Lloyd Ruby and George Snider. At the end of qualifications, Andretti's 1964 Ford earned the pole, and Billy placed an outstanding second.

Norm Nelson was always the man to beat.

(Courtesy USAC archives)

Norm Nelson, who began the race from the fourth position, led 47 laps during the afternoon and drove to victory. He was four laps ahead of second-place finisher Scotty Cain's '64 Mercury. The third through fifth spots went to Andretti, McGriff, and Jim Cook. Billy's #22 Dodge held the lead for 25 laps, but engine woes forced him out of the race on the 59th lap. He placed 21st overall.

The 1965 USAC Stock Car season had come to an end. Norm Nelson had a great year and rightly earned the championship with six race wins. The second and third season-ending positions went to Paul Goldsmith and Don White. Foster was able to fully display his talents during the season and was rewarded with the division's Rookie of the Year Award. He came in sixth in total points, recording two top-five and eight top-ten finishes.

THIRTY

The 1966 Champ Car Season – First Two Races

The first event of the 1966 USAC Champ Car season came on March 20th at Phoenix. The 'Jimmy Bryan Memorial' was scheduled for 150 laps on the one-mile paved track in the desert surrounds of Avondale, Arizona.

Billy returned to the cockpit in the #66 Vollstedt/Ford entered by Jim Robbins. Following the qualifying session of 23 cars, Foster could only muster enough to start the race from the 16th position. The front row was comprised of pole winner Mario Andretti's Brawner/Ford and Don Branson's Gerhardt/Ford.

Following the green flag, Andretti led the first 46 laps before a spin took him out of the running two laps later. Jim McElreath, driving a Brabham/Ford for John Zink, then took over to lead the final 104 laps and grab the win. The only other driver to complete all 150 laps was Rodger Ward, finishing second in John Mecum's Lola/Offy.

(Jay Koch Collection)

During the afternoon, there were a number of cars dropping out due to mechanical issues, spins or accidents. As a result, there were only nine cars running at the end. Foster drove a steady race throughout the day, completing 147 laps, and finished seventh. His winnings only amounted to $576, but he earned an important 90 points toward the driver's championship.

The next race came on April 24th at Trenton. For this 150-lap event, Billy would drive the Eisert/Chevy owned by J. Frank Harrison. For the second race in a row, Foster qualified 16th of 22 cars. Andretti would start from the pole. It turned out to be a short day for Foster, as he retired after just one lap because of suspension woes. Ward drove to victory that day, ahead of Johncock and McElreath.

Now it was time for Billy to gear-up for his sophomore year at Indianapolis.

THIRTY-ONE

The 1966 Indianapolis 500 – Prerace

As it was in that era, the 50th running of the Indianapolis 500 drew over 50 entries, all vying for a position on the 33-car starting field. The entry list included a whopping 22 rookies, but their ranks would decline drastically in the days before qualifications took place. Several rookie entries were declined by the Speedway due to a driver's lack of experience.

Three-year veteran Johnny Rutherford was forced to sit out the 1966 event due to injuries he suffered in a serious crash in early April at Eldora. The Mecom Racing Team was fielding drivers Walt Hansgen, Rodger Ward and Jackie Stewart. Sadly, Hansgen died from injuries from a crash while testing at LeMans, France. Formula One standout Graham Hill was named as his replacement.

Practice for the 'Golden Anniversary 500' opened on Saturday, April 30th. The cold and rainy weather over the first few days held on-track activities to a minimum. On May 2nd the weather had cleared up enough for the mandatory rookie test, comprising ten laps each at 135, 140, and 145 mph.

Art Pollard and Billy Foster sharing a moment at Indy in 1966.

(Racing Wheels photo)

Making his first driving appearance at Indy was Billy Foster's close friend Art Pollard - and Art became the first to pass the 145-mph test. His #66 Vollstedt/Offy was far from being a first-timer, as it was the same chassis as raced at the Brickyard by Len Sutton in 1964 and Billy in 1965. An Oregonian, Dick Compton, had purchased the car from Rolla Vollstedt and installed an updated Offenhauser engine.

As Art would say in an interview: "I really know now why they call us rookies. Until you have driven at Indianapolis, you definitely are one."

Vollstedt submitted two entries, with Jim Robbins listed as the owner of both cars. Foster's would be the #27 Vollstedt/Ford sponsored by Autotron Electronics. The #66 Vollstedt/Ford, with sponsorship from Bryant

Heating & Cooling, would be in the hands of rookie Cale Yarborough – the burly and fearless NASCAR driver from South Carolina. Though he had never raced an open-wheel car, Vollstedt felt Yarborough could do the job.

In his book *The Rolla Vollstedt Story*, Rolla made a humorous observation of Cale:

"When running at Indianapolis, on the front straight as you approach Turn One, there are numbers 3, 2, 1, and then the gate. When you get to the gate, you are pretty well into One. The guys used to tell where they would get off the gas by the numbers. Well Cale, after he got warmed up and taken a few laps, he was driving it past 1, past the gate, and he was getting it sideways coming out of the turn. Bob Sowle, in his Hoosier slang, says, 'Tell you one thing – that Cale he ain't allergic to getting them sideways.'

Anyway, I brought him in because I was afraid he might crash. I said to him, 'Cale, here they don't drive the cars that deep and get them crossed up. They kind of get off the gas and then pick it up a little earlier in the corner.'

He says, 'Oh. How's my times?' 'Well', I said, 'you are running 159 mph', which was fastest of all my cars. And he says, 'Maybe my way ain't so baaad.'"

Cale Yarborough

(IMS photo)

1966 marked an era of ever-increasing speeds at Indy, thanks to the proliferation of rear-engine chassis, more powerful Ford and Offenhauser engines and better tire technology. Once time trials were completed there would be only one front-engine, turbocharged Offy roadster in the field, driven by Bobby Grim.

Friday, May 13th, was the final day of practice before Pole Day. Andretti's Hawk/Ford shattered the unofficial track record by over five miles-per-hour with a lap of 167.411. With rain hampering most of the day, Clark's Lotus/Ford was second quickest with a speed of 165.7 mph.

On a chilly Saturday – the run for the pole – 18 cars completed qualifying runs. Mario Andretti kept his pace from the day before and grabbed the first position with a four-lap average of 165.889 mph. Joining him on the front row at the start of the race would be Jimmy Clark in second and George Snider's Lotus/Ford in third. A.J. Foyt experienced a crash but would return on Sunday with a speed of 161.355, placing him well back in the 18th starting position.

Billy Foster had a respectable four-lap run to place twelfth and would start the '500' from the outside of the fourth row. The team had been experiencing handling problems with the car, which were corrected after running a feature race at Milwaukee. The team found that the inboard rear front pickup-point was flexing in the chassis. After being reinforced, the car became much better.

Inside of the fourth row would be Jerry Grant, with Jackie Stewart's car in the middle. Overshadowing the day was the death of driver Chuck Rodee. On his second warm-up lap, he lost control in Turn One and backed into the outside wall. He died from his injuries at the hospital.

The second weekend of qualifications filled the 33-car field. On the final day two drivers, Ronnie Duman and Larry Dickson, managed to "bump" their way into the race.

For Art Pollard, Duman's speed ended the month for the popular Pacific Northwest driver. When proceedings ended at 6 p.m. on Sunday, the qualifiers represented the fastest starting field in Indianapolis history.

Billy qualified in the 12th position for the 1966 Indy 500

(Jay Koch Collection)

(Jay Koch Collection)

Now it was time to prepare for the "Greatest Spectacle in Racing." The race would be broadcast live on the Indianapolis Motor Speedway Radio Network to over 1,500 stations worldwide. Veteran chief announcer Sid Collins would be joined in the booth by Len Sutton, replacing Freddie Agabashian as the broadcast's 'driver expert'.

**Billy's 1966 nose cone autographed by Rolla Vollstedt:
"To the Good Old Days."**

(Author photo)

THIRTY-TWO

The First Lap Incident

All the trials and tribulations of the month of May came together on race day, as the field lined up behind the Mercury Comet Cyclone GT pace car.

Through the parade and pace laps, everything looked good. The drivers lined up neatly, three-by-three across the eleven rows of growling race cars. With Billy Foster on the outside of the fourth row, he was directly behind Don Branson in the third row, and ahead of Graham Hill on the outside of row five.

As the pace car, driven this year by Benson Ford (grandson of Henry Ford) exited onto pit lane, the field picked up speed as it accelerated towards the green flag. Chief starter Pat Vidan then waved the start of the contest, and pole-sitter Mario Andretti shot out in front as he approached the tricky Turn One. Jackie Stewart was just behind in the second position.

And then, all hell broke loose as the rest of the field was passing the start/finish line.

Reviewing race footage of the major mishap, taken from the Turn One area, Billy's car abruptly veers right and makes impact with the outside wall as other cars begin to scatter. Other drivers, now going at full steam, careened across the track – with parts and wheels flying in all directions.

When all the dust and debris settled, the track was a mess and the red flag was displayed to halt the survivors as they appeared out of Turn Four. Eleven cars were wiped out before they were able to get to Turn One. Fortunately, there were no serious injuries to the drivers involved, nor any spectators or crew members. A.J. Foyt injured his hand after scrambling out of the way over the catch fence on the outside wall.

Besides Foster and Foyt, the other drivers involved were Don Branson, Gary Congdon, Dan Gurney, Cale Yarborough, Arnie Knepper, Al Miller, Bobby Grim, Larry Dickson and Ronnie Duman.

The melee just after the green flag.

(Press photos)

In one post-wreck interview with a disgruntled Dan Gurney, he told the reporter: "Collectively, I don't really know who is to blame. I don't think you can blame it on any one person, but they're all using very, very poor judgment. It's not very difficult to drive down a little straight piece of track here with a few cars. There shouldn't be any trouble at all. We're all supposed to be good drivers. I don't think they have the judgment of a flea for all I'm concerned."

And in an interview with A.J. Foyt, he remarked: "What happened today was not called for. It's just one of the guys was too eager and I don't think had enough experience, and it just caused a lot of cars to get tore up. It was really ridiculous what happened and I'm just glad nobody got hurt real bad."

The remains of Billy's racer.

(Jay Koch Collection)

In the days following the race, many fingers were pointed at Billy for causing the big wreck, including several media outlets. Veteran driver Don Branson didn't hold back any punches when he said: "It happened because Foster tried to go outside Johncock when there just wasn't any room. He got into Johncock, and that's all there is to it."

This article appeared in the May 31st, 1966 edition of *The Indianapolis Star* newspaper:

Billy Foster, 28-year-old British Columbia driver starting his second 500-mile race, was taking most of the heat for the spectacular 16-car pileup seconds after the start of yesterday's race.

Most of the combustion was being generated by his fellow drivers. But Foster was just as certain that the Speedway's biggest smashup since the 1958 first-lap crash that killed Pat O'Connor was not his fault. Immediately after the wreck that put 11 cars out of the race but resulted in no major injuries, Foster told reporters, "All I know is that someone hit me on the right rear and I ended up going into the wall. I guess that started the whole mess."

Foster started the race on the outside of the fourth row. The consensus was that his Jim Robbins Special ran up over the Weinberger Homes Special which Gordon Johncock started on the outside of the second row. But later, Foster said he had already passed Johncock when "somebody came by me on the inside and pushed me toward the outside. My right-rear wheel bumped Johncock's left front. Then my rear end went to the left and then back to the right and I hit the outside wall along the fuel tanks. If the wall had been 10-feet farther out, I would have missed it. I don't know who was on the inside of me and pinching me out."

Then, obviously incensed over the accusations, Foster said, "I'm positive someone hit me. I'm not in the habit of spinning in the middle of the main straightaway."

Johncock's only comments were that Foster "ran right over the top of me. He hit my left-front wheel." Other driver's versions varied but veteran Don Branson, whose Leader Card entry started on the outside of the third row – just in front of Foster – left no doubt that he believed Foster was at fault. "No one forced Foster into Johncock. He just ran over him. His right rear went into Johncock's left rear and there they went. Some guys ought to have more sense. You'd think when they get in this race they'd have to have some sense, but they sure as hell don't show it."

Also, on May 31st, this *Associated Press* report appeared in *The Oregonian* newspaper:

Billy Foster, Canadian from British Columbia, was blamed by some drivers Monday for the wreck that eliminated about one-third of the racing field on the first lap of the Memorial Day 500. Foster, in an interview, said it was not his fault. He added, "Someone on my left moved to the outside, and I moved with him, to avoid his hitting me. As I moved over my right rear tire hit Gordon Johncock's front tire. That's what they tell me."

Foster said the first time he knew he was involved in the wreck was when he hit Johncock. He said he was traveling about 140 to 150 miles per hour when he wrecked.

Foster indicated that he will try again to win at Indianapolis next year. "My chances for winning were really good this year," he said. "My car was running well." Foster, who ran his first Indianapolis 500 last year, said he will race again Friday night in Grand Rapids, Mich. And again, on Sunday. Foster drove a year-engine Ford entered by Rolla Vollstedt of Portland, Ore.

Another review and opinion of the accident appeared in the June 13th, 1966 issue of *Sports Illustrated Magazine.* The author was Bob Ottum:

A Reckless Dash to Disaster

The safest part of the Indianapolis 500-mile race is the moment when the band plays Back Home Again in Indiana. After that, when 33 cars try to make it around the first lap, it gets a lot less folksy. And this week, back home in the world's most expensive junkyard, there were growing indications that the old routine would never be the same again.

As always, the race had begun with 33 cars arranged in 11 rows of three each. But while cars at the back of the lineup were still getting the green flag, most of the others were spinning out of control. Drivers began whomping each other on the main straightaway, and the sky was falling with tires, suspension parts and pieces of engines.

When the panic settled, the crowd looked down on 11 cars lying helpless with backs and bellies broken and five others that would have to go to the pits for minor repairs. None of the drivers was killed. This was not a miracle, as was emotionally suggested at the time, but a tribute to modern chassis, which wrap around the drivers like tubular envelopes. But debris winging into the crowd had injured five spectators who were not as well protected.

The disaster seemed all too familiar to Indy. Two of the last three races have gone bad at the start. Two years ago, a first-lap crash killed two drivers and demolished seven cars. In 1958 driver Pat O'Connor was killed. Fifteen cars were involved on that ominous first lap, and eight could not continue.

The fiasco at this year's Indy was followed by impassioned argument over which driver had done what to whom. Several movies made on Memorial Day have since settled the question. They clearly show that a number of drivers, contrary to explicit instruction and common sense, were trying to win a 500-mile race in the first 500-yards.

The United States Auto Club's spokesman, Jim Smith, reconstructed the accident this way: Pole man Mario Andretti brought the field down toward the line at about 110 miles-per-hour. "I think I crossed the line at about 125," Andretti says, "and I was still in low gear. I have a gearbox that will take me up to 135 before I pop it into high."

Behind Andretti, drivers Billy Foster (fourth row) and Johnny Boyd (fifth row) both swung to the inside as the field roared up to the line. Driver Gordon Johncock (second row) lagged badly at the start and was passed by four others: Jim McElreath and Chuck Hulse, from the third row, plus Jackie Stewart and Jerry Grant from the fourth row. As they crossed the starting line, Foster appeared to be a half a car length ahead of Johncock and Boyd, running between them. Hulse was riding directly in front of Foster, roughly in the center of the track.

As Hulse cleared Johncock, he moved toward the outside, seeking more running room, thus leaving a hole up the middle. Both Foster and Boyd went for it, Boyd veering sharply to his right to get into the spot. Foster apparently reacted instinctively. He swung hard to the right to avoid Boyd, cutting in front of Johncock and slamming into the outside wall. The impact sheared the nose cone and two wheels from Foster's car.

As Foster churned along the wall, it appeared for an instant that the field – now accelerating fast – would make it through. But then Mel Kenyon (sixth row) began a deadly inside spin as he swerved to miss the nose cone. The spin threw him into the path of Don Branson (third row), who had started directly behind the slow-moving Johncock. Branson tried to swing inside and ran underneath Gary Congdon (sixth row).

Thus, with Foster coming back off the wall on the outside, with Kenyon spinning down the center and Branson and Congdon piled up on the inside, the track was effectively blocked. The other drivers came pouring in on them. "Keep in mind," said one of the survivors, "that the accident was getting ready to happen long before the cars crashed. Jockeying around before the race starts is illegal, remember?"

Standing in the garage after the pile-up, wearing a warmup jacket, Billy Foster said, "There was an opening. I don't know who it was, but whoever was on my left moved up, and I had to swing out to avoid hitting him. That's when someone bumped me in the right rear and I spun into the wall." Had he hit Johncock in the process? Foster shrugged, "I don't know. I hit him. He hit me. What's the difference?"

The sharpest criticism of last week's ghastly start come from two of the most experienced drivers. They had an excellent view; they were in the middle of it. Driver Dan Gurney, builder of the American Eagles, who moves in the separate worlds of Indy and Grand Prix racing, was one. Houston's A.J. Foyt, twice the Indianapolis 500 winner and perhaps the best driver on the track, was the other – and he was going to stay shouting mad for a long time.

While the crash still boiled on, now and then zinged a crippled racer past the place where his own car lay crushed against the wall, Foyt had climbed out, taken a quick look around and scrambled over the fence and into the stands. The accident had not injured him, but climbing the fence he banged up both knees, and the next day they were badly swollen. "I ain't never, ever going to run in one of these races again," said Foyt, "unless I can start from up there in front. You got to be free to drive clean away from those crazy sons of bitches. This is supposed to be a 500-mile race. This first lap ain't no drag strip, you know."

Gurney said, "Those clowns. Ridiculous. I was hit four times in there. Four times. Wouldn't you think that a bunch of grown men, all supposedly experienced race drivers, could drive together down a simple stretch of straight road? Unless we put these people under control, fewer and fewer owners are going to want to race at Indy. They won't be able to afford Indy, to risk their huge investments on an unsanctioned drag race down the main straightaway. They will simply stay away."

"I'll tell you what," says Andretti, speaking as the fastest man of the season. "The people who run Indy must really punish the man found out of position at the start. The penalty has to be severe enough to stick. Say you pull a guy out of racing for six months or a year – suspend him. It is his living, and he'll do like you say. And then you'll see 33 cars come up to the start like they're supposed to."

Rodger Ward agrees. "Let's assume we could pinpoint the blame for this year's crash on someone," he says. "If the steward was able to say, 'Sir, you will now undergo a one-year suspension,' you would see some drivers exercise a little more caution."

The perils of the first lap were enough to make a new elder racing statesman of Ward, who drove through the tangle and decided it would be his last lap. "Maybe it's because my age (45) won't let me gamble," he said when it was over. "But the start of the accident came right beside me. I saw Foster go into the wall. I saw that he had some help getting there. And I simply had to drive in there and take my medicine with everyone else."

At the awards banquet the next evening, Ward made a short but effective speech. "I promised myself the day this stopped being fun, I would quit," he said. "Well, yesterday it stopped being fun."

On June 2nd, 1966, a special screening of motion pictures of the accident was attended by several USAC officials, including President Tom Binford, Director of Competition Henry Banks, and Rhiman Rotz – a referee for the Championship Division. Also attending was reporter Dave Overpeck of the *Indianapolis Star* newspaper.

In an article that appeared on June 3rd, 1966, Overpeck described how the film clip was taken with a telephoto lens positioned at the end of the front straight. The short clip was viewed several times – in regular speed, slow motion, and frame-by-frame. The following is Overpeck's opinion of the incident, after viewing the footage:

1. The field was in fairly good position when Benson Ford maneuvered the pace car into the pits. Then first, Johnny Boyd from the middle of the fifth row and then Foster from outside the fourth row ducked to the inside as they passed the pit gate north of the starting line.

2. Gordon Johncock, starting outside the second row, lagged badly at the start and was passed by Jim McElreath and Chuck Hulse from the third row and Jackie Stewart and Jerry Grant from the fourth.

3. As they crossed the starting line, Foster appeared to be half a car length ahead of Johncock and Boyd and between the two. Hulse was immediately in front of Foster and just about in the middle of the track.

4. As he cleared Johncock, Hulse moved to the outside, leaving a hole in the middle of the track. Foster and Boyd both went for it. Boyd veered sharply to his right toward Foster, but he did not appear to contact the latter's car.

5. Foster seemed to catch Boyd's move out of the corner of his eye and reacted instinctively. He swerved to his right, ran over the front end of Johncock's car and slammed into the outside wall, ripping off two wheels and his nose cone.

6. For an instant it looked like the field would be able to get by Foster as he hugged the wall. Then Mel Kenyon began an inside spin as he tried to miss the nose cone as it bounced back across the track. Kenyon may have had a push from Gary Congdon, who tried to slip between him and the outside wall.

7. In any event, Kenyon's spin put him in the path of Don Branson. The latter had to dart violently to the inside and ran underneath Congdon's car near the inside wall.

8. At that point, with Foster disabled on the outside, Kenyon spinning in the middle of the track and Branson and Congdon piled up on the inside, the course was almost completely blocked. Cars behind started plowing into those already involved.

9. Eventual winner Graham Hill, riding high on the track when Foster went into the wall, ducked inside the latter and rode a fairly high path through the rest of the trouble with Roger McCluskey trailing right behind him.

10. Foyt was in front of Hill and McCluskey but elected to try to go through on the inside. Branson and Congdon closed that hole, but another up higher was opening up when Foyt was clobbered from behind by Arnie Knepper, who was trying to miss the trouble on the inside. Foyt's disabled car was knocked outside into the path of Al Miller's machine and both rode into the outside wall.

11. Dan Gurney was through the trouble but was hit from behind by the ricocheting cars of Congdon and Knepper in bang-bang order. He then went into the path of Cale Yarborough, while Congdon bounced off into the path of Bud Tingelstad.

12. Joe Leonard, with the track blocked in front of him, spun in the middle of the track and was hit by Carl Williams, who bounced clear and continued on around the track. Ronnie Duman was trapped on the inside and spun into the wall. Bobby Grim was boxed outside and looped into that wall. Larry Dickson was also caught in the jumble, but just who he hit and/or what he hit was not clear.

13. Just when it appeared all exits were blocked, a hole opened as Yarborough and Knepper slid to the inside and Miller and Foyt followed the wall. This allowed Al Unser, Eddie Johnson, Jim Hurtubise and Bobby Unser to slip through.

Overpeck's conclusion was that: "It would be wrong to attach any blame to the actions of either Foster or Boyd. The green flag was out, and the race was on. Both were racing, and both went for the same hole. It was like two people trying to go through the same door at the same time."

Henry Banks, speaking for the USAC officials, did not want to offer any definite conclusions before viewing other films taken from other angles of the wreck. "We have a lot of time to look this thing over very carefully," Banks stated, "so we can make the necessary recommendations to improve the situation next year."

Overpeck noted that Banks indicated he thought the start was too slow and left the impression that the possibility of a two-abreast start instead of three would be considered. Of course, today, we know that change has never taken place.

Billy Foster had his opportunity to voice his thoughts on the incident in an interview with reporter Jack Kiser of the *Philadelphia Daily News* that appeared on June 3rd, 1966:

"Sure, I wanted to move up in position as quickly as possible, but I wasn't trying to right then. Somebody on my left – I don't know who it was – moved to the outside wall and I eased into it. But just as I got there Gordon [Johncock] moved outside and my rear tire caught his right front tire and all hell broke loose.

Another split second and I would have been past him. I'm thankful nobody was hurt and I'm sincerely sorry that all those cars were knocked out. But remember, mine was knocked out too, and I'm not crying. That's just the breaks of the game."

Following all the scrutiny by the United States Auto Club officials, Billy was properly vindicated of the claim he was the sole cause of the incident. On July 2nd, 1966, this notice appeared in the *Competition Press* newspaper:

USAC Lifts Indy Blame from Foster

INDIANAPOLIS, June 12 – Blame for the multiple first-lap crash in the Memorial Day 500 cannot be attributed to any one driver. In a special bulletin released by USAC Director of Competition Henry Banks concluded that the first-lap accident was not the fault of any specific driver, but rather the result of a number of circumstances in which no one could be blamed directly. Many hours were spent by top USAC officials repeatedly viewing several motion picture sequences of the wreck, in slow motion, reversed and frame-by-frame.

The consensus seems to be that the pace car brought the 33-car field down to the starting line much too slowly. Several cars were fitted with multi-speed gearboxes, and at this low speed were able to use their enormous accelerative advantage of the two-speed cars with their resultant slower pickup. The differential produced a great deal of weaving and hustling for positions.

Billy Foster, who was generally blamed for the accident by several other drivers and officials alike, did appear to be slicing his way up through the field in his Vollstedt/Ford, passing a number of two-speed cars, when his way became suddenly blocked.

From the accident films, it was apparent that he could either bear left or move straight ahead and, in either instance, almost without doubt hit another car, or turn to the right and risk contacting the wall. In a split-second decision he chose to turn into the wall. Upon contact, he instantly lost his two right wheels, and the fiberglass nose of his Vollstedt was torn completely off.

Those cars directly behind him got by, but rookie Mel Kenyon suddenly found himself face-to-face with the Vollstedt's gyrating nose piece. Kenyon instinctively veered left and in do so tapped another car which launched the snowball accident.

Commenting on the remarkable fact that none of the drivers was more than bruised in the accident, Rodger Ward noted that the flying wheels that filled the sky during the crash were a probable indication that the drivers were not getting full impact shock.

USAC officials are reported to have said that the greatest regret, apart from the accident itself, was the attitude of several drivers in trying to pinpoint the blame onto one driver before the facts were fully known and studied. The accident threw considerable credit upon research work done by major tire companies in rubber fuel bladders, following the tragic accident that claimed the lives of Eddie Sachs and Dave MacDonald in the 1964 race.

Suggestions put forward to alter the starting format and avoid a repetition of this accident have been numerous. They include spacing the rows further apart, lining the cars up in twos or even using a single-file start. Other veteran observers here feel that the answer is to employ a high-powered pace car with a professional driver at the wheel. These suggestions will be considered at USAC's rules committee meeting in September.

THIRTY-THREE

1966 Indy 500 – Conclusion

To facilitate the cleanup following the accident, the race was under the red flag for nearly one and one-half hours. The remaining field of 22 cars realigned for the restart. After several warm-up laps, the now single-file field accelerated as Pat Vidan displayed the green flag for the second time.

But then, Johnny Boyd crashed in Turn One and the yellow lights came on immediately. Boyd climbed out unhurt, but his car joined the growing number of thrashed machines.

Following another restart, Mario Andretti held the lead through the 16th lap when his car started smoking. A pit stop to change spark plugs didn't solve the problem, and the pole-sitter was forced to retire on the 27th lap. Meanwhile, Chuck Hulse and George Snider tangled on the backstretch on the 22nd lap, ending both drivers' day.

When Andretti first slowed, Jimmy Clark took over the lead through lap 64. Lloyd Ruby was running second and Parnelli Jones was third. Preparing to enter the pit lane Clark spun, but received no damage and was able to continue. Ruby inherited the lead for the next eleven laps.

When he pitted, Clark regained the lead position. Two-time Indy champion Rodger Ward retired his Lola/Offy on the 74th lap, thus ending the popular veteran's long driving career. Parnelli Jones lasted until lap 87 before dropping out with a wheel bearing failure.

At the midway point of the race, perennial favorite Lloyd Ruby was leading ahead of Clark. For the next 50 laps, these two changed positions back and forth, depending on pit stop timing. Around lap 150 though, Ruby's car slowed, and he had to park it in the pits after 166 laps. A broken cam stub had failed.

Rookie Jackie Stewart had been charging – eventually passing Clark – and took over the lead on the 151st lap in his Lola/Ford. Graham Hill was just behind. With only ten laps to the finish, Stewart began losing oil pressure and he slowly pulled to the side of the track. From that point forward, Hill was unchallenged for the victory. Only four cars completed all 200 laps. Clark, McElreath and Johncock followed Hill across the finish line.

With his victory, Graham Hill became the first rookie to win the '500' since 1928, when Louis Meyer came home first driving a Miller chassis. Meyer covered the 500 miles in just over five hours at an average speed of 99.482 mph. In 1966, Hill accomplished the same feat in three hours and thirty-seven minutes at an average of 144.317 mph.

(Headline courtesy of The Indianapolis Star)

Though this edition of the Indianapolis 500 was now complete, there was no slack in the schedule for the Champ Car series regulars. A 100-lap race at the Milwaukee Mile was taking place the next weekend.

THIRTY-FOUR

1966 USAC Champ Car Season – Second Half

For unknown reasons, Billy did not make the starting field for the 'Rex Mays Classic' at Milwaukee on June 5th, 1966. He is listed as "failed to qualify, withdrew, or driver changes." Mario Andretti dominated the event, leading all 100 laps.

It turned out to be a great day for Foster's pal Art Pollard. He was driving a Gerhardt/Offy that was co-owned by NASA astronauts Gus Grissom and Gordon Cooper, along with racing veteran Jim Rathmann (the 1960 Indy 500 Champion). Pollard drove to a fourth-place finish after qualifying seventh.

The following weekend the Champ Cars arrived at Langhorne Speedway for a 100-lap event on the one-mile paved oval. Billy qualified his #27 Vollstedt/Ford in tenth and completed all 100 laps to secure a fifth-place finish. Once again, Andretti led every lap for the win, followed by McElreath, Leonard, Branson, and Foster. Billy's result was good for $1,342 in winnings and 100 driver points.

The 1.5-mile oval at Atlanta International Raceway on June 26th was the next event for Foster and the Vollstedt team. A large field of 40 cars assembled, all competing for 30 starting positions. For this event, Vollstedt entered a second Ford-powered chassis – the #66 for Bobby Unser.

Andretti's Dean Van Lines Special, except for Indianapolis, was having a stand-out season. Once again Mario won the pole with a speed of 169.014 mph, with Johncock's Gerhardt/Ford setting the second quickest time. The second row would consist of Branson on the inside in another Gerhardt/Ford alongside Foster. Pollard's Gerhardt/Ford qualified fifth. Bobby Unser qualified 23rd.

Rolla Vollstedt recalled a humorous incident that took place the night before the race:

"That evening at our motel, I was in the swimming pool when Billy walked past in his driving suit. I promptly pushed him into the pool, driving suit and all. Billy left, and shortly returned wearing my brand-new sport coat over his driver's suit. He hollered at me to get my attention as he dove into the pool! So much for my new sport coat."

In front of a race day crowd of 27,000 spectators, Andretti jumped away at the start, but he and his best friend Foster had a great time dicing together. Midway through the distance, Foster made a routine pit stop. Soon thereafter, the Vollstedt crew signaled Unser to come in. During the pit stop, chief mechanic Grant King tightened a leaking fuel injection line and then a crewman signaled Bobby to go. However, the refueling hose and nozzle were still connected to the car. Unser returned to the track with parts of the refueling system still attached, which brought out a cautionary yellow flag.

During this period Andretti pitted and gained an insurmountable lead over Foster. As Vollstedt remarked, "We created the yellow that allowed Mario to win."

Andretti was credited with leading all 200 laps and came away with the winner's trophy. Foster drove a great race to finish second, one lap down to Andretti, while Johncock finished third. Unser earned the 14th position with the second Vollstedt entry, but Pollard had to drop out on the 64th lap due to a fire that occurred during a pit stop.

Close buddies Billy Foster and Art Pollard in 1966.

(Ralph Hunt Collection)

Of interest is the post-race report that appeared on July 16th, 1966, in the *Competition Press* newspaper:

Andretti Marches Through Georgia

Like Julius Caesar or even William Tecumseh Sherman, Mario Andretti came and he saw and he conquered in winning the Championship 300 at Atlanta International Raceway by more than a lap over Gordon Johncock. The 1965 national champion set his sixth qualifying record in as many races and never relinquished the lead in sweeping to his third straight victory in the Dean Van Lines Brawner Hawk/Ford.

Andretti set a qualifying mark of 169.014 Friday and proceeded to go out on Saturday and turn the 1.5-mile high-banked track at 169.992 in an effort to reach the predicted qualifying speed of 170 mph.

Andretti's three straight wins is an admirable feat, but still a long way short of Foyt's incredible string of seven-straight in 1964. Andretti, a complete unknown two years ago, has set qualifying records and earned the pole position in each of the six 1966 championship trail races, winning at Milwaukee, Langhorne and now Atlanta.

Andretti said high banks make a race even tougher than the flat tracks, forcing the driver to work all the time. "You can't relax for one second here," the tired driver gasped in victory circle between gulps of ice water. "The straights at Indy give you a chance to relax, but there isn't any time for that here. I was running steady laps between 158 and 162 mph. I just want to thank God and my mechanics for the car holding up," Andretti said with one arm draped around his twin brother Aldo's shoulders. "Other than worrying about the car holding up, I didn't have a real challenge," he said.

The Nazareth, Pa. driver jumped into the lead on the first lap, but Tommy Copp's rear-engined Offy smacked the guard rail in the second turn, rupturing his outside gas tank and spraying flaming fuel more than 500 yards down the track. The Fresno, California driver suffered second-degree burns on the face and hands but was reported in satisfactory condition. The caution flag came out for more than 20 laps, and the field made four false starts before the official starter turned them loose.

Andretti dueled briefly with Art Pollard in the Pure Oil Special after the restart, but steadily pulled away from the pack, and by lap 75 had lapped the entire field except Billy Foster. Foster provided the only real threat to the low-flying Andretti. "I had trouble with a fuel valve and I had to operate the valve manually. But I couldn't do that and get through traffic, so I ran good and I ran sour," Foster said.

Foster's troubles were not limited to fuel valves. Running in second place with five laps to go, Foster ran out of gas and was forced to make a last-minute pit stop as Andretti took the white flag. Foster was penalized three laps for allegedly passing while under the caution flag on one of the three occasions the flag was thrown during the 300-lap event. Foster indicated he would protest the ruling which put him back of Gordon Johncock in the final standings.

Four-time USAC champion A.J. Foyt qualified his rear-engined Ford at better than 165 mph in his first appearance after suffering burns on his face and hands at Milwaukee June 4th. Foyt dropped out after two laps. "I had the wrong gear in my car. I turned 800 too many revs on the first lap and all I would have done was blow an engine," Foyt said. The 96-degree heat very obviously bothered the tender burn scars from the Milwaukee accident – they were puffed and red when Foyt climbed from the car.

Art Pollard and astronauts Gus Grissom and Gordon Cooper narrowly escaped serious burns when Pollard's car caught fire during a pit stop. Pollard suffered slight facial burns but neither Grissom nor Cooper was hurt. Al Unser qualified the Mecom Lola/Ford which Graham Hill drove to victory at Indy in the fourth spot, but suspension problems sidelined the car with less than 30 laps remaining and Unser running in third position.

Bobby Unser drove the same rear-engined Vollstedt/Ford that Cale Yarborough drove at Indy until the car gave up the ghost with only 13 laps remaining and Unser in fifth place. Unser was black-flagged when he toured the track at more than 155 mph dragging a piece of hose about three yards behind the race car.

Al Smith of Dayton, Ohio pushed his supposedly obsolete front-engined Offy to a qualifying speed of 161.628 mph, good for fifth spot in the field of 30 cars. Smith hung on for a fifth-place finish and the best showing of the day for an Offy.

Al Unser and his mechanic George Bignotti wanted to file a protest Friday afternoon after track officials persuaded USAC officials to extend the qualifying period for an hour.

Andretti and two other drivers bettered Unser's time, the fastest turned in before the 4 p.m. deadline, and Foyt/s record of 166.314 from last year.

Track temperatures reached more than 130-degrees during qualifying on Friday and Saturday, nine degrees warmer than last year. Andretti collected $16,000 in his tour of AIR at an average speed of 139.319 mph, almost 2 mph slower than Johnny Rutherford's record time in last year's 250-mile event.

As mentioned in the article, the results were still up in the air following the race, as Vollstedt and Foster would protest their three-lap penalty for passing under a yellow flag. Rolla Vollstedt explained in his autobiography:

"I protested this action to the Chief Steward, Harry McQuinn, saying, 'Harry, surely Billy Foster didn't gain three laps by passing a slower car under the yellow.' Harry replied, 'I had to go three laps in order to hurt you, because Mario and Billy were three laps ahead of third place.'

I appealed Harry McQuinn's decision to the United States Auto Club's Board of Directors. After hearing my appeal, the Board restored our second-place position, points and money. Then they added insult to injury by fining Billy $2,500."

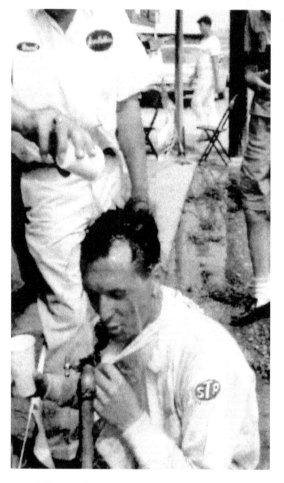

Billy cooling off at Atlanta with help from Grant King.

(Jay Koch Collection)

Following this decision regarding the Atlanta finish, Billy had earned $8,500 and 480 driver points.

The next Champ Car race that Foster competed in came on July 24th at Indianapolis Raceway Park in Claremont, Indiana. The 80-lap 'Hoosier Grand Prix' was held on IRP's challenging 1.875-mile road course.

Though he held little road racing experience, Billy qualified the Vollstedt/Ford 12th on a grid of 24 cars. Lloyd Ruby earned the pole position in a Lotus/Ford he was driving for Dan Gurney's All-American Racers team, with Andretti second quickest.

As the green flag fell Jim McElreath, in a Brabham/Ford, led the first six laps. From that point forward, other leaders included Roger McCluskey, Al Unser, Sr., Gordon Johncock and Mario Andretti, who led the final 38 laps to secure the victory. Foster hung in there and placed 13th, still running at the end, but was four laps down. His winnings were just $320, and no driver points were awarded.

It was back to the one-mile oval at Langhorne on August 7th for the 'Langhorne 150'. The top five qualifiers, in order, were Branson, McCluskey, Johncock, Congdon and Foster. For this event, Andretti was driving a second Vollstedt/Ford but only managed the 20th starting position. As Vollstedt explained:

"During qualifying, Mario sets a new one-lap track record and then crashed his car on his second qualifying lap. It so happened that I had a spare car there, my 1965 car. He and Billy were good friends, both rookies together in '65, so Billy got him to drive my 1965 car."

During the race, Roger McCluskey was dominant and led all but eight laps on his way to victory over Johncock and Al Unser, Sr. This day turned sour for the Vollstedt drivers on lap 33. We'll turn to Rolla Vollstedt for his description of the circumstances:

"Grant King was the mechanic on Billy's car and Harold Sperb was the mechanic on Mario's car. So, I notice that there's no tape on the fittings on either car. The tape keeps the fittings from coming loose. The guys say, 'We're not taping them anymore. Clint Brawer doesn't tape his, and A.J. Watson doesn't tape his, so we don't think we should have to. Those guys have gotta' know as much as we know!'

So I said, 'OK guys, you are the mechanics.' But when I did it, you went around and checked every fitting, and when it was tight you taped it. Sort of a double-check and that way none of them got by without being snugged. So guess what – in this race they weren't all snugged up.

Mario was running fourth and a hose came off! And if you look in your books, it will tell about the hose coming off of Mario's car. The oil spilled and as a result he got black-flagged. The next lap, Billy spun in the oil and crashed in the infield and ran into a big culvert. Because the fittings weren't taped, it took both cars out. I said, 'Now, will you tape the fittings!?'

The result was Foster finishing in the 20th position just in front of Andretti. Their combined earnings were a mere $184.

In late August, Foster's next Champ Car contest was back at the Milwaukee Mile for the 'Tony Bettenhausen 200'. During qualifying Billy placed his Vollstedt/Ford, entered by Jim Robbins, ninth on the grid. His Northwest compatriot Pollard had a fine run in his Gerhardt/Offy to qualify sixth.

Coming as no surprise, Andretti would start the 200-lap event in front of the field with a speed of 111.497 mph. Johncock would start second. The complete field was made up of 26 cars.

The first half of the race witnessed a duel between Andretti and Johncock, who diced for the lead several times. It was Andretti, though, who led the way for the final 93 laps to earn another victory for the season. Johncock followed in the second position, with Leonard, McElreath, and Foster rounding out the top five. Pollard ran well to finish seventh. Billy's earnings were $2,001 plus 200 additional points towards the driver's championship.

On Labor Day weekend of 1966, Foster secured a sprint car ride for the 'Ted Horn Memorial' 100-lap race on the one-mile dirt track at the DuQuoin State Fairgrounds. In a field of 18 cars, he qualified 16th in a Silnes/Offy owned by Dayton Steel Wheel founder George Walther. Bobby Unser was on the pole, registering a quick lap of 95.102 mph in a Blum/Offy.

The one hour-long race featured four changes for the lead between McCluskey, Bobby Unser, Arnie Knepper, and Tinglestad. Tinglestad, driving a Meskowski/Offy, led the final eleven laps for the win, followed by Dick Atkins' Watson/Offy. Foster finished four laps down in the ninth position, earning $657 in prize money and 40 championship points.

September 10th was another dirt track event for Billy – the 'Hoosier Hundred' – at the Indiana State Fairgrounds. This week he was behind the wheel of a Meskowski/Offy entered by businessman Jake Vargo.

Foster qualified eighth out of 18 entries but was forced to drop out of the race on lap 40 due to a loss of oil pressure. He finished in 15th place. Foyt started on the pole and led the first 97 laps in another Meskowski/Offy but was passed by Andretti's Kuzma/Offy just three laps before the end. The final order of finish was Andretti, Foyt, and Knepper.

With only a few more Champ Car races remaining in the 1966 season, the teams returned to New Jersey on September 25th for the 'Trenton 200'. Behind the wheel of his #27 Vollstedt/Ford, Foster qualified sixth in the 26-car field. Coming as no surprise, Andretti locked in the pole position with a speed of 115.333 mph and would share the front row with Al Unser's Lola/Ford.

Billy held his own during the early stages of the 200-lap race, as several drivers were eliminated either by crashes or mechanical failures. Ignition problem's ended Billy's day on the 84th lap and he placed only 18th, earning just $337. It was continued success for Andretti, who led all but one lap in his drive to victory. Al Unser finished second followed by Foyt in the third spot.

With a few weeks break in the schedule, USAC scheduled an exhibition (non-points) race on October 9th at Fuji International Speedway in Shizouka, Japan. The international event featured acclaimed drivers from both Formula One and Champ Cars, along with many of their wives who made the long plane trip.

For many, it was their first experience in a foreign land – as Vollstedt described:

"I remember Billy and Mario and Grant King and I ended up in a restaurant at Mt. Fuji. We needed Grant to help us figure out how to use chopsticks."

Thirty-two drivers made qualifying attempts, but ten failed to start the race: Mario Andretti, Dick Atkins, Jimmy Clark, Wally Dallenbach, Bob Harkey, Gordon Johncock, Rich Muther, Art Pollard, Al Unser Sr. and Bob Wente. As Vollstedt added:

"That track had a hell of a horseshoe, and actually ran clockwise, backwards from Indy. The problem with that was that a lot of engines seized, because the oil pump pickup was designed for going counter-clockwise."

The official results show that Foster's car failed with "rear-end" issues, but according to Vollstedt's account:

"What really happened was that the magneto rotor broke off. Grant King was supposed to take off the magneto and put on the battery ignition, which was proven to work. The magneto was still experimental, especially where the rotors were concerned. But we told Billy and the press that the rear-end had gone out, especially so that Billy wouldn't kill Grant King."

Billy at Fuji International Raceway.

(John Feuz Collection)

The series returned to the West Coast for the 'Golden State 100' on Sacramento's one-mile dirt oval on October 23rd. Foster was again entered to drive the #52 sprint car sponsored by Vargo Excavating, but he either failed to qualify or the car was withdrawn.

California driver Dick Atkins scored the victory ahead of Chuck Hulse and Larry Dickson. Just one month later, Atkins was killed in a sprint car crash at Ascot Park in California. The wreck also took the life of veteran driver Don Branson, who had planned to retire from racing at the end of the season.

The Champ Car season finale came on November 20th at Phoenix for the 'Bobby Ball Memorial' - 200 laps on the one-mile paved track in the desert. Bobby Ball was a Phoenix native who died following a wreck that occurred in 1953.

Forty-four cars showed up for qualifications. Of the 26 cars that made it into the field, Foster timed in tenth-quickest. Mario Andretti was on the pole in his Brawner/Ford with a speed of 122.158 mph. Lloyd Ruby's Eagle/Ford was second quickest, followed by the Shrike/Offy driven by Parnelli Jones.

With Andretti easily ahead in points for the driver's championship, the race was billed as a showdown between Gordon Johncock and Jim McElreath for the second position. But during qualifying, that story went out the window when Johncock spun his Gerhardt/Ford into the wall, demolishing the front of his car. All McElreath now had to do was to finish the race to gain the runner-up spot in the overall standings.

A record crowd of nearly 15,000 spectators were ready for an afternoon of close competition, but on-track incidents and mechanical failures left only seven cars running when the checkered flag waved. During the same time though, the fans were greatly entertained by a duel between Andretti and Jones.

Over the 200-lap event, there were five yellow flags. The most spectacular crash occurred on the third lap when Ralph Liguori flipped his dirt track Offy into the pit wall when Pollard spun out of the fourth turn. Bud Tingelstad tried to avoid the carnage but was hit by Liguori on the front straight. According to one account, Tingelstad's car came apart and scattered debris for 50-yards down the track. Liguori's stronger car survived with a bent roll bar and minor body damage. No one was injured. Pollard straightened out his car, roared down pit lane and rejoined the race.

During the first yellow flag period, Jones made a quick stop in the pits for a check-up, but when the race restarted, he was positioned near the back of the field. Andretti was again out front, but over the ensuing laps Jones made a charge up through the ranks. By lap 40 he was in second. Around this same time, Foster was in the eighth position.

Jones slowly closed in on Andretti. On the 71st lap, there was another caution when Gary Congdon spun into the wall. After seven laps under the yellow flag, the track went green and Jones was ready to pass Andretti. Another yellow came out when Greg Weld spun into the wall. When the race was again restarted on the 85th lap there were only twelve cars left running. Jones and Andretti were side-by-side going into the first turn, and then Jones pulled out front and the crowd went wild!

With Jones still barely leading on lap 133, Andretti made a successful pass in the third turn. As they raced down the front straight Jones' engine blew, spewing a ball of flame. He had been running without brakes for the preceding ten laps and when he pulled the car out of gear, he reported that it was "like stepping on the accelerator." His car shot into the wall, briefly climbed it, and then bounced back down to the track surface. Andretti led the final 68 laps to victory, with Al Unser Sr. and Jim McElreath following in order.

Alas, Billy Foster's Champ Car season ended on the 123rd lap when his car's rear-end failed. He was credited with 12th place, earning $674 and 20 driver points.

(John Feuz Collection)

After the overall results were tallied for the 1966 USAC Champ Car season, Mario Andretti was crowned the champion for the second year in a row. In 15 races, he recorded eight wins, nine pole positions, led 1,142 laps and amassed 3,070 points. His total earnings were $94,856.

640 points behind Andretti was Jim McElreath, who recorded just one win but had numerous top-five and top-ten finishes. Just four drivers raced in all 15 contests: Andretti, McElreath, Bobby Unser and Bud Tingelstad.

Billy Foster finished tenth in the standings, earning 930 points and $24,872 in winnings. Though he recorded no wins, Billy finished in the top-five three times and placed in the top-ten in five events, completing 1,097 laps.

Now with two Champ Car seasons under his belt, other teams were noting his potential. Who knew what the 1967 season would hold for the 'Victoria Flash'?

THIRTY-FIVE

Billy's Friends Remember – Jay Koch

In 1952 Jay Koch was born into a racing family in Portland, Oregon. His dad, George 'Pops' Koch, was a master racing mechanic who spent many years working for Rolla Vollstedt. Jay's uncle, Ernie Koch, was one of the top drivers to hail from the Pacific Northwest.

As a teenager, and because of his father's involvement with the Vollstedt Champ Car team, Jay spent much of his time traveling to races around the country, walking in the shadows of Billy Foster. Today, Jay is a racing historian and has a massive collection of memorabilia. He shared with us a few memories of his close ties with Foster, particularly at the USAC race at Atlanta.

"One of Billy's best races was at Atlanta in 1965. He had tire-tested down there in early 1965. I think that gave him an advantage with the newer car. Foyt asked [the crew], 'How'd you get this battleship going so fast?' My dad held his finger to his lips so I wouldn't say anything, but they had qualified on nearly a full tank of fuel onboard."

"I rode with Billy to the race track that morning," Jay continued. We stopped at some little town, as he was trying to find some duct tape. Billy got a guy out of church to open up the hardware store. I remember him saying he was going to try to push Foyt as hard as he could until Foyt broke."

"The trouble in the race was that the crew made their fuel stop a lap late and the engine quit as they were refueling. By the time they plugged in the starter they were way behind. He [Billy] just couldn't catch Rutherford. Mario passed Billy on the last lap – Billy thought Mario was just trying to unlap himself – otherwise Billy may have tried harder. We ended up third."

Jay was in the Indianapolis grandstands in 1966, when the big first-lap accident happened on the front straight. "I was sitting right across from where it happened," said Jay. "I didn't know that Billy was involved at first – it happened so fast – until they picked up the nose cone. Afterwards, I didn't really get a chance to talk to Billy. I was in the garage area after the race and just saw pieces of the bodywork in the trash can."

In his travels from track to track with his father, a young Jay had grown very fond of Billy, who left quite an impression on the teenager. Jay was in Minnesota when he got word of Billy's fatal accident. "My step-mom told me," he remembers. "My dad was working on the cars for Dayton Steel Wheel and that's how he heard about it. It still hurts, even to this day."

George ('Pops') Koch and Rolla Vollstedt began working together in their early days of racing.

(Jay Koch Collection)

Ernie Koch in the cockpit at the Milwaukee Mile in 1960.

(Jay Koch Collection)

THIRTY-SIX

The Story of 'Old Bess'

Gordon Alberg was fortunate in obtaining the 1965 Vollstedt/Ford that, during its heyday, was raced by an elite group of Indy Car drivers, including Billy Foster. 'Old Bess', as it is known, is the crown-jewel in his amazing car collection.

Len Sutton piloted 'Old Bess' in the car's debut at Indianapolis in 1965.

(Rolla Vollstedt Collection)

The car competed in its first Indianapolis 500 in 1965, with Len Sutton in the cockpit. He qualified 12th but, due to spending much time in the pits with fuel injector nozzle issues, Len finished 12th, 23 laps down to winner Jimmy Clark. Sutton next raced the car at Milwaukee and Trenton, and then abruptly ended his driving career.

(Len Sutton Collection)

Upon Sutton's retirement, Rolla Vollstedt named Foster as the full-time driver of the #16 for the rest of the 1965 season and again during 1966.

(Rolla Vollstedt Collection)

Following Indianapolis in 1966, in late June Bobby Unser drove 'Old Bess' (now #66) in the 200-lap Atlanta 300 in Hampton, Georgia. With Jim Robbins as a sponsor, that weekend Unser was a teammate of Foster, who was in his now-regular #27 Vollstedt/Ford, also sponsored by Jim Robbins.

Foster scored a fine second-place finish behind Andretti, while Unser finished 14th after suffering engine woes on the 164th lap.

At Langhorne in August of 1966, Rolla Vollstedt enlisted Mario Andretti to drive 'Old Bess'. Billy Foster would be driving Vollstedt's newer car, built in 1966, the #27.

During time trials Mario set a new one-lap track record in his primary car – the Dean Van Lines Special – but crashed on his second qualifying lap. Vollstedt had brought along his 1965 chassis as a spare. Billy talked his close friend Mario into driving that car in the race, which he qualified in the 20th position. Foster would start the race from the fifth position.

Andretti's day was cut short on the 33rd lap due to an oil hose coming loose, for which he was black-flagged. The next lap, Foster spun in the oil and crashed into the infield, hitting a big culvert. It was a disappointing day for the Vollstedt team, with Foster finishing in 20th place and Andretti in 21st.

Rare photo of Mario Andretti preparing to race 'Old Bess' (carrying #66) at Langhorne in 1966).

(Rolla Vollstedt Collection)

The chassis was converted to a Super Modified, with Chevy V8 power, in the late 1960s. Vollstedt ran it in Portland, Salem and Eugene, Oregon; Boise, Idaho, and Victoria, Edmonton, Alberta and Lethbridge in Canada.

In the summer of 1970, the team installed a rear-wing and entered the car in the 1970 Copper Cup Race at Phoenix International Raceway. In his autobiography Vollstedt described the outing:

"We decided to run 'Old Bess' at Phoenix in the 1970 Copper Cup race. Being an ex-Indy 500 rear-engine race car, it looked rather strange and quite small on the track surrounded by the numerous large, roadster-style Super-Modifieds. The majority of these Super-Modifieds were from the east coast and elsewhere and were powered with oversize big-block Chevrolet engines that were located to the left side of their chassis, hanging out of the frame.

The track was one-mile long, the same track on which the Indy 500 cars ran. This day we ran two 50-lap heats. I know we qualified first. They ran a reverse grid with 30 cars and that meant 'Old Bess' started at the back. Tom drove very successfully but finished second in the first heat because somebody rammed into the back-end of the car and split the oil tank. We came into the pits and made a hasty repair. We went back out and finished second.

Then prior to the second heat, we repaired the tank by putting some RTV 'huckey puck' on it, layers of tape, more 'huckey puck', and more tape. The officials let us start [the second heat], and at the end of the second lap we came in for the officials to inspect the repair and allow us to go back out again. We came from last twice and won the race. We won first overall for the two events and won a beautiful trophy."

Tom Sneva in the highly-modified 'Old Bess' on the way to winning the Copper Classic in 1970.

(Rolla Vollstedt Collection)

The car was subsequently sold to a Larry Kramer, who took the car to Trenton, New Jersey for the first USAC Championship race of 1971, again with Tom Sneva behind the wheel. Rain came along, so the race was postponed to the following weekend. During that race the car did not finish due to mechanical problems.

Down the road 'Old Bess', which was by now in very poor condition, was purchased by Bruce Russell of Portland, Oregon. Vollstedt's son Kurt restored the chassis, while Harold Sperb fashioned new aluminum bodywork. Russell got an Indy Ford quad-cam V8 from A.J. Watson and Grant King, which was then installed by Kurt Vollstedt. Finally, the car was painted by Tom Black of Portland.

The next long-time caretaker of the car was Don Shervey of Vancouver, Washington, who displayed the car frequently – including driving it in various vintage racing car events. Several years ago, Shervey sold the car to Alberg.

According to Rolla Vollstedt, the official record books show that this chassis started 151 races, driven by many standout drivers, on the Champ Car circuit during the 1960s.

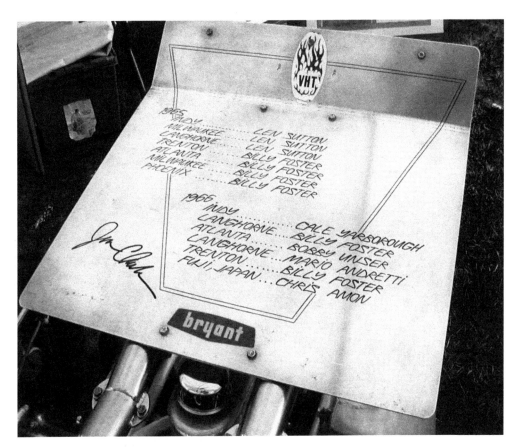

All the drivers who spent time in the cockpit of Old Bess

(Author photo)

In an interview with *Shaw TV*, Gordon described his long affinity with 'Old Bess'. He spoke with the enthusiasm of a kid in an ice cream store:

"Having this car puts me on cloud nine. There's no air dams, no spoilers and the engine sound is just unbelievable."

Gordon first witnessed the car on the track at Indianapolis in 1965, when Len Sutton was behind the wheel. "I was in the grandstands. When this thing came down the front straight, the beer can I had in my hands was vibrating. Back then the race cars made 500-horsepower at 10,000 rpm – they just screamed."

Gordon chased 'Old Bess' for the last 30 years, yearning to add it to his auto collection. "My love for old cars goes back to childhood," he said in the interview. "By the time I was four years-old I was taking things apart, but I couldn't put them back together again. I eventually learned. I became a machinist and welder for my career, and that was right in line with what I like to do."

Though the cockpit is tight for Alberg's tall frame, he has little difficulty inside. "It's like putting on my best sports jacket and going out to a dance. 150 miles-per-hour in a car like this is like driving 60 miles-per-hour down the freeway. I'm dying to feel the acceleration."

Gordon's dream is to someday drive it at the Indianapolis Motor Speedway in a vintage Indy Car event. During its long career, a number of famous racers have competed with it at one time or another – Mario Andretti, Johnny Rutherford, Gordon Johncock and Tom Sneva. All went on to be Indianapolis 500 champions.

A restored 'Old Bess' as she appears today.

(Author photo)

THIRTY-SEVEN

The 1966 USAC Stock Car Season

Beginning in 1963, the traditional start of the country's professional stock car season began in late January at the fast and challenging road course at Riverside International Raceway in California. Sanctioned by NASCAR – and for several years following known as the 'Motor Trend 500' – the event drew numerous entries from teams and drivers representing both NASCAR and USAC.

The track was known as a dangerous course. It had a long, downhill back straightaway and a slow, 180-degree turn nine that was especially hard on a car's brakes.

In 1964, NASCAR champion Joe Weatherly died when he lost control entering Turn Six, hitting the steel barrier broadside and suffering fatal head injuries.

During the 1965 running of the 'Motor Trend 500', A.J. Foyt suffered a brake failure at the end of the straight and his car flew off-course and dropped into a lower area, going end-over-end at high-speed. Crash crews first assumed that he was killed in the accident, but fortunately A.J. survived, though with serious injuries.

Road racing ace Dan Gurney practically owned the event during the 1960s, emerging as the winner in four consecutive years (1963-1966) driving Ford products. In 1967 Parnelli Jones interrupted that streak, but in 1968 Gurney recorded his fifth win. Other notable drivers that have won stock car races at Riverside include Richard Petty, A.J. Foyt, Bobby Allison, Mark Donohue, David Pearson and Cale Yarborough.

The record for the greatest number of stock car victories at Riverside is held by Hershel McGriff, who then hailed from the little town of Bridal Veil, Oregon. His fourteen wins at the track in NASCAR-sanctioned events is an amazing feat. Now a long-time resident of Arizona, McGriff was inducted into the West Coast Stock Car Hall of Fame in 2002 and the Motorsports Hall of Fame in 2006.

The Hoerr and Foster team was among the 44 entries for the 1966 edition of the race on Sunday, January 23rd. Their well-prepared 1965 Dodge was sponsored by the Illinois Dodge Dealers, and Billy qualified 12th quickest. The top three starting positions, in order, went to David Pearson's '65 Dodge, Dan Gurney's '66 Ford and Curtis Turner's '66 Ford.

Riverside 1966 Parade Lap: Dan Gurney's Ford on the pole. Foster's Dodge, starting in the 9th position, indicated by the arrow.

(Daryl Foster Collection)

The 185-lap race took a little over five hours to complete, with two caution flag periods. Throughout the run, the lead was tossed back and forth between Pearson, Turner, and Gurney - with Gurney dominating the second half of the contest on his way to another victory. Foster had a competitive day, credited with 181 laps and a seventh-place finish – sandwiched between Jim Hurtubise and Ned Jarrett. His winnings amounted to $1,275.

The first USAC-sanctioned stock car event of the year came on April 17th at Langhorne Speedway. The 150-lap race drew just 19 entries, with returning champion Norm Nelson on the pole in his 1966 Plymouth. Despite his many career victories, Nelson had never won at Langhorne.

At the drop of the green flag Jim Hurtubise, starting from the second position in his Plymouth, grabbed the lead and held it for the first 90 laps, though Foster and Nelson were chasing closely behind. Billy then took command until the 136th lap when a tire blew. Nelson raced by and held the lead until the checkered flag. Hurtubise came home in the runner-up position. Foster was running at the end, four laps down to the leader, and finished fifth.

Next up was the 'Yankee 300' race on the first of May at Indianapolis Raceway Park, with the 160-lapper drawing 25 entries. Starting on the pole was the 1966 Plymouth of Paul Goldsmith, alongside

Don White's 1966 Dodge Charger. During the race, Billy's '65 Dodge led the most laps (54), but he finished second behind Norm Nelson. Those two drivers were the only ones to complete all 160 laps. The average speed of the event was 93 mph. Foster pocketed $3,003 of the $15,000 race purse.

On the fourth lap of this race, four people were injured when the car driven by Herb Shannon hit the starter's stand and careened into the crowded pit area, injuring three members of Goldsmith's pit crew. According to one report Shannon, who was not injured, lost control on the main straight when his engine locked up. The impact with the starter's stand knocked starter Jim Shipman to the ground, but there were no major injuries. Later, on the 65th lap, Jim Hurtubise's car hit the outer guard rail of the first turn and flipped over. Hurtubise was not injured but his car was demolished.

Billy Foster protecting his lead ahead of eventual winner Norm Nelson at Indianapolis Raceway Park.

(Photo courtesy of C.V. Haschel)

Berlin Raceway in Marne, Michigan hosted the next USAC stock car event on June 3rd. The statistics list just seven cars running the 100-lap race on Berlin's half-mile dirt oval. Don White started from the pole and led the first 60 laps but was overtaken by Norm Nelson, who registered another win for the season. Billy's Dodge finished in the second position.

Foster's schedule during June of 1966 was fully focused on the Champ Car Series, with races at Milwaukee, Langhorne, and Atlanta, demanding his full attention. The next event for the stock cars would not take place until July 2nd at the Indiana State Fairgrounds.

Labeled the 'Sesquicentennial Classic', the 100-lap race on the fairgrounds' one-mile dirt oval drew 30 entries. Don White's '66 Dodge Charger grabbed the pole position during qualifying. Mario Andretti and Jim Hurtubise flew up from Daytona for the race, only to find their cars had not been delivered to the track. For unknown reasons, Foster could not make a qualifying attempt, but officials allowed him to start from the back of the field.

13,343 spectators watched as White led the first 63 laps, but then Norm Nelson was up front for the next 37 go-arounds. At the end of the race, Nelson's Plymouth was the first car to see the checkered flag, with White in second. Billy had a steady charge up through the field and drove home in the seventh position, though earning only $619 for the day's work. The average speed of the race was 83.97 mph.

The stock car contingent celebrated the Fourth of July with a 100-lap event on the half-mile dirt track at the Brown County Fairgrounds in DePere, Wisconsin. In a field of just 16 cars, Nelson once again started on the pole and led all 100 laps in the race that took just a little over 45-minutes to complete. Finishing second was Gary Bettenhausen in a '66 Dodge Charger, while Foster finished third in Rudy Hoerr's Dodge.

It was back to the famous Milwaukee Mile on July 10th with a 200-lap feature on the challenging paved oval. Forty-five cars were entered, though seven would not qualify. During the race accidents, mechanical woes, and black flags eliminated 20 of the competitors. Don White's Dodge was the dominant car, leading 159 laps on his way to victory. Though we don't know Billy's starting position, he finished fifth behind White, Nelson, Hurtubise and Jack Bowsher. The winner was awarded $5,683.

The stock car series celebrated the Fourth of July with a 100-lap event on the half-mile dirt track at the Brown County Fairgrounds in DePere, Wisconsin. In a field of just 16 cars, Nelson once again started on the pole and led all 100 laps in the race that took just a little over 45-minutes to complete. Finishing second was Gary Bettenhausen in a '66 Dodge Charger, while Foster finished third in Rudy Hoerr's Dodge.

It was back to the famous Milwaukee Mile on July 10th with a 200-lap feature on the challenging paved oval. Forty-five cars were entered, though seven would not qualify. During the race accidents, mechanical woes, and black flags eliminated 20 of the competitors. Don White's Dodge was the dominant car, leading 159 laps on his way to victory. Though we don't know Billy's starting position, he finished fifth behind White, Nelson, Hurtubise and Jack Bowsher. The winner was awarded $5,683.

Billy Foster and Don White.

(USAC photo)

The September 10th, 1966 edition of *Competition Press* offered this full race report of the Milwaukie event:

White Tops Great Dane at Milwaukee

Fast driving and quick pit work gave Don White victory in a 200-mile USAC late model stock car race over the one-mile State Fair Park oval here today. White's '66 Charger dominated the event in winning by 14.5 seconds from Norm Nelson's '66 Plymouth. White averaged 90.980 mph for the distance, although slowed down by two lengthy periods run under the caution flag. Jim Hurtubise, Nelson's teammate, took third, followed by Jack Bowsher's independent 1966 Ford, the only competitive Ford Motor Company product in the race.

Nelson was the only driver capable of catching White when the Charger made its second pit stop on lap 176. But the Ray Nichels crew got White back on the course in fast style, and the Iowan needed only to maintain his margin to the finish.

It appeared that it was going to be White's day from the start. During qualification he shattered Nelson's four-day-old, one-lap time of 35.671 seconds, or 101.058 mph.

White took the lead on the opening lap after a tight scramble into turn one. He was closely followed by Andy Hampton's '65 Dodge. On lap three Nelson moved into second spot and the fifth time around was joined by Hurtubise. The top trio moved steadily away, leaving Hampton to do battle with Billy Foster's '65 Dodge and J.C. Kotz's '65 Plymouth.

As the field stretched out, Rick Kleich's engine blew in his '64 Ford, spraying the entrance to the south turn with oil and parts and leaving the Ford broadside across the track. The caution flag closed everyone up again, and at the drop of the green it was a new race.

No sooner were things underway again when a crash involving three slower cars jammed up the south turn again. It was at this point that Nelson, Hurtubise and Bowsher chose to pit, leaving White comfortably ahead. By lap 46 Nelson caught Foster, who was running second, and the two gave the 15,124 spectators something to cheer about as they ran side-by-side. Fourteen laps later Hurtubise caught Foster and then, shortly after, Nelson, to move into second.

White led Hurtubise by some 10-seconds when the yellow light came on briefly on lap 71, and White and Foster took the chance to pit. Hurtubise emerged the leader and Nelson, who in the meantime had managed to shake Bowsher, was in second.

White's stop was a quick one and it was obvious, as he roared through the pack, that to beat him Hurtubise, who was four seconds ahead on lap 118, he would have to step up the pace. Hurtubise came in on lap 122 with White in second, only to discover a boiling radiator. This cost him that race, forcing as it did a lengthy pit stop.

White was comfortably in the lead, with Nelson some 30 seconds in arrears on lap 130. But instead of losing time, White began to add to his lead, finally lapping Nelson on lap 152. It was then he made his second stop some six laps later that the outcome of the race was in the balance. This was hardly a delicate one, however, as White was unable to make up any further time between that point and the finish.

On July 22nd, Berlin Raceway again hosted another short, 50-lap race with a total purse of $7,500. The finishing order was White, Hurtubise, Nelson, Foster, Bay Darnell and Bettenhausen.

On July 30th, Hoerr and Foster traveled across the border to Canada to participate in the 'Kawartha 250' on the demanding road course at Mosport International Raceway in Bowmanville, Ontario. The event consisted of two, 50-lap heats on the 2.5-mile track with the teams vying for a piece of the $20,300 purse.

In the first heat, Sal Tovella's 1965 Plymouth led all 50 laps, with Billy finishing close behind in the second position. These two were followed by Roger Regeth and Norm Nelson. The second heat was dominated by winner Don White's '66 Dodge, with Nelson the runner-up and Mario Andretti finishing third. This time, Foster could only manage a seventh-place finish.

Race program cover and a promotional photo of Billy with a '66 Dodge Charger at Mosport.

(Photos courtesy of Canada Track and Traffic)

A post-race report, written by Sid Priddle for *Stock Car Magazine,* gave a full perspective of the event:

The 'Kawartha 250' marked the first return of USAC racing stocks to Canada since 1962; also the first time a professional sponsor promoted a stock car race on this track, resulting in a turnout of 30,000 fans. In '62, a similar event promoted by an amateur car club was a flop.

To most Canadians, USAC drivers other than the big names such as Andretti, are strangers. But the fans who attended the first Kawartha 250 will follow the fortunes of these men for some time to come. They saw one of the most exciting shows ever at six-year-old Mosport, where sports car races involving the leading drivers of the world have been staged.

More important is the fact that Mosport will go down in the USAC record books as "the place" where Chicago's Sal Tovella chalked-up his first USAC victory. For Tovella, an independent, it was his greatest day on the USAC circuit, as he brought his 1965 Plymouth into first place. Tovella was so happy he could hardly talk. "Man, this is the greatest place in the world. Why, I'm so happy I could cry," stammered the overjoyed 37-year-old driver.

However, no one can convince Sal that it was his steady driving that earned him the victory. In fact, he feels he owes a vote of thanks to his wife, Ruth. "In all my 16 years of racing, my wife had never worked in my pit – until today. She can work there anytime, now."

Don White was favored to take this race. White was driving Ray Nichels' Dodge Charger, and he won the pole position and was by far the fastest man on the circuit during both 50-lap heats of the race. "I raced here in 1962, and no doubt that helped me remember the course," Don explained.

The fact is, White had the race wrapped up, with only four laps to go, when his engine's crankshaft broke, and he had to retire. The 250-mile event was divided into two 125-mile heats. White won the first heat, then on lap 46 of the second, he had to call it quits. White ended up with a disappointing third-place finish.

"This isn't the first time this has happened," White said. "I've been leading a 100-lap race for 99 laps and had something break." In the second heat, White appeared to be pushed by Canadian ace Billy Foster (obviously a favorite with the fans), as the latter made a bid for first place.

White, however, said that Foster didn't bother him. "I had real good pit stops and I wasn't concerned about Foster catching me, because he seemed to be having handling problems. In the first heat, I had a 30-second lead, and I figured from that I could have gone faster if necessary, but I didn't want to hurt the car."

Foster disagreed and said he would have caught White, only flat tires (three in the second heat) put him out of contention.

Flat tires, incidentally, seemed to be the problem of the day. Many drivers complained of stones being thrown onto the pavement by cars taking unorthodox lines through the corners. White, however, said that stones didn't bother him at all. While many of the cars were running with hard tires, White said his compound was in-between. Mario Andretti's Charger suffered a flat tire at the beginning of the second heat, after he had placed third in the first. But Mario's other problems kept him from being a threat.

Andretti flipped his car after only three laps of practice. Although the car was badly smashed, Ray Nichel's crew is to be commended for putting it in shape within six hours, and Andretti was able to qualify. Most of the damage, other than the body, was done to the suspension, and this is what finally gave out on Andretti late in the second heat.

Tovella was able to grab-off almost $3,000 (the other part of the purse went to the first heat winner White), for his efforts. His non-factory Plymouth didn't have the power to match the big guns, but Sal explained that his car handled exceptionally well; of the utmost importance in conquering the rolling, twisting, winding Mosport circuit.

The idea of the two heats was well-received by all drivers. As Tovella accepted the Coca-Cola trophy he said, "I like the two-heat idea. It's great from the safety angle, and it came in real handy for me. I was up late last night watching television and boy; did I feel tired in that first heat. Funny, though, I don't feel tired anymore."

Two weeks later, on August 14th, there was another 150-lap event at Milwaukee. Forty entries took the green flag, and Norm Nelson took home another winner's trophy after leading every lap with his Plymouth. One lap down in second place was the Ford of Jack Bowsher, while White, Foster and Darnell rounded out the top five finishers. For their fourth-place run, Hoerr and Foster collected $1,192.

Just four days later, USAC held another race at the same track, but this time the length was increased to 200 laps. Another large field of 39 cars was on-hand and there were 18 drivers who completed the event, which took a little over two hours to run. White's '66 Charger started from the pole and raced on to victory, with Nelson just behind in second place. The next three across the line were Hurtubise, Bowsher and Foster, who was three laps down to White. Billy's winnings this day amounted to just $691.

The stock car's hectic schedule during this period of the 1966 season included a return to the Illinois State Fairgrounds just the next day, August 19th. Only three of the 24 cars entered completed all 100 laps on the dirt oval, with a finishing order of White, Nelson and Foster. This was White's day in the sun as he led all but one lap. The average speed of the race was 90.222 mph

It is about 225 driving miles from Springfield, Illinois to the Indiana State Fairgrounds. It was there on August 26th that the USAC series staged 100 laps of competition. Thirty cars timed in for the 'State Fair Century' race and Billy achieved his first pole position of the season in Rudy Hoerr's #22 Dodge. During the race Foster led for 15 laps, but for unknown reasons, he slipped back to an eighth-place finish, three laps down to winner Don White. Finishing second and third were Norm Nelson and A.J. Foyt, who was driving Jack Bowsher's '66 Ford.

Billy going full-tilt in Rudy Hoerr's Dodge at the Indiana State Fairgrounds.

(Foster Collection)

Labor Day weekend in 1966 found the stock cars at the DuQuoin State Fairgrounds for another 100-lapper. It was Don White on the pole who raced on to take the win over Nelson and Foster. The event took a little over one-hour to complete with a race average of 85.91 mph.

By finishing third, Rudy and Billy left the track with $2,143 in prize money. The next day at the fairgrounds, Billy would finish ninth in USAC's Champ Car event driving a Meskowski/Offenhauser sprint car for owner George Walther.

Only three races remained in the season for the USAC stock cars – Langhorne on September 11th, Milwaukee on the 18th, and the finale would be on the road course at Wentzville, Missouri on October 9th. Foster would be unable to compete in the last race because the Champ Cars would be appearing at the Mt. Fuji, Japan circuit that same weekend. Though they had yet to win a race, Rudy and Billy were having a gratifying season while accumulating valuable championship points.

The race at Langhorne was scheduled for 250 laps, and 20 cars made up the field. This time around it was the Norm Nelson-owned '66 Plymouth, driven by Jim Hurtubise, which ruled the day. Starting from the third position, Hurtubise led 190 laps in his run to be the first under the checkered flag. Nelson started his own Plymouth from the pole and led 35 laps, but finished third behind Foster, who was two laps down to the winner. The race was completed in 2.5-hours at an average of 99.656 mph.

Thirty-nine cars posted qualifying times for the 250-lap race at Milwaukee. Leading the way, as usual, was Norm Nelson in his strong #1 Plymouth. Don White qualified in the second slot and Foster would start the race from the fourth position. White led most of the laps and ended his day by pulling into victory lane. The only other driver on the same lap was Billy, finishing his stock car season with a strong second-place finish for Rudy Hoerr. The third through fifth positions went to Bowsher, Nelson and Foyt.

For the second year in a row, Norm Nelson was crowned USAC's Stock Car Champion. Don White finished second in the overall points standings, and Billy Foster placed an outstanding third for the season. Butch Hartman picked up the Rookie of the Year honors.

"Dad and Billy ran 29 races during 1965 and 1966", Irv Hoerr remembers. "They did really well, especially on the road courses. I worked on the crew as a tire changer, but in late 1966 I went to basic training. I spent one year of active duty in the Air Force and then five years in the Air Guard.

At first the team got little factory support, but eventually Chrysler began furnishing engines," Irv explained. "Dad bought used racing cars. One was a year-old car from noted stock car builder Cotton Owens. The first car Dad got fresh from the factory was the 1967 Dodge Charger he and Billy would debut at Riverside in January 1967.

Unfortunately, it was there that Billy lost his life."

THIRTY-EIGHT

January 20th, 1967 – The Last Lap

Today, perhaps the most anticipated racing event of a new year – at least in North America – is the annual Rolex 24-Hours of Daytona in late January. The large and fascinating field is made up of internationally-based sports cars, teams and drivers.

Back in the 1960s though, the nationally-highlighted event of a new racing season was the Motor Trend 500 at California's Riverside International Raceway. The first running of this event took place on January 20th, 1963 and was a NASCAR-sanctioned Grand National occasion.

One unique aspect of this race was that it drew top drivers not just from NASCAR, but also USAC stock cars and open-wheel ranks. Men such as Richard Petty, Fireball Roberts, Ned Jarrett and Fred Lorenzen would race side-by-side with the likes of A.J. Foyt, Parnelli Jones, Jim Hurtubise and Troy Ruttman. And then there was Californian Dan Gurney, who was superb in any type of machine he commanded, including Formula One. He was brought in to drive for the powerful Holman-Moody Ford factory team.

Riverside's 2.7-mile serpentine road course was regarded as a real challenge for light and nimble sports racers, so imagine the strains it would hold for the heavy, powerful but somewhat crude stock cars of the day. On this Sunday afternoon, everyone would be hoping to endure a grueling 185 laps in front of a reported 52,500 anxious spectators.

Forty-four cars qualified for the field, led by pole-sitter Paul Goldsmith in the Ray Nichels-built '63 Pontiac with a one-lap speed of 99.59 mph. Sharing the front row was A.J. Foyt, who was also driving a second Nichels Pontiac. Rounding out the top-five were Fireball Roberts, Len Sutton and Joe Weatherly – all also in Pontiacs. Ned Jarrett was the highest-qualifying Ford in the eighth position and Gurney would start his Ford eleventh. The top Chevrolet was in the hands of Dave MacDonald (13th) and the fastest MOPAR product was Richard Petty's Plymouth (15th).

Mechanical failures and crashes ruled the day and just 21 cars were running at the end of the grind, which took nearly six hours to complete at an average speed of 84.965 mph. In all there were nine lead changes, with Gurney emerging the victor with a 36-second lead over Foyt in the second position. Gurney was dominant, leading a full 120 laps and earning $14,400 of the purse. Finishing third through fifth, in order, were Troy Ruttman, Fireball Roberts and Bobby Johns.

In the following three years of this event Dan Gurney was unbeatable, again driving Fords but now out of the Wood Brothers' stable. His record run was interrupted in 1967 by Parnelli Jones' Ford entered by Bill Stroppe. That day Gurney's Stroppe-built Mercury expired due to an engine issue after

143 laps. Gurney returned to Riverside's victory lane in 1968 for his fifth win in the Motor Trend Magazine-sponsored weekend. In 1969 it was King Richard Petty's turn for the trophy when he pushed his Ford (the Petty team had switched from Plymouth to Fords this one year) to a 25-second win over A.J. Foyt, who was driving a Ford for Jack Bowsher. Foyt would finally accomplish victory at Riverside in 1970 when his Ford took the checkered just 3.5-seconds ahead of Roger McCluskey, driving a Plymouth for Norm Nelson.

Though without a win during the 1966 USAC stock car season, the pairing of Rudy Hoerr and Billy Foster had a pretty darn successful year, finishing nearly every race they entered in the top-five, including three second-place showings. With this performance, Rudy Hoerr received his first, fresh-from-the factory, 1967 Dodge Charger which would make its debut at Riverside. Both the team and the driver shared much optimism with their new #22 Dodge. After all, the previous year Billy qualified their old '64 Dodge 12th and finished in the seventh spot upon their first visit to the track.

But tragically, that optimism would be short-lived. During a practice session on Friday, January 20th, something went horribly wrong. Billy had been recording top-ten lap times, but on one flying circuit he experienced a reported brake drum failure.

According to observers, he was coming off the mile-long backstretch straightaway when the mechanical issue occurred at an estimated 140 mph. He apparently tried to sideswipe the retaining wall in turn nine in an effort to slow his Dodge, but he hit the wall so hard it ripped all the sheet metal off the left side.

In that era driver-side window nets were not included in NASCAR-mandated safety equipment, and upon impact Billy's helmet impacted the hard wall, resulting in his fatal head injury. His wreck was strangely similar to that of NASCAR champion Joe Weatherly's fatal incident in 1964 during the running of this same event, when he also struck a retaining wall sideways. Along with not having a window net installed, Weatherly was also not wearing a shoulder harness because he was afraid of being trapped in a burning car.

Due to the nature of the injuries to Weatherly and Foster, along with those of Richard Petty at Darlington in 1970, NASCAR ultimately required window nets – but that was not until 1971. One must wonder why this ruling didn't take place immediately following Foster's crash?

The news reports describing Billy's tragic death appeared soon after across the United States and Canada, as in these examples from various news outlets:

Billy Foster Killed at Raceway

By Bruce Grant – Sun-Telegram Auto Editor

RIVERSIDE – Death dulled the glitter of preparations yesterday for tomorrow's Motor Trend 500-mile stock car road race at Riverside International Raceway. Canadian Billy Foster was killed instantly when his 1967 Dodge Charger crashed into the dirt-reinforced steel retaining wall on treacherous Turn 9.

The well-liked Foster was on a practice lap at the time of the accident. He was coming off the mile-long back straightaway when a front brake drum failed. The left side of his car hit the wall with such force that Foster's head apparently went through the window and struck the wall.

Raceway physician Dr. Irving Omphroy said: "Foster died upon impact of his car with Turn 9. He died instantly as far as we can tell." Cause of death was listed as massive head injuries.

The car is owned by Rudy Hoerr of Peoria, Ill. Foster, 29, is survived by his widow, Beverly, and three children, Debra, William and Kelly, of Victoria, B.C. He has been racing 12 years. A member of the U.S. Auto Club, Foster finished 17th in the 1965 Indianapolis 500 and was a principal in the 1966 first-lap smashup. He placed seventh in last year's Motor Trend 500.

Foster was the second driver to die in five years of NASCAR competition at Riverside. Joe Weatherly was killed during the running of the 1964 Motor Trend 500.

Foster Thursday had earned the No. 9 starting spot for tomorrow's race when he qualified his Charger at 105.297 miles per hour. NASCAR officials said yesterday that all qualifiers beyond the No. 9 spot would move up one position. Lee Roy Yarbrough of Columbia, S.C. led yesterday's five qualifiers with a speed of 106.009 mph in a 1966 Dodge Charger.

Victoria's Billy Foster Killed in Stock Practice

RIVERSIDE, Calif. (CP) – Billy Foster of Victoria, whose superior driving skill never quite made up for his ill luck, died Friday in a mass of twisted metal while braving the danger he considered part of a race car driver's job. Foster, 29, died of massive head injuries when his car slammed into a retaining wall during a practice run for the Motor Trend Riverside 500 stock car race here Sunday.

His skill and love of the sport earned him the United States Auto Club's rookie of the year honors in 1965, but bad luck kept him from becoming one of the world's leading drivers. He was never unaware of the danger – he said it "is part of the job. It's my job, and I can't do anything else."

In 1965, he became the first Canadian to qualify for the 500-mile Indianapolis Memorial Day race. He dropped out on the 90th lap when a water line in his rear-engine Offenhauser burst. He qualified again in 1966 and barely got over the starting line when he became involved in a 16-car pileup at the first turn.

Foster was the second British Columbia driver to die racing in less than a year. Bob McLean of Vancouver was killed when his auto caught fire at Sebring last year.

Brake Drum Failure Blamed for Foster's Crash

RIVERSIDE, Calif. (AP) – Billy Foster suffered massive head injuries when his car slammed against a retaining wall as he approached turn No. 9 while travelling at an estimated 135 to 140 miles an hour. His car, a 1967 model owned by Rudy Hoerr of Peoria, Ill., hit the wall as he started to turn to the right. The left side of the car slammed broadside with such force that all the sheet metal on that side was ripped off. There was no car near his.

A spokesman said the apparent cause of the crash was brake drum failure. Foster started to brake on a mile-long straightaway where speeds of 160 mph are reached, but as he began to make the right turn, his car rammed broadside against the retaining wall. The car struck with such impact that Foster's helmet hit the wall, inflicting the head injuries.

A spokesman for the track said Foster's car was equipped with specialized safety brake drums – common to racing stock cars – but that they apparently failed at the turn.

This tribute appeared in a publication named *The Charger*, by editor Bill Marvel:

Riverside, California – Last Friday afternoon there was a friendly poker game taking place in the garage area here as crews and driver took advantage of a lull in the practice sessions. A slim uniformed driver, who many in the world of racing had grown to know and appreciate for his ability, desire and unassuming ways, wandered in.

Not having any money in his uniform, he borrowed a dollar and jumped into the game with his usual happy enthusiasm. A few hands later a member of his pit crew called him to take a few practice laps. "Leave the cards as they are. I'll be back in a few minutes, this won't take long."

With these words he headed for the pit area. Those dealt cards were never played for a "few minutes" later. Billy Foster was fatally injured in the high-speed number nine turn and the world of racing was dealt a hard blow.

Monday morning, Mario Andretti stood with me in the press room as he waited to pose for some Ford P.R. shots, and we discussed the death of Billy. Andretti was possibly Billy's closest buddy and as we talked, Mario, with the heart of a champion held back his emotions.

"It's ironic you know, only last week we (Billy and Mario) were driving over from LA and Billy was discussing how fortunate we were to have things going so well for us," Mario continued. "Billy was always very appreciative of his success and he said to me 'now that we are really making good, we don't want to get killed, we should enjoy things.' He was trying to talk me out of running the sprints. You know he always worried about me and the sprinters."

Many words will be said about Billy as last respects are paid to him, but I believe that Mario summed it really well with the statement, "He was a real racer."

The staff of *The CHARGER* would like to join the racing fraternity in offering to Mrs. Foster and Billy's family our deepest sympathies. May God be with them.

Wednesday, January 25th, 1967 was a cold, miserable day in Victoria, but the weather didn't sway hundreds of people, from all walks of life, to attend Billy's memorial.

(Victoria Times Colonist)

This reflection of the day appeared in the *Victoria Times Colonist:*

Hundreds Say Farewell

More than 500 friends Wednesday paid final tribute to Billy Foster, Victoria's car racing ace who died in a California crash last week.

"We are remembering him not as a man who was able to win a race but as one who was able to discipline himself to great character," Rev. Dr. S.J. Parsons told the overflow crowd of mourners at McCall Bros. Chapel. A mile-long procession followed the casket to Hatley Memorial Gardens, where the snow was falling lightly during a dull and chilly afternoon.

Born and raised in Victoria, he had an impressive record, including that of being the first Canadian, in 1965, to qualify for the Indianapolis 500.

Dr. Parsons, from Centennial United Church, had special words for his wife and three children: "I think of the wife and those children who were in the bleachers – and he became what he became because they were cheering him back there." He said Billy Foster was a man determined to win, a man who gambled with his life, "the very precious thing he owned."

"Billy is calling on us not only to see the goal and get going in the arena, but he is calling on us to get going on a better world."

The first mourners were in the chapel an hour before the service started at 1:30 p.m. Even with 150 extra seats, many were standing in the adjoining covered concourse. The flowers came from all over Canada and the United States – his racing associates, mechanics, sponsors and suppliers. Names like Chrysler, Ford, Goodyear, Firestone, plus dozens from local groups and friends, were on some of the 150 floral tributes.

Billy's Friends Travelled Far to Pay Tribute

By Hal Malone, columnist

They said goodbye to Billy Foster on a cold, raw, wet day Wednesday, 575 of them. Drivers, mechanics, car makers, friends filled McCall's Chapel and formed a mile-long auto cortege paying final respects to the Victoria man who rose to the top in the world of auto racing before being killed in a crash last Friday at Riverside, Calif.

From distant parts of the United States and Canada came more than 100 people in the high echelons of Billy Foster's world. There was two-time U.S. national driving champion Mario and Andretti and his crew; Bill McCrarey of Akron, Ohio, chief of Firestone's racing division; Chuck Hulse, fifth in last year's Indianapolis 500 and a Goodyear representative.

Norm Ellefson of Edmonton, CAMRA king and the racing Rasmussens of Edmond, Eldon and Arnold; Ralph Monhay, Vancouver driver; Grant King, formerly of Victoria, Foster's chief mechanic on the United States Auto Club circuit; John Feuz of Portland, mechanic in Foster's halcyon Pacific Northwest racing days; Geoff Vantreight of Victoria.

There were floral tributes upon floral tributes, 174 in all, the largest number in the chapel's history. Some were in the form of a giant checkered flag, the traditional "last lap" symbol for drivers. And others depicting No. 27, the number he made famous.

Pit crews, drivers and mechanics formed a floral honor guard as active pall bearers Mario Andretti, Grant King, Rudy Hoerr, Ed McDonald, Rolla Vollstedt, Reg Midgely, John Feuz and Jim Haslam carried the casket from the chapel. Then they stepped into their cars and in a driving rain went to Hatley Memorial Gardens for their final goodbyes.

In the days that followed the memorial, there were several well-written articles that paid tribute to the fallen Victoria driver. Some of these follow, attributed when possible:

Billy Foster

'I've Lost the Best Friend I Ever Had'

By Doug Peden

If you don't think Billy Foster was a special kind of man you should talk to Mario Andretti, the two-time U.S. national car racing champion from Nazareth, Pa.

From the time they met as rookie drivers at the famed Indianapolis 500-mile race in 1965, Mario and Billy were buddies. It was a rare, almost-instant type of friendship that seemed to grow in depth as the months went by – until last Friday.

That was the day Foster was helplessly trapped by brake failure as his machine hurtled toward a turn at better than 140 miles per hour. The car crashed into a retaining wall and Foster, the Victoria driver with a touch of greatness, was dead. That was the day Andretti's former fun-filled world of screaming rubber and roaring engines suddenly became sad and lonely.

Mario was in Victoria Tuesday, joining dozens of other famous men of the automobile circuits in paying final tribute at Foster's funeral. Friends and admirers of Foster, probably more than 100, from Boston, Akron, Peoria, Indianapolis and other places, arrived in the city to say farewell.

All were sad. But none seemed more forlorn or more helpless than Andretti, the slender little man who becomes such a fearless giant behind a wheel that he has won the national title in both his years on the big-time sprint car circuit.

"Words are hard to find," said Andretti, "but I'll tell you one thing. I've lost the best friend I ever had, in racing and away from the track. What makes it the hardest is that Billy was loved so much by everyone. If he hadn't been that way this would have been easier. He was a great driver and a wonderful man. More than that; he was a special kind of a man, a very easy man to get to know. Everybody seemed to like him instantly."

"I don't make friends easily, but Billy and I were buddies right from the start. He had a special way about him and he's the only really close friend I ever had. We talked about this several times, but we were confident it wouldn't happen to us. Now it has happened, and I doubt if things will ever be the same."

'He Was One of the Best'

By Brian Doherty

Geoff Vantreight, a close associate of Foster for years and his mechanic during the Japanese-style 500 late last year, said: "I was certainly surprised. He was a smart driver. I didn't think he would ever get it." Reg Midgley, manager of Western Speedway and a close friend, said: "He was one of the best. He never lived long enough to hit his peak."

Bing Foster, another friend but no relation of the friendly, freckled-face speed king, said: "I can't understand what happened – it seems to me it must have been mechanical trouble. The success of Billy's driving was largely because of his exceptionally fast reflexes. I have never seen a driver respond so quickly. It kept him out of trouble."

Midgely continued, "He was the idol of every car racing enthusiast – he had all the talents. He didn't find much luck down there ever [the United States] but he was doing what he wanted to do. He won everything up here. His biggest success? Being a Canadian and getting as far as he did. He had to sell himself to the Americans and he didn't get any financial aid from Canada. Being able to do that was something. In his mind he knew the danger. He wasn't fooling himself. He knew what was involved."

Foster began racing before he was old enough to drive on the road, at 15, on the Shearing track at Cobble Hill. He moved to the Western Speedway about 11 years ago, driving in the aggressive manner that became his trademark.

After marrying his childhood sweetheart Beverly, he gave up racing and took a job with the Government Forest Service. That didn't pay enough money and he went to work at his father's garage on Fernwood. Racing called him back and he said to one interviewer: "Now I've found a way to make money without manual labor. It sure is a better way to make a living than getting $200 a month working for the government." He and Beverly got a $2,000 loan from the bank where she worked, and they used the money to buy Billy's first racing car. One of the biggest stepping stones in Foster's career came in 1961 when he went to Edmonton for the Gold Cup race in Jim Haslam's car, recalled Bing Foster.

Billy Foster – a Superb though Jinxed Driver

By Bob Lightower, *Competition Press & Autoweek*, February 25, 1967.

Billy Foster was not just a good driver. Billy Foster was a superb driver. Nor was Billy Foster just an unlucky driver. Billy Foster was a jinxed driver.

Long after the crunching scars left by the fastback Charger have been erased from the turn nine boiler plate, everyone from the Hoosier Auto Racing Fans club to Rolla Vollstedt to Mario Andretti will ponder the ever-promising but ever-painful racing career of Billy Foster.

Billy Foster will be missed not just because he was affable; a thoroughly well-liked personality in a dangerous profession. Most drivers are affable, thoroughly well-liked personalities. Only for a few days in his short span as a race driver was Billy Foster NOT an affable, thoroughly well-liked personality.

After Indianapolis and the starting line disaster, blame was tentatively thrust at Foster. After all, he'd been the first man to lose a wheel in what shortly became a mad rainstorm of wheels. But Foster was so aboveboard the only real mark against him was, at best, a questionable one; he was a cunning gin rummy player. Therefore, the yoke of blame was almost immediately lifted. Billy Foster made a most unconvincing villain.

Billy Foster will be remembered as the driver who was on his way, but never arrived.

No driver in the last few seasons – with the exception of the late Bobby Marshman – performed so brilliantly yet achieved such meager success.

Billy Foster could have been another Mario Andretti. It was no coincidence Foster was Andretti's closest friend in a sport where – perhaps wisely – drivers are not supposed to be friends. But Andretti and Foster were friends.

During last years Can-Am at Riverside they embarked in partnership with a McLaren-Ford. It was never successful, but Mario never doubted both the car, and Foster, would soon be very successful.

Who, Mario was asked late last season, would be his most serious threat in championship cars in 1967? Andretti had little doubt. "Billy Foster. You'll be hearing a lot from him next year."

Like Andretti, Foster was not a spectacular chauffeur on the few dirt tracks, although also, like Andretti, he was fast becoming one. The paved, super-speedways of USAC – the faster the better – were Foster territory. It showed.

Not that Foster won races. He didn't even finish races, owing to a sickening record of mechanical failures, and his personal failure to align himself with that most important racing basic: luck. But whoever saw Foster run races at Atlanta, the Dixie stock car track which has humbled Indianapolis by becoming the fast championship car venue of all, could only roll their eyes and mop their brow. Billy Foster was a flier.

Rolla Vollstedt made an ironically perfect mechanic for Foster. If Foster was the most ill-starred championship car pilot, Vollstedt has always been the most singularly unlucky mechanic on the USAC circuit.

Vollstedt was never unwilling to express his admiration of Foster. And at Phoenix last November, the last contest where Vollstedt and Foster were to run as a team, Vollstedt summed it all up in one emotion-dripping burst:

"Know who's going to win the race today? Billy Foster; Billy Foster is going to win the race today. After what he's been through, he has to win the race today. But Billy Foster did not win that day.

In stock cars, Foster had been USAC's rookie of the year in 1965, and in last season's Riverside 500 had fired-up spectators by keeping a three-year-old Dodge in contention. They could tell he was much more than just a good driver. This year they found out, tragically, he was also a jinxed driver.

THIRTY-NINE

A Fitting Tribute

In June of 2016, at the grand opening of the Vancouver Island Motorsport Circuit, the memory of Billy Foster was deservedly honored. In attendance at this gala event were members of his family and some of his old friends. I'm sure as he looked down upon them on this perfect day, he had a huge smile on his face.

Located in Cowichan Valley, B.C., the circuit is open to the public to enjoy motorsport and driving experiences at all skill levels, unique driving programs, facility rentals and community events. The site features a state-of-the-art 15,000 square-foot clubhouse equipped with a full-service commercial kitchen. (www.islandmotorsportcircuit.com)

The track itself is a 2.3 km (1.42 mile) circuit with five different track configurations, skid pad and four pit garages. Also available is an off-road experience course. The challenging road course was designed by Tilke Engineering, which has provided services to race tracks around the world.

The facility was established by Dr. Sylvester Chuang and Peter Trzewik, principals with the GAIN Group of Companies, a consortium of eleven auto dealerships on Vancouver Island, the Villa Eyrie Resort, Cowichan River Lodge, the Vancouver Island Motorsport Circuit, and the AWIN Group of Companies with fourteen dealerships in Ontario, Canada.

The event featured an esteemed guest list, including acclaimed race drivers Danny Sullivan and Max Papis. A highlight of the day was the visit by Billy's cousin – the world-renowned composer and musician, David Foster. A Victoria native, David is twelve-years junior to Billy and is the son of Morry and Eleanor (Vantreight) Foster.

In 1963, at the age of 13, David enrolled in the University of Washington music program. From that point forward, his musical career advanced rapidly. In 1974 he moved to Los Angeles and went on to create for and perform with the top-echelon artists in the industry.

In 1985 David composed the score for the film *St. Elmo's Fire,* which was followed by several other movie scores. His many works included "*Winter Games*", the theme song for the 1988 Winter Olympics in Calgary, Alberta. Some of the musicians and groups David has written or produced songs for include Earth, Wind & Fire, Chicago, Celine Dion, Whitney Houston, Michael Jackson, Kenny Loggins and Peter Cetera. For his continuing work, he has acquired a number of Emmy, Grammy, Golden Globe and Academy Awards.

Thirty-one years ago, he established the David Foster Foundation, a non-profit organization dedicated to providing financial support for non-medical expenses to Canadian families with children in

(L to R) Sylvester Chuang, Debra Foster, David Foster, Bev (Foster) Hill, Peter Trzewik.

need of life-saving organ transplants. In three decades the Foundation, under Chief Executive Officer Mike Ravenhill, has assisted over 1,100 families with children in need of major organ transplants and provided much-needed dollars in direct family support. In 2006, the Foundation became a national organization, expanding to help families across Canada. (www.davidfosterfoundation.com)

(L to R): Billy Foster Jr., David Foster, Danny Sullivan.

Billy Foster's younger cousin - renowned musician and composer David Foster.

(L to R): David Foster, Debra Foster, Jen and Billy Foster Jr.

(Photos in this chapter are courtesy of the Vancouver Island Motorsports Circuit)

FORTY

Billy Foster's Championship Car Results

1964 Season

August 23:
    Tony Bettenhausen 200 – Milwaukee, WI.
    Flynn/Offy (Walt Flynn)
    Started 18th – Finished 16th (181 of 200 laps – running). Earnings: $700
    Winner: Parnelli Jones – Lotus/Ford

September 27:
    Trenton 200 – Trenton, N.J.
    Flynn/Offy (Walt Flynn)
    Started 21st – Finished 7th (193 of 200 laps – running). Earnings: $1,470
    Winner: Parnelli Jones – Lotus/Ford

November 22:
    Bobby Ball Memorial – Avondale, AZ.
    Flynn/Offy (Walt Flynn)
    Started 22nd – Finished 21st (32 of 200 laps – spin). Earnings: $136
    Winner: Lloyd Ruby – Halibrand/Offy

1965 Season

March 28:
    Jimmy Bryan Memorial – Avondale, AZ.
    Eisert/Chevy (J. Frank Harrison)
    Started 11th – Finished 24th (12 of 150 laps – engine). Earnings: $79
    Winner: Don Branson – Watson/Offy

April 25:
    Trenton 100 – Trenton, N.J.
    Eisert/Chevy (J. Frank Harrison)
    Started 7th – Finished 7th (86 of 87 laps – running). Earnings: $911
    Winner: Jim McElreath – Brabham/Offy

May 31: **Indianapolis 500** – Indianapolis, IN.
Vollstedt/Offy (Jim Robbins)
Started 6th – Finished 17th (85 of 200 laps – manifold). Earnings: $9,936
Winner: Jimmy Clark – Lotus/Ford

June 20: **Langhorne 100** – Langhorne, PA.
Vollstedt/Offy (Jim Robbins)
Started 13th – Finished 5th (100 of 100 laps – running). Earnings: $1,764
Winner: Jim McElreath – Brabham/Offy

July 18: **Trenton 150** – Trenton, N.J.
Vollstedt/Ford (Rolla Vollstedt)
Started 8th – Finished 20th (45 of 150 laps – crash). Earnings: $129
Winner: A.J. Foyt – Lotus/Ford

August 1: **Atlanta Championship 250** – Hampton, GA.
Vollstedt/Ford (Rolla Vollstedt)
Started 2nd – Finished 3rd (167 of 167 laps – running). Earnings $5,700
Winner: Johnny Rutherford – Watson/Ford

August 8: **Langhorne 125** – Langhorne, PA.
Watson/Offy (Jim Robbins)
Started 7th – Finished 17th. 98 of 125 laps – running). Earnings: $190
Winner: Jim McElreath – Brabham/Offy

August 14: **Milwaukee 150** – West Allis, WI.
Vollstedt/Ford (Rolla Vollstedt)
Started 12th – Finished 20th (40 of 150 laps – engine). Earnings: $100
Winner: Joe Leonard – Halibrand/Ford

August 22: **Tony Bettenhausen 200** – West Allis, WI.
Vollstedt/Ford (Rolla Vollstedt)
Started 15th – Finished 26th (7 of 200 laps – mechanical). Earnings: $186
Winner: Gordon Johncock – Gerhardt/Offy

September 18: **Hoosier Hundred** – Indianapolis, IN.
Meskowski/Offy (David McManus)
Started 15th – Finished 12th (97 of 100 laps – running). Earnings: $995
Winner: A.J. Foyt – Meskowski/Offy

September 26: **Trenton 200** – Trenton, N.J.
Kurtis/Offy (Tassi Vatis)
Started 15th – Finished 24th (16 of 200 laps – engine). Earnings: $141
Winner: A.J. Foyt – Lotus/Ford

November 21: **Bobby Ball Memorial** – Avondale, AZ.
Vollstedt/Ford (Rolla Vollstedt)
Started 10th – Finished 13th (188 of 200 laps – running). Earnings: $603
Winner: A.J. Foyt – Lotus/Ford

1966 Season

March 20: **Jimmy Bryan Memorial** – Avondale, AZ
Vollstedt/Ford (Jim Robbins)
Started 16th – Finished 7th (147 of 150 laps – running). Earnings: $864
Winner: Jim McElreath – Brabham/Ford

April 24: **Trenton 150** – Trenton, N.J.
Eisert/Chevy (J. Frank Harrison)
Started 16th – Finished 22nd (1 of 102 laps – suspension). Earnings: $112
Winner: Rodger Ward – Lola/Offy

May 30: **Indianapolis 500** – Indianapolis, IN.
Vollstedt/Ford (Jim Robbins)
Started 12th – Finished 24th (0 of 200 laps – crash). Earnings: $9,554
Winner: Graham Hill – Lola/Ford

June 12: **Langhorne 100** – Langhorne, PA.
Vollstedt/Ford (Jim Robbins)
Started 10th – Finished 5th (100 of 100 laps – running). Earnings: $1,342
Winner: Mario Andretti – Brawner/Ford

June 26: **Atlanta 300** – Hampton, GA.
Vollstedt/Ford (Jim Robbins)
Started 4th – Finished 2nd (199 of 200 laps – running). Earnings: $8,500
Winner: Mario Andretti – Brawner/Ford

July 24: **Hoosier Grand Prix** – Clermont, IN.
Vollstedt/Ford (Jim Robbins)
Started 12th – Finished 13th (76 of 80 laps – running). Earnings: $320
Winner: Mario Andretti – Brawner/Ford

August 7: **Langhorne 150** – Langhorne, PA.
Vollstedt/Ford (Jim Robbins)
Started 5th – Finished 20th (34 of 150 laps – spin). Earnings: $92
Winner: Roger McCluskey – Eagle/Ford

August 27: **Tony Bettenhausen 200** – West Allis, WI.
Vollstedt/Ford (Jim Robbins)
Started 9th – Finished 5th (197 of 200 laps – running). Earnings: $2,001
Winner: Mario Andretti – Brawner/Ford

September 5: **Ted Horn Memorial** – DuQuoin, IL.
Stillness/Offy (George Walther)
Started 16th – Finished 9th (96 of 100 laps – running). Earnings: $657
Winner: Bud Tinglestad – Meskowski/Offy

September 10: **Hoosier Hundred** – Indianapolis, IN.
Meskowski/Offy (Jake Virgo)
Started 8th – Finished 15th (40 of 100 laps – oil pressure). Earnings: $70
Winner: Mario Andretti – Kuzma/Offy

September 25: **Trenton 200** – Trenton, N.J.
Vollstedt/Ford (Jim Robbins)
Started 6th – Finished 18th (84 of 200 laps – ignition). Earnings: $33
Winner: Mario Andretti – Brawner/Ford

October 9: **Fuji 200** – Shizuoka, Japan
Vollstedt/Ford (Jim Robbins)
Started 6th – Finished 9th (70 of 80 laps – rear end).
Winner: Jackie Stewart – Lola/Ford

November 20: **Bobby Ball Memorial** – Avondale, AZ.
Vollstedt/Ford (Jim Robbins)
Started 10th – Finished 12th (123 of 200 laps – rear end). Earnings: $674
Winner: Mario Andretti – Brawner/Ford

FORTY-ONE

Billy Foster's USAC Stock Car Results

1964 Season

November 14:   **Ascot Park** – Gardena, CA.
1963 Mercury   (no owner listed)
Started 10th – Finished 5th
Winner: Parnelli Jones – 1964 Mercury

November 29:   **Hanford Motor Speedway** – Hanford, CA.
(no car or owner listed)
Finished 13th
Winner: A.J. Foyt – 1964 Dodge

December 6:   **Ascot Park** – Gardena, CA.
1964 Plymouth   (no owner listed)
Started 13th – Finished 24th   (13 of 300 laps)
Winner: Rodger Ward – 1964 Mercury

1965 Season

July 4:   **Illiana Speedway** – Schereville, IN.
1965 Dodge   (Rudy Hoerr)
Started 6th – Finished 6th
Winner: Norm Nelson – 1965 Plymouth

July 11:   **Milwaukee Mile** – West Allis, WI.
1965 Dodge   (Rudy Hoerr)
Finished 8th   (197 of 200 laps – running). Earnings: $873
Winner: Norm Nelson – 1965 Plymouth

August 15:   **Milwaukee Mile** – West Allis, WI.
1965 Dodge (Rudy Hoerr)
Finished 13th (146 of 150 laps – running). Earnings: $363
Winner: Paul Goldsmith – 1965 Plymouth

August 19:   **Milwaukee Mile** – West Allis, WI.
1965 Dodge (Rudy Hoerr)
Finished 10th (192 of 200 laps – running). Earnings: $454
Winner: Norm Nelson – 1965 Plymouth

August 20:   **Illinois State Fairgrounds** – Springfield, IL.
1965 Dodge (Rudy Hoerr)
Started 5th – Finished 17th (55 of 100 laps)
Winner: Bobby Isaac – 1965 Dodge

September 5:   **DuQuoin State Fairgrounds** – DuQuoin, IL.
1965 Dodge (Rudy Hoerr)
Finished 10th. Earnings: $704
Winner: Paul Goldsmith – 1965 Plymouth

September 7:   **Indiana State Fairgrounds** – Indianapolis, IN.
1965 Dodge (Rudy Hoerr)
Finished 3rd (100 of 100 laps – running). Earnings: $1,600
Winner: A.J. Foyt – 1965 Ford

September 19:   **Milwaukee Mile** – West Allis, WI.
1964 Dodge (Rudy Hoerr)
Finished 7th (244 of 250 laps). Earnings: $818
Winner: Jim Hurtubise – 1965 Plymouth

October 10:   **Mid-American 200** – Wentzville, MO.
1964 Dodge (Rudy Hoerr)
Finished 8th (52 of 71 laps – crash). Earnings: $358
Winner: Don White – 1964 Ford

October 24:   **Langhorne Speedway** – Langhorne, PA.
1964 Dodge (Rudy Hoerr)
Started 2nd – Finished 4th (Led 63 of 250 laps – running)
Winner: Paul Goldsmith – 1965 Plymouth

November 28:   **Hanford Motor Speedway** – Hanford, CA.
　　　　　　　1964 Dodge (Rudy Hoerr)
　　　　　　　Started 2nd – Finished 21st (59 of 134 laps – engine)
　　　　　　　Winner: Norm Nelson – 1965 Plymouth

1966 Season

April 17:   **Langhorne Speedway** – Langhorne, PA.
　　　　　　1965 Dodge (Rudy Hoerr)
　　　　　　Finished 5th (146 of 150 laps – running)
　　　　　　Winner: Norm Nelson – 1966 Plymouth

May 1:   **Indianapolis Raceway Park** – Clermont, IN.
　　　　　1965 Dodge (Rudy Hoerr)
　　　　　Started 5th – Finished 2nd (Led 54 of 160 laps – running). Earnings: $3,003
　　　　　Winner: Norm Nelson – 1966 Plymouth

June 3:   **Berlin Raceway** – Marne, MI.
　　　　　1965 Dodge (Rudy Hoerr)
　　　　　Finished 2nd (100 of 100 laps)
　　　　　Winner: Norm Nelson – 1965 Plymouth

July 2:   **Indiana State Fairgrounds** – Indianapolis, IN.
　　　　　1966 Dodge (Rudy Hoerr)
　　　　　Started 30th – Finished 7th (100 of 100 laps). Earnings: $619
　　　　　Winner: Norm Nelson – 1966 Plymouth

July 4:   **Brown County Fairgrounds** – DePere, WI.
　　　　　1966 Dodge (Rudy Hoerr)
　　　　　Finished 3rd (100 of 100 laps). Earnings: $560
　　　　　Winner: Norm Nelson – 1966 Plymouth

July 10:   **Milwaukee Mile** – West Allis, WI.
　　　　　　1965 Dodge (Rudy Hoerr)
　　　　　　Finished 4th (197 of 200 laps). Earnings: $1,679
　　　　　　Winner: Don White – 1966 Dodge

July 22:   **Berlin Raceway** – Marne, MI.
　　　　　　1966 Dodge (Rudy Hoerr)
　　　　　　Finished 4th. Earnings: $1,679
　　　　　　Winner: Don White – 1966 Dodge

July 30:	**Mosport International Raceway** – Bowmanville, Ontario, Canada
	1966 Dodge (Rudy Hoerr)
	(Heat One) Started 2nd – Finished 7th
	Winner: Don White – 1966 Dodge
	(Heat Two) Finished 2nd
	Winner: Sal Tovella – 1965 Plymouth
August 14:	**Milwaukee Mile** – West Allis, WI.
	1965 Dodge (Rudy Hoerr)
	Finished 4th (148 of 150 laps – running). Earnings: $1,192
	Winner: Norm Nelson – 1966 Plymouth
August 18:	**Milwaukee Mile** – West Allis, WI.
	1965 Dodge (Rudy Hoerr)
	Finished 5th (197 of 200 laps – running). Earnings: $691
	Winner: Don White – 1966 Dodge
August 19:	**Illinois State Fairgrounds** – Springfield, IL.
	1966 Dodge (Rudy Hoerr)
	Finished 3rd (100 of 100 laps – running)
	Winner: Don White – 1966 Dodge
August 26:	**Indiana State Fairgrounds** – Indianapolis, IN.
	1965 Dodge (Rudy Hoerr)
	Started 1st – Finished 8th (Led 15 of 100 laps). Earnings: $1,119
	Winner: Don White – 1966 Dodge
September 4:	**DuQuoin State Fairgrounds** – DuQuoin, IL.
	1965 Dodge (Rudy Hoerr)
	Finished 3rd. Earnings: $2,143
	Winner: Don White – 1966 Dodge
September 11:	**Langhorne Speedway** – Langhorne, PA.
	1965 Dodge (Rudy Hoerr)
	Finished 2nd (248 of 250 laps – running)
	Winner: Jim Hurtubise – 1966 Plymouth
September 18:	**Milwaukee Mile** - West Allis, WI.
	1965 Dodge (Rudy Hoerr)
	Started 4th – Finished 2nd (250 of 250 laps – running.) Earnings $3,790
	Winner: Don White – 1966 Dodge

FORTY-TWO

The Victoria Auto Racing Hall of Fame and Museum

The Victoria Auto Racing Hall of Fame came to fruition when a few racers were discussing the long history of motorsports in the area. Those conversations spawned the idea of recognizing the achievements of the many local racing personalities of the past.

The initial meeting was held on June 19th, 1984 at the Ross Rockett residence and included Rockett, Bill Smith, Ted MacKenzie, Frank Kitto, Norm Wilcox and Barrie Goodwin.

From this early beginning, the Hall of Fame was established as the first of its kind in Canada that was solely dedicated to the sport. In 1991 the Hall of Fame became an integral part of the Museum facility, which is located beneath the grandstands at Western Speedway.

The annual Induction Ceremonies and Racer's Reunion are held each February, on the weekend following the Daytona 500.

Top: The Committee establishing the Victoria Auto Racing Hall of Fame in 1984.

Bottom: Andre Cottyn, founder of Western Speedway, cuts the ribbon to open the Victoria Auto Racing Hall of Fame and Museum in 1991.

(Barrie Goodwin Photos)

Following are those individuals that have been inducted into the Victoria Auto Racing Hall of Fame, year-by-year:

1984 Inductees

DAVE COOPER, a local Victorian, was introduced to the sport of auto racing by Eric Foster, former owner of a Fernwood Avenue Garage. Cooper drove his first race in 1941 at the Langford Speedway. He started driving street stocks, such as a 1936 Chrysler, and later turned to big cars. A plumber by trade, Dave became involved with the building of Western Speedway in 1953 by volunteering to install all the plumbing work.

Also in 1953, Cooper placed first in season points for both the stock car and big car classes. In 1954 he repeated as the season champion for stock cars, along with holding the track record and being voted as Most Popular Driver. As the winner of the Gold Cup Race in 1955, the "Flying Plumber" also repeated as track champion.

Cooper was virtually unbeatable during 1957. On his way to becoming the track champion for the third time, he won the Gold Cup, the Roy White Memorial, the Six-Mile Perpetual Trophy, the Corby Cup and the championship race. 1958 was nearly a carbon-copy of the previous year, as Dave repeated as track champion.

In 1959 Cooper won the Dick Willoughby Memorial Trophy and ended the year in fifth-place in the standings. Following a brief retirement, he moved into super stock racing and competed throughout the Pacific Northwest on a limited basis. Dave Cooper retired from active competition in 1974.

ANDRE (ANDY) COTTYN moved from Manitoba to Langford in 1938 as a young man who had a deep and abiding love for auto racing. In the early 1950s, Andy had the courage and foresight to carve out Western Speedway from a raw, 62-acre tract of land off Millstream Road. With no money, he sold his logging equipment and borrowed from the bank and his brother George to finance his dream. His son George helped to clear the site for the future facility.

The track, a 3/8-mile oval, held its first race on May 22, 1954. For the 1957 racing season, the track was paved and reconfigured to a flat oval with the size reduced to 4/10ths of a mile, as it remains today.

In the fall of 1966, Andy Cottyn sold the speedway to a group of local businessmen and racing enthusiasts. He retained shares in the speedway and was on the board of directors. Andy played a major role in the building of a steel and cement-structured grandstands in the late 1970s. The $250,000 project (at the time) made it one of the most ambitious privately-financed undertakings in Vancouver Island sports history.

BILLY FOSTER began racing at Victoria's Western Speedway in 1954. He drove his 1934 Ford stock car to a tenth-place finish in the point standings at the end of that season. He won his first main event on July 24.

Over the next seasons, Billy continued to hone his incredible racing skills. He began driving for Jim Haslam in 1960 and ended the year fifth in overall points. Foster was voted Most Popular Driver, won the July Cup race, earned the Roy White Memorial Trophy, won the championship race and ended the season third in championship points.

In 1962 Billy moved up to driving the more powerful super-modified cars, winning the Gold Cup, the Daffodil Cup and finished the season as champion. He then turned his attentions to driving in the newly-formed Canadian-American Modified Racing Association (CAMRA) and competed throughout the Pacific Northwest during the 1963 season. He again was the victor in the Daffodil Cup race in Victoria and was crowned CAMRA Champion at the end of the year.

In 1964, Foster won the Strawberry Cup race and finished second in CAMRA points. He was given the honor of a Life Membership in the Vancouver Island Track Racing Association (VITRA). In August of 1964, he qualified for his first United States Auto Club (USAC) event at the Milwaukee 200 in Wisconsin.

Billy qualified for his first Indianapolis 500 in 1965, driving a Vollstedt/Offy that was previously raced by Len Sutton. Amazingly, he was the sixth fastest qualifier in the two-year-old car. He received the Citizen of the

Month Award from the Victoria Chamber of Commerce during the month of May. Billy also began competing in the USAC Stock Car Division, driving for Rudy Hoerr, and was named Rookie of the Year in 1965.

Billy continued to make a name for himself in both USAC stock cars and championship cars during 1966, including a second qualifying effort for the Indy 500. Unfortunately, he was involved in a multi-car accident just as the green flag was waved.

Billy Foster lost his life in a practice run for a NASCAR-sanctioned stock car race at Riverside California in January of 1967.

BING FOSTER (no relation to Billy Foster) was known throughout his career in the sport as "The Golden Voice of Auto Racing". He began his early association with auto racing in the 1940s, serving as the track announcer at Digney Speedway, just outside of Vancouver, B.C.

He later moved to Vancouver Island and re-established his hobby by becoming the announcer for Shearing Speedway, near Duncan. He continued in this capacity for the life of the speedway, which meant commuting to the track each weekend from Victoria.

When the Western Speedway opened in 1954, Bing Foster became that track's official announcer. The first three years or so were rather tough, as Western was a dirt track and the dust created by the cars sometimes made for difficult car identifications.

Bing continued as the track's announcer for 26 consecutive years. During his time there, he made a point of going over his notes, visiting the pit area prior to each meet to ensure he had each driver's correct information.

He became involved with other members of the Vancouver Island Track Racing Association (VITRA) to promote entertaining track-side activities. Bing's attention to detail and his clear speaking voice were a delight for the spectators and added greatly to the total racing program.

GARY KERSHAW developed his initial driving skills while competing in go-karts at an early age and began his racing career at Western Speedway in 1961. He drove a 1932 Ford stock car to a sixth-place finish in the season's point standings, earning the Rookie of the Year title.

In 1962, Kershaw returned with his stock car and finished the year second in the overall standings. This same year, he drove a Ford flathead-powered modified that won the year-ending championship race.

Returning to stock cars in 1965, he drove his 1953 Ford to a fifth-place finish in the championship. After racing in Victoria with the Victoria Auto Racing Association (VARA) for the next two years, Gary drove a 1955 Chevrolet stock car to an impressive record in 1968. He won nine out of the fifteen main events for his class and ended the year as the points champion. During that season, Kershaw won the Corby Cup (most main event wins), the Billy Foster 100 Trophy, the Best-Appearing Crew Award, the Best-Looking Car Award, the Most Popular Driver Award, the VARA Competition Sports Trophy and the championship race trophy.

Gary moved up the super-stock class in 1969, winning the July Cup and finishing the year as the season's champion. Turning his attention to competing in the open super-stock class throughout the Pacific Northwest in 1971, Kershaw set a track record in Victoria in June and then made a name for himself as the first Canadian to win the Permatex 200 stock car race at Riverside, California. He was the International Drivers Challenge Champion and was voted Victoria's Male Athlete of the Year.

Gary was nicknamed 'The King' after winning an impressive 21 main event victories in a row in the stock car class at Western Speedway. In subsequent years he raced in selected international races, including running a 1930 Ford coupe with the Old Time Racers Association.

AL SMITH began his racing career in 1956 at Western Speedway. He won his first main event in June of 1958, followed up by winning the next two. Al also won that year's Gold Cup and finished fourth in the season's points championship.

1959 saw Smith win the July Cup, the Championship Race and placed third in the overall points standings for the year. Al was voted Most Popular Driver in 1960 while being crowned the season points champion.

In 1961 Al Smith turned his driving talents from the stock cars to the modified sportsman class. He raced on the very competitive Canadian American Modified Racing Association series during 1963. Along with being the track record holder in Victoria, Al finished a credible fifth-place in CAMRA's season-ending points standings. He continued racing successfully with CAMRA and the Washington Racing Association (WRA) over the next several years.

DICK WILLOUGHBY began his first year of racing at Western Speedway in 1954 with a 1934 coupe. Unfortunately, his initial driving luck was not great, as he demolished three cars in his first year of competition. For the 1955 season, his crew fastened a pair of roller skates to the top of his race car in case he decided to continue to do roll-overs. He went on to finish sixth in the season's points standings.

1956 turned out to be a banner year for Willoughby, as he won a record three consecutive main events and ended the season with a total of six main event victories. Dick's superb record earned him and his crew the 1956 championship. In 1957, he had the distinction of being the first main event winner on the newly-paved track surface, along with being named Most Popular Driver.

Dick Willoughby lost his life in an unfortunate skin-diving accident in July of 1959. Every year thereafter a trophy in his honor – the Dick Willoughby Sportsmanship Trophy – has been presented at Western Speedway.

1985 Inductees

FRANK KITTO became involved in auto racing in Victoria in the early 1950s, along with becoming a life-long member of the Vancouver Island Track Racing Association.

In the beginning, Kitto was the owner and crew member of a 1933 Chevrolet stock car that was driven by Dave Francis at Western Speedway. Through the ensuing years, he served as an active member of VITRA, holding various executive positions and as a volunteer.

Frank ultimately became the official pit boss at the speedway and held a reputation for level-headed decisions, fairness, and congeniality. Everyone from competitors to race fans all respected Frank and appreciated the job he did and the accomplishments he achieved. One of those was designing a new time-in sheet which made setting the race lineups much more streamlined and efficient.

In 1984 Frank Kitto became one of the founding members of the Victoria Auto Racing Hall of Fame.

BOB VANTREIGHT began his racing career in the late 1940s at Victoria's Langford Speedway. He came from a family that was involved in the sport, so his interest and knowledge were a natural process. His brother competed regularly in a big car at Langford.

Bob is primarily recognized as a fierce competitor behind the scenes, being involved with owning, constructing and maintaining his own race cars for many years. Despite working on a limited budget, his true racing heritage came through, as he always seemed to be able to field a race car.

In 1964 Vantreight turned his attention from stock cars to modifieds by building a GMC-powered car for driver Dick Varley. In the following years Bob built numerous super-modifieds, with each one more sophisticated and competitive than the previous model. These cars have competed throughout the Pacific Northwest.

In the early 1960s Bob served as a crew member for Billy Foster. During his long career, Bob was also associated with other well-known drivers such as Al Smith and Ray Pottinger, in addition to Bob's own son Gerry.

DICK VARLEY was another Victoria-based driver who began his racing career in 1952. During his racing career, Dick drove nearly every type of oval track racing machine.

Commencing in 1955, he made the top-ten in points for seven years running. In 1958 he teamed up with mechanic Grant King, and that year this combination ended second in overall season points. The following year at Western Speedway, Varley won the 40-lap Gold Cup race, and at year's end took home the Most Popular Driver and Best-Looking Car awards.

1986 Inductees

JIM HASLAM began his involvement with auto racing in the 1940s at Victoria's Langford Speedway. He was among the enthusiasts who helped Andre Cottyn build Western Speedway, which brought big-time racing back to Victoria.

Haslam's auto wrecking yard was located in near proximity to the speedway and was a haven for racers looking for that elusive part. It was also a great meeting place for out-of-town competitors. In addition, Jim provided the wrecker service to the track in the late 1950s and early 1960s. His other involvement included serving as a car owner, sponsor and crew member for many racers.

Haslam was most notably associated with Billy Foster. Billy drove Jim's 1933 stock car, followed by a modified sportsman car. Jim then joined Billy as he competed throughout the Pacific Northwest on the CAMRA circuit and eventually accompanied Billy to the Indianapolis 500 in 1965.

Jim was honored by the Vancouver Island Track Racing Association with a Lifetime Membership, an award not given out lightly. He was also a member of the Golden Wheels Fraternity. In later years, Haslam was involved with the racing career of his son, Roy, who established himself in stock cars, super stocks and open wheel classes.

LEN 'DIGGER' O'DELL began his driving career at Langford Speedway, then moved to Shearing's Speedway and finally to Western Speedway. Known primarily as a stock car driver, Digger also competed in a few big car races in the Victoria area.

In the very first race at Western Speedway in May of 1954, O'Dell drove his Ford coupe to a second-place finish in the day's main event. During that season, he also was victorious in the championship race. Because he was drafted into the U.S. Army in 1955, he had to take the year off from racing.

One year later Digger returned to competition. His best year came in 1957 with an impressive string of nine consecutive trophy dash wins, five main event victories, and ended the season second in points. In 1958, his season-ending standing was in the third position.

Digger O'Dell was a renowned mechanic and engine builder, able to get the most out of a flathead Ford V8. He built and maintained engines for many of the top drivers at Western Speedway. Later, he was also instrumental in starting his son Rick in the racing game, who became one of the top drivers in the Pacific Northwest.

GEOFF VANTREIGHT was a great supporter and sponsor of auto racing in the Greater Victoria area. Additionally, Geoff contributed much of his time and effort to keep the sport alive throughout the region.

From the earliest days at Western Speedway, it seems like the name Geoff Vantreight has been displayed on many race cars - often two or three in one season. Some of the racers that he has supported over the years include Mike Newton, Al Smith, Mike Currier, Ran Hancock, Dick Midgley and Roy Smith.

Vantreight worked closely with master car builder Grant King to establish both the Daffodil Cup and Strawberry Cup Awards at Western Speedway. Geoff also made a significant contribution to the sport in 1966 when he headed a group of businessmen that purchased the Speedway from original owner Andre Cottyn. Geoff then served as Western Speedway president for the next 16 years.

1987 Inductees

RON MAYELL attended his first auto race in 1932 at a race track in Nanaimo. In 1935 he became the Safety Inspector for the British Columbia Automotive Sports Association (BCASA), which sanctioned races at Langford Speedway. In 1946, at Langford, Ron took on the starter duties.

Mayell was one of those who attended the meeting to form the Vancouver Island Track Roadster Association in 1948. The offshoot of this organization became the Vancouver Island Track Racing Association (VITRA).

Ron became the club president in 1954 but served in many other capacities over the years. He was the official timer and scorer in the control tower, displaying his technical skills by building an electronic timing device that proved to be very accurate.

In 1966 Mayell became one of the shareholders in the Western Speedway 1966 Ltd. That partnership purchased the track from Andre Cottyn. Ron went on to serve as president of the Victoria Chapter of the Golden Wheels Auto Racing Fraternity, along with serving as the official starter for the Old Time Racers Association.

1988 Inductees

ROSS SURGENOR joined the Vancouver Island Track Racing Association in 1963, and his first year of driving in competition began one year later. He campaigned a 1938 Buick with a straight-eight engine in the stock car class. He was awarded the Dick Willoughby Sportsmanship Trophy.

In 1965, Surgenor switched to a 1950 Ford coupe which proved even more successful than the Buick. He won the championship race and ended up first in overall season points. 1966 saw Ross competing primarily in Nanaimo with VITRA, and he once again was crowned season's champion.

Ross moved up to the new super-stock class in 1968 and gained another championship with a 1958 Ford. He repeated that feat in 1970 with wins that included the July Cup, the Sponsor's Trophy, the Corby Cup, the championship race, and was the track record holder for his class.

Driving a 1969 Ford Torino, Surgenor won the prestigious Canada 200 race in 1972. The 1973 season found him second in points in the International Drivers Challenge event. Additionally, he qualified for the Permatex 200 in Riverside, California. He also won the Rainier Sportsman 250, the Belmont Stakes Race at Langley Speedway and the B.C. Super Stock Championship.

Following a brief retirement from racing, he returned behind the wheel of an OTRA (Old Time Racers Association) race car, competing throughout the Pacific Northwest for several seasons and winning his share of events.

1989 Inductees

PHIL HENDRY began his racing activities when he became a member of the Vancouver Island Track Racing Association in 1952. He went on to serve as the official starter at Western Speedway from 1956 to 1972.

In this position, Phil always displayed a certain class that earned him the respect of the drivers, and his flamboyant style of flagging always added greatly to the show. He passed along his talented moves and expertise to the younger starters who apprenticed under him and subsequently took over the responsibilities when Hendry retired.

Phil was known to be involved in many club activities. He was a fixture in the Victoria May Day parades, was involved in 'fun' activities at the track and was known to take the wheel in special events (such as demolition derbies) and was renowned as the king of the Western Speedway fireworks displays. Over the years, Phil Hendry also held a number of key positions for VITRA.

BRUCE PASSMORE and his family moved to Victoria in 1945 from Moose Jaw, Saskatchewan. In 1946 he became involved with an old race car and drove it in the two scheduled race meets at Langford Speedway. The following year, Bruce mortgaged everything so that he could purchase Langford Speedway.

In preparation for holding events every Saturday night, he built additional grandstands, repaved the track, installed an electric-eye timing device and commissioned the building of six new race cars for the season.

Just 25 years-old, Passmore scheduled 17 events which led to a total season attendance figure of over 40,000 fans. As a testimony to his abilities, he amassed a $30,000 race track, a $40,000 apartment block and a new yellow convertible in just two years.

Bruce owned and operated Langford Speedway for the next three years. He promoted many international events and his race track was billed as the only paved big car facility on the West Coast. Langford Speedway also had the distinction of being the first paved race track in Canada.

Bruce also kept his hand on the steering wheel by racing his own stock cars at Shearing Speedway, and then at Western Speedway. He retired from the sport to devote his time and energies to a newly-acquired business - Speedway Motors. This was the oldest Volkswagen dealership in Canada.

REG MIDGLEY joined the auto racing scene just after Western Speedway opened its gates in 1954. Over the years, he has done just about everything a person could do at a race track, except the obvious thing - he has never driven a race car. Midgley has been a car owner, track official, club executive member and finally, a race track promoter.

In 1961 Reg served his first term as president of the Vancouver Island Track Racing Association. He was also president of the Canadian American Modified Racing Association during the early 1960s. This was the series that served as Billy Foster's road to the Indianapolis 500.

In late 1966 Reg became the promoter of Western Speedway, a position he held for a number of years. One of his accomplishments was bringing in 'name' drivers to compete, including Bobby Allison, Rodger Ward, and Janet Guthrie.

In 1970 Midgley was instrumental in developing and promoting a Northwest racing series called the International Drivers Challenge, with both a super stock and super modified division.

Aside from his promoter's duties, Reg spent much of his time behind the microphone at Western Speedway as the track's announcer. He also headed up the International Pro Stock series in the late 1970s. He served as president of the Western Auto Racing Promoters Association. In 1983 Reg received the Victoria Sportsman of the Year Award.

1990 Inductees

NIBBS ANDERSON competed out of the Nanaimo area in the late 1950s and early 1960s. Starting his racing career as a car owner and mechanic, he employed notable drivers such as Ray Pottinger wheeling his beautifully-prepared machines.

Anderson then turned his talents into the driving end of the sport, beginning with a 1934 Ford coupe. At the end of the 1962 season he placed third in points. He won the Roy White Memorial Race in Victoria and was voted Most Popular Driver for the year.

Nibbs graduated to the modified sportsman class in 1963 and through 1965 participated in the CAMRA circuit as well as the local Inter-City Modified circuit. He then retired from active competition.

In 1980 Nibbs was convinced to join the Old Time Racers Association. He was given a 1934 Ford coupe which he meticulously restored to look exactly like the original car he drove in 1962. He competed in his first OTRA event in June of 1981 and attended virtually every scheduled Northwest event with the organization until his retirement in the early 1990s.

In addition to competing and winning many races with this car, Nibbs Anderson used his expertise in assisting fellow racers with the building and refurbishing of carburetors, distributors and other vital components to keep their performance at a maximum.

DICK MIDGLEY is known primarily as a race car builder and mechanic. He did have a very limited stint at driving in the early 1960s, earning the nickname of 'The Bird' after trying to fly one of his cars.

Dick began his racing career working with driver Dave Cooper during the 1950s at Victoria's Western Speedway. In 1959 he built his first race car – a 1934 Ford coupe – for driver Dick Willoughby. Future cars were built in conjunction with Grant King.

Midgley graduated to becoming the chief mechanic of the famed 'Daffodil Special' super modified race car. This Geoff Vantreight-owned car campaigned in the Canadian American Modified Racing Association series with Al Smith as the driver.

Dick was one of the first car builders in Victoria to construct a super-stock racer. In the 1970s he turned his attention to NASCAR competition, fielding cars at several major Winston Cup tracks such as Daytona and Riverside. His drivers included Bobby Allison, Dave Marcis, Roy Smith, Norm Ellefson and Ross Surgenor. In 1989 Midgley's car won the Busch Pole Award at Phoenix International Raceway with Roy Smith driving. Dick's cars have also competed in many international events, including Australia and Japan.

1991 Inductees

BILL SMITH, SR. began his career in racing when he joined the Vancouver Island Track Racing Association at the age of 16. The next 28 years found him competing in jalopies, stock cars, B-modifieds and super-stocks. Early on he drove for Andre Cottyn, the owner of Western Speedway.

In 1960 Bill won the Rose City Cup in Portland, Oregon. 1961 proved to be his most successful year when he built a new race car equipped with an engine built by Grant King. In 1963 Smith was voted Most Popular Driver at Western Speedway.

Years later, in 1975, Bill traded the piano he loved to play for a new race car. Bill became president of the Vancouver Island Track Racing Association in 1984 and again in 1986. He built a new race car for his son, Bill Jr. Bill, Sr. had injured his neck after two bad accidents. Senior moved on to become president of the Pro Stock Car series in 1991 and carried on in an executive capacity with the organization.

The 1999 racing season saw Bill, Sr. taking on the biggest challenge of his racing history as he became co-promoter of Western Speedway. His wife Connie was by his side managing the concession stands and overseeing the books.

JIM STEEN began his racing career at the age of 16 along with his cousin, Billy Foster. Jim was doing practice laps at Western Speedway in his first race car and had a mishap occur in turn one. The car rolled over, the seatbelt broke, and Jim ended up on the race track with the car landing on top of him. At the time he was not expected to live more than an hour after the incident. His parents were rushed from up-Island with a police escort, but Jim proved everyone wrong by surviving.

For most of his driving career, Steen was a one-man crew, driver and owner. He typically competed on a shoe-string budget but was always there and always part of the show. In 1964 Jim moved from the ever-popular stock cars to the B-modified class. In the following years Jim drove a variety of car types.

1972 found Jim driving a new stock car. At the first race of the season, he was involved in an accident which saw his car flipping and rolling nine times down the backstretch at Western Speedway. Being the true racer that he was, Steen was back out with his car the following week.

During the 1973 racing season at the speedway, Jim was honored with a celebration of his 20 years of continuous racing. He started the year with a two-car team in 1976, with his son Kerry the driver of the second car. They continued racing together for several years.

Jim Steen holds the record of the longest continuous competitor at Western Speedway, a record that will likely never be broken.

1992 Inductees

JACK SMITH built his first race car in 1911 at the tender age of 15. That first effort produced a bicycle-wheeled contraption powered by a motorcycle engine. In 1919 Jack set out on a brilliant racing career where he built, maintained and drove his own race cars to two successive Alberta, Canada championships. He then relocated to Victoria where he constructed more cars and won the British Columbia, Northwest, Victoria and Vancouver titles.

Smith's many talents enabled him to manufacture many of his own engine parts, producing pistons, camshafts, head, crankshafts, valves, and rods of his own design. In 1927 he turned his attention to outboard boat racing, winning 14 of 15 events.

Concerned with the dwindling interest in the sport of auto racing, Jack was instrumental in forming the British Columbia Automotive Sports Association (BCASA). This organization would become the parent club from which all present British Columbia clubs have sprung. His last race, which he won, was at the one-mile Colwood Horse Race Track in 1933.

Jack Smith was convinced that the rear-engine racer would be the car of the future. He constructed a pair of these in his tiny basement shop and raced them at Langford Speedway in the late 1940s. His drivers were Howie Stanley and Vern Bruce.

During his later years Jack made daily visits to the shop of Mike Hitchcox, where a rear-engine 'sidewinder' chain-driven race car was being constructed. It's safe to say that Jack Smith had quite a bit of influence in this design.

ROY SMITH started racing cars at Western Speedway in 1964. In 1967 he followed in his older brother Al's footsteps by graduating to the more powerful and sophisticated super-modifieds.

Roy won the Inter-City Modified Championship in 1968, was fourth in points on the Northwest Canadian American Modified Racing Association series and won the Daffodil Cup Race in Victoria. He repeated as the Inter-City Champion in 1969 and 1970.

Roy won all three major modified races in Victoria in 1971 - The Daffodil Cup, The Strawberry Cup and The Billy Foster 100. In 1974 and 1975 Smith was crowned the International Driving Challenge Champion.

Roy made the switch to late model stock cars in 1976 and competed in the Daytona 500 for the first time, finishing 22nd. He returned the following year and finished 20th.

In 1980 Roy raced a late model stock car and set a track record at Western Speedway and won the Canada 200 race. At the end of the racing season, he was crowned the NASCAR Winston West Points Champion – a first for a Canadian. He repeated again in 1982. That same year Roy made his third visit to the Daytona 500. This time he was sponsored by his many fans and corporations located in Victoria. At the end of 500-miles, he earned a tenth-place finish and was the highest-placing Pontiac.

1993 Inductees

HARVEY CHIPPER began his racing career as a crew member on Jim Haslam's cars which were driven in 1961 and 1962 by Billy Foster. In 1967 Harvey built a 1955 Chevy stock car and, together with driver Roy Haslam, won the Western Speedway Stock Car championship that year.

In 1968 Chipper sold the winning six-cylinder Chevrolet engine to Gary Kershaw, who won the 1968 championship with it. Harvey moved up a class to super-stocks, again teaming with Roy Haslam, to win the championship. The next year Kershaw joined Chipper and went on to win another championship.

Harvey then built a race car to compete on the NASCAR tracks throughout the Pacific Northwest. Working again with Gary Kershaw, the pair performed very well where they raced, including Riverside, California. In 1971 they returned to Riverside and were victorious in that year's Permatex 200, the first Canadians to do so.

Chipper built two new cars for the 1972 season, one of which Kershaw drove to many local wins. The second car - the 'Olympia Express' - was built for Hershel McGriff of Portland, Oregon. That car handily won during its first outing at the Portland Speedway.

Harvey built another new car for Kershaw for the 1973 and 1974 seasons. The second year the team won virtually everything at Western Speedway, including the Sponsor's Cup, the Billy Foster Stock Car Trophy, the July Cup, the Corby Cup and, of course, the season's championship. Harvey earned the Mechanic of the Year Award at Western Speedway in 1975. George Steward drove Harvey's car in 1977, winning seven of eleven events entered.

Chipper joined forces with Roy Smith in 1978, and the pair took home the Winston West Championship trophy. The effort was repeated in 1980. 1981 saw Harvey receive the NASCAR Mechanic of the Year award, a first for a Canadian.

FRANK 'CORKY' THOMAS began his racing involvement with motorcycles, where he was an outstanding racer who won on a regular basis. During that time – the 1930s – he competed against riders like Frank Bayliss and Bill Rainsford.

Corky expanded in the automobile side of motorsports. Although he had the means to have a first-class machine, he instead chose to follow his personal guidelines and compete with second-hand equipment. He was a regular on the local scene at Langford Speedway, and later at Shearing Speedway near Duncan, British Columbia.

Thomas was truly one of the characters of the sport, much the same as was Eddie Sachs at the Indianapolis Motor Speedway. The caption for a local newspaper advertisement in 1947 read: "Corky Thomas, one of the most popular drivers of the Langford Speedway, sits in the "Lucky Lady". Corky and his noisy lady are a combination that has delighted crowds with repeated exhibitions of attempting to pass cars just a little bit faster."

An excerpt from the *Daily Colonist* newspaper of May 21, 1950, stated: "Bundled up fans, however, yelled encouragement to Corky Thomas, who placed last in the 'Lucky Lady'. He had quite a battle with Cooper for the position." Three days later, the race results showed that Corky had finished third in the main event, which had been won by Bob Simpson.

Corky Thomas always had his shop doors open to his fellow racers. He was an all-around good guy and was always willing to lend a hand. He remained active and involved in the sport until the early 1960s when he retired from auto racing.

1994 Inductees

GRANT KING began his involvement in auto racing at Langford Speedway in the late 1940s, when he built his own car and had Bung Eng as his driver. King also worked with driver Bob Simpson over the next few years, winning many races. Grant also campaigned a stock car at Shearing Speedway in 1950.

During the 1950s King competed with stock cars at Western Speedway and teamed with driver Dick Varley from 1959 to 1961. The duo won numerous races using a powerful GMC engine in the 'Kersey Peanut Butter Special.' In 1961 Grant began designing and building his own 'Kingo' go-karts while still working with Bob Simpson and the sprint car.

1963 saw King construct five new super-modified race cars at Geoff Vantreight's small shop. These cars had illustrious careers throughout the Pacific Northwest. One, the #7 Daffodil Special, was campaigned for many years in Victoria by Al and Roy Smith.

Grant moved to Portland, Oregon in 1963 to work with Rolla Vollstedt, who was preparing a rear-engine Offy Championship Car for driver Len Sutton. During this time, Grant became quite familiar with the Offenhauser engine and traveled to Indianapolis with the team.

Over the following years, King set up a race shop in Indianapolis and became a car mechanic for car entrants like Jim Robbins, A.J. Watson and Andy Granatelli. He formed his own company - Grant King Racers, Inc. - and built cars for many of the car owners and drivers of the day. He built sprint cars, midgets, and Indianapolis-type cars. It is estimated that Grant produced over 250 complete racing machines.

Grant King was killed on December 18th, 1999 in an automobile accident in Indiana.

TONY VAN DE MORTEL started racing in 1966 with a 1950 Ford stock car. He was named VITRA Rookie of the Year, while also becoming a shareholder in Western Speedway when Andre Cottyn sold the track.

In 1967 Tony raced a 1955 Chevrolet stock car to a tenth-place overall finish to end the season. The next year, he purchased a super-modified race car and competed on the CAMRA circuit, ending the year sixth in points and as Rookie of the Year. At the end of the 1969 season, he came home fourth in the CAMRA points race.

Van De Mortel relocated to Spokane, Washington in 1970 to assist car builder Jim Tipke in the construction of super-modified cars, including a new CAMRA roadster for himself. Part-way through the year, Tony took over as CAMRA's president. Aside from his duties in this position, in 1971 he raced whenever possible. He won the International Drivers Challenge Race in Victoria, and then sold the car the same night.

The years 1972 through 1976 saw Tony working on various racing-related projects, including USAC midgets and sprint cars on the east coast.

Van De Mortel became manager of Western Speedway in the fall of 1976, where he was instrumental in the construction of new grandstands. He also stopped zoning changes to ensure the continuance of auto racing in the Victoria area. From 1977 to 1981, Tony served as the promoter and general manager of the speedway. He introduced 'Hit-to-Pass' racing as well as the Pepsi Challenge Series. He was also the driving force to send driver Roy Smith to the Daytona 500 in 1980, spending countless hours promoting this opportunity to the city and gathering monetary sponsors and support.

1995 Inductees

JACK 'DIGGER' CALDWELL first donned racing togs in 1937 after purchasing a four-cylinder Chrysler sprint car from Phil Foster, Billy Foster's uncle. This was an ideal beginner's car - not too fast, but a good-handling car that was almost always still running when the checkered flag fell.

In 1939 Digger bought a four-cylinder Chevy sprint car from Langford Speedway promoter Jack Taylor. Digger flipped this car while he was on a test run. Fortunately, the car was one of the first of its kind that was equipped with a roll bar, so he was unhurt. He went on to place well with this car until racing was cancelled during World War Two.

Returning to action in 1946 Digger equaled Langford's track record of 18-seconds flat. Out of 17 main events he won 14, placed second twice, and grabbed one third-place finish. Digger also scored seven consecutive clean sweeps that included the helmet dash, the heat race and main event.

Caldwell relocated to Seattle in 1947 and ran a heavy schedule with midget cars. This lasted until mid-season, when a lucrative job offer in Victoria lured him back north again. He raced the rest of the season in the Davis sprint car.

He returned to the United States in 1948 and continued his involvement in racing until his retirement in 1959. During this timeframe, Caldwell earned the nickname of 'The International Complication'.

Digger was known as a true sportsman, a gentleman and a 'class' individual. In later years, he was involved with the Golden Wheels Club in the Northwest and served as Master of Ceremonies at many of their banquets. Digger Caldwell passed away in January 1993, but his driving expertise and memories lives on with many of his friends in the auto racing fraternity.

EARL POLLARD began his racing career in Vermillian, Alberta in 1950. His first car was a 1932 Ford - basically a chassis and drive train with no bodywork. In those early days, Earl won his share of trophies driving stock cars, jalopies and modifieds. He was instrumental in getting a track built in Vermillion and later on having it paved.

He then raced a 1936 Ford until 1954. He and his fellow racers ran a 460-mile circuit every two weeks, competing in Edmonton, Lloydminster, Battleford and Saskatoon. Pollard was the most consistent entrant with second and third-place finishes all season in his #77 racer.

In 1965 the Pollard family relocated to Victoria, BC. He began his successful Western Speedway career in 1966 driving a 1951 Ford and won that year's championship. In 1968 Earl served as vice-president of the Victoria Auto Racing Association. Additionally, he built two new stock cars – one for himself and the other for his 14-year-old son Larry. The family duo ran several novelty races, as Larry was too young to compete.

Earl and Larry ran as a team in 1970, driving identical white 1956 Ford stock cars. At the end of the season the pair finished second and third in points. Larry was just one point behind his father. Earl finished third in points at the end of the 1971 season while winning the July Cup, the Dick Willoughby Memorial Sportsmanship Award and was voted Driver of the Year.

For the 1972 season Earl turned his attention to builder and crew chief for Larry's super stock car. He continued holding this position over the next several years.

As well as building a car for himself in 1982, Earl traveled to North Carolina with Larry and spent the next four years working with Richard Childress and Richard Petty, while also assisting Larry with his Busch Grand National race car. Pollard returned to Victoria in 1987 and promptly built a race car for his daughter Lois, who competed in the mini-stock class. Larry got the racing bug again and built another car for himself.

1996 Inductees

BUD GREEN began racing cars at Langford Speedway in 1936, first driving Phil Foster's 'Speedway Special' – a four-cylinder flathead Chrysler-powered car. Bud suffered the most serious spill of his career in May 1938, when he flipped end-over-end several times in heavy traffic during an A-main event. After several months of recuperation, Bud was released from the hospital in a full body cast.

Returning to racing in 1939, Bud scored enough points to capture the British Columbia Championship – and repeated the feat for the following two seasons. In the mighty midget racing boom in 1945, Bud's 'rockem, sock-em' driving style gained much attention. Fortunately in 1947, his car owner was Les Wasilchen. Les was a proprietor of an auto re-build shop, and Bud's car was thoroughly crunched at least once a week during the season.

Green then began devoting more of his time to driving his favorite sprint cars again. He was driving a Cadillac-powered sprinter for owner Mac McBurnie at Yakima, Washington's 1/8th-mile track early in 1950. Bud's determination to take the lead began to wear on Mac's nervous system – to the point that when he watched Bud drive the new sprint car in the first turn without backing off, the owner popped a full roll of Tums into his mouth and began chewing, paper and all!

After a brief stint in hardtop racing Bud ended his racing career at Western Speedway in 1957. In later years Bud Green was involved with the Golden Wheels Fraternity. He raced a restored vintage sprinter at meets throughout the Pacific Northwest and enjoyed the fellowship of his many racing friends until his passing.

PIKE GREEN started driving race cars in 1946 behind the wheel of Stu Pringle's sprint car. In his first race, he qualified in the top-four and wound up in the trophy dash. The highlight of Pike's early career was winning the first-ever 50-lap main event at Langford Speedway in 1946. There were over 40 cars entered from throughout the West Coast. He ended his rookie season by earning second-place in the season standings.

Early in 1947 Green drove the #25 sprint car for Tacoma's Chuck House. This proved to be a very good car and he did well with it. He won a 40-lap main event at Aurora (Playland) Speedway in Seattle with this sprinter. In these years Pike piloted many race cars, winning a number of main events at Langford Speedway.

Pike drove a sprint car named 'The Stinker', which derived the name from an oil company sponsor. He delighted in winning with this car as it had a small, 110 cubic-inch engine that competed against more powerful machines on quarter-mile tracks. His first time out at Shearing Speedway found him winning the main event.

Pike and his brother Bud were referred to as 'The Brothers' by many famous racing personalities that included racing announcer Ted Bell, hydroplane pilot Bill Muncie and racing mechanic Grant King. Green was quite involved with many public relations activities for the sport and had written numerous newspaper articles and kept statistical information, clippings and racing results.

Pike and Bud Green retired from active racing in 1960, but then became involved in hydroplane racing and won Seattle's Seafair Trophy for Limited Hydroplanes in 1964.

NEIL MONTGOMERY started in the sport in the spring of 1960. He had to get a waiver signed by his parents because he was not 16-years-old. In 1963 Neil won the jalopy class championship race at Western Speedway and finished the season ninth in points. In 1964 he won the July Cup and was third in points at season's end.

1965 found Montgomery switching from jalopies to B-modified cars and was the track record holder. The next year he returned to stock cars and won the VARA championship race.

In 1970 Neil built a Ford late model stock car and ended the season ninth in points. In 1971 and again in 1974 he competed in the super-stock class, finishing eighth in points both years. He had a superb year in 1975 and finished second in the championship.

The next few years found Montgomery assisting on Roy Haslam's crew while racing periodically for Terry Forsythe in the stock car class. He teamed up with Russ Lejeune in the early 1980s and drove a Camaro super-stock car. In 1987 Neil was honored with the VITRA Art Golding Dedication Award.

Neil and Lejeune again teamed up and built an IMCA modified car for his son Trevor to drive during 1989, and traveled to races as far away as Anderson, California. In 1992 the team had a two-car stable with both of Neil's sons handling the driving chores. Neil was given the nickname 'The Chief'.

Neil Montgomery always made time to help his fellow competitors. He has built engines, helped with chassis setups and often just 'being there' to listen and assist others in the sport.

1997 Inductees

RICK O'DELL followed his father, 'Digger', into the auto racing scene. He earned the Victoria Auto Racing Association's Rookie of the Year honors in 1966 for stock cars. In 1967 Rick ended the season fourth in stock car points, along with the Sponsor's Trophy. In 1968 O'Dell won the Roy White Memorial Trophy and finished the year second in points.

Rick served as vice president of VARA in 1969. He also switched to the super stock class and held a track record for the new Figure-8 class. In 1970 he won the Most Popular Driver Award and ended the season fourth in points. 1971 saw O'Dell win the Corby Cup, the Sponsor's Trophy, the championship race, the Most Popular Driver Award and was the super stock points champion. The 1972 season was nearly a carbon copy, and he repeated as the champion.

Rick O'Dell competed in the open super-stock classes with some success in the 1980s while traveling to various tracks around the Pacific Northwest. The cars he drove were always first-class in appearance and performance.

BILL PRICE teamed up with Keith Jackson and brother Charlie in 1964 with a 1950 Ford. Bill was nominated as the driver at their third race, which required his mother to sign a waiver because he was underage. He won three B-trophy dashes during his rookie season of 1965. The next year Bill ended the season in the fifth position in VARA points with a newer 1952 Ford. He won his first A-trophy dash with a 1953 Ford stock car.

For the 1969 season Price drove the ex-Gary Kershaw 1955 Chevy stock car. He was chosen Driver of the Week in May, won the Corby Cup (most main event wins), earned the Sponsor's Trophy, won the CFAX Most Popular Driver Award, was a track record holder and tied Mel Marshall for the season championship. Bill moved up to the late model stock car class in 1970 and competed successfully there for the next several seasons. In 1976 he won the super-stock championship by a large margin. During that year he won the July Cup, the Sponsor's Trophy, the Roy White Memorial Award and was again voted the CFAX Most Popular Driver.

Price raced only occasionally in 1977. He served on the executive board of the Vancouver Island Track Racing Association (VITRA) as a director. He then became vice president of the organization in 1978 and 1979. He served as president of VITRA from 1980 through 1990. Bill also was president of the Victoria IMCA organization and sat on the board of directors for the Old Time Racers Association (OTRA). He also drove OTRA race cars in the mid-1980s and later campaigned an IMCA race car.

1998 Inductees

RUSS LEJEUNE, after an initial involvement as a crew member, turned his attention to driving super stock cars in 1971, earning the Rookie of the Year Award. During the years 1975-77 he acted as crew chief for the Vantreight #7 super-modified car that was driven to many victories by Roy Smith. 1978 saw the pair move to late model stock cars. The combination set a track record at Victoria's Western Speedway and won the Canada 200 race.

In 1980 and 1981 Lejeune and Smith captured the NASCAR Winston West Championship titles. Roy would say of Russ, "He's the best fabricator I know, and also one of the best crew chiefs I have worked with. Because of the many innovative changes he made and the thought he put into things, I won many more races. By his preparation and attention to detail, he made me look good."

In the early 1990s, Russ joined forces with Neil Montgomery and built an IMCA modified car for Neil's son to race. In 1992 this team ventured into dirt track sprint car racing by constructing a car for Trevor to race at Cassidy Speedway near Nanaimo. In 1995 a second car was built and both Neil's sons, Trevor and Jeff, raced at Cassidy.

A highlight for Lejeune and the team took place in 1997 when they captured the prestigious Daffodil Cup Race in Victoria. With the victory the team clinched the NSSRA points championship.

Through the years Russ' company – Lejeune Engineering – has been involved in the construction of many race cars and components. He has supplied the many parts and pieces to racers on the Island and is a well-respected fabricator and innovator.

RAY POTTINGER was a very popular Nanaimo driver and a top competitor. In 1954 he drove his 1934 Ford coupe stock car to a sixth-place final spot in the Western Speedway points championship. The following year he finished fourth in points for the season.

Again in 1956 Ray ended the season fourth in points at Western Speedway, where he also won the Gold Cup race. During the year he also competed in Nanaimo, Skagit and Digney. For the next several years he maintained his consistency on the track.

In 1960 Pottinger moved up to drive a DeSoto-powered super-modified race car. The next year he earned the division's season championship. From 1962 to 1965 Ray raced super modifieds locally as well as throughout the Pacific Northwest. In 1966 he drove the #44 super-modified. Along with his driving duties, Ray became president of the Mid-Island Auto Racing Association (MIARA) and took on the promotional activities at the race track. His wife Vi sold tickets and son Lance sold programs.

1968 saw Ray pilot a superb #23 super modified for Prince George car owner Barry White. They campaigned successfully on the Canadian American Modified Racing Association (CAMRA) circuit throughout the Pacific Northwest. From 1973 to the time of his retirement from racing, Ray drove Bob Vantreight's super-modified car.

1999 Inductees

ALLAN and **JOHNNY DALBY** were well-known in the Northwest racing circles, beginning in the mid-1930s. The brothers were inducted into the Hall of Fame together as a tribute to their contributions to racing, along with recognition of their sons and grandsons who have also chased the checkered flag.

The Dalby mark of excellence has been etched in the framework and engines of many different racing machines, from sprints, midgets, stock cars, sports cars and even a 266-class hydroplane.

In the early years famed car builder and owner Grant King studied much of the Dalby's work. At that time the Dalby Special was a radical departure from the conventional in that it was designed specifically for paved track use, presenting a much lower profile than the contemporary dual-purpose machines.

Though the Dalby brothers did not follow the same paths in racing in later years, they both held a long-time involvement in the sport. Johnny was active in the Seattle area building and working on cars, and even took a job on the technical committee with NASCAR's Grand National West series. In 1976 he joined his two sons, Steve and Jan, who were driving stock cars and began driving himself. His grandchildren were active in quarter-midgets. Johnny also enjoyed being active with the Northwest Golden Wheels Fraternity with his restored midget race car.

Living in Victoria, Allan was a supporter of his two sons, David and Wayne, who had become involved in auto racing at Western Speedway. Allan also served on the crew of an Old Time Racers Association race car and, in 1990, traveled with the troupe to a racing series at Flamboro Speedway in Hamilton, Ontario, and then to the CNE Stadium in Toronto.

ROY HASLAM worked as a crew member on his father Jim's modified racer that was driven by Billy Foster in 1961. He began driving Jalopy Class cars midway through the 1965 season.

Racing in Nanaimo in 1966, Roy was named VITRA's Driver of the Year and finished the season seventh in points. In 1967 Haslam was named stock car champion, winning the Roy White Memorial, the Billy Foster 100 and the Corby Cup. The next season he moved up to the super-stock class, winning the July Cup and coming home third in points at the end of the year. 1970 found him finishing sixth in late model points. He also won the Canadian 100 go-kart race at Westwood.

Over the next several decades Roy Haslam proved to be a most successful driver in the super-stock ranks, winning a number of prestigious titles. These include the Carling Challenge Open Series Championship, the Pepsi Challenge Championship, the Can-Am Late Model Championship and the Island Super Stock Series Championship. His many wins include multiple victories in the Canada 200 race.

WALTER WAKELYN got his start in racing in 1939, serving as the mechanic for Stu Pringle. He continued in this role in 1940 and then joined the Royal Canadian Navy where he spent the war years.

Wakelyn resumed his racing activities in 1946 at Victoria's Langford Speedway, teaming up with good friend Jimmy Dempster. Walt and Jim ran the #1 Winfield sprint car and had great drivers such as Digger Caldwell and Jack Spaulding. Digger was the driver in 1946 and was virtually unbeatable. Out of the 17 main events that year, the car scored 14 wins, two seconds and one third. It also held the track record and had seven clean-sweeps (trophy dash, heat race and main event) - quite an enviable record for the team! As well as the excellent preparation of the car and its flawless performance, the team also held the distinction of being the first in the area to wear uniforms.

When Langford Speedway closed, racing shifted to Shearing Speedway. Walt traveled up the Island every weekend to serve as pit boss during the 1950 season. When Western Speedway opened in 1954, Walt and Jimmie Dempster were the track's safety committee. Wakelyn was also building race engines for several teams. He built quite a few flathead Ford engines as well as other types, such as a 302 cubic-inch GMC for Ken Dobey.

Walt retired from active racing for a time, but the bug hit him again in the 1980s. He became involved with Ron Douglas and vintage race cars. He was a member of the Northwest Golden Wheels Fraternity and the California-based Western Racing Association.

2000 Inductees

MIKE CURRIER became interested in auto racing as a fan of Phil Lambrick in the early 1950s at Western Speedway. In 1958 he built his first race car, a 1935 Ford coupe, and had Wally Lum as a driver.

Mike graduated to become an owner and builder of a modified sportsman car in 1961. This Fiat-bodied racer had a Buick engine and was driven by Bob Fiddick. The team competed in the Gold Cup race in Edmonton where they finished seventh.

During 1965 Mike ran a 1950 Ford in the jalopy class with his brother John doing the driving. The following year Mike made the long tow to race in Nanaimo every weekend, this time with his brother Bill behind the wheel.

Currier then took some time off from owning and maintaining race cars to become a track official. He worked the pit entrance gate in 1967 and 1968, and then turned his attention to becoming an assistant pit boss for the next two years. Mike served as vice president of the Vancouver Island Track Association in 1969.

For 1970 Currier built a 1957 Ford Fairlane super-stock car, with Ron Hancock as the driver. In 1972 the pair finished sixth in the season's point race. 1973 saw Mike join forces with his brothers Pat and John to compete with a 1969 Ford Torino super-stock car. With John as the driver, the team finished the year within the top ten in points. Mike again held the position of Vice President of VITRA in 1974 and was awarded the Member of the Year trophy.

In 1975 he became involved with the Old Time Racers Association and was the owner of a 1930 Ford. Gary Kershaw, Dave Johnson, Roy Haslam and Bill Price were among the drivers who piloted this car during the next few years.

Following a brief retirement, Mike owned and campaigned a 1933 Oldsmobile with OTRA. Shortly after the formation of the Victoria Auto Racing Hall of Fame in 1984, Mike Currier became a director of the enterprise.

BOB SIMPSON began his racing career in 1946, driving a Model T-based car at the Willows race track and then at Langford Speedway. In 1947 he bought the #16 car from Bob Wensley and Charlie Flitton. It was powered by a Dodge engine with a Laurel head. He also raced this car in 1948.

During 1949 Simpson drove for Jack Greenwood in a flathead Ford-powered sprint car. In 1950 he drove for Seattle's Gene Fanning, also running a flathead Ford engine. He had a serious accident with that car, nearly losing an ear. Bob spent six weeks in the hospital but when he was released, he jumped into Greenwood's car for the championship race at Langford.

Commencing the 1952 season at the Shearing Speedway, Bob drove Grant King's #1 car to victory on the opening night of the season. In 1953 Dick Marks bought this car and then teamed up with Simpson to take the racer on the United States circuit.

When Western Speedway opened in 1954 Simpson set fast time, won the dash and placed second in the main event, driving King's #77 car. Two days later Bob won the main event in this same car. During the season

Bob set three track records. At the season-ending championship race he won the dash, the heat, and was again second in the main event. He ended the year winning the Bardahl Trophy as track champion, and the Bert Sutton Memorial Trophy.

Simpson continued to drive for Grant King in 1955 and 1956, then purchased Rolla Vollstedt's #27 car in 1957. After racing this car, he sold it to Eddie Kostenuk in 1960. Bob then joined forces with Bill Walters in 1961 and drove super-modified cars until his retirement from racing.

Over his driving career Bob Simpson raced and won throughout the West Coast, usually traveling with Del Fanning. They raced at tracks located in Edmonton, Great Falls, Boise, Seattle, Portland, Phoenix and Los Angeles. Beyond driving, Bob was deeply involved with the BCASA as well as being a program sponsor with his Saanich Arm Logging Company.

2001 Inductees

TED MACKENZIE began his racing involvement in 1954 at Western Speedway when he teamed with driver Bob Bowcott to run a 1934 Ford coupe. The following year he joined Gerry 'Pussycat' Sylvester and fellow crew members Billy Lees, Frank Addison and Bill Sims. The team, commonly referred to as the 'Fat Five', finished the season in the fifth points position.

In 1956 Ted became the car owner and again had Gerry handle the driving chores. They finished the year third overall in the points tally.

After discovering that car ownership was too time-consuming Mackenzie turned his attentions to officiating at Western Speedway, becoming a corner man in 1957. At this time, he also began taking racing photographs. In 1960, as vice president of the Vancouver Island Track Racing Association, Ted took over the president's position, vacated by Dave Francis, who had moved out of town.

In 1962 Ted and Dick Midgley together ran a modified sportsman car dubbed the 'Flintstone Flyer.' This Buick-powered race was driven by Gerry Sylvester. During 1964 and 1965 Ted as the pit boss at Western Speedway. From 1966 through 1969, he was a member of the crew for Geoff Vantreight's super-modified that was driven by Al Smith. Mackenzie then served as the assistant starter at Western Speedway in 1970 and 1972.

Ted also worked on Dick Midgely's crew and traveled to many international events throughout North America. As such, Ted did his fair share of driving the tow rig as well as working on the race car as a crew member. A few of the drivers he worked with included Norm Ellefson, Dave Cooper, Ross Surgenor, Roy Smith, Bobby Allison, Hershel McGriff and Dave Marcis.

In 1983 Ted Mackenzie was one of the original committee members who initiated the formation of the Victoria Auto Racing Hall of Fame. He served on the Hall of Fame committee until his retirement in 1991.

GARY MADDEN became involved with the sport at Western Speedway when his first competitive season as a driver came in 1968 when he won the stock car mid-season championship race. 1970 found him drive to a fourth-place finish in season points. He also won the N.W. Insurance Agencies Trophy and was voted of having the Best Appearing Stock Car.

In 1973 Madden ran in the claimer division and finished in the top-ten of season-ending points. He also ran a 1965 Beaumont in the super-stock class. 1974 was a banner year for Gary, as he set a track record for the claimer class, won the championship race, and was crowned as season points champion. He competed in the final demolition race of the year and won in front of over 3,700 fans. He also won the enduro race that year. Madden competed in the Demolition class for several more years.

After racing on a limited basis, he became president of the Vancouver Island Stunt and Demo Drivers Association (VISDDA) in 1985. The same year he was also the champion in the demolition car class. He continued as club president in 1986 and was instrumental in forming the demo truck racing class. He built and raced a truck, winning the most main events, and was voted Member of the Year. He again served as president in 1987.

In 1988 the club changed its name to the Lower Island Track Racing Association (LITRA). Madden was the driving force behind the creation of the $299 claimer class. He continued as club president through 1990 when he was awarded the LITRA Member of the Year. In 1991 Gary was awarded a lifetime membership.

Gary resumed the presidency of LITRA in 1995 and 1996, becoming a seven-time club president. In 1996 he restored the 1957 Chevrolet stock car formerly driven by Art Reedy and donated it to the Victoria Auto Racing Hall of Fame. He went on to become involved with the International Mini Stock 4's class.

DENNY RAND started in racing in 1961 when he teamed with Alex Smith and Rob Duncan with a 1934 Ford stock car. He only drove the car once – rolling it over – thus ending his driving career. Duncan took over the driving duties. Following a brief break Denny returned to racing in 1964, crewing on a 1951 Dodge coupe driven by Fred Best. The team campaigned this car for four years and was awarded the Best Appearing Crew Award in 1964 and 1966.

In 1968 the team switched to a very quick super-modified car purchased from Ray Pottinger. They competed on the Inter-City Modified circuit as well as in some CAMRA race meets over the next two years.

Rand teamed up with Roy Haslam in 1970 and worked with him until 1981. That year he was awarded the Dick Willoughby Sportsmanship Trophy, and the following year he helped build the weigh scales at Western Speedway. In 1973 Denny served as vice president of the Vancouver Island Track Racing Association. The following years found Rand traveling to races around the United States along with Haslam. In his last year with Roy, the combination won the 1981 Speedweek Northwest Championship along with the Canada 200 race.

Denny Rand then spent several years away from active competition to devote more time to his growing family and to build a successful business. He was an avid NASCAR fan, traveling to events throughout the United States.

In 1996 he became very interested in Trevor Montgomery's NSSRA sprint car and joined the crew with Neil Montgomery and Russ Lejeune. The team won the Daffodil Cup and went on to lock in the NSSRA Championship. In 1997, Denny was on the promotions committee for NSSRA and helped bring a field of cars to Saratoga and Western Speedway. He continued working on the car's crew, as well as serving as a NSSRA director until June of 1999.

2002 Inductees

BARRY RANKIN started as a crew member on a 1951 Dodge stock car in 1964. The car was driven for four years by Fred Best and was crewed by Denny Rand, Lawrence Fox and Ken Holding. As the car was owned by the Checkmates Car Club, Barry even tried out as a part-time driver of the car.

In 1966 he gave up the pit activities and went to work for Reg Midgley in the promotional side of the sport, assisting with the program and other various duties around the race track.

The next year Rankin's duties expanded substantially as he learned most of the tasks associated with the management and administration side of racing - program sales, concessions, media reports and some of the promotional tasks. He performed the job of track recorder for two years and compiled statistics for all the car classes and drivers. On occasion he was also the track announcer, a duty he again assumed in the mid-1980s with Butch Behn.

Under Barry's direction the logistics of organizing out-of-town shows into Victoria, including media coverage, hotel room bookings and managing special events. He became Western Speedway's assistant manager in 1971. A decade later he served as track manager and announcer at Western Speedway through 1983.

Rankin was also an executive of the Western Auto Racing Promoter's Association, a position he held for over ten years. When the International Driver's Challenge (IDC) Race Series was organized, Barry worked on the statistics for both series (super-stock and sprint cars). He remained in this position for the duration of the series.

JACK TAYLOR was responsible for bringing international sprint car racing to Canada on a regular basis, and Victoria became widely known as 'Canada's Auto Racing Capital.'

As a big car owner in the early 1930s, Jack campaigned a Ford sprinter in BCASA-sponsored meets at two local horse tracks - Willows and the Colwood Mile. The capacity crowds didn't escape his attention, especially when he was approached to build a speedway on a large tract of land he owned near Langford Lake. With the combination of the Depression-era and the island location of Victoria the risks were enormous, but Jack was willing to gamble. The BCASA members volunteered and turned out in full-force, and the construction of Langford Speedway began in 1935. The grandstands were built by Taylor with the help of Andre and George Cottyn.

After opening in 1936 the 3/8ths-mile track proved to be successful beyond anyone's expectations, due largely to Jack's abilities. He acted as his own promoter, track manager, publicist, announcer and car owner. To augment the meager local field of about a dozen sprint cars, he offered a generous guarantee of $25 to any sprinter from the United States.

Competitors came flocking in from Seattle, Portland, California's Bay Area and Los Angeles. The local field of cars swelled to around 25 in number, but Jack continued to offer the appearance bounty to those in the U.S. – thus maintaining the international flavor of the events.

Some of the legendary drivers that raced at Langford include Jimmy Wilburn, Rajo Jack, Wally Schock, Einar "Swede" Lindskog, Johnny McDowell, Allen Heath, Chick Barbo, Tommy Legge, Adolph Cans, "Cactus" Jack Turner and Shorty Scovell.

Track lighting was installed in 1937 using 150-watt bulbs. The track also became the first paved facility in Canada, thanks to a $1,500 donation by Frannie Morse. As sprint car racing was his mainstay, Taylor turned down most other racing association's request to appear. His weekly Saturday events were attracting near-capacity crowds. In October of 1940, the season ended with a split midget/sprint car race. Other types of cars occasionally appeared on the same program with the sprints.

Langford Speedway ceased operation after the 1941 season for the duration of World War Two. During that time the facility was used by the military, and then in 1945 was purchased by Bruce Passmore.

Jack Taylor was instrumental in providing the great early history of auto racing in the Victoria area.

2003 Inductees

KEITH CAHILL began racing at Western Speedway in 1979 at the age of 16, competing in the demo car class. In his first outing he placed second in the main event and won the Best Appearing Car Award. The next year he won the total destruction championship. At the end of 1981 Keith was the championship-winning driver in the demo car division.

In 1982 Cahill drove a hobby stock car, as well as a late model stock car. In 1984 he was part of a three-car team competing for the first time at the Pacific National Exhibition in Vancouver, B.C., winning the championship. Over the subsequent years, and known as 'The Masked Banana', Keith Cahill continued his winning ways racing demo cars and trucks, earning well over 300 trophies. He also served as the flagman for two years at Western Speedway.

LARRY POLLARD began working as a crew member with his father in Alberta, Canada and then moved to Victoria in 1966. He built his first stock car in 1967 at the very young age of 13 but had to wait until 1970 to be old enough to compete. In his first event at Western Speedway he won his heat race and finished second in the main event. He ended the year as the highest-finishing rookie. The next year Larry won the championship race and the stock car title.

Moving up to super-stocks in 1972, Pollard won five out of fifteen trophy dashes and at year's end was the highest-placed rookie, finishing fifth in points. In 1973 he came home fourth in local super-stock points, and then moved to the open competition class in 1974. 1975 found Larry winning two of the Carling Series races plus the Billy Foster Memorial race, which he also won the next season. Larry was voted the VITRA Driver of the Year in 1978.

For 1979 Pollard promoted and ran the outlaw open super-stock class where he won three main events and scored a clean-sweep at Langley Speedway. Additionally, he served as president of the Capital City Auto Racing Group.

Larry gained NASCAR attention while crewing on Roy Smith's winning Winston West operation for two years, which included racing in the Daytona 500. He joined the Richard Childress organization as a crew member for Ricky Rudd in 1982. Then he moved to the Richard Petty enterprise and was co-crew chief for Petty's three victories in 1983. In 1984 Larry became the crew chief for Phil Parsons, who finished the season second in rookie points to Rusty Wallace.

Pollard drove NASCAR Grand National cars in 1985 and 1986, finishing third and ninth in points. In 1987 he became the first foreign-born driver to win a NASCAR Busch Series Grand National race at Hampton, Virginia. He also competed in four Winston Cup events.

Larry Pollard was seriously injured in a 1988 incident, and then raced on a very limited basis in the following years.

2004 Inductees

EDDIE KOSTENUK, in 1948, drove the Chuck House #25 car, the #6 Dalby Special and came in third in the Labor Day finale at Langford Speedway. In the opening race of 1949, he set second-fastest time, was second in the dash and won his heat race.

In May of 1950 Kostenuk drove Grant King's car to a fifth-place finish at Portland, Oregon. The following week he was third at Langford and duplicated that result again on July 5th. He won the race in late July. During this year he also traveled on a weekly basis to Digney Speedway to compete in the midget races and for both 1950 and 1951, ended the season as points champion.

In early June of 1953 at the big car meet at Shearing Speedway, Eddie won the dash, the heat and placed second in the main event. He scored numerous wins in 1954, and in 1955 placed first in the Western Canada Big Car Championship.

Moving ahead to 1959, Kostenuk became the president of a newly-formed go-kart association and won the first race at Island View Beach. He raced his own Ranger-powered roadster in 1961 and won the last big car race that was held at Western Speedway in late July.

In 1962 at the age of 33, Eddie passed his United States Auto Club rookie tests and entered the Indianapolis 500, joining teammates Rodger Ward and Len Sutton. Unfortunately, his bid to qualify was shattered when he was struck in the goggles by a bird while on a practice run at 140 mph. After recovering, he ran the Centennial 100 Modified race in Victoria, setting a track record and winning the race.

In 1963 Kostenuk returned to Indy, but a lack of funding forced him to turn the City of Victoria Special car over to Johnny Rutherford. During his USAC years he appeared in races at DuQuoin, Syracuse, Trenton, Milwaukee, and Phoenix. His best finishes were an eleventh and twelfth.

DON SMITH, whose father was a motorcycle fanatic, joined his brothers who were all riding bikes at a very young age. The family also had a yard-full of cars and a small race track. By the time he turned eight in 1965 his love or racing had developed, as he had his own car to 'race' on the backyard dirt track.

During the 1970s Don competed in some total destruction derbies, and then became involved in stock car racing in Nanaimo in 1979, winning the Rookie of the Year title. For the next three years he became a mechanic at Western Speedway, wanting to learn how to assemble the race cars. During this time Smith built a roadrunner-class of car for his brother Steve to drive.

In 1986 the brothers purchased a 1970 Chevy Nova stock car and achieved three consecutive class championships. In 1986 Don was the Stock Car Driver of the Year, the Mechanic of the Year, the championship race winner and the season points champion. The next year Smith won the Billy Foster 100, the July Cup, the Corby

Cup, the Stock Car Special Event, the championship race and was again the season's champion. He repeated the same feat in 1988.

Don moved up to the Can-Am Pro Stock class in 1990 and won races at Prince George, Quesnel, Ephrata and Western Speedway. He finished second in points for the year. Staying with the Can-Am series, he was crowned champion in 1992.

Smith joined the 13-race Northwest All Stars Tour in 1993, racing at Spanaway, Ephrata, Stateline and Wenatchee in Washington State. He won the Gillette-Thrifty Foods 200 at Western Speedway. In 1995 he campaigned in the late model super-stock class. He became the points champion in 1997. During 1998 Don Smith competed in the Northwest International Racing Association Series.

DAN WADE and his brothers had their first taste of racing when their parents took them to Shearing Speedway in the mid-1950s. This fascination with auto racing continued from 1955 to 1971, as Dan was an avid spectator at both Western Speedway and throughout the Pacific Northwest.

In 1972 Wade and his three brothers purchased a stock car. Al Wade drove and became the crew chief. They ended the season sixth in points and won the Rookie of the Year Award. Over the next several years the team won nine main events, including the Roy White Memorial race, and finished second in points.

In 1975 the Wades purchased Rick O'Dell's 1963 Plymouth super-stock car and finished seventh in points. Dan also crewed for O'Dell at NASCAR and IDC events.

Wade became president of VITRA in 1977 and was instrumental in the creation of the Island Series for Stock Cars and Super-Stocks. He was also voted VITRA Member of the Year. The next two years Don doubled as both a car owner and VITRA president. In 1976 Don began organizing tours to the Daytona 500 which continued for many years.

In 1986 Dan Wade once again became a car owner for his son Lance, driving a VITRA bomber car, which they raced over the next several years. Dan and his brother Roger purchased a super-stock car in 1989 and converted it into a pro-stock, racing at Western Speedway and the Fall Classic at Yakima. During 1990 and 1991 Dan helped his son Lance raced in the International Pro Stock Series and the Can-Am Late Model Series.

From 1992 through 1999 Dan joined forces with his brothers Roger and George to field a team for Lance to compete in the Winston West Series of NASCAR. They even tried to qualify for NASCAR's Brickyard 400 at Indianapolis.

2005 Inductees

JOHN EDGETT, a successful businessman, supported numerous racing drivers and teams and played a big part in their many wins and championships.

John began his involvement with auto racing in 1968 as a mechanic and pit crew member with Harvey Brown at the Oyster River Speedway, located north of Courtenay, B.C. They raced a 1956 Chevy stock car in the local events. In 1973 Edgett was the crew chief for Harvey Brown on the Connie Mangles Special when they competed in the first International Driver's Challenge races for super stock cars.

1976 found John join forces with George Stuart and Phil Bickle when they formed the Island Racemasters Team. He then worked with Harvey Chipper and Dave Smith (Chipper-Smith Racing) to field a car for George Stuart to race in the NASCAR Winston West series – the first Canadians to win a Winston West event. John then ran an Open-competition Camaro late model stock car that was driven by both Rick O'Dell and Roy Smith.

In 1980 Edgett became a car owner and hired drivers Gary Kershaw and Roy Smith to race his car, which won many Winston West races and championships. In 1982 John was the sponsor and crew chief for Roy Smith, driving the 'Pride of Victoria' car in the Daytona 500, where they finished in tenth place. Without John's support, Roy would probably not have been able to compete at Daytona.

In the early 1990s, John sponsored and was the crew chief for Lance Wade. They began with late model sportsman cars and then moved up to Winston West. In 1993 Wade finished third in the Coors Lite 500

Winston West race at Monroe, Washington. He also earned the pole position and finished fourth at a race in Tri-Cities, Washington.

In 1994 Edgett sponsored Lance for the inaugural Brickyard 400 at Indianapolis, and also aided with sponsorships for Gary Smith in various events during the 1990s.

BILL HITCHCOX began racing go-karts at the age of 12. He transitioned to claimer cars at Western Speedway in 1975 when he won the Ted Birtwhistle Memorial Trophy, was named Rookie of the Year and ended the season third in points. In 1976 he advanced to the hobby stock class and won the N.W. Insurance Agency Trophy, the Corby Cup, the championship race and was crowned the season's champion. 1977 found Hitchcox move to the super-stock class where he captured another Rookie of the Year Award.

The next two years Bill competed in the Northwest Open Competition Super Stock Series where he earned numerous top-five finishes. He raced in the NASCAR Northwest Late Model series from 1980 to 1983. In 1980 he won at six different tracks and had two top-five finishes. 1981 saw him become the first Rookie of the Year to win the overall Northwest Championship with six main event victories. He also was crowned the Yakima Speedway champion. The following year he repeated as the overall Northwest Champion with five main event wins, becoming the first Canadian and second driver to win back-to-back championships.

Hitchcox campaigned in NASCAR's Winston West series in 1984, placing third in his first outing at Monroe, Washington. He continued in Winston West the next two years before managing Ron Ward's NASCAR Southwest operation where the team won the 1987 Madera Speedway championship in California. Bill participated in the Northwest Pro Stock series in 1988 and 1989, when he won both Fall Classic races in Yakima, Washington. He raced in the NASCAR Northwest Tour series in 1990 and 1991, and then switched to the NASCAR Late Model series in Yakima over the next two years. After a successful season Bill moved to Kannapolis, North Carolina.

Bill raced in the Big-10 Late Model Sportsman Division at Concord, North Carolina in 1994 and 1995. He won his first race, a 100-lapper at Concord, then qualified on the pole for his second event and finished second. After moving to Concord, where he worked as a CNC machinist, he raced in 200-lap events, always finishing in the top-ten.

GEORGE 'G.B.' STERNE won the Western Canada Motorcycle Hillclimb Championship in 1931. He did not compete in any events until 1954 when at the age of 42, he began racing sports cars with an MG-TC roadster. He joined the Sports Car Club of British Columbia (SCCBC) in 1955 and raced at Abbotsford and other circuits. G.B. was the owner and operator of a Standard Chevron station in Sidney, which in 1956 became the first home for his fledgling Morgan dealership. He began racing a Morgan 4-seater in 1957 and the next year won his first race as well as the International Conference of Sports Car Clubs (ICSCC) championship.

During the nineteen years he competed Sterne drove Morgan cars exclusively. In 1963 he drove a Morgan Super Sport; in 1966 he ran a Morgan Plus Four Competition model; in 1969 a Morgan Plus Eight; and in 1972 a Morgan 4/4 1600. G.B. retired from driving at the end of the 1975 season.

In 1974 he won his 389th trophy – 170 of which were for finishing in first place. Through the years he also achieved a number of SCCBC and ICSCC championships. Included in his race wins was a first overall placing in the 1964 Westwood Enduro with co-driver Dave Ogilvy. He and co-driver Richard Evans won the Index of Performance Award in the 1968 Enduro. In 1972 Sterne and his son Robert qualified for the CASC National Championship at Mosport, Ontario. The pair drove nearly 3,000 miles towing a small trailer of racing tires behind their race cars so they could compete at this meet.

In 1969 G.B. was nominated for the *Columbian Newspaper* 'Sportsman of the Year' Award. In addition to his driving talents, he was a charter member of the Victoria Motor Sports Club and, on two occasions, served as president. He also served, for five years, as vice president for ICSCC and the novice license director for three years.

George's wife Lydia was an active partner during his racing career. She did lap scoring, timing and some corner work duties.

2006 Inductees

ROCKIE COLLINS began racing a demolition car at Victoria in 1974. The following year he ran a stock car and finished eighth in season points. In 1976 he moved up to super-stocks. His best year in this class came in 1982, winning two main events, awarded the Best-Looking Car and Crew honors and finished the season third in points. Rockie drove Dick Midgley's car in the 1982 Winston West Grand National race in Victoria, where he finished fifth.

Collins participated in the Northwest Super Stock series starting in 1983 and earned the Driver of the Year and Best-Looking Car trophies. He finished fifth in the Canada 200 race and was crowned the season champion.

In 1985 he had five main event wins along with the Popular Driver Award. He won the Roy White Memorial race and finished second in points for the season. In 1986 he again finished second in points with three main event wins. He gained the Popular Driver Award, won the Billy Foster trophy and placed fifth in the Canada 200 Northwest Tour race. In 1988 Collins raced in pro stock, was second in points and again was named Most Popular Driver. He had top-ten finishes at Yakima, Portland, Monroe, and Tenino. He won two main events in Port Angeles.

Rockie switched to IMCA modified cars in 1991, winning championships both that year and the next. In 1993 he led in points until the last race of the season when he ended in third place overall. In his last year of driving in 1999 he finished as the Pro Stock Points Champion.

During his racing career, Rockie Collins was excellent with chassis set-ups and knew how to make cars run quickly. In addition to Western Speedway, he competed at Grandview Bowl, Cassidy and Saratoga on Vancouver Island; Vernon and Penticton on the British Columbia mainland; Port Angeles, Tenino, Skagit, Monroe and Yakima in Washington; and Anderson, California. He drove for Gordie Alberg, Skip Crawford, Larry Johnson, Roy Wilson, Butch Behn, J.R. Edgett, Dick Midgley, Dave Smith, George Kormandy and Jim Smith. He also crewed for St. James Davis, Dave Marcus, Janet Guthrie and Bobby Allison.

ROB SCOTT first came on the scene at Western Speedway in a 1973 demolition derby. During the next two years he served as crew chief for Gordie Stone. In 1976 he drove Dave Bennett's car in a jalopy class race and won the main event. In 1977 he drove in the hobby stock class, winning the championship. The next year he won the stock car championship.

In 1982 Rob was again crowned the stock car champion. In 1984 he won the hobby stock championship and was named the Mechanic of the Year, an award that he earned again in 1989.

In 1990 Scott joined the ranks of the Old Time Racers Association (OTRA), traveled to Hamilton and Toronto for the East-West Challenge, and emerged as the western points champion. He drove the Milt Barnes #32 car and won numerous main events throughout the Northwest. He was voted Mechanic of the Year in 1991 and 1992.

In 1994 Rob moved to the IMCA Series and won six features out of nine entered at Western Speedway - on his way to capturing the championship. He also received the Driver of the Year and Mechanic of the Year Awards, plus the Corby Cup for most main event wins. Scott was crowned the 1995 open-wheel champion along with being named Rookie of the Year, and a third-place finish in national IMCA points. His impressive IMCA record found him becoming the first British Columbia driver to win the national title in 1996, a feat he repeated in 1997 and 1999. He was the IMCA champion at Saratoga in 1996 and 1997, as well as the Salmon Classic winner and Western Speedway champion in 1997 and 1998. He won the British Columbia IMCA series championships in 1998 and 1999.

Scott joined the WILROC Sprint Car and Super Modified series in 2000, driving the Ron Douglas roadster to three consecutive fifth-place finishes, along with winning four main events.

Through his career Rob competed at Western Speedway, Grandview Bowl, Cassidy, Saratoga and Tri-Port Speedways on Vancouver Island; Penticton, Prince George, Quesnel, Vernon and Williams Lake in British Columbia; Port Angeles, Skagit, Spanaway, Tenino and Wenatchee in Washington; Portland and Roseburg in

Oregon; Stateline in Idaho; Kalispell in Montana; Medicine Hat and Race City in Alberta; and Flamboro and CNE Stadium in Ontario.

GERRY VANTREIGHT did not begin his competitive racing career until he was 24. He was closely associated with the sport through family ties – especially with his father, who was a long-time race fraternity member, car owner and builder.

Gerry started driving in 1977 without rising through the traditional ranks of jalopies or stock cars, but as a driver of the powerful super-modifieds. Sharing the driving duties with Al Vantreight Gerry appeared in only five races but was still considered a rookie on the Canadian American Modified Association (CAMRA) circuit.

With Al's guidance and his own familiarity with the race car, Gerry was an instant success. In his debut at Evergreen Speedway in Monroe, Washington, he won the B-dash, was third in the heat race and came home fifth in the A-main event. He ended his first season in 12th place in the Washington Racing Association (WRA) points standings, just one position behind Al.

Over the next year and a half Vantreight honed his skills and gained the necessary driving experience to be a strong contender on the CAMRA circuit. He was the fastest qualifier for the 1979 Daffodil Cup race in Victoria but was forced out with mechanical issues. The next CAMRA race in Victoria was the Strawberry Cup where Gerry set fast time, won the A-dash, came home third in his heat race and the 50-lap main event.

In the following seasons Gerry raced throughout the Pacific Northwest and scored numerous top-ten finishes. In 1983 he was involved in a major crash at the Portland Speedway in Oregon. He hit the wall at 130 mph but escaped with a broken collar bone, nerve damage in his neck and a car about five-feet shorter than it was before the race. At the time he was in second place in CAMRA points.

A major highlight in Gerry's career took place in 1985 when he was crowned the USAC northwest champion. The next year he finished the season third in points. After competing in cars built by his father for the majority of his career, the team purchased an 870-horsepower, methanol-fueled machine for the 1989 Northwest Super Modified Racing Association season.

In subsequent years Gerry drove for the Veenstra family, based in Boise, Idaho.

2007 Inductees

RICHARD GRAHAM joined the Vancouver Island Track Racing Association at the age of 16. He first worked on a super-modified car and then owned a 1932 Ford stock car driven by Wally Lum. He then became part-owner of a 1955 Chev super-stock driven by Roy Haslam.

In 1969 Richard became involved with driver Gary Kershaw and shared car ownership with Harvey Chipper and Dave Smith. This group raced four cars between 1969 and 1971 – a 1955 Chevrolet, followed by 1964, '65 and '69 Chevelles.

The team competed throughout the Pacific Northwest, winning many main events and several championships. They won championships in Victoria in 1968 and 1969. On their second trip to Riverside, California in 1971, they captured the Permatex 200 race and went on to win the Northwest IDC championship.

Graham left active racing to look after his business and family responsibilities, but still provided sponsorships and tow money to keep in touch. In the early 1980s he began visiting Skagit Speedway with his family to watch the sprint cars and for several years sponsored their event called 'A Few Dollars More'.

In 1986 Richard and his younger son joined the Langley Midget Association and began racing a quarter-midget at various Northwest locations. They won championships in 1988 and 1990, then moved up to half-midgets from 1990 to 1993. In their first season the car scored many close finishes and captured four championships. He and his son also ran mini-sprints, winning three championship races in 1993.

The next progression was to sprint cars in 1994. Richard's son was named Rookie of the Year at Skagit in 1994 and in San Jose, California in 1995, where they also set the all-time track record and won a feature race in 1996. The family duo had now teamed up with Henderson Motorsports in California – a highly competitive organization.

In 1996 the team driver was Ronnie Day, who achieved three wins and eight podium finishes. The next season saw Roger Crockett in the cockpit, who earned two wins and six podium finishes. In 1998 they won the 360 Nationals at Skagit Speedway.

In 1999 the Henderson Team had Steve Kent as their driver. The result totaled 40 wins with 57 podium finishes from 1999 to 2006, and numerous championships.

TOM HAMILTON began racing in the early 1960s in an Austin-Healey Sprite and an MG Midget. In 1964 at the age of 33 he placed second in the Gymkhana Class in the British Columbia Region of the Canadian Automobile Sport Club. In 1965 he graduated to a powerful Sunbeam Tiger and held a record of 38 wins in 54 events entered.

In 1967 Tom began racing his famous Shelby GT350R sponsored by Brown Brothers Motors of Vancouver, B.C. Over the next two seasons Hamilton and his sponsor were an unbeatable combination, capturing over 40 podium finishes in the process. Not content with winning the sedan or B-production contests, they changed carburetors, wheels and tires, and other components in order to compete in various other categories. The result was a large number of wins at Vancouver's Westwood road circuit.

Hamilton won five northwest driving championships in 1968 along with two International Conference titles, two BC Regional Championships and the overall Royal City Club title. This year marked the high point of his road racing career. In 1969 Tom won the Mt. Douglas Hill Climb in Victoria – a feat that was also accomplished by Billy Foster in 1962.

In 1970 Tom left sports car racing and turned his attention to oval racing at his home track – the Oyster River Speedway (which became Saratoga Speedway). He started with a B-class car and then moved to the A-class in 1972. He also raced at Western Speedway and Langley Speedway. His winning ways prevailed as he earned four championships while being victorious in numerous heats and feature races. The media dubbed him 'Terrible Tommy' after some particularly aggressive racing moments which earned him eight black flags.

Tom Hamilton retired from active driving in 1976. In 2005 he was reunited with Carroll Shelby and his freshly-restored Brown Brothers GT350. Tom was invited to test-drive it again at the California Speedway. He hadn't lost any of his driving skills as he hit 165 mph, which would have placed him third on the grid for the next day's racing event. He asked, "So how do I get started in vintage racing?"

DAVE SMITH was bitten by the racing bug after watching his first demolition derby at the age of eight. By 1972, at the age of 17, he learned the sport of racing and was building demo cars to run at the Chemainus Gravel Pit.

In 1973 he competed in derbies around Vancouver at Duncan, Lake Cowichan, Courtenay, Victoria, Chemainus and Nanaimo. Dave then joined the newly-formed 'crash-to-pass' series at Western Speedway and went on to win the 1979 championship and Driver of the Year Award. In 1980 Smith was part of the three-car team which competed at the PNE.

In 1982-83 he won the three car PNE Championship, then raced in the 200-lap enduro race in 1985 at Western Speedway and came home the winner in the 120-car field.

For the 1981 season Smith moved to racing a 1934 Ford with the Old Time Racers Association. He ran this car throughout the Northwest, winning many events including the last race held at Grandview Bowl. He became involved with Fraser Carmichael and Joe Pullen to spearhead the purchase of Cassidy Speedway.

Moving up from the OTRA class Dave transitioned into sprint cars at Cassidy, winning numerous events and championships from 1995-1997. Dave always loved pavement, so he ventured into the NSSRA program, competing for two partial seasons and then one complete season. In 1998 Dave finished third in points and won the Most Outstanding Effort Award.

When the WILROC series was formed in 2000 Dave Smith joined and owned cars that competed until 2006. He claimed the 2000 WILROC championship with driver Dave Emmerson. He ran cars in two classes - a

360 sprint car at Skagit Speedway and an asphalt car with WILROC. Beginning in 1999 he was mentoring other young race drivers such as Britt Gillett, Randy Makowski and Todd Heikes. Smith was also specializing in rebuilding and modifying engines and chassis.

In 2001 Dave's team with driver Todd Heikes made history south of the border when the captured the overall 360 Sprint Car championship in Washington State. No other Canadian had ever accomplished this feat.

2008 Inductees

FRASER CARMICHAEL began his racing career at Nanaimo's Grandview Bowl in the mid-1960s when he drove stock cars. He became well-known for driving Fords that were purple in color. After racing stock cars, he moved into the newly-formed Old Time Racers Association (OTRA) in 1978.

Fraser drove a 1932 Chevrolet coupe that was owned by Victoria's Norm Wilcox and sponsored by Coca-Cola. This combination proved to be very successful, netting many fast times and wins throughout the Pacific Northwest. In 1985 Carmichael ran in a 7-11 Race of Champions race at Victoria's Western Speedway, where a group of past champion drivers competed in five events driving various types of cars at each race. At the end of the year Fraser was the points winner for this yearly series.

Carmichael continued racing with the OTRA until 1989. In addition to his coupe he periodically drove several sedan race cars. Later, he and a handful of others were instrumental in the re-establishment of auto racing in the mid-Vancouver Island area. After the untimely closing of Grandview Bowl, Fraser and his group set about acquiring suitable property in the Nanaimo area to build a race track, and the Cassidy Speedway was born.

Fraser Carmichael wore various hats in this operation at one time or another. He also again donned a driver's suit to help get the newest class – the winged sprint cars – up and running at Cassidy. His tireless efforts in all aspects of the sport have done much to enrich motor racing on Vancouver Island. He continued to own and sponsor a sprint car until the political closure of Cassidy Speedway.

TREVOR MONTGOMERY was first involved with BMX bicycle racing along with assisting with his dad's race car. Trevor began his auto racing career at the age of 16 in the Western Speedway street stock class. He went on to win back-to-back championships in 1987 and 1988.

At age 19 he moved up to the IMCA Modifieds, becoming the Western Speedway champion in 1989 and the Canadian IMCA champion in 1991. His first sprint car ride found him competing on the dirt at Nanaimo's Cassidy Speedway and earned a third and second-place in the yearly championships.

Trevor then moved to pavement sprint cars at age 26 and became the first Canadian sprint car winner at Calgary's Race City Speedway. He began racing with the Northwest Supermodified and Sprint Car Association (NSSRA) where he established himself as a very talented and dedicated driver. He set all-time race records at Campbell River's Saratoga Speedway and at Victoria's Western Speedway. The latter broke Davey Hamilton's old record set seven years previously with a Super Modified car.

Montgomery's last sprint car was built by Victoria's Russ Lejeune, who also served as a crew member on the NSSRA circuit. His father assisted by building the engines for this car. In all he won 11 of 18 races over a two-year period. In 1997 Trevor won the prestigious Daffodil Cup race in Victoria – a feat he repeated in 1999 and again in 2003. He also won the Strawberry Cup event in 1998 and 2002.

While competing on the NSSRA circuit he won the season championship in 1997. Trevor Montgomery was the first Canadian to succeed in this series and he clinched it in front of his hometown fans at Western Speedway. He won his second NSSRA title in 1998 at the Tri-Cities Speedway in Washington State. The next season Trevor's third-place finish at the last race at Meridian Speedway in Boise, Idaho earned him his third NSSRA points title despite missing one race during the year. With more than 50 feature race wins and numerous other awards, Montgomery established himself as one of the premier race car drivers in the Pacific Northwest.

ANDY YOUNG came into the sport at the young age of 14. He became involved with the super-modified race car of Tony Mortel, who was racing on the Canadian-American Modified Racing Association circuit. Soon thereafter Andy built his own car for the super-stock series in Victoria with Teddy Mortel driving. After one-year Young joined the Ross Surgenor crew in the open super-stock series and the NASCAR Northwest Sportsman series. The team was very successful, winning races from Portland, Oregon to British Columbia, including the Rainier 205 event at Monroe, Washington. The team won the International Driver's Challenge and competed in the Permatex 200 at Riverside, California.

During those years Andy also was involved in NASCAR's Winston 500 at Riverside, working with drivers such as Roy Smith, Hershel McGriff, Ross Surgenor and Jimmy Means. After a successful career with Surgenor Andy was hired as a tire changer on Roy Smith's crew. He also prepared many race cars over the years by doing bodywork and paint. Young's first year with Roy Smith was very rewarding as they won the NASCAR North Sportsman championship and placed tenth overall in the Winston West points race.

In 1980 the team won the Winston West championship and continued to do so the following two years. The 'Flying Aces' set many records and won a number of prestigious races over a ten-year period. Andy Young's most memorable moment with Roy Smith was the opportunity they had to compete in the Daytona 500 in 1982. He was instrumental in the fund-raising efforts for the 'Pride of Victoria' car, which finished a respectable tenth in that race.

2009 Inductees

TERRY FORSYTH began racing at age 13 by driving go-karts at Nick's Island View Beach track in Victoria. In 1965 when he turned 16, he began driving stock cars at Western Speedway, where his first ride was in a Hudson. Over the next three years he teamed up with Glen Hewitt and raced a Ford to one top-ten finish.

In 1970 Terry moved up to the newly-created super-stock class. He raced a 1955 Chevy to an eighth-place finish in the standings. In 1971 he finished the season in second place overall.

Forsyth also was an assistant starter in 1971 and 1972. That year he purchased a 1965 Chevelle formerly driven by Gary Kershaw. He got off to a great start in 1973 by winning five out of the first seven feature races. The next season he raced in a total of 26 events and won the 1973 class championship. Terry also placed second in the Most Popular Driver voting and won the Billy Foster 100 race, the Sponsor's Trophy and the Carling Challenge race.

Following this successful season Terry had many memorable highlights during his racing career. Championships and top finishes came at tracks such as the Portland Speedway and elsewhere. He finished fifth in Bakersfield, California behind drivers such as Neil Bonnet, Bobby Allison, Roy Smith, Bill Schmidt and one place ahead of Donnie Allison. He finished in the ninth position at Phoenix, Arizona following Richard Petty all race long. Forsyth competed at 26 different tracks and was also involved in racing promotions.

In 1978 Forsyth joined with Reg Midgley, Bob and John Beadle to form International Productions, Inc. The company won a contract to oversee the motorsports operations at Evergreen Speedway in Monroe, Washington. Terry was also involved with Midgley with the IDC Series for several years, working as pit boss. He assisted Ted Pollack with the Yakima and Portland Speedways.

Terry also participated for many years in fund-raising with VITRA for handicapped children. Additionally, he crewed for Dick Midgley, traveling many times to Riverside International Raceway and Ontario Motor Speedway in California, and Daytona, Florida. Drivers he worked with include Dave Cooper, Roy Smith, Dave Marcis and Hershel McGriff.

ROCKY HORNE began his association with auto racing in 1984 at Western Speedway when he was a crew member for a demolition car. Little did he know at that time that his sharp and quick-witted demure would escalate him to a much higher level. With a little coaxing, the 1985 season found him interviewing drivers, crew members and fans at the speedway.

In 1986 Rocky became the full-time announcer for promoter Butch Behn, kicking off an impressive 24-year career announcing for all the later Western Speedway promoters. He worked both sides of the counter as a parts provider to the racers at Mid-Island Engines, as well as Lejeune Engineering. When he was announcing fans would go home knowing more of the workings of racing engines and suspensions. He shared his knowledge with the fans and provided very good information of the racing that was taking place.

In 1995 Horne built a Chevy Monte Carlo Thunder Car, drove it himself for a few races and then handed the wheel to Randy Price to finish the season. 1996 found Rocky working on an IMCA modified with Rob Scott. He built and owned a stock car for the 1997-98 seasons with Robbie Haslam driving. Rocky then purchased a sportsman car which Jeff Montgomery raced throughout the 1999-2000 seasons. The pair then moved up to a sprint car for the next two years.

From a young age Rocky Horne always had his fingers in something mechanical, including a Kelly Road Texaco air compressor, which accounts for his missing digit! Despite this shortcoming his passion for the sport and ability to connect with the fans and the racers which placed him in a very select group. He had an uncanny knack of assigning a nickname to the racers and promoters alike.

Beyond the track Rocky acted as master of ceremonies at countless racing functions throughout the course of his career. The years of service he has provided the racing fraternity can be coined as nothing short of immeasurable.

TONY JOHNSON began racing at Western Speedway in 1967. In 1970 he finished the season fifth in total points. The following year he moved up a spot to finish fourth at the season's conclusion. 1972 saw his 1956 Ford win the stock car points championship. During that year he also won the Roy White Memorial and Good Samaritan 100 races. In 1973 Tony was again crowned the stock car champion, competing in 15 events and winning the title over 38 other competitors in the division.

In the latter part of 1973 Johnson moved into the super stock class with a 1964 Ford previously driven by Bob Collins. He finished the season fifth in super stock points and was voted Rookie of the Year. In 1975 Tony became the champion in the super stock class along with winning the July Cup.

The following years found Tony stepping up into other classes where he realized success. He drove in the open super-stock late model class, competed in the 1987 season racing a 1929 DeSoto with the Old Time Racers Association, and later moved on to the IMCA modified class where he posted many victories. He completed his racing career in 2008, ending the season with the Saratoga Speedway IMCA championship.

JACK SPAULDING, a Seattle, Washington native, traveled to Langford Speedway in 1938 to race with Swede Lindskog, Woody Woodford, Bert Bloomgren, Chuck Barbo, Lew McMurtry, Claude Walling, Wes Moore and Wally Schock.

He moved to Vancouver, British Columbia in the early 1940s and successfully raced at Langford through the 1950 season. During those years Spaulding registered 22 main event wins, capturing numerous trophies and championships along the way.

During the following years Jack added to his long list of racing accomplishments at Shearing Speedway in Duncan and at Western Speedway in Victoria. He retired from competition in 1955.

A program feature from Langford Speedway described Jack Spaulding as: "The Little Man with the Big Cigar. He was the 'old man' of racing. Jack has been a favorite with the racing fans for a good many years, not only because of his driving ability, but for the color and thrills he injects into every race he enters. Pilots with his class are at a premium and are eagerly sought by racing car owners. Jack seems to get the utmost out of every car he drives and usually ends up leading the field across the finishing line."

BILL VATER began his racing career in 1964, joining with Norm Edger to race a jalopy at Nanaimo's Grandview Bowl over a four-year period. In 1968 he joined forces with Fred Bull in Port Alberni where the duo won the Mid-Island Auto Racing Association (MIARA) championship.

Bill then built a claimer car in 1973 for Bill Powell and they won every main event that season along with the MIARA claimer championship. Vater also served on the MIARA executive staff for the 1973-74 seasons. The next year he built a stock car for Bill Drummond and the pair finished third in the points standings.

Vater attended Southard's Racing School in California in 1975 and then built a new car for Bill Smith in 1977. In 1978 he built another car for Orton Ker and they captured the Western Speedway stock car championship.

From 1979 to 1991 Bill used his building talents by constructing ten cars, including two dragsters, plus various performance chassis components. He partnered with Bill Zdebiak in 1991 and 1992 on an IMCA modified car which was driven by Gary Smith. The next year, Vater became a sole owner of the car and Smith earned all three Island championships – Western Speedway, Cassidy and the Island Series.

Midway through 1994 Bill rented a NASCAR Northwest Tour car from Ron Eaton, with Gary Smith driving in three races. He then purchased and rebuilt the car for the 1995 season, where the team finished third in the NASCAR Northwest championship points race. In 1996 Lance Wade drove the car in four events which included a win in Yakima, Washington.

In 1997 Vater sold the car back to Ron Eaton and became a crew member for Ron. The next season he crewed for a number of racers before being invited to a trip to Japan to work on the Wade Motorsports Winston West car for NASCAR's Coca-Cola 500 at Twin Ring Motegi - an opportunity he considers to be a highlight of his career. In the years following Bill Vater continued to be a crew member for Eaton, as well as helping other racers both on the track and at his race shop.

2010 Inductees

DAVE FERGUSON first became involved with auto racing in 1965 in Victoria. He provided many years of continuous service to the area's racing community. The drivers and crews came to know him as a hardworking, generous and dedicated individual always available to assist anyone needing help.

Dave came to Victoria from Sarnia, Ontario in his late teens, first working as a gas jockey, and then in 1964 began working at OK Tire when he was 19 years of age. He was taught to hand-true racing tires and became one of only two Victorians to do the job proficiently. He became the guy most racers relied on to take care of their racing tires. Many Friday nights he would stay late on his own time to ensure the drivers had their tires ready for Saturday night's racing activities.

After working at four different locations Ferguson purchased the Six Mile Tire Store in 1995, and the racers always followed him. Many race cars have been sponsored by his establishment. Over the years he has likely been associated with 75% of all cars, drivers and crews that have entered the back gates at Western Speedway, and every class of car would be on the list.

Through the years he worked with many of the top teams and drivers that have competed in the Victoria surroundings. He has also served as a crew member for various teams not only in British Columbia, but other venues around the United States.

LOU MELIN spent a great deal of his time at Western Speedway by being a spectator, working on his friend's race cars, racing his own cars and eventually teaching his son to race. His first drive was a mechanics' race in 1989 when he was just 14. He then moved to demo cars in 1985 where he won two heat races and one main event in his first year. After several seasons he was named the season points champion in 1989 and again the next year.

Melin sat out part of the 1991 season but still recorded two main event wins. In 1992 he again won the championship and the Goodwin Trophy. He then upgraded to the thunder car class at Western and, in 1995, won the Rookie of the Year, Driver of the Year and the championship.

There was a special Friday night 100-lap event at the speedway, which he won. The next day he went to Saratoga Speedway to win a 100-lap race.

Lou competed successfully in thunder cars for the next three seasons. In the year 2000, he joined the sportsman series class. His proudest day came when his son Mike began racing in a hornet car and soon won a main event.

GORD STONE began crewing for his brother Dave's claimer car in 1972, and then began his own driving career at age 17 at Western Speedway. He raced a 1953 Studebaker claimer car, won ten heat races and ended up 37th in points. The next year he changed to a 1956 Dodge, followed by a 1957 Ford that he totaled during his third year of competition.

1976 found Gord driving a 1956 Ford hobby stock car, finishing the season second in points. He moved up to the stock car class in 1978 with a '66 Ford Mustang. After two races he upped the track record twice, finished second in his first two trophy dash races, won two fast heats and one main event.

At the end of the 1978 season Stone was the stock car champion. He also won the NW Insurance Agency Trophy, the 60-lap Andy Cottyn Appreciation Trophy, the Billy Foster Trophy, the Best-Looking Car Award, the Corby Cup and the championship race. He repeated as champion in 1979 and 1980 driving a 1970 Javelin. He was awarded the VITRA Driver of the Year Award as well as the Promoter of the Year Award. In 1982 Gord Stone and his Javelin moved up to the late model stock car class, finished eighth in points for the season and was presented with the VITRA Mechanic of the Year Award.

2011 Inductees

ROSS ROCKETT began his racing involvement in 1958 when he crewed on a 1934 Ford, and then the team upgraded to a B-modified in 1964. He also worked with Jim Malloy's super-modified car for three seasons.

Ross was a crew member on stock cars in 1966 and 1967, moving to a super-modified that raced on the CAMRA circuit over the next several years. He worked as a track official at Western Speedway, serving first as an assistant pit boss, pit boss, and corner man. Additionally, he was a VITRA club executive member, promoter, car owner and unofficial Western Speedway club historian. On two occasions Ross was awarded the VITRA Promoter of the Year Award.

In 1977 Rockett was a founder of the Old Time Racers Association (OTRA), held the club leadership post until 1994, and was the owner of three cars that competed in the series – a 1932 Chrysler, a 1933 Dodge and a 1929 DeSoto. He was awarded a lifetime membership in the club and also submitted racing reports to *Racing Wheels*, a weekly publication based in Victoria.

In 1984 the Victoria Auto Racing Hall of Fame was formed – the first of its kind in Canada. The initial formation meeting was held at Rockett's residence. He was instrumental in producing the yearly souvenir program along with controlling the museum's website and the Hall of Fame Museum adjacent to Western Speedway.

In 1999 Ross joined the Hall of Fame as a director. In 2000, he was the co-founder of the WILROC sprint car and super-modified series, which became very competitive and popular in the Pacific Northwest. After six successful years of involvement, they retired in 2006.

Ross Rockett's primary interests continued, being on the board of directors of the two halls of fame and being a true auto racing historian of Vancouver Island auto racing dating back to before the 1920s. He was also a member of the Sprint Car Hall of Fame in Knoxville, Iowa and enjoyed collector cars.

DAVID SMITH got his start in racing during the mid-1960s, hanging around Digger O'Dell's place after school. He could sometimes be a nuisance and was often summoned to do any dirty job required. One of his first tasks was cleaning out Harvey Chipper's tool box. He helped Harvey on a 1955 Chevy stock car for Roy Haslam, and they built a '55 Chevy super-stock driven by Gary Kershaw.

In 1970 they pair built a 1965 Chevelle in a one-bay shop on Atkins Road. They took the car to Riverside, California where David burned his hands while fueling the car. Returning to Riverside the next year they won the Permatex 200 race. Around the same time, while heading to practice, Smith and Chipper were broadsided by a speeding car. While recovering in the hospital, David read all the literature he could get his hands on about chassis design and race car technology.

This experience clearly changed Smith's life and he was ready to take on the world of racing with a new focus. He traveled south to work with famed NASCAR builder Ralph Moody. A short time later he returned to Sidney, British Columbia to continue honing his skills. Along with Chipper, Jim Tweedhope and countless others he continued building race cars, including the car driven by Gary Kershaw, which won 21 main events in a row. A bounty was put out for anyone that could beat the car.

David worked with Roy Smith in winning the NASCAR Winston West Championship. They broke the track record with a Camaro at the Westwood road course. In 1983 the team appeared at the Riverside 500 race in California, qualifying in the sixth position alongside Bill Elliot, who went on to win the race.

David Smith's cars held many track records and were victorious around the Pacific Northwest with a number of well-known drivers. He eventually started a business - Professional Components - building parts for race cars, Zodiac boats and ambulances. David was always known to be a little eccentric and a little wild, but there were not many people in the racing world that could design or build a car like he did.

BERT SWEETING began his racing experience in his family's garage in the mid-1960s when he had just received his driver's license at age 16. He built his first dragster two years later along with Fred Carver and Larry Whitman. Victoria's Golden Knight Car Club was where he met Gary Shepheard and the two quickly became best friends and set a goal to build a car together. It was to be a Double-B gas dragster to compete against the National Hot Rod Association's (NHRA) best in the hotly-contested Division 6.

An apprentice welding fabricator by trade, Bert and Gary built their tube-frame rail after seeing a photo of a dragster on the cover of a national hot rod magazine. With Sweeting doing the driving chores and Shepheard tuning the car, they were primed for success. He and NHRA's top driver and world record holder, Gary Beck, would go head-to-head in the national races for over half a decade. Drag strips they competed at were in Mission, Bremerton, Puyallup, Seattle, Edmonton and Bamberton.

Beck was a consistent winner, but Bert beat him at an event at Van Isle Dragway in Bamberton in 1969. The 26-year-old, who was an Esquimalt Dockyard welder and fabricator, took his home-built dragster to the one-eighth mile drag strip and posted two out of three wins in front of a boisterous crowd of 2,000 spectators.

Not long after that victory Sweeting retired from competition, as his wife Marie was expecting their second child. He focused his attention on helping other drivers and teams building their own cars. In 1971 he started his own welding business – Nomad Welding – and turned his attention to oval track race cars. He built roll cages for Ross Surgenor, Harvey Chipper, Dave Smith, Gary Kershaw, Rick O'Dell, George Stuart and many others. The welding expertise he learned from his own dragster was now being applied to help other local driver's safety in NASCAR competition. Bert Sweeting is the first drag racer to be inducted into the Victoria Auto Racing Hall of Fame.

2012 Inductees

GORDON ALBERG began his involvement in 1960 when he was a member of Jim Gallaugher's historic race car at Western Speedway. He started as a driver in 1961 with a 1934 Ford stock car. During that season he spent many hours with George 'Spin' Sheridan and Donny Wilson from Wilson and Proctor Company, building Ford flathead engines with all the performance tricks. Gordon also admits that he was living his dream – racing against all the drivers he idolized when he was a young teenager. Those included Dave Cooper, Dick Varley, Gary Kershaw, Jerry Sylvester, Al Smith, Billy Foster and others.

After an unfortunate accident during the mid-season at Western Speedway, Alberg had to stay away from the cockpit for several weeks, so the next weekend Billy Foster drove the car. Foster claimed the fourth-fastest time and a clean-sweep in winning the dash, the fast heat and the main event. Dave Cooper then drove it in Nanaimo the following Wednesday and scored a win in the main event. The next weekend the car appeared at the Haney, Vancouver track and Tom Urdley won the main event. Gordon got back into the cockpit the next week.

In July of 1963 the stock cars traveled to the SeaTac Speedway in Seattle to put on their own program. Gordon drove his #56 car, winning the main event. Another big night for him was the 50-lap stock car championship at Western Speedway, where he ran very well - except for a last-lap 'shot' he received. He ended the 1963 season ninth in points and received the speedway's Rookie of the Year Award.

Alberg upgraded into a B-modified car from Bob Vantreight. Along with driving it for two years, Gordon was also very involved with building components for many racers. His first modified race was in Nanaimo, where he set fast time, won the dash and was second in the main event.

Six weeks later he went to Boise, Idaho, with Reg and Anne Midgley, accompanying Billy Foster. Gordy decided to assist Foster's crew there and went on to help in Pocatello, Salt Lake, Denver, and back again to Pocatello and Boise. Their second racing excursion was to Edmonton, Salt Lake and Denver. Billy won all but three of the main events and had clean sweeps at four of the tracks.

Gordon Alberg continued for many years and was involved with building and supplying numerous racing parts and equipment for many well-known racers. Today his impressive car collection includes the 1965 Vollstedt/Ford Championship Car first driven by Len Sutton in 1965 and Billy Foster in 1966.

TIM CHRISTY began competing in the demo cars at Western Speedway at the age of 16 in 1981 and continued for the next nine years. His racing career became very impressive during the 1990s and 2000s. He originated with a Cassidy Speedway track record in 1987, then upgraded to claimer cars in 1991. In 1992 he finished second in points and in 1993 won the claimer championship with the most main event wins. In 1994 Tim upgraded to the stock car class and finished seventh in points.

Christy received the Member of the Year Trophy in 1995, finishing fifth in the season standings. The next year he was the stock car champion and Driver of the Year. He repeated this record run in both 1997 and 1998.

1999 found him moving up to the late model class and he went on to win that year's championship and Rookie of the Year honors. The year 2000 found Christy winning his fifth-straight championship and Driver of the Year Award. One more championship came in 2001 and his crew chief earned the Mechanic of the Year Award.

The next few years found Tim with many more trophies to add to his collection. In 2004 he won the Winn River Invitational 100-lap race at Shasta Speedway in California, and in 2005 he won the DeWalt Miller Springs Mainland Late Model championship. He placed second overall in the Katana Racing Series from 2006-2008. He finished third overall in 2009 when competing in the ARCA West series. After retiring from active racing, Tim Christy became a committee member for the Victoria Auto Racing Hall of Fame.

AL CLARK has a tremendous history with all the racing situations he was involved with. Originally born in London, England, he lived in Victoria since the age of three. Years later he was one of the most successful drag racers at Mission Raceway. In 1961 he joined the Quarter Milers Car Club and in 1962 drove a 1948 Chevy coupe to high school. He began drag racing driving the Quarter Milers C/Dragster at Arlington, Washington and San Cobble, Vancouver Island.

In 1963 Clark fired up his dragster and raced it down the front straight at Western Speedway on a Wednesday afternoon. During 1964 he raced at Arlington, San Cobble and Pacific Raceway in Kent, Washington. He also helped organize the Quarter Milers Autorama. In 1965 he started a metal fabricator and boilermaker apprenticeship at the DND Dockyard while he continued to race. He went on to become the show chairman for the Quarter Milers' Autorama.

Al drove the second dragster to appear at the Mission track and continued to drive the Quarter Milers dragster. He had purchased the car from the club and won his own class championship at Mission. In 1967 he started running at the new Van Isle Raceways in Mill Bay where he won many match races against dragsters from other areas. During the 1968 season Clark set the track record at Van Isle racing the fuel-injected Chevy C/Dragster to a time of 9.76 seconds at 144 mph. He won the Competition Eliminator title six times.

In 1969 Al built a B/Dragster for Brian Roberts and Bill England. The next year he raced an E-Class dragster equipped with a straight-eight Buick engine. From 1971 to 1974 he raced a B-Class rail with an injected Chrysler Hemi engine, reaching a top speed of 148.68 mph in 9.21 seconds.

Al Clark retired from drag racing in 1974 when he sold his equipment. In the following years he was a show chairman for the International Show Car Association from 1974 to 1988, and then produced his own shows in 1991 and 1994. He also spent time building street rods and formed his Deuces Northwest Street Rods Company in 1996. In 1998 Al became the coordinator of the Northwest Deuce Day events in Victoria.

2013 Inductees

JOHN BIGGS was an owner of Victoria Auto Wreckers when one of his employees, the late Bob Bissenden, approached him to build a race car. In his words, "Much to the disapproval of my dad, I agreed to Bob's idea and this started a very successful partnership over the next twelve years. In order to race at Western Speedway, you had to belong to the Vancouver Island Track Racing Association."

After he joined, John never missed a meeting in order to learn all there was to know about racing and the rules. The first car John and Bob built was a 1949 Ford stock car. They raced that car between Grandview Bowl in Nanaimo on Friday night Western Speedway on Saturday night every weekend for five years. VITRA then started a new super-stock class and in order to compete, they built a 1957 Ford.

During Biggs' twelve-year span he was elected VITRA president in 1968, 1971 and 1972. In this position he was responsible for representing VITRA at the Western Speedway board of directors' meetings, as VITRA owned 10% of the facility. Additionally, he actively promoted racing in the area. Some awards presented to John over the years include Mechanic of the Year in 1968, Sportsman of the Year in 1966 and Member of the Year in 1968 and 1971.

John Biggs met and made many friends while racing and as the head tech had to make some hard decisions. Some of these proved him unpopular, but rules were rules and had to be strictly adhered to. As John said, "I enjoyed this time of my life, being part of VITRA and the fellowship and, if I was young (a lot younger), I would not hesitate to do it all again."

BOB COLLINS started going to the race track with his father in the mid-50s to the early 60s. In 1966 he joined VITRA and served as a crew member for a 1955 Ford stock car owned and driven by Al Hitchcox. The following year Bob decided to build a car of his own - a 1949 Ford powered by a Mercury flathead engine. His goal was to learn to become a competitive driver and that year saw him become one of the fastest B-main drivers.

In 1968 Collins found himself qualifying in the middle of the 35-car A-main class. This was more competitive than ever and provided some exciting racing. Most of these cars were six-cylinder powered and the days of the flathead V8 were numbered, but not for Bob. He vowed to run a Flathead forever! Bob's wife Kathy has a racing jacket made with 'Flat Head Forever' printed on the back and she wore it proudly to support her husband. That season found Bob splitting the year between the A-main class, starting at the front of the field, and the B-main class starting at the rear.

Collins was gaining confidence in his driving ability and in 1969 was qualifying in the top-six of the field. He qualified ninth for the Billy Foster 100 in late July but on the 75th race lap his faithful Mercury flathead blew up. He had worked hard to make the engine competitive against the six-cylinder cars at Western Speedway.

Bob then built a Ford six-cylinder motor which made him even more competitive over the remaining season, finishing the year third in points. In 1969 many drivers had a tough decision to make, as the stock car class was no longer the premier class. A new super-stock division was taking over in 1970.

To compete in this new class Collins made allowable modifications to his outdated Ford. In 1971 Bob and his brother Gary teamed up to build a new car for the season powered by a 312 cubic-inch Mercury, going on to finish fifth in points. The brothers made other improvements for the 1972 season, finishing seventh in points.

1973 found Bob bring out a slick-looking 1964 Ford. Though the cost to stay competitive was high the car was in the top four all season. He sold this car at the end of the season. In 1974 he switched from driving to be a crew chief and engine builder for a new open super-stock car that was owned and driven by Terry Forsyth. With Bob's help Forsyth would go on to win the Blitz-Weinhard series and finish second in overall IDC points. Collins did win the VITRA Mechanic of the Year Award for his efforts.

Bob returned to the driver's seat, winning events in a 1959 Thunderbird. In 1977 the Island Super Stock Series was born. He and his crew built a 1968 Mercury Cougar to run (the first pony car to race at Western Speedway) that went on the win the super stock championship.

Bob Collins retired from racing and turned his full attention to building engines for other racers. In 1975 he began his own business – High Performance Engine – building oval track and street engines. He retired from this occupation in 2009.

BILL DRUMMOND began racing at the age of 28 in 1966, with only six races left in the season - towing his 1949 Ford over the Malahat to Victoria. He raced in the jalopy division and finished 42nd in a field of 52 drivers. In 1967 Bill would race at both Western Speedway and Grandview Bowl. For the first time in the association's history a tie occurred for top owners. Bill jointly accepted the O'Keefe's Old Vienna Brewing Company Trophy for most A-dashes and the Globe Hotel Trophy for most main events. He also received the Simpson-Sears Trophy for the 50-lap stock car championship and the MIARA Trophy for Best Appearing Stock Car. He finished the season second in points.

In 1968 Drummond built a 1956 Chevrolet and raced primarily in Nanaimo, with the occasional race at Western Speedway, winning several main events and trophy dashes. By the end of the season the body of the car was ready for the junk pile, but it kept him in the number two spot in points for the second year in a row. In 1969 he built a second '56 Chevy that would carry him once and for all into the front rank of competitors. He would break an axle and roll end-over-end, make the necessary repairs, and go on to win a 30-lap main event. At season's end Drummond was voted Most Popular Driver and finished first in points at Grandview Bowl.

The year 1970 would find Bill's car displaying a big #1. Following the first two races of the season he pulled the head from the engine and found a wrist pin had broken. It was at 3 p.m. on a Sunday afternoon and the only remedy was a new motor – simple enough – but not when the next race was early in the afternoon of the next day. By the time Bill and his crew found a new block and new parts were delivered, it was just before midnight. They worked all night building a new engine and had it installed by early in the morning. They made it to the track just 30 minutes before time trials and Bill went on to win the trophy dash and main event. By the end of the season Bill would emerge at the top of the points standings once again.

Bill Drummond would dominate the stock car races during 1971. He won most of the dashes, heats and main events for the third consecutive year and was voted Most Popular Driver on the Vancouver Island circuit. He won the championship race for the fourth time but would fall short by finishing second in points at the end of the season.

In 1974 Bill drove in the super-stock class for Bill Vater, ending the year third in points. The next year he continued to drive for Vater but retired from racing at the end of that season. In 1977 Bob Powell brought Drummond out of retirement in order to drive his hobby stock car, though he only participated in a few races. But that just got Bill going again and in 1978 and 1979 he would be in his own car again racing Island Series super stocks in Victoria and Nanaimo. He finished both years third place in points but retired from action the second time at the season's end.

HAROLD SJOSTROM began racing jalopies in 1960, eventually ending his racing career on the CAMRA circuit in 1978. He competed in stock cars during the 1961 and 1962 seasons. In 1963 he moved to B-Modifieds racing cars of his own design. He is well remembered for starting from the back of the field and winning the B-main, which qualified him to start at the back of the A-main and going on to the win in that event.

In 1964 Harold built a new B-modified car powered by a Pontiac V8, and that season was one of his best. He won Sportsman of the Year, Most Popular Driver, most main events, and was B-modified champion at Grandview Bowl.

Sjostrom had an inventive side and as a welder, coming up with quite a few innovations for the cars he built. At the same time, he designed and built a third axle system for logging trailers that allowed them to carry more logs on each trip. Despite keeping busy raising a family, building axles, modifying trailers and running his welding shop, he found time to put his building talents to work on a new A-modified racer for 1965, another for 1966 and a new offset B-modified car for 1967.

This new race car worked well for him. He won the Inter-City championship against race drivers from Langley, Victoria and Nanaimo. He set new speed records at each facility along with scoring wins at many other tracks.

In 1970 Harold built a new car for the CAMRA series using a 311 cubic-inch Chevy for power. From that year through 1975 he ran in the A-modified division and competed at Portland, Boise, Salt Lake City, Edmonton, Prince George, Langley, Victoria, Nanaimo and William's Lake. Following this hectic schedule Harold was picked by Ken Svendson to drive Ken's new #09 racer in the CAMRA series from 1976 to 1978, adding to his large trophy collection along the way.

2014 Inductees

JOHN COPP, as a teen growing up in Vancouver, B.C., took an early interest in racing - often sneaking off to Digney Speedway in Burnaby. He decided to start racing in 1951 and prepared a 1929 Pontiac. His career ended before it began because he couldn't get his parents to sign the permission slip.

Twenty years later a chance meeting with Roy Haslam and Denny Rand started a long relationship with the racing community. John became involved sponsoring Haslam's 1967 Chevelle through Garden City Auto, along with helping other drivers that included John Forsyth and Billy Price. The Garden City Auto name became well-known during the 1970s and 1980s, not just through stock cars and open-comp cars on and off the Island, but as a lap sponsor at Western Speedway.

When Roy, Terry, the crews and families traveled off-Island Copp also took his family along, competing at over 20 tracks in British Columbia, Alberta, Saskatchewan and throughout the United States. The team returned home with many wins and championships which made John a proud man.

John Copp liked everyone to enjoy the racing, but always strived for the best in competition. That's just what it was the night he put Gary 'The King' Kershaw in the old black Camaro and Roy Haslam in the new white Camaro, which turned out to be a great fan draw and fun night of racing. John's friends remember an approachable, yet imposing man with a strong handshake and long thick cigars.

After Garden City Auto became Garden City Suzuki, Copp found a new avenue of racing. For two years he supplied his son Steve and Roy Haslam with Suzuki 4x4s to compete in the Boomerang 250 off-road racing in Nanaimo, bringing home first-place trophies for their class.

JOE MACMURCHIE was a multi-talented member of the racing community as a driver, builder, mechanic and dyno. He grew up around automobiles as his father had an automotive business. Joe started with road racing on dark country roads in cars he and Lamont Brooks put together - an apple box for a seat, no exhaust and no lights - only the moon and stars to navigate by. The pair graduated to the quarter-mile drag racing scene on the old Bamberton cement road in the 1950s and then the new strip the Quarter Milers Car Club acquired in 1967. Joe's race cars included a 1953 Oldsmobile, a Model A, and 1968 and 1969 Camaros.

In 1968 MacMurchie was a mechanic for Lamont Brooks at Westwood when a fateful crash took the young Victoria driver's life. Joe was devastated, vowing never to be involved in racing again. A few years later though, when Roy Haslam needed a mechanic and partner, Joe caught the racing bug once more. Together they built a car and partnered for that one season.

Joe then began to build and race his own cars over the next several years for several classes, including sportsman, super-stock and even one year of NASCAR. Joe crewed for and raced against such notable drivers as Lamont Brooks, Bob Low, Dave Cooper, Roy Haslam, Neil Montgomery, Jack Jeffries Gary Kershaw, Dave Smith, Rick O'Dell and Don Dowdy.

MacMurchie's father, a VITRA tech man, was the driving force that got the infield scales at Western Speedway and Joe helped install them. Years later when there were disagreements at the track and the scales were going to be removed he stepped in, having them carefully dismantled and transported to his property to be stored. Later, Tony Mortel needed to be a tech man for the IDC. Joe agreed as long as they would reinstall the proper scales he had kept.

More years passed as other matters got into the way, racing wasn't as important to Joe until the WILROC sprint cars needed a tech crew. MacMurchie was called on again and, after a short stint with WILROC, he teamed with Neil and Jeff Montgomery and the #33 crew that competed on the Northwest Sprint Car Racing circuit.

DICK MILLER began a 20-year involvement with racing on Vancouver Island when he first sold chips in the stands at Western Speedway in the early 1950s. It ended when he retired from the executive board of MIARA. Dick's progress into racing was slow and steady. He worked as part of the pit crew for Frank Dyer in 1955 and 1956 with driver Lamont Brooks. In 1957 he crewed for the #98 car driven by Billy Foster, and his final year on a pit crew was with Frank Dyer when Brian Wilson drove the car and became the champion that season.

The experience Miller gained during this era helped speed things up for him and in 1963 he graduated to driving in the Nanaimo-Victoria circuit. He placed fourth in his rookie year with Roy Haslam as his crew chief. Traveling between Victoria and Nanaimo in 1964 with his orange 1949 Ford, Dick won 28 trophy dashes - ten of them in a row.

In 1964 Roy Haslam won his first race driving the same in the mechanic's race in Nanaimo. In another race that year Dick loaned Ross Surgenor his spare radiator only to go out and damage his own. Since he was far enough ahead in points Miller sat out the main event that Surgenor went on to win. Dick finished the season as the 1964 stock car champion. The inaugural Billy Foster Memorial Race at Western Speedway was the first and only rollover wreck for Dick. It took place when a car exiting the pits spun him out of control and he proceeded to do the Western roll.

Miller's work place transferred him to Nanaimo in 1966, where he continued to race. Here he won a number of main events and dashes driving cars for several Central Island teams, including Skip Hallgarth, Bobby Courser and John Green. John retired from racing near the end of the 1960s but served on the executive committee of MIARA until 1972.

HANK NEILSON was just 19 years old when he arrived in Nanaimo from Copenhagen with his family in 1951. By then he had already completed his apprenticeship as a mechanic and machinist. Soon after arriving Hank joined his father and brother to begin operations of Mountain View Service, which was a very successful business for many years.

Encouraged by Ray Pottinger in 1952 Hank put his skills to work building a race car. He began racing at Shearing Speedway in 1953 on the newly-paved track in a 1934 Ford. One night during his first year of racing and after winning the B-main Neilson was invited to race in the A-main, which we went on to win. He also helped put Nanaimo on the racing map by winning a number of main events against many Victoria drivers such as Digger O'Dell, Dave Cooper, Roy Pottinger and Dick Varley.

Over the years Hank built his own engines and cars, using his experience to improve performance and reliability. The overheating issues of the flathead Fords were solved when Hank and others removed fins from the dual water pumps that were restricting flow through the thermostat housing.

When the new Western Speedway dirt track opened in Langford, Neilson raced at both tracks. It was at Western when Hank discovered a weakness in the spindles on his '34 Ford which caused him to lose a couple of wheels. He suffered a roll-over that put him in the hospital for two weeks with a severely broken arm. True to his racing spirit he worked out the problem and returned to the track with a stronger truck axle. Hank was obviously fearless, because that wasn't his only roll-over and he has several Rollover Crests to prove it.

The mid-1950s found Hank, Wally Illott and a few others devoting time and effort to successfully have the Grandview Bowl built in Nanaimo. They were instrumental in forming MIARA, where Hank served on the executive committee. On the newly-paved Western Speedway Hank held the first track record - at least for a short time since he was the first driver to time-in. He was narrowly edged out of first-place in 1955 by Dick Varley in the 100-lap championship race at Western.

Hank Neilson went on to win many races in Nanaimo and Victoria when he drove several more of his 1934 Fords until 1960. The Ford retired that year, but Hank did not. He drove when needed for several drivers, such as Nibbs Anderson, Ray Pottinger and Red Burk. Hank could jump into a car and drive it competitively, keeping them in the points and scoring more wins along the way.

NORM WILCOX realized his first experience with racing in the early 1960s, riding down Miller's Hill in a homemade go-kart built by Harvey Chipper. He began crewing in 1963 on a car owned by Frank Dyer, where one of his first jobs was to put heads on the old flathead Ford. Norm and Roy Haslam put them on "backwards" while driver Dick Miller, who was under the car installing the transmission, fell asleep.

In 1968 Wilcox and Gary Kershaw built the beautiful #21 Mallock and Mosely 1955 Chevy. They had three goals for the season: win the championship, the Billy Foster 100, and grab the Best Appearing Car Award. In the end, they won all three.

Kershaw moved up to the super stock class in 1969 so Norm teamed with Billy and Charlie Price. They bought Kershaw's former car and with Billy in the driver's seat, proceeded to tie Mel Marshall for the championship. The Price/Wilcox team then moved to super stocks in 1970 and finished the season third in points with the '55 Chevy.

The next year the car was rebuilt and adapted 1964 Chevelle bodywork. With Billy still driving they finished sixth in points and again won the Best Appearing Car Award. Continuing for one more season the Price/Wilcox team earned a third-place finish in standings at the end of the year.

Norm's interest had changed by 1976 and the vintage stock cars from the 1930s and 40s became his focus. Within a few years he was rebuilding the first of several old-time racers. The #1 Coca-Cola car that had been driven by Bill Halliday in Nanaimo was purchased from Dean Cramb. Wilcox rebuilt the car and Gary Kershaw was the first to drive it at Western Speedway. The next year the Old Timer Racer Club was formed. In the following years Norm built four more Old Timers, selling them to Fraser Carmichael, Dave Smith, Mike Currier and Wayne Townsend.

Norm Wilcox comes up with numerous ideas and some have been implemented for the betterment of the racing community on the Island. His best thought came in 1983 when he said, "The auto racing community should have a Hall of Fame."

Friends agreed and in 1984, a Hall of Fame committee was formed and inducted the first seven Hall of Fame members at Western Speedway. In 1984 Norm started the 7/11 Race of Champions for former Western Speedway champions.

Thanks in part to Norm, each year's new inductees receive a blue jacket with the Hall of Fame crest emblazoned on it. At the induction ceremony each member is interviewed and photographed. A newspaper insert in the *Victoria Times Colonist* regarding the induction is also Norm's idea. After fifty years and counting Norm Wilcox remains active in the racing community and he remains an advisor to the Hall of Fame committee.

2015 Inductees

FRED BEST and four friends formed a car club called the Checkmates in the early 1960's and went on to try auto racing. In 1964, using Fred's 1951 Dodge, the club ran in the jalopy class at Western Speedway. The Checkmates joined the Vancouver Island Track Racing Association (VITRA) as a requirement to drive or be on a pit crew at the speedway. Fred did well in his six-cylinder Dodge against the popular and quicker Ford flathead V8s. By the end of the season Fred and his friends were seventh in the point standings, earning the jalopy class Rookie of the Year and the Checkmates won the Best-Looking Crew Award.

For the 1965 racing season Fred drove the #7 Plymouth, winning heats and finishing well in the A-mains against the Fords at both Western Speedway and Grandview Bowl in Nanaimo. The class had grown to over 70 cars, so each night saw three or four main events being run. Car clubs were popular during that era, so the Junior Chamber of Commerce and the Victoria Police Department sponsored a Road-E-O at the Town and Country parking lot and twelve Island clubs participated. Best and his friend Ken Holding won top honors in the three-hour skills competition and the Checkmates Car Club took home the Top Car Club Trophy.

The 1966 racing season witnessed big changes. The jalopy class was now the stock car class and VITRA tried bargaining with Western Speedway for additional prize money. Things did not go well, so VITRA decided to race only at Grandview Bowl. A new group, the Victoria Auto Racing Association (VARA), formed at Western Speedway. Fred was on the VITRA executive committee, so he raced at Nanaimo. Suddenly auto racing's future was at stake in Victoria. A compromise was reached during the summer when a syndicate, headed by Geoff Vantreight, purchased Western Speedway. Both clubs were persuaded to complete the 1966 race season together. Fred continued on the executive committee to help keep racing alive at Western Speedway.

After racing jalopies and super-stocks Best wanted to drive something faster. In 1968 he drove a Super A-Modified with Inter-City Modifieds. He also tried sports car racing, driving a 1967 Camaro on the new road course at Western along with the Westwood road course on the mainland. Fred and Bob Lowe also entered the Camaro in the South Vancouver Island Road Rally and picked up the win.

In 1968 Fred served as vice president of VITRA and then as president in 1969, where he proved to be a strong leader for the racing community. He continued racing Inter-City Modified but tried the Super-Modifieds in the Canadian American Modified Racing Association (CAMRA) at various Pacific Northwest tracks. He finished fifth in the 150-lap Daffodil Cup race.

One practice evening in 1970 he came down the front stretch nearing the Western Speedway track record when the throttle locked wide-open, slamming the car into the mountain at the end of the front straight. The safety crew got Fred out and transported him to the hospital, after which he spent several days at home recovering. The car was a write-off and the incident ended Fred's driving career. He continued to stay involved in racing at Western as a four-time VITRA president. He also served as pit boss and was the race director of the International Drivers Challenge Super Stock Series.

DON GORDON began his many years of involvement at Western Speedway by crewing for Greg Court from 1979 until the end of the 1982 season. The pair won several races and set track records but never managed a championship. In 1983 through 1994 Don served as crew chief for Roy Haslam. They won numerous races, broke track records and clinched championships throughout the Pacific Northwest during those years.

Switching duties at the track in 1994 Gordon became General Manager of All Fun Recreation Park and Western Speedway. He worked long and hard taking care of the vast property for Fran Wile until the park closed in 2007.

The racing season of 1998 found Don running the track with Matt Sahlstrom. That was the same year when big changes took place at the facility. Don oversaw and assisted installing a new drainage system, repaving and rebuilding of the track, and rewiring the infield. He was instrumental in getting the new lighting around the track installed in 2006. Among the many things Don Gordon did for the race fans was to institute the free season's pass for all Victoria Auto Racing Hall of Fame members. Thanks to his knowledge, expertise and hard work, Western Speedway was refurbished into a great racing facility to be enjoyed by racers and fans for years to come.

WALTER ILOTT remembered, "My interest in auto racing began as a spectator and goes back to Duncan at a track called Shearing Speedway. I believe that I was still going to high school at the time," said Wally Ilott of Nanaimo, British Columbia.

Five years and a chartered accountant's degree later Wally was immersed in the sport. In 1956 he joined MIARA as a member of Red Burke's crew. Later that year Nibbs Anderson introduced Wally to Bob Ibbotson, a machinist. "With Bob's expertise and Cowie Machine's sponsorship, my car #17 was born," said Wally. On September 1, 1956 Wally ran his first race on Western Speedway's clay track.

Wally Ilott was a driver, a pit boss, a starter, part of the safety and technical committee, a participant in promoting the construction of Grandview Bowl, and president of MIARA. Being a chartered accountant, it was a perfect fit for Wally to assume responsibility for all of the club's financial affairs during these years. He volunteered his services in this area until 1969.

If you ask Ilott, he will tell you he wasn't much of a driver - just a guy who loved the thrill and skill of the ride and being at the track. His closest brush with a trophy came in May of 1958 when he came home fourth in a main event behind drivers Ray Pottinger, Digger O'Dell and Bill Temple. However, Wally's wife Fay owns a first-place trophy for a Powder Puff race.

Wally's 15-seconds of fame came in May of 1957 when he made the headlines in several Vancouver Island newspapers: *"Ilott Uninjured in Speedway Spill"*. Competing before a crowd of 2,100 spectators Wally did a double end-over-end on the backstretch of the third heat. He recalls Phil Hendry pulling him from the car. As the headlines stated, Wally was uninjured, but the car took a beating.

With the support of Harry Roberts of Paramount Autobody, the frame was straightened, and Wally and Bob Ibbotson rebuilt the car. Sometime later they built a new car. "We got the frame for free and paid five-dollars for the battery," Wally recalls. Down the road, the sale of this car didn't stop Wally's enthusiasm for the sport. By invitation he began driving in main events for Art Clarke and later he drove John Muckle's car.

Ilott's family has their own memories of MIARA. Fay's parents were avid fans who attended all the races, while Wally's parents only attended one race - when their son missed a turn due to a broken steering and drove straight off the end of the track. Fortunately, Wally was uninjured. Wally and Fay's children have fond memories of getting French fries from the concession stand and circling the track in the back seat of their dad's 1965 Mustang sitting aside the pretty trophy girls after the main events.

"In my view my contribution to the club came mainly from my financial and administration services," said Wally. He was awarded Sportsman of the Year in 1965, a special appreciation award in 1968 and a lifetime membership in 1969.

HARRY ROBERTS began racing in 1954, under the rules of BCASA because Nanaimo did not have an association. They raced at Shearing in Cobble Hill, which was a very rough track. Harry raced there for two years until the Western Speedway dirt track was opened.

The first car Roberts raced was a 1935 Ford which he described as "a real tank, but it was our first try at racing." The next car was his first #13 racer which was a 1935 Ford that he drove at Western. Harry's cars were always green in color and carried the #13.

In 1958 Roberts was elected president of MIARA and negotiated with the City of Nanaimo in building Grand View Bowl. He continued to race at the now-paved tracks in Nanaimo and Victoria until 1960. The last car he drove was painted with a candy apple lacquer paint and Bing Foster dubbed it 'The Apple Green Baby.'

In 1960 there was no time for racing. That year two of Harry's three children contracted polio and had to stay in the Queen Alexandria Solarium in Victoria. Harry continued to stay active in racing.

2016 Inductees

BUTCH BEHN was just a toddler in 1950 when his family moved to Port Alberni from Hamburg, Germany. After completing high school, Butch worked in Alberta for a short time, but returned to Victoria in 1968. That same year, he watched his first car race at Western Speedway.

After working a short time in a Victoria sawmill, Butch started his own business - Behn's Disposal, later becoming Behn's Enterprises. Over the years Butch crewed for or sponsored various race teams including those for Larry Pollard and Rick O'Dell and was part-owner of a NASCAR Winston West car.

From 1986 until 1997 Butch took on the operations of Western Speedway. Along with the regular Saturday night racing he brought special feature events: the NASCAR Northwest Tour, the Can Am's, Tractor Pulls, All Star Super Stock Tour and Demo Derbys. He promoted more than just racing by managing two open-air rock concerts that drew more than 10,000 people each time at the Speedway.

In 1989 with the track showing its age, Behn began a major renovation project. The first challenge was a complete rebuild of the front stretch followed by repaving the back stretch, a new grandstand wall, replacement of the old wooden grandstand and a new section of grandstands added at turn one. Most of the work was done by volunteers and donated equipment and some of the funding coming from Butch's company.

Race teams found that Butch always seemed to be there when help was needed. Crews were able to use the state-of-the-art frame straightening machine at his auto repair shop at no charge. Oftentimes he assisted a crew that was short on funds with free tires so that they could make the next race.

In 1995 Butch purchased South Sound Speedway in Tenino, Washington. He continued to operate and promote Western Speedway until the end of the 1997 season, then relocated his family to Tenino.

TRACY and **TERRY CESSFORD**, twin brothers whose team became known as 'TNT Racing', began their involvement at age 15 by joining VITRA and crewed on their older brother Dan's Demo car. In 1969 while still helping Dan, Tracy began racing Demos with Terry as his crew.

For more than 30 years the TNT Racing brothers drove and crewed in many various racing classes and worked with many drivers.

The brothers held many accomplishments through the years, both on and off the track. Their first year in 'B' Hobby Stocks they finished only two points behind dominating Gord Smith.

Tracy did most of the driving with Terry serving as crew chief through the early 1980s. As they gained experience, they moved up the racing ladder, competing successfully in the hobby stock, stock cars and super stock classes – as well as the IMCA Modifieds.

In the Canada 200 stock car race in 1983 they qualified fifth, one position ahead of Roy Smith, and finished 13th. In 1995 TNT Racing was the force behind OTRA's $10,000 Phone Book Drive which raised funds for Queen Alexandra Children's Hospital.

Tracy won Driver of the Year in 1987 while Terry earned the Mechanic of the Year award. Through the years the Cessford brothers acquired six Rookie of the Year awards, broke track records in several classes and won more than 160 races. The brothers were later mainstays in the Old Time Racers Association class.

Unfortunately, Terry was diagnosed with cancer in 2012 and passed away the following year.

GERRY FLESH was introduced to racing by his father at Grandview Bowl in Nanaimo when he was just four years of age. He has been a spectator, an official, a crew member, a builder and a driver for over 55 years.

Gerry's first job, when he was 14 years-old, came in 1970 as a flagman at Grandview Bowl. The next season he drove the cement truck, watching the racing from the infield. Following knee surgery in 1974 he operated the time clock. The next year found him performing Assistant Starter Flagman duties with Ken Ozero.

Flesh became Vice President of MIARA in 1977 and began crewing on Dave Johnson's Island Series Super Stock for several seasons. From 1977 through 2015 Gerry crewed for several drivers.

Over the years Gerry accomplished more than just being a crew member. He built a Modified car in 1981 but blew the engine on practice night and scrapped that car. In 1985 he borrowed a car to run the last stock car race at Grandview Bowl. At the first Cassidy Speedway Dirt Cup in 1990 he was the Assistant Flagman. That September he held the first meeting in his kitchen to form the Central Island Modified series for Cassidy Speedway.

Gerry built three frames and suspensions in his basement for Jack Mowatt, Don Barrasky and himself and won the MIARA Sportsman of the Year award in 1991. After racing for a season, he sold his car to Wady Heckford and joined the Wade Winston West Team. While still crewing for the Wades in 1994, he built a second Modified to run in a few races on the IMCA circuit. This same year he traveled with the Wade Team to the Brickyard 400 in Indianapolis. In 1997 Gerry handed over his modified racer to his son Ryan but stayed aboard as the crew chief.

In the following decade Gerry served as Crew Chief on a Wilroc Lites Sprint Car from 2011 through 2014. In 2015 he was the series' Director of Competition.

2017 Inductees

SCOTT AUMEN began racing stock cars on the Cassidy Speedway dirt track in 1992. He continued doing so for several years until being offered a ride in Darren Kennedy's sprint car, when he became "hooked." Now in the sprint car at Cassidy Scott earned a few championships. The Northern Sprint Tour then became a mainstay for Scott. During that time, he won feature events at the speedways in Skagit and Yakima, Washington.

In 2000 he made his way to the A-Main at Alma, Washington in the World of Outlaws race along with Sammy Swindell and Steve Kinser. Although they were much faster, Scott was thrilled to have just made it into the event.

For a time Aumen drove at a number of tracks in a Tony Menard VMac car. When the Cassidy track closed in 2005, taking away mid-island racing, Scott turned his sights to the local Wilroc Sprint Car Series. Western Speedway is where Aumen built a resume that would be the envy of many drivers in the series.

In March 2007 Scott joined the ASA/NSRA at Evergreen Speedway in Monroe, Washington. On opening night, driving a Withcomb/Stewart/Turner car with a brand-new engine built by Neil Montgomery, he won the Doug James Memorial Race. This was his first experience at Evergreen's big track and the first race in this series on the pavement.

Scott continued to be a champion racer from 2006 through 2011 on tracks in British Columbia, Washington, Oregon and Utah.

The driver from Duncan, B.C. hit the track at the Rocky Mountain Raceway in Utah in September 2013 for the inaugural "Salt City 200". The event marked the first 200-lap winged sprint car race of the modern era and offered the second-richest purse for a pavement sprint car race in the nation. Scott came home the victor with $7,500 of earnings in his pocket - the biggest win of his career.

JIM McKAY has been involved in racing since 1982 when he raced in a few Demo Car races. In 1983 he built a Datsun 510 Mini Stock to race at Western and Saratoga Speedways. He then built a Datsun 610 Mini Stock in 1985 and ran locally and in Washington State. Beginning in 1989, with a Nissan 200SX, he won four consecutive championships.

At the end of the 1993 season Jim sold that car and switched to 'slicks and the big carburetors' on a Nissan 200SX Mini in order to run the Pro-4 West Tour at Spanaway, Washington, finishing tenth out of 36 cars from the Pacific Northwest. Following that he built a tube-frame car to run the Washington Pro-4 Series that was sanctioned by the Foreign Stock Car Racing Association. He finished third overall in 1998, second in 1999 and won the championship in 2000.

In 2002 McKay built a Nissan 240SX for Kyle Vantreight and in 2005 Kyle won the championship. Jim raced in the 2003 Pro-4 Shootout at Chaparral Speedway in Boise, Idaho where he qualified sixth in a field of 27 cars and finished second. Also that year Jim began driving Norm Wilcox's roadster in the Wilroc Winged Sprint Car Series.

Over the next few years McKay made improvements to the car and managed to win some events. In 2007 Jim purchased Norm's roadster but in 2009 that car was badly damaged and he lacked the funds to rebuild.

From 2009 to the present Jim has been crewing on the Montgomery Team's NSRA sprint cars. He was able to drive a spare Montgomery winged car in the 2013 Daffodil Cup race. McKay has also been on the executive board for both Mini Stock and Wilroc Sprint cars. In ten straight years of racing he has never finished lower than third in points. He pioneered the use of factory fuel injection in the Mini Stock class and in 2015, received the Don Mouner Memorial Award for Mechanical Excellence.

JOHNNY SUTTON, a kid from Langford, was at the go-kart track pretending to be his racing idols Gary Kershaw and Roy Haslam when someone pushed him in front of an oncoming kart. He landed in the hospital for a few days, which concerned his dad John Sutton Sr. – who was afraid his son would end up being afraid of cars. So together the father and son built a go-kart and Johnny learned to weld, set-up and tune the Briggs & Stratton engine.

On the first race day of 1981 they took their #22 kart to Western Speedway, only to fail the pre-race inspection. John Sr. was a boiler maker at the shipyard and the kart resembled a "battleship". Fortunately, the Capital City Kart Club gave them a rule book and let them run on the backstretch to figure things out. Father and son worked to have their kart ready for the Turkey Race in October, where Johnny finished third and won two Cornish game hens.

In 1992 the Suttons moved up to the two-cycle division where John Sr. worked with and became friends with Gary Kershaw and Roy Haslam. These new friends encouraged the Sutton's to visit other tracks since Johnny proved to be a good racer. Johnny raced in his first Gold Cup race in Yakima that year. In 1984 he was a full-time Gold Cup entrant in the Junior 2 class. The highlight of the year came during a race in Calgary in which he ran ahead of a young unknown driver named Paul Tracy.

From 1985 through 1992 the Sutton family (with Mom as the videographer) raced at every track in Western Canada and the Pacific Northwest. In doing so they logged 350,000 in a Chevy Suburban towing an 18-foot trailer.

The ultimate highlight of Johnny's career came in 1989 when he achieved professional status and was listed as an international Kart Federation Expert - the highest award given in karting. Some of his competitors included Tony Stewart, Scott Pruett and Greg Moore.

In the early 1990s Johnny raced in the open-wheel Bel-Ray Drivers Search in Shannonville, Ontario, finishing second. With endorsements from Greg Moore and Paul Tracy Sutton secured a spot in the Players Development Program and a tryout in the Indy Lights Program. Despite high results there were no offers to move ahead.

Johnny's final years of racing were low-funded for 'The Giant Killers' team. Despite racing just part-time they remained competitive and won an international event in Sacramento. After 22 years of racing Johnny retired from racing.

DARREN YATES began his racing career in 1991 preferring to work and crew on cars until the day he drove one lap of the track. Following that experience, racing became a part of his life for the next 25 years.

Darren started racing Demo cars and trucks, but once he watched a sprint car practice, he decided IMCA Modifieds would be the class he would like to try. At Cassidy Speedway, after watching Dave Conway and Dave Emmerson battle on the dirt, he bought Emmerson's car in 1996. Darren then drove in 30 races a season for the next two years at Cassidy, Western, Saratoga, Skagit, Penticton and Port Hardy.

In the fall of 1998, he built a Modified from scratch in his garage, learning more than ever about fabrication, chassis design, tinwork, engineering, suspension and engine building. He raced in this class through the year 2000 and then knew it was time to move up to Sprint cars.

That winter Darren purchased the 'pink car' from Jody High - a car that Ken Haskell had driven the previous two seasons, and Ross Moore joined Darren's team. Once the 2001 season began Darren placed second to Emmerson in his first race. The next few years his team raced at as many tracks as they could afford. In 2011 he won the 'last' Winged Wilroc Championship. From 2012 until 2014 Yates participated in the NSRA series.

In 2015 he elected to run the full season, racing at Western Speedway, Meridian, Post Falls, Spokane, Roseburg and Evergreen. When his engine blew up at Evergreen Speedway he decided it was time to retire from racing. Darren stated that the part of racing he truly values are the people he met during his 25 years in the sport.

2018 Inductees

JERRY FERRIE 's racing journey started in 1970 when he purchased a 1954 Ford jalopy. Along with the car came his introduction to Earl Pollard and his son Larry. Earl took Jerry under his wing and passed on some of their combined racing knowledge, giving Jerry a head-start. Earl ran the #99 car and Larry's was #98, so Jerry decided his first car would be #97.

Ferrie's first crew included his older brother, Lyle, and Rick Cudby. The advice from the Pollards that first year made such an impression on Jerry that he finished tenth in points and was named Rookie of the Year.

The 1971 season witnessed Jerry taking his Jalopy success and move up a class. He built his own car, a 1957 Ford Super Stock. Gone was the stenciled, hand-painted car, replaced by a car with a real paint job courtesy of his new sponsor, Save-Way Paint and Body Shop.

Jerry's crew chief Rick Cudby then caught the itch to drive for himself and build his own new Stock Car. With Rick moving on, Ferrie needed a new crew member and his other brother Larry came on-board, making it a true "family affair." Jerry was making quite a name for himself, finishing third in the Most Popular Driver standings.

For the 1973 season Ferrie added Russ Blackstock, Fred Best and Bernie Leblanc to his crew. The combined team built another new car, a 1966 Mercury Comet with McDonalds Bread as their sponsor. Jerry and his crew launched the much-loved "bread toss" for fans. As a fan favorite the bread toss has continued to this day, now with Island Bakery.

The 1976 season brought more crew changes. Russ Hancock and Wayne Campbell signed up to help build another new car, this time a 1964 Ford Fairlane. Jerry's experience told him a shorter wheelbase car was what was needed. In the meantime, Jerry and his wife Judy welcomed their eldest daughter Andrea to their crew and for the first year of her life, Jerry was a stay-at-home dad. However, the two were said to be spotted at the various auto wrecking yards searching out used parts for the race car.

All the hard work and laps run were starting to pay off. Jerry won his first Main Event as well as the Dash and fourth in the Heat. The crew's hard work earned Jerry the "Best Looking Super Stock" award that year.

1977 found Jerry become even more competitive as the laps went by. A highlight for him was winning the "Roy White Memorial Race" and running strong – week in and week out. Crew member Russ Blackstock was awarded the "Mechanic of the Year" award for his efforts.

For the 1978 season another new car was built, a 1968 Ford Mustang, and Jerry and his wife welcomed a second daughter, Kimberly. The Mustang brought a new sponsor on board, which was Reg Midgley AMC. Spending more time with his family, Jerry ran a limited race schedule. As racing became more of a drain on his pocket book Jerry sold the Mustang but kept up his involvement with racing and helped Dan Wade with his son Lance, who was starting his own foray into racing.

In 1995 Ferrie "scratched the itch" one more time. His oldest brother Larry passed away in 1994, so to honor his brother who had told him at the 1994 IMCA Championship night, "You need to race these." Jerry did so, purchasing a car from Neil Montgomery and Russ Lejeune. He campaigned for two seasons. The car was competitive and well- maintained. Jerry also shared the seat time in the #65 IMCA car with Lance Wade, giving him the opportunity to hone his skills in an open-wheel race car.

Sadly, Ferrie passed away at Western Speedway after suffering a heart attack in 1966, after he took his final checkered flag.

KEN EMERSON 's earliest memory of his interest in racing began by winning several trophies while competing at Van Isle Dragways in the late 1960s and early 1970s in his 1965 Corvette.

In 1972 Ken began racing with Doug McKenzie. The next year he teamed up with Jerry Forsyth and served as crew chief, where he remained for six years. Ken then began crewing for Dick Midgley of Midgley Motorsports in 1979. Their first race was at Riverside in California with Hershel McGriff behind the wheel. Today, Ken remains a crew member with the Midgely team.

Ken happily spent evenings and weekends driving from his home to work on Midgley's race cars. Ken is a talented and dedicated individual, working voluntarily and tirelessly. His expertise includes bodywork, paint, engines, chassis, mechanical and electrical components. He would often stay awake until the early morning hours putting the finishing touches on the race car. He would then do his share of work once the team arrived at the track – and was often a tire-changer during the race.

The list of drivers and other crew members Emerson has worked with over the years is extensive. He has never tired of racing and has always been keen to share his talents with young racers. Ken's even disposition and ability to deal with all personalities has served him well.

DAVID MORIS attended his first race at Grandview Bowl in Nanaimo at the age of nine and remained a spectator through 1971. In 1972 he saw an advertisement in the local newspaper asking, "Have you ever had the urge to race?" The ad was placed by the Mid-Island Auto Racing Association (MIARA), along with a set of rules for their new Claimer Class which was starting that season. David had been waiting for this opportunity.

Just 15 years-old, David purchased his first car for $25 – a 1958 Ford Fairlane 500 with a 332 cubic-inch V8. He enlisted the help of Robbie Robertson, who welded in the roll bars and drove the car in the first races until work called him away. Dave drove his first three races that year and blew three engines. With Danny Downer crewing, Dave finished his first season 24th in points out of 58 participants.

For 1973 Dave purchased a 1957 Pontiac six-cylinder model from Nanaimo Auto Wreckers for $75. With this car he won his first trophy dash along with a few heat races, finishing the season 35th in points. In 1974 Dave bought a Pontiac V8 that he placed into a 1957 Chevrolet. With a little assistance from another competitor, he put the car into the wall in its first main event. Dave's next car was a '55 Chevrolet.

Through the next few seasons Moris continued to race a variety of cars. In 1976 he won trophies for the Most Main Event wins and was MIARA's Points Champion. For 1978 Dave participated in the Island Stock Car Series. In MIARA, he again had the most main event wins while also serving as a MIARA director. In 1979, the last season for the Island Stock Car Series, Dave finished second in the point standings and received MIARA's Driver of the Year Award.

Moving ahead a few years, Moris and Bob Powell built a 1968 Chevelle stock car for the 1983 season at Western Speedway. Altogether Dave won ten Main Events, five Trophy Dashes and was crowned the speedway's Stock Car Champion. This was the first driver from Nanaimo to accomplish this feat since Ray Pottinger did so in 1961.

For several seasons during the 1990s, Dave successfully competed around the Pacific Northwest in Dwarf cars. 1998 was his last year in racing.

GEORGE WADE 's auto racing career spans 46 years. His parents, Les and Ruby, started taking George to Western Speedway when he was just eight months old. Their favorite drivers were Dave Cooper and Billy Foster.

Wade's first personal experience with racing came in 1968 when he built a go-kart that he used to race down the "big hill" that led into Jordan River, where he grew up. The kart displayed the #27, after Victoria's legendary racer Billy Foster.

In 1972 the Wade brothers (Dan, Alan and Arnie) bought a 1956 Ford stock car from Harvey St. Hilaire, which was driven by Al Wade and his brother, George, rounding out their crew. The finished the year sixth in VITRA Stock Car points and Al received the Rookie of the Year honors. In 1973 they finished 11th in points.

In 1978 George was on the VITRA membership committee and looked after the back gate at Western Speedway. This year the Wade brothers finished second in the championship points standings. In 1975 the Wade brothers bought Rick O'Dell's 1963 Plymouth and competed in the Super Stock class, placing seventh in points.

Between 1977 and 1981 George wrote and submitted race reports for Western Speedway and the *Racing Wheels* newspaper. He also crewed with his brothers on a new 1973 Dodge Challenger built for the Super Stock class and driven by Al Wade.

George served as the Race Director for Western Speedway for a total of 19 years, between 1982 and 1997, and then again from 2001 through 2015. His responsibilities included selling advertising and submitting race reports and press releases. In 1985 George received a VITRA special promotion award and the recipient of the "Meeres Equipment Promoter of the Year" award.

Between the years 1986 and 1998 George was a crewmember on Lance Wade's Street Stock, when not officiating at Western Speedway. From 1989 to 1992 George served as crew chief on Lance's Pro Stock, owned by brothers Dan and Roger. In 1991 the team won the inaugural "Montana 200" at Montana Raceway Park, taking home the $10,000 in prize money.

George wrote the first set of rules for the MISS (Merchants International Super Stock) Late Model series which ran between Port Angeles, Washington and Western Speedway. He was also the series' Race Director. The MISS Late Models raced for a few years and were eventually renamed the International Pro Stock Series.

In 1992 George wrote a set of rules for a new Thunder Car class at Western Speedway. The Thunder Cars were later renamed Stock Cars in 1998.

From 1992 to 1999 George Wade was the crew chief on the Wade Racing NASCAR Winston West team. They raced at many of the tracks throughout the Pacific Northwest, California and Arizona. One of his highlights was making the trip to the Indianapolis Motor Speedway to qualify for the 1994 inaugural running of the NASCAR Brickyard 400.

In 1998 George became the Race Director at South Sound Speedway in Tenino, Washington. The next year he moved to Tenino and held the position of the speedway's Manager.

From 2000 to 2003 he served as General Manager at Evergreen Speedway in Monroe, Washington. From 2004 to 2007 George was the General Manager at Shasta Raceway Park in Anderson, California. His following position, from 2007 through 2010, he was the General Manger at Grays Harbor Raceway in Elma, Washington prior to returning to Western Speedway in 2011. In 2013 George was an inductee in the North Sound Racing Hall of Fame.

If that wasn't enough, from 2007 to 2015, he served as President of the WARPA (Western Auto Racing Promoters Association) and today remains an active member.

Today, George lives in Monsanto, Washington and is going into his third year as the promoter at Wenatchee Valley's Super Oval in Washington.

2019 Inductees

Don Carmichael
Barrie Goodwin
Mike Grute
Bill O'Kell
Robert and Melvin Pallister

ABOUT THE AUTHOR

BOB KEHOE

A native of Portland, Oregon, Bob Kehoe is a freelance automotive journalist and photographer who wrote his first car column for his high school newspaper. Following a stint in the U.S. Coast Guard and a career in the high-tech industry, he turned to automotive writing on a full-time basis, beginning with the *Oregonian* newspaper in 1994.

Additionally, he has written for other publications including *Speedvision Online, DRIVE! Magazine,* and *eBay Motors*. He has held positions as Media Coordinator for an SCCA Pro Racing Series, and Public Relations Coordinator for a producer of major hot rod shows. He published his first book, *Art Pollard – The Life and Legacy of a Gentleman Racer –* in 2016.

Bob and his wife Karen reside in Hillsboro, Oregon and Eloy, Arizona.

INDEX

A

Addison, Frank · 24, 78, 334
Agabashian, Freddie · 259
Agajanian, J.C. · 234
Alberg, Gordon · 1, 5 , 7, 41, 131, 137, 145, 281, 348-349
Alexander, Ed · 178
Allison, Bobby · 174, 215, 287, 324-325, 334, 340, 344
Allison, Donnie · 344
Amato, Joe · 158
American Automobile Assn · 68, 243
American Challenge Series · 247-248
Amick, Bill · 253
Amick, George · 193-194, 216
Anderson, John · 215
Anderson, Nibbs · 125-127, 129, 324-325, 354, 356
Andretti, Aldo · 238
Andretti, Dee Ann · 12, 238
Andretti, Jeff · 238
Andretti, Mario · 5, 7, 12, 23, 158-159, 176, 181, 189, 203-204, 214-215, 222-223, 225, 227, 229, 231-242, 253-255, 257, 260, 264-265, 269, 271-278, 283, 286, 289, 292-293, 299, 301-304
Andretti, Michael · 12, 159, 238
Andrus, Mel · 129, 142, 154
Arnold, Cal · 149
Ascot Park · 68, 244-245, 250, 277, 313
Atkins, Dick · 242, 276-277
Atlanta Int'l Raceway · 232, 271-274, 279, 282, 289, 304, 310-311
Atlantic Speedway · 69
Aumen, Scott · 358
Autotron Electronics · 231, 234, 256

B

B.C. Automobile Sports Assn. · 21, 46, 52, 56, 58-59, 323, 326, 334, 336, 356
Baker, Jim · 164
Balboa Stadium · 68
Banks, Henry · 266-267
Barber, Jerry · 133
Barbo, Chick · 49, 55, 336
Barcelle, Len · 125
Barrasky, Don · 358
Basset, Ray · 162
Beadle, John · 344

Behn, Butch · 357
Bennett, Don · 125
Benson, Chris · 75
Berlin Raceway · 289, 291, 315
Berry, Jim · 116-117, 120, 122
Best, Fred · 335, 355,360
Bettenhausen, Gary · 189, 253, 290
Bigelow, Tom · 189
Biggs, John · 350
Billy Vukovich Memorial · 244
Binford, Tom · 266
Blackstock, Russ · 360
Blake, Smokey · 113
Bloomgren, Bert · 53, 65, 345
Blum/Offy · 181, 275
Blume, Walter · 30, 32-33
Bobby Ball Memorial · 236, 277
Booth, Percy · 157
Bowcott, Bob · 334
Bowell, Doug · 95-97, 117-121
Bown, Dick · 253
Bowsher, Jack · 290-291, 293-294, 297
Brabham, Jack · 206, 219
Brabham/Offy · 176, 231, 233, 309-310
Branson, Don · 177, 181, 235-236, 238, 254, 260, 262-263, 265-266, 277, 309
Brawner/Ford · 234, 236, 254, 277, 311-312
Brickyard 400 · 338-339, 358, 362
Brix, Harry · 248
Brooks, Lamont · 78, 108, 352-353
Brown County Fairgrounds · 289-290, 315
Brown, Brownie · 60-63, 73
Brown, Don · 119
Browne, Bob · 136, 139, 142, 162
Bruce, Verne · 60-62, 73-74, 326
Bryan, Jimmy · 180, 243, 309, 311
Bryant Heating & Cooling · 234-235, 257
Bunyan, Barry · 44
Burgess, Bob · 110, 113-114
Burke, Red · 94-95, 97, 111, 114-118, 121, 123-124, 356
Busch Grand National · 100, 329
Buttera, Jim · 37

C

Cahill, Keith · 336
Cain, Scotty · 253
Caldwell, Jack 'Digger' · 8, 17, 50-56, 59-62, 68, 110, 328-329, 332

Calistoga · 195
CAMRA · 25, 27, 42-43, 199-100, 112, 125, 127-129, 138-141, 143-151, 156, 158, 162, 167, 169, 171-172, 174, 200, 301, 319, 321-322, 324, 328, 332, 332, 328, 332, 335, 341, 347, 351-352, 355
Canada 200 · 323, 326, 331-332, 335, 340, 357
Canadian Automobile Racing Enterprises · 180
Canadian Motorsports Hall of Fame · 160, 162
Card, Dick · 129, 142-143
Carman, Richard · 213
Carmichael, Don · 363
Carmichael, Fraser · 343
Carnegie, Tom · 232
Carson, Fred · 51, 54-55, 114
Cawthorne, Benny · 118
Cazier, Pete · 143
Cessford, Tracy and Terry · 357
Chamberlain, Barry · 125
Champion Spark Plug Series · 247
Chapman, Colin · 180
Cheesbourg, Bill · 246
Childress, Richard · 100, 329, 337
Chipper, Harvey · 5-7, 87-89, 90, 100, 326-327, 338, 341, 347-348, 354
Christie, Bob · 246-247
Christy, Tim · 349
Chuang, Dr. Sylvester · 305
Clark, Al · 349
Clark, Jimmy · 204, 225, 229, 239, 257, 269, 276, 281, 310
Clarke, Bob · 127-129, 135-136, 138-139, 161
Clarke, Bobby · 114-120, 124-127, 147
Cobble Hill · 19, 21, 24, 39, 43, 46, 71, 77-78, 303, 356
Cochran, Bob · 150
Christy, Tim · 349
Collins, Bob · 150
Collins, Don · 349
Collins, Rockie · 340
Collins, Sid · 232, 259
Colwood Mile · 46, 336
Compton, Dick · 256
Congdon, Gary · 260, 265-266, 278
Conway, Ed Conway · 56
Cook, Len · 125
Cooper, Dave · 5, 7, 13, 17-25, 30, 59-63, 73, 75-78, 96-97, 111, 114-120, 122-123, 127, 129, 132, 135, 156, 206, 273, 319, 325, 327, 344, 348-349, 353, 362
Cooper, Gordon · 271
Cooper/Climax · 206, 219
Copp, John · 352
Copp, Tommy · 273
Copper Cup · 128, 141-143, 153-154, 161, 172, 283
Corby Cup · 22, 90, 319-320, 323, 327, 330-332, 338-340, 347
Cottyn, Andre · 46, 79, 85, 91-92, 99, 319, 322-323, 325, 328, 347
Coutts, Al · 123
Cox, Greg · 158
Crockett, Roger · 342
Crow, Bill · 41, 85, 141, 150, 154, 156, 200
Crowell, Palmer · 1, 150, 195-197, 206
Cudby, Rick · 360
Currier, Mike · 322, 333, 354

D

Daffodil Cup · 41, 43, 88, 97, 100, 124, 127, 130, 144-145, 154, 169, 185, 200, 319, 322, 325-326, 328, 331, 335, 341, 343, 355, 359
Dalby, Allan & Johnny · 57, 332
Dallenbach, Wally · 276
Dans, Adolph · 49
Darnell, Bay · 291
David Foster Foundation · 306
Davidson, Bill · 158
Day, Ronnie · 342
Dean, Al · 238
Dean Van Lines Special · 225, 236, 238, 271-272, 283
DeBock, Errol · 172
Desereaux, Bob · 125
Destobel, Gary · 125
Deveca, Willy · 212
Dickson, Larry · 258, 260, 267, 277
Digney Speedway · 46, 81-83, 320, 337, 352
Dippel, Judy (Pollard) · 5
Dippolito, Dave · 47
Dobrey, Leo · 60
Donker, Bob · 194
Donohue, Mark · 287
Dory, Tom · 175
Dover Downs · 100
Dowdy, Don · 175, 353
Douglas, Ron · 114, 333, 340
Drummond, Bill · 351
Dudley, Max · 129
Duman, Ronnie · 170, 181, 258, 260, 267
Duncan, Rob · 335
DuQuoin State Fairgrounds · 235, 244, 251, 275, 294, 314, 316
Duray, Gus · 33-36
Dyer, Frank · 353-354

E

Eagle/Ford · 216, 277, 312
Eastholm, Ted · 115
Eaton, Ron · 346
Eckman, Jack · 127
Eddie Matan Memorial · 152
Edgar, Norm · 126
Edgett, John · 338
Edmonton Gold Cup · 22, 40, 42-43, 129, 142-143, 153-154, 156-157, 163, 165, 169, 303, 319-321, 331, 333, 359
Edson, Marc · 150
Ehlers, Mike · 150
Eisert, Jerry · 180
Eisert/Chevy · 180-181, 255, 309, 311
Ellefson, Norm · 5-7, 42, 61, 97, 127, 129, 147-150, 152-153, 156-158, 161-164, 168-172, 174, 301, 325, 334
Elliot, Bill · 348
Emerson, Ken · 361
Eng, Bung · 17, 58, 60-62, 182, 327
Erbes, Bob · 194
Erickson, Carl · 3

Erickson, Roy · 109
Evans, Richard · 339
Evergreen Speedway · 341, 344, 358, 360, 362

F

Falardi, Gil · 115, 118
Fanning, Del · 8, 17, 61-63, 73-74, 92-93, 108-110, 113-114, 334
Fanning Jr., Del · 113
Fanny Bay Drifters · 117-119, 123-124
Feenstra, John · 153
Ferguson, Dave · 346
Fernwood Esso · 7, 13, 25, 87
Ferrie, Jerry · 360
Feuz, John · 5-6, 40, 88, 132-133, 138, 153, 164, 176, 188, 193-201, 203-206, 209, 301
Fiddick, Bob · 333
Firestone · 215, 224, 301
Flesh, Gerry · 357
Flitton, Chub · 93
Flying Saucer · 61, 65
Flynn, Dick · 193, 243, 256, 331
Flynn, Walt · 176, 224, 238, 309
Flynn/Offy · 176-177, 238, 309
Ford, Benson · 260, 266
Forsyth, Terry · 344
Foster, Alan · 5
Foster, Bev · 2, 5, 10-12, 26, 87-89, 223, 298, 238, 242, 303
Foster Jr., Bill · 2, 5, 11, 238
Foster, Bing · 132, 303, 320
Foster, Daryl · 4, 5, 8
Foster, David · 16, 306
Foster, Debra · 2, 10-12, 241, 256, 319
Foster, Eric · 3, 5, 7, 9-10, 16-18, 59-60, 319
Foster, Gladys · 3, 5, 9, 15
Foster, Kelly · 2, 5
Foster, Kelly · 2, 5
Foster, Lionel · 5
Foster, Morry · 5, 7-8, 306
Foster, Phil · 3, 5, 7-8, 34, 74-75, 85-86, 94, 111, 162, 323, 328-329, 337, 356
Foster, Stephen · 3, 5-7, 9, 15-16
Fox, Lawrence · 335
Fox, Tom · 126-127, 144
Foyt, A.J. · 104, 158, 176-177, 180-181, 186, 189, 215, 218-219, 222, 225, 232-236, 238, 244, 250-251, 257, 260-261, 265-267, 273-274, 276, 279, 287, 294-297, 310-311, 313-314
Friedkin, Thomas · 215
Frumento, Jack · 52, 54-55
Fuji International Raceway · 167, 214, 276, 295, 312

G

Gagnon, George · 125
Gallia, Lyle · 116
Gerhardt/Ford · 254, 271, 277
Gerhardt/Offy · 158, 188, 271, 275, 310
Geyser, Don · 75
Giddings, Bill · 30, 33, 36-37
Gilmore Stadium · 65, 68-69, 367
Glenny, Bob · 6, 140
Golden State 100 · 236, 277
Golden State 200 · 170
Golden Wheels Club · 329
Goldsmith, Paul · 244, 251, 253, 288, 296, 314
Goodwin, Barrie · 6, 147, 317, 363
Goodyear · 175, 178, 186, 208-209, 215, 224, 301
Gorder, Bud · 97, 129, 148, 156, 172
Gorder, Mike · 150
Gordon, Don · 355
Graham, Richard · 341
Granatelli, Andy · 170, 187, 219, 328
Grandview Bowl · 7, 41, 43, 107-130, 147-148, 340, 342-343, 345, 350-352, 354-358, 361
Grant, Jerry · 215, 223, 257
Grays Harbor Raceway · 362
Green, Bud & Pike · 8, 51, 53-59, 62, 64-65, 68, 73, 329-330
Greenwood, Jack · 333
Gregg, Bob · 1, 18, 74, 1127-129, 143-144, 146, 148, 150, 158, 169, 172, 189, 194, 196-197
Gregory, Masten · 203, 223, 239
Grey, Don · 125
Grim, Bobby · 103, 214, 257, 260, 267
Grissom, Gus · 271, 273
Gruman, Dorothy · 65
Grute, Mike · 363
Gurney, Dan · 180, 225, 234-235, 251, 260-261, 265, 267, 274, 287, 296

H

Haas, Dick · 248
Halibrand/Ford · 234, 251, 310
Halibrand/Offy · 177, 309
Hall, John · 132
Hall, Karen · 133
Hamilton, Ken · 150, 189
Hamilton, Tom · 342
Hampton, Andy · 291
Hancock, Ron · 333
Hanford Motor Speedway · 244, 253, 313, 315
Hanks, Sam · 68
Hansen, Dick · 5, 7, 25
Hansen, Mel · 68
Hansgen, Walt · 202, 256
Hanson, Phil · 143
Harkey, Bob · 103, 276
Harrison, J. Frank · 180, 255, 309, 311
Haskell, Ken · 360
Haslam, George · 59, 63, 74
Haslam, Jim · 13, 16, 22, 40, 87-88, 131-132, 301, 303, 319, 322, 326
Haslam, Roy · 89, 326-327, 330, 332-333, 335, 341, 347, 352-355, 359
Hastings Park · 46

Hayes, Red · 127
Hayhoe, Jim · 169-170
Healey, Jim · 35-37
Heath, Allen · 49, 336
Heikes, Todd · 343
Heller, Bill · 73-75, 93
Hendry, Phil · 5, 7, 74-75, 85, 323, 356
Henham, Wes · 125, 127, 145
Hill, Graham · 256, 260, 266, 269, 273, 311
Hissett, Bob · 165
Hitchcox, Bill · 339
Hodges, Gerald · 162-163, 169, 175
Hoerr Racing Team · 247-248
Hoerr, Ann · 246, 248
Hoerr, Irv · 5, 246-248, 295
Hoerr, Rudy · 7, 139, 159, 240, 245-248, 250-251, 290, 294-295, 297-298, 301, 313-316, 320
Hoerr, Scott · 5, 30, 246-248, 345
Holding, Ken · 335, 355
Holdridge, Sid · 54-55
Holman-Moody · 251, 296
Hoosier Grand Prix · 274
Hoosier Hundred · 103, 235, 276
Hopkins, Bud · 118-119
Hornaday Sr., Ron · 253
Householder, Ronnie · 68
Hucul, Cliff · 150, 156
Huffaker/Offy · 232, 236
Hulse, Chuck · 264, 266, 269, 277, 301
Hurt, Bob · 223
Hurtubise, Jim · 219, 232-233, 250, 252-253, 267, 288-289, 291, 295-296, 314, 316
Hyde, Bill · 1, 18, 108-110, 113-114, 195-197

I

Ibbotson, Bob · 356
Illiana Speedway · 250, 313
Illinois State Fairgrounds · 234, 251, 294, 314, 316
Illot, Wally · 108, 114, 354, 356
IMCA · 163, 189, 330-331, 340, 343, 345-358, 360-361
IMSA American Challenge Series · 247-248
IMSA Champion Spark Plug Series · 247
Indiana State Fairgrounds · 235, 251, 276, 289, 294, 314-316
Indianapolis Motor Speedway · 169, 192, 220, 259, 286, 327, 362
Indianapolis Raceway Park · 216, 232, 244, 247, 274, 288, 315
International Driver's Challenge · 335, 338, 344
Inland Empire Cup · 148
Inland Empire Motorsports Hall of Fame · 162
International Motor Sports Assn. (IMSA) · 246-247
Isaac, Bobby · 250-252, 314

J

Jack, Rajo · 49, 336
Jacobi, Bruce · 103
Janett, Frank · 129

Jantzen Beach Arena · 194, 199
Jarrett, Ned · 288, 296
Jeffries, Jack · 353
Jesmore, Pat · 150
Jimmy Bryan Memorial · 180, 254
Johncock, Gordon · 233, 235, 255, 262-267, 269, 271-272, 275, 277
Johns, Bobby · 203, 223, 232, 239, 296
Johnson, Blim · 60
Johnson, Dave · 333, 358
Johnson, Eddie · 229, 267
Johnson, Tony · 345Joiner, Carl · 253
Jones, Len · 125
Jones, Parnelli · 144, 176-177, 180, 225, 234, 238-239, 241, 241, 244, 251, 269, 277, 287, 296, 309, 313
Jones, Tom · 158
July Cup · 90, 95, 319-320, 323, 327, 329-332, 337, 345

K

Kalevala, Kajia · 7, 77-78, 80-83
Kawartha 250 · 292
Kayno, Ray · 30
Keen, Mel · 124, 126-127, 156
Kent, Steve · 342
Kenyon, Mel · 223, 231, 264, 266, 268
Kershaw, Gary · 89, 100, 320, 327, 331, 333, 338, 341, 344, 347-348, 352-354, 359
King, Al · 109
King, Doris · 190
King, Grant · 6, 36, 58, 62, 85, 97, 100, 109, 114, 134-136, 139, 155, 158, 176, 178, 182-192, 200-203, 207, 214-216, 224, 239, 246-247, 264, 266, 271, 275-276, 284, 297, 301, 321-322, 325, 327-328, 330, 332-334, 337
Kingfish/Offy · 188-189
Kinser, Sheldon · 189
Kinser, Steve · 358
Kitto, Frank · 317, 321
Klein, Sam · 162
Knepper, Arnie · 103, 203, 223, 239, 260, 266, 276
Koch, Ernie · 102-103, 109, 113, 165-166, 197, 200, 211, 216-217, 279
Koch, George 'Pops' · 279
Koch, Jay · 5-6, 8, 279
Koeppel, Mike · 248
Kostenuk, Eddie · 7, 40, 60-62, 75, 77-78, 93, 102-106, 123-124, 177, 198-199, 334, 337
Kotz, J.C. · 291
Kramer, Larry · 284
Krause, Glen · 115-117, 119, 124
Krisiloff, Steve · 189
Kurtis/Offy · 105, 235, 311
Kuzma/Offy · 235, 276, 312
Kuzmanich, Kuzie · 253

L

Laing, Ray · 109-110
Laird, Jimmy · 51, 53-54, 59
Lambrick, Phil · 94, 111, 333
Langford Speedway · 7-8, 17, 24-25, 46-67, 71, 78, 85, 91, 102-103, 182-184, 230-231, 233, 244, 252-253, 271, 273, 283, 288-289, 295, 310-319, 321-324, 326-330, 332-333, 336-337, 345, 354, 359
Langhorne Speedway · 244, 252-253, 271, 288, 314-316
Langhorne 125 · 233
Langhorne 150 · 275
Langley Speedway · 43, 323, 337, 342
Larson, Doug · 150, 162
Latta, Charles · 30, 33
Lazier, Buddy · 248
Leblanc, Bernie · 360
Legge, Tommy · 49, 54, 336
Lejeune, Russ · 330-331, 335, 343, 361
Leonard, Joe · 103, 203, 223-236, 239, 244, 251, 267, 271, 275, 310
Liguori, Ralph · 223
Lilac Cup · 155, 162-163
Lindskog, Swede · 7, 50-52, 56, 59, 64-69, 336, 345
Lola/Offy · 254, 269, 311
Long, Ed · 178
Lorenzen, Fred · 244, 296
Lott, George · 30, 32-33, 36
Lotus/Ford · 176, 181, 225, 232, 234-236, 238-239, 257, 274, 309-311
Low, Bob · 353
Lower Island Track Racing Assn. · 335

M

MacDonald, Dave · 202, 219, 268, 296
MacKenzie, Ted · 6, 192, 317, 334
MacDonald, Dave · 202, 219, 268, 296
Madden, Gary · 334
Maffeo, Pete · 107
Malloy, Jim · 97, 124, 127-129, 142-148, 150, 156-158, 169, 171, 187, 189, 347
Malone, Hal · 179, 301
Mantz, Johnny · 243
Marcis, Dave · 325, 344, 344
Marshall, Mel · 331, 354
Marshman, Bobby · 176, 303
Martin, Dick · 207
Matan, Eddie · 163
Matan Memorial · 127, 156, 164, 169
Mathouser, Bob · 225
Mawle, Bob · 95-96, 99, 111, 114, 119, 121, 123-124
May, Les · 150
Mayall, Ron · 56, 323
Mays, Rex · 68, 106, 189
McCabe, Frank · 125
McCelland, Dave · 117-119
McClure, Del · 197, 206
McCluskey, Roger · 170, 181, 214, 232, 236, 244, 266, 274-276, 297, 312
McCoy, Jack · 253
McDowell, Johnny · 48-49, 68, 336
McEachern, John · 164
McElreath, Jim · 176, 181, 231, 233, 236, 254-255, 264, 266, 274, 277-278, 309-311
McGee, Jim · 214
McGowan, Frankie · 109, 194
McGreevey, Mike · 223
McGriff, Hershel · 89, 174, 253, 287, 327, 334, 344, 361
McKay, Jim · 358
McKenzie, Doug · 361
McLellan, Jack · 126
McLeod, Bert · 62
McManus, David · 235, 310
McMurtry, Lew · 50-52, 54-56, 59, 62, 66, 68, 345
McQuinn, Harry · 274
Means, Jimmy · 344
Mears, Rick · 214, 222
Mecom, John · 254
Mecom Racing Team · 256
Melin, Lou · 346
Meskowski/Offy · 234-235, 276, 310, 312
Meskowski, Wally · 102
Meyer, Louie · 269
Michigan Int'l Raceway · 158-159, 244, 289
Mid-America Raceways · 241, 253
Midgley, Darrell · 100
Midgely, Dick · 41, 117, 334
Midgley, Reg · 11, 180, 301-302, 324, 335, 344, 360
Mid-Island Auto Racing Assn. · 41, 112, 120, 122-123, 125-126, 128, 332, 345, 361
Miller, Al · 260, 266
Miller, Dave · 75
Miller, Dick · 127, 353-354
Miller, Fritz · 48
Milner, Jack · 115-116, 118-119, 124-127, 130, 148
Milo, Chic · 124
Milo, Gene · 129
Milwaukee Mile · 176, 186, 230, 234, 237, 244, 250-252, 270, 275, 290, 313-316
Minnesota State Fairgrounds · 161, 170
Monhay, Ralph · 125-126, 130, 148, 150, 156, 169, 172, 301
Monroe Speedway · 44
Montgomery, Neil · 330-331, 335, 353, 358, 361
Montgomery, Trevor · 343
Moody, Ralph · 348
Moore, Greg · 359
Moore, Joe · 52-55
Moore, Wes · 52-53, 55, 345
Moore, Verne · 21, 77
Morgan, Bob · 167-168, 171
Moris, David · 361
Morris, Frawny · 48
Morse, Frannie · 336
Mortel, Teddy · 344
Mortel, Tony · 169, 172, 344, 353
Mosport Int'l Raceway · 292, 316
Motor Trend 500 · 287, 296-298

Mowatt, Jack · 358
Mt. Douglas Hillclimb · 7, 22, 88, 131-132, 342
Muckle, John · 356
Mullaly, Lloyd · 126
Mumua, Mickey · 150
Muncie, Bill · 330
Muther, Rich · 276

N

NASCAR · 89-90, 100, 161, 174, 215, 223, 232, 243, 248, 250, 257, 287, 296-298, 320, 325-327, 331-332, 335, 337-339, 344, 346, 348, 353, 357, 362
National Sprint Car Hall of Fame · 192
Naylor, Glen · 142, 150, 172
Nehl, Tom · 208
Naylor, Glen · 142, 150, 172
Naylor, Tom · 150
Neitzel, Chuck · 148, 172
Neilson, Hank · 76, 96-108, 115-121, 123, 353-354
Nelson, Bill · 76
Nelson, Dusty · 172
Nelson, Ken · 21-22, 76, 78
Nelson, Louie · 34
Nelson, Norm · 244, 250-253, 288-289, 291-295, 297, 313-316
Newcomer, John · 188
Newman, Paul · 216
Newton, Mike · 75-77, 322
Nichels, Ray · 253, 291, 293, 296
Nish, Terry · 129, 142
North, Henry · 30, 33-34
Northwest Golden Wheels Fraternity · 332-333
Nyborg, Brent · 172

O

O'Connor, Pat · 263-264
O'Dell, Len 'Digger' · 109, 111, 322, 347, 353, 356
O'Dell, Rick · 330-331, 338, 348, 353, 357, 362
Offenhauser · 102-103, 174, 180, 184, 186-188, 197, 201, 203, 206-207, 212, 216, 219, 225-227, 238, 256-257, 294, 298, 328
O'Kell · 363
Old Bess · 8, 301-306
Old Time Racers Assn · 320, 323-324, 331-333, 340, 342-343, 345, 347, 357
Oldfield, Oldfield, Barney · 243
Olds, Don · 60-61
Olympia Express · 89, 327
Ontario Motor Speedway · 190, 216, 244, 344
Osborn, Howard · 194
Owens, Cotton · 232, 295

P

Pallister, Melvin · 363
Pallister, Robert · 31, 339, 363

Papis, Max · 306
Parsons, Johnny · 68
Paschal, Jim · 233
Pascoe, Carmen · 109
Passmore, Bruce · 21-22, 24, 56-58, 60, 62-63, 73-78, 324, 336
Pearson, David · 287
Peets, Ray · 127, 129, 143, 146, 152, 157
Permatex 200 · 89, 100, 320, 323, 327, 341, 344, 348
Pescod, Doug· 153, 164
Petty, Richard · 100, 287, 296-297, 329, 337, 344
Phoenix Int'l Raceway · 105, 177, 180, 216, 283, 325
Pikes Peak Int'l Hillclimb · 244
Pinkham, Pinky · 65
Pilkey, Arley · 132-133
Pocono Raceway · 151, 158, 244
Pold, Paul · 114
Pollard, Art · 1, 139, 143-144, 150, 153-154, 156, 165, 170-171, 178, 187-188, 223-234, 236, 256, 258, 271, 273, 276
Pollard, Earl · 329
Pollard, Larry · 100, 336-337, 357
Porter, Don · 108
Porter, Marvin · 250
Portland Speedway · 1, 17
Pottinger, Ray · 5-7, 30, 39-45, 75-76, 95, 97-98, 108-119, 121-127, 129, 146-147, 152, 155-158, 223, 296, 321, 324, 331-332, 335, 353, 356, 359, 361
Powell, Bob · 351, 361
Price, Bill · 331
Price, Randy · 345
Pruett, Scott · 359

Q

Quarter Miles Car Club · 9-10

R

Rand, Denny · 335, 352
Randol, Keith · 166
Rankin, Barry · 335
Rasmussen, Arnold · 164
Rasmussen, Eldon · 5-7, 41, 88, 97, 127, 129-130, 143-144, 146-154, 156, 164, 169, 215
Rathmann, Jim · 271
Ravenhill, Mike · 306
Razzelle, John · 133
Reedy, Art · 335
Regeth, Roger · 292
Rex Mays Classic · 271
Richter, Roy · 65, 69
Riverside Int'l Raceway · 23, 89, 287, 296-297, 344
Robbins, Jim · 187, 203-204, 219, 223, 231, 233, 236, 254, 256, 263, 275, 282, 310-312, 328
Roberts, Fireball · 296
Roberts, Harry · 95, 111, 115-119, 121-122, 356
Roberts, Jim · 127, 144, 146, 150
Robertson, George · 127, 129, 141-144, 147-148, 150, 153-154, 156, 169, 172

Robertson, Robbie · 361
Robinson, Harold · 202
Robinson, Stan · 143
Robison, Don · 5, 6, 197-198, 201, 206, 212
Rockett, Ross · 317, 347
Rodee, Chuck · 257
Rohn, Heather · 15
Romano, E.J. · 30
Rose, Larry · 116
Rose, Sylvia · 16
Ross, Jack · 30, 32-37
Rotz, Rhiman · 266
Roy White Memorial Race · 324, 360
Ruby, Lloyd · 177, 180, 231-232, 235, 244, 253, 269, 274, 277, 309
Rudd, Ricky · 100, 337
Rumley, Jack · 76
Rummings, Fred · 114
Rupp, Mickey · 203, 223, 239
Russell, Bruce · 284
Russing, Roy · 69
Rutherford, Johnny · 103, 105, 233, 238, 256, 274, 286, 310, 337
Ruttman, Troy · 296

S

Sachs, Eddie · 203, 214, 219, 268, 327
Sahlstrom, Matt · 355
Sacramento Fairgrounds · 102-103, 236, 277, 359
Salt Lake City Fairgrounds · 141, 143, 154, 171
Sauer, Sam · 143
Schmidt, Bill · 344
Schock, Wally · 49, 336, 345
Schornhurst, Bill · 172
Scott, Rob· 340
Scovell, Art · 18
Scovell, Shorty · 49, 59, 336
Scovell, Vi · 18, 41, 195, 332
Selley, Don · 150
Sewall, Fred · 5, 213, 216
Shannon, Herb · 246, 289
Shasta Raceway Park · 362
Shaw, Glen · 48, 66
Shearing Brothers · 71-74
Shearing Speedway · 7, 19, 20-21, 24, 39, 43, 71, 73-80, 134, 320, 324, 327, 330, 333, 337-338, 345, 353, 356
Shelby, Carroll · 215, 342
Shelton, Monte · 206
Shervey, Don · 285
Shipman, Jim · 289
Silnes/Offy · 275
Simon, Dick · 150, 168, 213, 216
Simpson, Bob · 19-21, 60-63, 73-74, 92-93, 108-109, 113-114, 123-124, 183-185, 327, 333-334
Sims, Bill · 334
Sjostrom, Harold · 99, 125-126, 351
Slogar, Tony · 116, 127-130, 148-149

Smith, Al · 42, 94, 97-97, 111, 116-122, 124, 127-130, 142, 144-145, 147-148, 150, 156, 273, 320-322, 325-334, 348
Smith, Alex · 335
Smith, Bill · 97, 99, 116, 317, 346
Smith, Bob · 111, 115, 117-119, 121, 124
Smith, Dave· 338, 340, 341-342, 348, 353-354
Smith, David · 347
Smith, Don · 337
Smith, Jack · 24, 48, 54, 58, 62, 73, 78, 326
Smith, Roy · 97, 100, 185, 322, 325-328, 331, 334, 337-338, 344, 348, 357
Sneva, Blaine · 150
Sneva, Jan · 149-150
Sneva, Jerry · 8, 51, 59, 133, 144, 150, 156, 189, 203, 215, 239, 264, 266, 348, 360
Sneva, Tom · 6, 43, 56, 100, 116, 126-127, 144, 150, 156, 158-159, 167, 170, 173-174, 187, 189, 214, 283-284, 286, 349
Snider, George · 189, 203, 218, 223, 235, 239, 253, 257, 269
Souders, George · 227
South Sound Speedway · 357, 362
Sowle, Bob · 186, 202, 216-218, 257
Spaulding, Cliff · 152, 165
Spaulding, Ernie · 61-62
Spaulding, Jack · 8, 21, 54-56, 59, 60-62, 65, 76, 92, 332, 345
Speedway Park · 143, 152, 156-157, 164
Sperb, Harold · 197-198, 211, 213, 275, 284
Springbank Speedway · 161-162
Stanley, Howard · 58
Starks, Bill · 143
Stedelbauer, George · 152, 157-158
Steen, Bill · 5
Steen, Jim · 5, 12, 14, 40, 137, 325
Sterne, George 'G.B.' · 339
Stevens, George · 152, 164
Stevens, Gig · 223
Steward, George · 327
Stewart, Jackie · 167, 256-257, 260, 264, 266, 269, 312
Stewart, Tony · 359
Stone, Gord · 347
Strawberry Cup · 99, 319, 322, 326, 341, 343
Strong, Billy · 153
Stroppe, Bill · 244, 296
Stuart, George · 338, 348
Stutz Special · 30, 32, 34-36
Sugai, Art · 185
Sullivan, Danny · 306
Surgenor, Ross · 323, 325, 334, 344, 348, 353
Sutton, Bert · 48, 50-51, 56, 67, 74, 93, 334
Sutton, Johnny · 359
Sutton, Len · 1, 6, 103-104, 178-179, 184, 186, 194, 196-199, 201-202, 204, 206-207, 211, 216, 219, 223, 229, 230-231, 238, 256, 259, 281, 285, 296, 319, 328, 337, 349
Svendson, Ken · 352
Sweeting, Bert · 348
Sylvester, Gerry · 334
Symes, Jimmy · 50-52, 67-68

T

Taylor, Frank · 152-153
Taylor, Jack · 46, 48, 50, 53-55, 66, 328, 336
Taylor, Jud · 50, 56
Taylor, Oscar · 114, 117-119, 122
Taylor, Ralph · 62
Ted Horn Memorial · 275
Temple, Bill · 111, 356
Templeman, Shorty · 183, 211, 243
Texas World Speedway · 158, 244
The Matan 100 · 163
The Willows · 7, 28-36, 46, 56, 333, 336
Thomas, Frank 'Corky' · 8, 61-63, 73-74, 76, 93, 109-110, 114, 123, 327
Throckmorton, Bill and Stephanie · 192
Tinglestad, Bud · 177, 267, 276-278, 312
Tipke, Jim · 167-168, 169, 170-174, 328
Tony Bettenhausen 200 · 105, 176, 238, 275, 309-310, 312
Tony Bettenhausen Memorial · 234
Tony Slogar Memorial · 126-130, 148-149
Tovella, Sal · 251, 292, 316
Townsend, Wayne · 354
Trenton 200 · 104-105, 188, 276, 309, 311-312
Trenton Speedway · 176, 232, 235
Trzewik, Peter · 305
Turner, Curtis · 287
Turner, Jack · 49, 336

U

Undra, Rhineardt · 125
United States Auto Club (USAC) · 1, 103, 127, 144, 174, 180, 189, 219, 243, 264, 267, 274, 298, 301, 319, 337
Unser Sr., Al · 189, 203, 222-223, 239, 244, 246-248, 267, 273-276, 278
Unser, Bobby · 219, 232, 236, 244, 267, 271, 273, 275-276, 278, 282
Unser, Jerry · 180, 223, 244

V

Van Camp, Eric · 153
Van De Mortel, Tony · 328
Van Humbeck, Larry · 111, 114, 117-118
Vancouver Island Motorsports Circuit · 305
Vancouver Island Track Racing Assn. (VITRA) · 9, 16, 23-24, 41, 78-79, 85-86, 99, 154, 319-321, 323, 328, 330-333, 337-338, 344, 347, 350-351, 353, 355, 357, 362
Vantreight, Bob · 41, 43, 88, 123, 134, 136, 321-322, 332, 349
Vantreight, Don · 55
Vantreight, Geoff · 100, 124, 185, 200, 301-302, 322, 325, 328, 334, 355
Vantreight, Jerry · 8, 17, 52-55, 57, 59, 62-65, 72-73
Vargo, Jake · 276
Varley, Dick · 7, 9, 75-78, 95-97, 109, 111, 114, 116-118, 120-121, 134, 155, 185, 321, 327, 348, 353, 354
Vasser, Jimmy · 170

Vater, Bill · 345
Vatis, Tassi · 106, 235, 311
Veith, Bob · 225
Victoria Auto Racing Assn' · 320, 329-330, 355
Victoria Auto Racing Hall of Fame · 5-6, 8, 14, 64, 90, 99, 106, 136, 192, 317-318, 321, 333-355, 347-349, 355, 357, 362
Vidan, Pat · 194, 229, 260, 269
Vogler, Rich · 189
Vollstedt, Kurt · 284
Vollstedt, Rolla · 1, 11, 102, 135, 165, 169, 176, 179-180, 184-187, 195-197, 205-206, 211-213, 216, 219, 223, 234, 239, 247, 251, 256-257, 263, 271, 274-275, 279, 282-283, 285, 301, 303-304, 310-311, 328, 334
Vollstedt/Ford · 230, 232, 234, 236, 251, 254, 256, 268, 271, 273-276, 282-282, 310-312, 349
Vollstedt/Offy · 106, 203, 209, 211, 225, 232, 2343, 236, 239, 256, 310, 319
Vukovich, Bill · 189, 243

W

Wade. Al · 338, 362
Wade. Dan · 338
Wade, George · 362
Wakelyn, Walter · 332
Walker, Bob · 133
Walker, Don · 156
Walkup, Bruce · 169-170
Wallace, Rusty · 337
Walling, Claude · 52, 54-56, 345
Walters, Bill · 20, 334
Walters, Don · 194
Walther, George · 275, 294, 312
Ward, Rodger · 103-104, 143, 176-177, 180-181, 199, 225, 227, 233, 238, 254, 256, 265, 268-269, 311, 313, 324, 337
Waring, Bill · 108
Warren, Bentley · 189
Watson, A.J. · 103, 180, 186, 201, 275, 284, 328
Watson/Ford · 181, 233, 310
Watson/Offy · 105, 181, 214, 229, 232-233, 235, 276, 309-310
Weatherly, Joe · 287, 296-298
Webb, Les · 24, 78
Weedman, George · 194-195
Weiss, Frank · 150, 172
Weld, Greg · 188-189, 223, 278
Wensley, Bob · 61, 63, 333
Wente, Bob · 276
Western Speedway · 7, 12-14, 16, 22, 24-25, 39-42, 44, 78-79, 85-89, 91-97, 99-102, 107, 109, 120, 127, 132, 134, 141, 145, 147, 152, 154, 174, 182-184, 199-200, 302-303, 317, 319-340, 342-362
Wheatley, Jingles · 117
White, Barry · 42, 332
White, Don · 253, 289-295, 314-316
White, George · 50
White, Marty · 150
Wilbur, Don · 169, 173-175
Wilburn, Jimmy · 49, 336
Wilcox, Ken · 124-125, 127-128

Wilcox, Norm · 317, 343, 354, 359
Wilke, Bob · 103
Williams, Carl · 223, 236, 267
Willis, C.H. · 31-32, 35-36
Willoughby, Dick · 22, 94-96, 114-115, 319, 321, 323, 325, 329, 335
Willoughby, Wayne · 125
WILROC · 340, 342, 347, 353
Willows Speedway · 28-36, 46, 56, 333, 336
Wilson, Brian · 99, 125-126, 353
Wilton, Norm · 117, 122, 124
Winston Cup · 100, 325, 337
Winston West · 100, 174, 326-327, 331, 337-340, 344, 346, 348, 357-358, 362

Y

Yarborough, Cale · 257, 260, 267, 273, 287
Yarbrough, Lee Roy · 298
Yates, Darren · 359
Young, Andy · 344
Youngstrom, Gordy · 109-110, 194
Yunick, Smokey · 113, 197, 208

Z

Zackett, Benny · 165
Zink, John · 176, 254

CPSIA information can be obtained
at www.ICGtesting.com
Printed in the USA
LVHW051243280720
661655LV00010B/632